Goodness and Justice

To my brother Constantine

Goodness and Justice

Plato, Aristotle, and the Moderns

Gerasimos Santas

 BLACKWELL
Publishers

Copyright © Gerasimos Santas 2001

The right of Gerasimos Santas to be identified as author of this work has been asserted in accordance with the Copyright, Designs and Patents Act 1988.

First published 2001

2 4 6 8 10 9 7 5 3 1

Blackwell Publishers Inc.
350 Main Street
Malden, Massachusetts 02148
USA

Blackwell Publishers Ltd
108 Cowley Road
Oxford OX4 1JF
UK

Library of Congress Cataloging-in-Publication Data

Santas, Gerasimos Xenophon.
   Goodness and justice : Plato, Aristotle, and the moderns / Gerasimos Santas.
      p. cm.
   Includes bibliographical references and index.
   ISBN 0-631-17259-9 (alk. paper) – ISBN 0-631-22886-1 (pb. : alk. paper)
   1. Good and evil – History. 2. Plato – Contributions in concept of good and evil. 3. Aristotle – Contributions in concept of good and evil. 4. Justice (Philosophy) – History. 5. Plato – Contributions in philosophy of justice. 6. Aristotle – Contributions in philosophy of justice. I. Title.

B398.G65 S36 2001
170 – dc21
                                                                    2001018133

British Library Cataloguing in Publication Data
A CIP catalogue record for this book is available from the British Library.

Typeset in 10½ on 12½ pt Bembo
by Best-set Typesetter Ltd., Hong Kong
Printed in Great Britain by T.J. International, Padstow, Cornwall

This book is printed on acid-free paper.

Contents

Preface   ix

1 Introduction   1

1   The Role of the Good in the Ancients and the Moderns   3
2   Science and Ultimate Good   9
3   Disputes and Questions about Good   12
4   The Aims and Limits of This Study   16
Notes   16

2 The Socratic Good of Knowledge   18

1   All Goods and their Socratic Rankings   20
2   The Dispute with Gorgias: Is Rhetoric the Greatest Good?   22
3   The Dispute with Polus about Power, Desire, and Good   25
4   The Dispute with Polus about Justice and Happiness   29
5   The Dispute with Callicles about Good and Pleasure   31
6   Conditional and Unconditional Goods   33
7   Socrates and Kant: Wisdom or the Good Will?   38
8   The Conditional Value of All Goods on Virtue in the *Meno*   41
9   Socrates and G. E. Moore on the Value of Knowledge   42
10 Goods, Wisdom, and Happiness   45
11 Is All Value Conditional on Virtue?   48
12 Was Plato Aware of These Socratic Problems?   51
Notes   53

3 The Good of Platonic Social Justice   58

1   The Great Questions of the *Republic*   59
2   The Functional-Perfectionist Theory of Good   66
3   The Application of the Functional Theory of Good to the City   75

4   The Definitions of the Social Virtues   84
5   The Role and Scope of Platonic Social Justice   90
6   The Good of Platonic Social Justice   93
7   The Application of Platonic Social Justice to Gender   95
8   Conclusion   103
Notes   103

4   *The Good of Justice in our Souls*   111

1   The Isomorphism Between Social and Psychic Justice   111
2   Plato's Pioneering Analysis of the Psyche   117
3   Psychic Justice and the Good of it   125
4   Plato and Hume on Reason or Passion as the Rule of Life   129
5   The Defense of Psychic Justice as Analogous to Health   133
6   The Criticism of the Democratic Individual   138
7   Which is Prior, Social or Psychic Justice?   150
8   The Structure of Plato's Ethical Theory   153
Notes   157

5   *Plato's Metaphysical Theory of the Form of the Good*   167

1   Opinion, Knowledge, and Platonic Forms   169
2   The Imperfections of the Sensible World   171
3   Forms as the Best Objects of their Kind to Know   178
4   Forms as the Best Objects of their Kind and the Form of the
    Good as their Essence   180
5   Function, Form, and Goodness   187
Notes   192

6   *Aristotle's Criticism of Plato's Form of the Good*   194

1   Aristotle's Arguments from Priority   196
2   Breaking up Goodness: Aristotle's Argument from Homonymy   200
3   Aristotle's Argument from Final and Instrumental Goods   205
4   The Attack on the Ideality of the Form of the Platonic Good   208
5   The Attack on the Practicability and Usefulness of the Platonic
    Good   212
6   Putting the Fragments of Goodness Back Together: Focal
    Meaning   214
Notes   219

7   *The Good of Desire, of Function, and of Pleasure*   224

1   The Concept of the Good   226
2   Different Orectic Conceptions of the Good   230
3   Aristotle's Functional-Perfectionist Theory of Good   236
4   Objections to Aristotle's Functional Theory of Good   241
5   Orectic, Hedonic, and Perfectionist Good   250
Notes   256

8   *The Good of Character and of Justice*   259

1   Is Aristotle's Ethical Theory Circular?   259
2   Did Aristotle Have a Virtue Ethics?   263
3   Aristotle's General Analysis of Virtue and Functional Good   269
4   Can Moral Virtue be Explicated by Functioning Well?   271
5   States of Character and Practical Wisdom   274
6   Aristotle's Analysis of Justice: Not a Virtue Ethics   278
7   Paucity of Practical Content: Justice and the Other Virtues   284
8   Summary and Conclusion   287
Notes   288

Bibliography   290
Index   297

Preface

My interest in theories of good began a quarter century ago, when I began to study and write about Plato's *Republic* and to read and sometimes teach John Rawls's *A Theory of Justice*. Their diametrically opposed views of justice, one meritocratic, the other egalitarian, were of course very evident. Less apparent but eventually clear was the opposition in their theories of good, one perfectionist and objective, the other relativistic or subjective. Equally interesting, the role of the good was very different in the two theories of justice; and Rawls, very much aware of the differences, fought hard to show that his subjective or relativistic theory of individual good did not damage the possibility of rational agreement on justice. Such differences in theories of good and the role of the good seemed well worth investigating.

Reading these two books at the same time also made me realize that they were probably the first and last (at that time) important books on justice and the good. And that important books in philosophy really belong to two contexts: not only their own cultural and intellectual times, but also the context of all the important books on the same subject. The historical context has been traditionally recognized and extensively used; and recently even revived in the setting of "contexualizing" important books, studying lesser documents, and perhaps even downgrading "great" books. But for understanding complex theories and recognizing fundamental advances, I believe the second context is essential. *A Theory of Justice* really helps us understand the *Republic*, even though Rawls barely mentions the work. (In his early years at Cornell, where I was a graduate student, Rawls taught interesting seminars on Hume's theory of justice and on Aristotle's and G. E. Moore's treatment of goodness, but not on Plato's ethics, though he knew Plato well.)

In this book I have tried to use both contexts, as far as my limited knowledge of the history of ethics allowed me. I hope that others, with more knowledge, time and energy, will continue to use both contexts.

It is difficult to acknowledge here all the scholars on whose work I have relied, in the use of both contexts. Earlier versions of parts of chapters were read at many conferences and other professional meetings, and I am indebted to many scholars in the audience for comment and criticism. Beyond the acknowledgments in the Notes and the Bibliography, I am especially indebted to Georgios Anagnostopoulos, Julia Annas, Dale Cooke, Mike Ferejohn, David Keyt, Fred Miller, Terry Penner, Jean Roberts and Charles Young. None of these good people are of course responsible for my views or for the errors of commission and omission that remain.

1

Introduction

> ... one deep division between conceptions of justice is whether they allow for a plurality of opposing, and even incommensurable conceptions of the good, or whether they hold that there is but one conception of the good which is to be recognized by all persons, so far as they are rational.... Plato and Aristotle, and the Christian tradition ... fall on the side of the one (rational) good. (Rawls, 1982, p. 160)

This is a study of Plato's and Aristotle's theories about good things, goodness, and the best life for human beings, with some comparisons with the moderns. I try to show that goodness was the most fundamental normative concept in the ethics of Plato and Aristotle. This has not always been apparent nor sufficiently appreciated, especially in Plato. In his early and middle dialogues the main ethical disputes are about virtue and happiness and they seem to take up all the ethical space. I argue that Plato held that virtue and happiness are derivative ethical concepts, to be explicated in terms of goodness. Plato actually *tells us* in the *Republic* that unless we know the form of the good we will not know that anything else, even virtue, is good. Indeed, goodness was one of Plato's discoveries. But his theory of the form of the good is obscurely stated, ontologically prolific, and not evidently put to work. I argue that he also has another theory of good, better known to us, the functional account which he actually uses to build up his theory of the virtues and their contribution to happiness. But he does not *explicitly* make this theory the foundation of his ethics, and it has not been appreciated as such, even though it makes the *Republic* a unified and more understandable work.

The fundamental role of the good is more evident in Aristotle, since unlike Plato he begins his ethics with the good, rather than virtue. But he rejects Plato's theory of a separate form of the good, and also the Platonic view that goodness is something which is present (immanent) in all good things, by which they are good. He breaks up goodness into fragments, and it is unclear how successful he is in putting the fragments back together with his theory of focal meaning. But his famous function argument shows decisively, I think, that functional good is his fundamental normative concept, in terms of which theories of virtue and happiness are built up; though he applies the functional theory differently from Plato by using his newly discovered psychobiology. And while Plato discovered goodness, Aristotle produced a fine analysis of the intricate concept of *the* human good.

I also try to show that both Plato and Aristotle fought subjective theories of good. That they fought hedonism is widely recognized if not universally agreed. But they also rejected, I argue, desire-satisfaction theories of good, something less evident but equally illuminating. They thought they discovered and used objective theories of good: Plato's perfectionist-formal theory of the good, and Plato's and Aristotle's perfectionist-functional theories. Both their attacks on subjective and relativistic accounts and their own theories were heavily influenced by Plato's discovery of universals, and by the medical and biological concepts of form or structure and function. In medicine and biology it seemed evident that pleasure and desire satisfaction did not always, nor even for the most part, coincide with what is good for human beings; whereas well functioning seemed fundamentally good, and the structures that contributed to well functioning also assuredly good.

If I am correct in these main contentions, then the ancients had already discovered and examined the three major theories of good that we know of: perfectionist formal or functional theories, hedonistic theories, and desire-satisfaction theories. And since they thought that goodness was the most fundamental concept in ethics, it is understandable that they favored what they thought were objective theories, and fought subjective or relativistic theories. For if goodness is the most fundmental concept in ethics, then all disputes in ethics are in principle amenable to reason, rationally solvable, if we can have an objective theory of good and sufficent information supplied by the sciences.

But though the ancients may have discovered all the major theories of good, they did not develop them all equally successfully. A series of brilliant British writers, the hedonistic utilitarians, elaborated hedonism further and showed how it can be used to build up theories of justice and happiness. And in the twentieth century advances in economic and decision theories make elaborate technical uses of desire- or preference-satisfaction theories. Equally important, the moderns have made major advances in understanding different structures for ethical theories, especially nonteleological structures. In such Kantian or contractarian structures, (nonmoral) goodness need not be so fundamental, and hedonic good or good as the satisfaction of desire can play an important role in making choices, without their subjective or relativistic nature doing damage to the central social concept of justice. The limited comparisons with the moderns I make in this book are not meant as complete studies, but are attempts to throw some light on the merits and limits of ancient and modern ethical theories.

In this chapter I sketch a wider philosophical and historical context in which my study belongs. I show some differences between ancient and modern ethical theories on the role of goodness, sketch some main disputes and questions about goodness, and indicate the aims and limits of this study.

1 The Role of the Good in the Ancients and the Moderns

Normative ethical theories about the good, the right, and the good person have not always related these three fundamental concepts in the same way (Rawls, 1971, pp. 24ff.). Nor have all disputes about them been present or equally emphasized in the history of ethics. Sometimes one set of disputes is "the problem"; at other periods "the problematic" comes from a different set, together with different perceptions of human nature and the human condition. Using "the ancients" and "the moderns" as convenient labels mainly for Plato and Aristotle and some figures of modern moral philosophy from Hobbes to Rawls, we can make some useful comparisons (see Sidgwick [1981, p. 106]; Berlin [1969, pp. xxxvii, 126]; Rawls [1971, p. 201]; Schneewind, [1993]).

From Plato's Socratic dialogues to Aristotle's *Politics* disputes about what is good and what a greater good occupied center stage. This is because the central ethical question of the period, how we should live, was thought of in terms of what is good or bad for human beings.[1] We should live the best life for human beings, and what that is depends on what is good and bad for human beings and on their order of importance. Though this question was sometimes stated in terms of happiness, it came to the same thing, for human happiness was conceived in terms of what is good for human beings, as *the* ultimate and sufficient human good. If the question was posed in terms of pleasure, this was so because pleasure was thought the only thing good in itself. If the issue was whether we should pursue and cultivate the virtues of character – and what these are – this too was conceived in terms the contribution of such virtues make to happiness or the ultimate good.

Once a basic distinction was made, between things good in themselves and good as means to such ends, between ultimate good and all other good, the shape of the solutions favored by Plato and Aristotle is pretty much the same. These solutions have three components.

First, all disputes about what things are good and what is their order of importance are factored into disputes about what is good as end or what is good as means or as both. This is how in Plato's *Gorgias* Socrates analyzes the dispute whether one is better off doing rather than suffering injustice: it depends on their relation to the good or happiness. When the issue is taken up by Callicles, the dispute about the good of justice turns on whether pleasure is the ultimate good and justice leads to that. Similarly, once Glaucon proposes the threefold classification of goods in the *Republic*, the issue about the good of justice becomes whether justice is good in itself, good only as means or part of happiness, or good as both.

Second, disputes about *ultimate* good are always treated as more fundamental and more difficult to resolve than disputes about means *to agreed-upon ends*. Once there is agreement on ends, disputes about means can be resolved by the sciences of number and measurement, as Socrates implied in the *Euthyphro* and explicitly claimed in the *Protagoras*. And all agree that we can make mistakes about good as means to given ends, so this notion has some objectivity. But disputes about ultimate good are deeper and more difficult to resolve. And yet unless they are resolved, the ancients thought, agreement about means is not enough to determine the best life for individuals and the best society. Moreover, disputes about ultimate good matter practically, beyond the academy: they can be deep causes of violent conflicts and wars, perhaps even among gods. Sparta and Athens disagreed deeply about the ends of life and the ends of the city-state, and because of that, about the order of importance of security, courage, knowledge, justice, education, industry and the arts, love, and beauty.

Finally, both Plato and Aristotle claim that disputes about ultimate good, *are* resolvable by advances in human knowledge. They are amenable to the divine element in a human, human reason; decisively so for Plato, at least reasonably so for Aristotle. Human good, perhaps even the good of the universe, is knowable by human beings, perhaps only by few very intelligent human beings with advanced educations, perhaps potentially by all. For Plato good can be known if the universe can be known; for Aristotle human good can be known if human beings and their place in the living kingdom can be known.

For the ancients, then, the concept of the good is fundamental in human life and disputes about it cut wide and deep. But fortunately, they thought, the good is knowable, and once human reason understands it, it is capable of directing human life, with assurance proportionate to our knowledge.

It may never have occurred to Plato or Aristotle, or any of the ancient philosophers, that we can have reasonable or rational agreement on *major means* to ultimate good even though we have no agreement on ultimate good itself. Nor that this might be enough for agreement on justice and other social and political ideals, such as stability and cooperation. This appears to be a discovery of the moderns.

John Rawls's theory of primary goods, major and universal means to human ends no matter what such ends are, and rational for any individual to want no matter what his or her final ends, was not oirginal with Rawls.[2] But it seems to be an original and important *modern* idea, going perhaps as far back as Hobbes's notion of "a person's power."[3] And so apparently modern is the idea, so central to nonteleological ethical theories, that by using such thin concepts of goodness as primary goods, we can determine the duties of justice, without agreement on ultimate ends.

The ancient Greek democracies, with their consensus on the values of freedom and equality of citizens, may have come close to these modern notions, but the philosophers of the time do not seem to have explored or exploited it. Plato expounds at least the seeds of these ideas in the *Republic*, but rejects them. And once he makes a distinction between the useful, as the necessary or best means to *any ends*, and the beneficial, as the necessary or best means to *good ends*, he abandons the useful as not admirable, not a central notion in ethics (*Hippias Major*, 295–7, Woodruff, 1982). And since social and political freedom can plainly be used for bad as well as good ends, it appeared to him to belong to the useful, not the beneficial. But this notion of the useful is the very notion that Thomas Hobbes, Talcott Parsons, Brian Barry, and John Rawls use; *and* all the notion of good they think is needed to reach agreement on fundamental principles of justice. Freedom, which was only a species of the useful for Plato, is the greatest primary good in Rawls (short of self-respect); and the parties to Rawls's Original Position need not know their final ends to reach agreement on fundamental principles of justice. Disagreements about ultimate ends remain important for the individuals' "comprehensive conceptions" of the good – which include final ends – but we do not need to resolve these disagreements in order to agree on justice.

It is not easy to explain these differences on the role of ultimate good in human life.

Henry Sidgwick noted "two different forms in which the fundamental problem of ethics is stated . . . an investigation of the true Moral laws or rational precepts of Conduct . . . [and] an inquiry into the nature of the Ultimate End . . . the Good or 'True Good' of man . . ." adding that "the former seems more prominent in modern ethical thought . . ." (1981, p. 3) He went on to claim that the ancients' central question was, "Which of the objects men think good is truly Good or the Highest Good?" while for the moderns it is, "What is duty and what is its ground?"; further noting that it is hard for us moderns to understand the ancients' question unless "we throw the quasi-jural notions of modern ethics aside" (1981, p. 106).

J. B. Schneewind's recent studies seem to confirm a modern shift from the concept of the good to that of duty as the central issue of morality. Schneewind agrees with Sidgwick's drawing of the difference and argues further that behind this shift was a perception, beginning with Grotius, of a new central problematic for practical philosophy: conflicts of interest among people and their resolution. In a striking passage, Grotius casually bypasses disputes about the best life and the best form of government, and proposes that the test of legitimacy for a government is rather free choice and consent (Schneewind, 1990, vol. 1, p. 102; Schneewind, 1993). Conflicts of interest were now clearly seen as part of the circumstances of justice, and religious and metaphysical controversies about the ends of life were thought of *as a permanent feature of modern societies*, not resolvable by advances in human knowledge, as the ancients supposed – a feature most recently and famously relied on by John Rawls (1993, e.g. pp. xvi–xvii). In response, a new conception of morality was developed, in which the role of justice was seen as the adjudicator of such conflicts of interest, a justice on which we could all agree without having to settle the metaphysical and religious controversies about the ultimate ends of human life. The "quasi-jural" concept of duty, perhaps inspired by the prevalence of natural law theories going all the way back to the Stoics and the Roman codification of positive laws, may have made possible the invention of nonteleological structures for ethical theories. In such theories the duties of justice can be determined without reliance on ultimate good.

Of course there are moderns who do have eudaimonistic or teleological ethical theories, perfectionists such as Spinoza and Leibniz, or the

British hedonistic utilitarians and the ideal utilitarian G. E. Moore. As Rawls defines them, ethical theories are teleological if (1) they define the good independently of the right and (2) define the right as what maximizes the good. Nonteleological theories deny (1) or (2) or both. Rawls's theory explicitly denies (2) (1971, pp. 24–5). Modern teleological theories seem to be more continuous with the ancients both on the central problem of ethics and the shape of its solution. The major problem of ethics is what is the best life for human beings, or the problem of the *summum bonum*, as J. S. Mill tells us in *Utilitarianism*. For some modern rationalists and for perfectionists the solution still lies in advances in human knowledge which can help us discover the ultimate human good; while the British empiricists turned inward and found the answer in the subjective ultimate good of happiness as pleasure.

But the moderns also have nonteleological theories with Kantian or contractarian structures, something the ancient philosophers did not explore or exploit. These structures may free the moderns from the tyranny of a single dominant final end for individuals;[4] and also from the tyranny of requiring agreement on the same final ends for all individuals, in order to have agreement on justice (Rawls, 1982, p. 160). We can have agreement on justice *and* allow the maximum possible freedom of "lifestyles" – lives with different ultimate ends – within the confines of the agreement on justice. In these structures questions about ultimate good are no longer of fundamental importance, as Sidgwick noted. Many recent writers in this tradition have turned inward once more and found individual good not in pleasure, but in the wide-open notion of desire or preference satisfaction; with the desires or preferences being variously sanitized by consistency, instrumental rationality, autonomy of desires, or some combination thereof (Rawls, 1971, ch. 7; Elster, 1985). An essential difference between hedonistic and desire-satisfaction theories of good is that hedonism still claims to tell us what is intrinsically good; whereas desire- or preference-satisfaction theories leave ultimate preferences or desires wide open and up to the individual. Such desire-satisfaction theories, using only formal and intrumental rationality, seem especially well suited for contractarian or deontological theories of justice.

But it is not easy to understand why, from Grotius to Hobbes to Kant to Rawls, philosophers have supposed that we need not resolve religious and metaphysical controversies about the ultimate ends of human life. Nor is it easy to see why these thinkers believed that such conflicts and controversies are permanent features of (at least democratic) societies, and that we cannot rely on advances of human knowledge to resolve them. How can anyone know that these conflicts are permanent? Or that advances in human knowledge will never resolve them?

One reason may have been the skeptical tradition from Hellenistic times to the present. Skepticism about ultimate good may have began even earlier with Aristotle's criticism of Plato's form of the good, which cast a shadow on all cosmic and metaphysical conceptions of the good. Pyrrhonic skepticism may have cast another, longer shadow on any nonsubjective conception of the good, on any value theory that went beyond "appearances." (Schneewind, 1991) When the concept of goodness was almost united with the concept of God in medieval times, all the skepticisms about God's existence and nature became transferred to the concept of goodness. The question of ultimate human good became entangled in religious controversies about the existence and nature of God and man's relation to God. Such controversies seemed to be a permanent part of the intellectual landscape of Europe, nowdays extending to the whole earth. Orthodox vs. Catholic, Catholic and Protestant, Islamic and Christian, Christian and Jewish, Hindu and Buddhist – is there a beginning or an end, historical or theoretical, to such conflicts? Spinoza and Leibniz seemed to resurrect the concept of goodness as perfection, and make it less dependent on any particular religion; but their making it inseparable from their controversial metaphysics did not create confidence in our ability to know ultimate good, and this tradition is not dominant.

Skepticism about the possibility of gaining knowledge of ultimate human good may have been a motivation for the invention of nonteleological ethical structures. But can we go as far as to say that such structures always presuppose or rely on such skepticism? Rawls at least seems to deny this for his theory of justice, claiming that his theory is neutral on such epistemological questions, and also neutral on metaphysical controversies about the universe and human life in it (Rawls, 1985, 1993). And this might be correct, *if* the problem of the choice of principles of justice in the original position has *a* solution with a veil of ignorance that hides the parties' final aims, whether the solution is Rawls's principles or other principles. For if there is such a solution, then rational agreement is possible on principles of justice without agreement on the ultimate ends of human life or on ultimate good.

Following Rawls's lead on skepticism, one might think that deontological theories can be neutral on the permanence of controversies about final ends of human life. We don't *need* to know that such controversies are permanent, nor assume it. What we do know is that such controversies have been present in human societies since historical time began and they are present now. If we can rationally agree on justice without having to resolve such controversies about the ends of human life, we can have just and stable societies which can allow for the maximum possible development of diversity and indviduality. We can have not only a separation of church and state, but also a separation of state and ultimate good. If and when human beings ever make discoveries about the universe and human life which enable them to resolve rationally disputes about ultimate good, let them rethink about justice and the form of ethical theories.

However, Rawls's neutral stance on ultimate ends of human life is still disputed. The latest criticism is that his theory of justice assumes either skepticism about knowledge of the good or subjectivism about the good, and thus it is not epistemologically nor ontologically neutral about ultimate human good.[5]

2   Science and Ultimate Good

To all this we can add that there are now scientists who think that we have already made significant advances in human knowledge, which significantly affect religious and metaphysical views about the ultimate ends of human life, specifically the advances in biology in the last century and a half.

The broader issue has a long history. There is a very old tradition in ethics according to which we need to know a lot about the universe and humanity's place in it in order to know what is good for human beings. That is the Platonic tradition, at least in the *Republic* and the *Timaeus*. Aristotle's famous function argument, based on his psychobiology, puts him in this tradition. Some medieval philosophers, Augustine and Aquinas, also belong to it, and in modern times Spinoza: his *Ethics*, cast in Euclidean form, begins with metaphysics, epistemology, and psychology, and deduces a perfectionist good from grandiose definitions and theorems about the universe and humankind.

The other major tradition, mostly modern and Anglo-American, teaches that ethics is an autonomous discipline which can be carried out independently of metaphysics and the positive sciences. According to some, this tradition begins with Aristotle when he does ethics dialectically, beginning with the opinions of the many and the wise, throwing out the ones that conflict with known facts, systematizing and explaining the rest. Sidgwick may be a good example: he seems to think of ethics as a discipline which prunes, makes consistent, and systematizes common sense about the good and the right. G. E. Moore is in the same tradition. His treatment of H. Spencer's attempt to have ethics come to terms with the theory of evolution is an illuminating example: he criticizes some of Spencer's reasoning, attributing to him the naturalistic fallacy, and seems content to leave things at that, as if that settled the matter (Moore, 1903, ch. 2). But even if Spencer did commit the fallacy, there might still be room for the theory of evolution to make a difference to ethics; as one can see, by contrast, in Aristotle, whose famous function argument seems to presuppose natural kinds, essentialism, and fixed species. Rawls, perhaps with important qualifications, seems also to belong to the Sidgwick–Moore tradition.[6]

Neither tradition is entirely clear on how much ethics is supposed to be either dependent or independent of science, metaphysics, or religion. Presumably no one wishes to maintain that the human good and the right are entirely independent of any facts ascertainable by the sciences. The alleged gap between fact and value, the modern Humean doctrine presumably at the basis of the claim of the autonomy of ethics, does not claim a total independence of value from fact – only that we cannot deduce value statements from factual statements *alone*; neither the empirical nor the formal sciences alone can *prove* to me what my good is or what I ought to do morally. But factual statements may enter a valid deductive argument with a value statement as the conclusion; and presumably the more concrete or specific our value conclusion, the more we will need factual premises in the argument for it. Thus a change in our knowledge of facts might well make a difference in our conclusions about what is the best thing for us or what we ought to do.[7]

An important example of this more concrete problem may be the relation between what is good for humankind and the nature of life. Nowadays, the most formidable challenge to both traditions concerning this relation comes not from metaphysics nor the rest of philosophy but from the empirical sciences, especially biology.

The theory of evolution seems to have dealt a major blow to the older, teleological, theological, and metaphysical global conceptions of human life. The idea that man was created almost perfect in the image of God seems contrary to the fossil record. Science finally has something big to say about the "meaning of life" and "the purpose" of human existence. The theory of evolution seems to destroy not only the transcendent creationisms of Plato and the Hebrew-Christian tradition, which postulated a sentient being who designed and created the cosmos and life with certain ends in view, but apparently even the immanent natural teleology of Aristotle, that final ends are built into organisms. What seems worse, science so far seems to give us nothing to replace these grand speculations: it is not that life has a different purpose from what Plato, Aristotle, or Aquinas thought it has; it seems that human life, as distinct from individual lives,[8] has *no purpose*.

We get a glimpse of some of this in the opening lines of Richard Dawkins's famous book, *The Selfish Gene*. The author boldly asserts that before Darwin there were only superstitious answers to three "deep problems: Is there meaning to life? What are we for? What is man?" And a few lines later he says that people still do not appreciate "its [Zoology's] profound philosophical significance. Philosophy and the subjects known as 'humanities' are still taught almost as if Darwin had never lived" (1976, p. 1).

It would be another bold person who was confident that we can find out what is good for human beings independently of various answers to Dawkins's three deep problems or to Darwin's answers to them.

But the challenge Darwin and Dawkins pose for the two traditions in ethics is different.

If we cannot know the human good without considering these deep problems, the modern tradition which teaches that ethics can be done independently of science is probably mistaken. And if what is good for humans depends on what they are, and Darwin's theory of the descent of humankind is roughly true, these modern theories of the good might turn out either to be incompatible with evolutionary theory or to be poorly grounded.

The challenge to the older tradition is equally formidable. If Darwin's answers to these deep problems are far more probable than Aristotle's theory of fixed species, or the Christians' belief in created perfect species, or Plato's theory of created *im*perfect species, then this tradition might be correct in thinking that ethics depends on answers to these deep problems, but wrong in its answers to them. Do the normative systems of this tradition then collapse on the ruins of their probably false assumptions about humanity and its place in nature?

Plato's and Aristotle's theories of the good would seem to provide good case studies for answers to this difficult question. Plato's theory of the form of the good is embedded in his epistemology, metapysics, and even his physics. Aristotle represents both traditions: sometimes he does ethics dialectically, seemingly independently of the rest of philosophy and of science. But in the function argument the ultimate good for man is deduced partly from his newly discovered psychobiology. A change in the psychobiological premises might bring with it a change in his account of the good. This book exhibits the dependence of Plato's theory of the good on his metaphysics and epistemology; and of Aristotle's theory of human good on his psychobiology. How far their ethics is compatible with modern physics and biology is an interesting and difficult question.

3   *Disputes and Questions about Good*

There may be a measure of agreement about goodness.[9] But there are many disputes and no end of them is in sight.

There are disputes about *what* things are good and what evil. Bodily and mental capacities and conditions, such as health, strength, and intelligence have always been prized, but there has been much disagreement about the social goods of freedom and equality, power and wealth, offices and honors. The moral virtues themselves, especially justice and temperance, have been seen by some, Callicles in Plato's *Gorgias*, for example, to be at best necessary evils. And such theological virtues as faith and hope have been thought by others, Freud for example, to be benevolent illusions. Even life and death enter the lists: according to Socrates death is not a known evil, and so not rational to fear.

There are even greater controversies about *priorities*: which goods are greater, which evils lesser. Is faith a greater good than knowledge? Knowledge than freedom, freedom than power, or health than wealth? Are the natural capacities of human beings more important than social goods, as the ancients thought? Is goodness of character an incommensurably greater good than external goods? Is the good of a community greater than the good of any individual in it? Since scarcity of resources can force choices between almost any goods, the need for priorities becomes crucial if the good is to be a guide to choice; security from criminals and education of the young are both good, but which should we put first if we cannot afford to increase both? In Plato's Socratic dialogues we shall see, in chapter 2, Plato's pioneering examination of priority disputes among his contemporaries.

Then there are disputes whether the vast *diversity of goods* allows for comparability, commensurability, or aggregation of goods and evils across times, something that might seem necessary if the good is to be choice guiding for individuals; and whether the diversity of goods allows for interpersonal comparisons of welfare, something that might seem necessary for social rational choices. As early as Plato's *Protagoras*, hedonism became theoretically attractive because it seemed to answer the need for commensurability of goods: pleasure was seen as the common currency, as it were, by which all goods could be measured, weighed, and ranked, as wealth can be measured and ranked by money.

There are even disputes about *distinctions* and classifications of good things, and *their* comparative importance. The oldest is among goods desired as means and goods desired as ultimate ends. But there are several others: between things good in themselves, or intrinsic goods and instrumental goods; and between conditional goods and things unconditionally good. Such distinctions have been used to systematize and make coherent different systems of value. Plato and Aristotle used the threefold means–ends distinction to determine the *form* of the best life. Socrates and Kant used conditional and unconditional goods to determine the sources of all value. G. E. Moore used the concept of intrinsic value to give shape to the major controversies about good. Once such distinctions are made, disputes take more specific forms: is pleasure the only intrinsic good as the hedonist claims? Is knowledge good for its own sake, as the ancients thought, or only good as a means, as the moderns tend to think? Is wisdom the only unconditional good, as Socrates claimed, or is it a good will, as Kant argued?

On a more abstract level yet, there are disputes about good*ness*: whether all good things have anything in common which makes them good, whether there is such a thing as good*ness*, as Plato and G. E. Moore supposed. Or whether there are *varieties of goodness*, and difficult to discover how they are related, as G. H. von Wright has argued. Or perhaps the term good is "said in many ways," and has only focal unity, as Aristotle supposed; or it is predicated of a wide variety of things, God and men for example, only by analogy, as some medievals thought. Here goodness becomes a battleground between logical realists and nominalists, and even within logical realists such as Plato and Aristotle, as we shall see in chapter 6.

Still at the level of critical ethics, there are disputes whether good and evil exist in nature, as some ancients tended to suppose; or these terms signify relations of human beings to objects, human attitudes of thought and feeling toward objects in the environment or other human beings, as Hobbes thought; or even that things are good or evil only by human convention. Here goodness becomes a battleground between ethical realists and subjectivists, and between relativists and absolutists.

These disputes about good suggest some *major questions* theories of good try to answer, if they are to be choice guiding; the questions give us some understanding of the *aims* and *scope* of a theory of good.

What things are good? This looks like the question one should begin with. It calls for the *kinds* of things that are good. Writers as diverse as Plato, Aristotle, and Hume, have identified goods of the soul such as pleasure, knowledge, and virtue; goods of the body such as health, strength, and beauty; and social goods such as property, honors, and offices. Hume uses this classification to indicate the scope of justice. Others, Rawls for example, have characterized natural primary goods such as intelligence and health, which are distributed by the "natural lottery," and social primary goods such as rights and freedoms, income and wealth, which the basic structure of society distributes justly or unjustly; this distinction is appealed to to explain the scope and role of justice. Chapter 2 discusses extensively the early Platonic theories about the kinds of things that are good, their systematic sorting, and disputes about priorities among them.

A second main question is, What is goodness? Usually, this question is interpreted Platonically: what is common to all good things, at least things good in themselves, by reason of which they are good? We can take one version of hedonism, for example, as an answer to it: since pleasure is the only intrinsic good, the quality of being pleasant (not the cause or source of pleasure) presumably is the same as the quality of being intrinsically good. But some writers, such as G. E. Moore, dispute that the question has an answer, a definition or analysis of goodness. Of course nominalists dispute the very question itself. Meta-ethical questions about good are often sparked by questions about goodness. I discuss Plato's and Aristotle's handling of this question in chapters 5 and 6. In chapters 3, 4, and 7 we also see an interesting account of functional good that may bypass the disputes about Platonic goodness, separate or immanent: what the moderns call a contextual definition, or definition in use, of a good thing of a given kind, a good eye, a good watch, a good citizen. The structure, though not the content, of these definitions is similar to the contextual definitions Rawls offers of something being good of a kind (1971, p. 399).

My last question is, What is *the* good of a person, the best life for a human being? This is the most complex of the three questions, and perhaps the most urgent and practical. It is the opening question of Aristotle's *Nicomachean Ethics* (hereafter *NE*). We would expect this part of a theory of good to tell how a person may reasonably discover the good life for her. Here all theories face difficult questions about principles of rational choice, about rankings and weights among goods, about the comparability and commensurability of diverse goods, and about aggregation of goods across times and across persons. In chapter 7 I discuss Aristotle's fine analysis of the concept of the human good and the diverse and disputed conceptions of it.

Our three questions can be related to each other in different ways. One tradition holds that to discover the best life for human beings, we must *first* discover what things are good and how they are distinguished, related, and ranked. And this suggests a proper order for investigating our questions, the order we stated them. In support of it we might say that our most concrete and sure-footed intuitions (or "considered judgements" in Rawls's term) are about what particular things and kinds of things are good; and so we do well to start with this question, as Socrates may have done. The question about good*ness* is more abstract, and in any case it has as constraints the answers we give to the first question: to find out what is common and distinctive to good things we need to know, or have confidence in, some sample of clearly good things; otherwise how would we construct and test any generalization? We could then have an interplay between answers to these two questions, and perhaps some theory about this interplay, such as Rawls's theory of reflective equilibrium. The third question about the best life for a human, perhaps the most practically important, is very complex and also seems to presuppose some answers to the first question: in some sense, the good life must be constructed out of things that are good and their order of importance. We certainly find this thought in Plato's *Symposium*, when he has Socrates define happiness as the possession of good and beautiful things.

But the tradition of virtue ethics, also found in Plato and Aristotle, might dispute this ordering of our three questions. Philosophers in this tradition might argue that to discover the best life for a person, and even to know what things are good and their priorities, we need to know *first of all*, what a good person is, what is good character. Actions and possessions will be good in so far as they promote a virtuous character, or the life of the good person. I shall discuss this controversy in chapter 8.

This is a bare sketch of the aims and scope of theories of good. But it is not arbitrary. The basic intuition is perhaps that good is supposed to be choice guiding, an intuition we find in all moral philosophers, from Socrates to Rawls. Our three questions are clearly relevant and even crucial for choosing rationally, that is, for selecting what is better for us. To do that we need to know what is good and bad and their relative rankings, weights and measures. And for long-range planning or for big decisions such as the choice of career, we need to think globally about the best or the happiest *life*. Answers to our first and third questions are clearly crucial to such choices. Conceivably we can make do without our second question, the very abstract question about goodness; but the price may be that we leave what could be the most fundamental concept of ethics shrouded in an impenetrable mystery.

4   *The Aims and Limits of This Study*

The first aim in this study has been to *reconstruct* Plato's and Aristotle's theories of good. A second aim has been to show how Plato and Aristotle used their theories of good to *build up* their theories of virtue, especially justice, and of happiness. And all along I have also tried some limited critical *comparisons* with the moderns, hopefully to illuminate the merits and limits of the ancient theories.

But this study makes no pretensions to being comprehensive, with respect to historical periods, writers, or problems. Most of the limits are set by the limits of the author's knowledge. Some choices have been made on the basis of what has been discussed extensively, what relatively neglected. Ancient hedonistic theories, for example, have received considerable attention (see Gosling and Taylor, 1982). And the dispute in Aristotle, whether in his view happiness is restricted to the virtue of theoretical wisdom or also includes the virtues of character, has had the benefit of many able scholars in the last quarter century.[10]

Notes

1   Aristotle opens *Nicomachean Ethics* with questions about the good and his *Eudemian Ethics* about happiness.
2   Rawls (1971, pp. 62, 92); Barry (1965, p. 176), who cites T. Parsons for support; the later Rawls (1993, p. 75) modified the idea, making it depend on the political conception of a person.
3   Hobbes's "a person's power" includes capacities and social powers, things necessary or useful no matter what one's final ends. See Kafka (1986, pp. 92–6).
4   Rawls (1971, p. 554): "Human good is heterogeneous because the aims of the self are heterogeneous. . . . [in dominant end theories of the human good] The self is disfigured and put in the service of one of its ends for the sake of system." The criticism might fit Aristotle, if his happiness is a noninclusive end.

5   In *Political Liberalism*, it is only "reasonable" comprehensive conceptions of the good that justice allows. This distinction has provoked new controversy (McCabe, 2000).

6   Rawls, 1971. The method of considered judgments in reflective equilibrium seems to be in the Sidgwick–Moore tradition. But argument from the original position relies considerably on the social sciences, especially economics and rationaldecision theory; and his conception of the sense of justice is informed by psychology and learning theory. The larger worldviews of biology and physics are not used as a relevant framework.

7   The connection between ethics and science might be different for the good and for the right. The scope of goodness seems far greater: goodness but not rightness applies to animals, their organs, plants, their organs, artifacts and many other things. So we need to understand a wider range of things to understand goodness.

8   Freud distinguishes the meaning or purpose of human life from the purpose or meaning of particular persons' lives. The former question has no known answer and may never have one, he says; and shrewdly remarks that we don't ask about the meaning of the life of animals, unless we mean to reply that they exist to serve humankind, which is indefensible (1953, vol. 21, ch. 2; Sullaway, 1970).

9   See Rawls (1971, p. 400) for a remarkable footnote claiming wide agreement on some parts of goodness as rationality, from Aristotle on.

10 See, e.g., Cooper (1975) for the impetus to the discussion; David Keyt's classic article (1983); the sophisticated treatment by Kraut (1989); and Crisp's analysis (1994).

2

The Socratic Good of Knowledge

The ancient Greeks believed in the power of personal qualities, character, and intelligence. These were the qualities of the Homeric heroes responsible for their leadership and success, admired by humans and approved by gods. Achilles was above all a man of bravery, high spirit, and touchy pride. Blessed with a cunning intelligence, Odysseus was a man of many ways, who could devise a strategem for any enterprise among friend and foe alike.

But the Greeks also believed in physical strength and beauty, noble birth, wealth and power, fame and glory. These were the good things of life and success and happiness would be inconceivable without them.

In the archaic period personal qualities and bodily and social advantages were all found together in the noble heroes. Odysseus and Agamemnon, Achilles and Ajax, the Trojan Hector, all have the virtues of character and intelligence, noble birth and physical stature, lands and flocks, power and fame. Their great lives and deeds were made possible by all of these goods. Lesser men are not highlighted in Homer, but in so far as they appear at all they reinforce this model. Odysseus' companions are not his equals in birth, wealth, or power, and they prove to be equally lesser men in wisdom and bravery.

The invention of money and the development of trade in the seventh and sixth centuries spread wealth beyond the landed aristocracies, to men of lesser birth and lesser deeds. These newly rich could make substantial material contributions to the defense and the adornment of their cities and could thus lay claim to honors and offices, esteem, and even virtue. Nobility and heroic deeds, which had been sure signs of character, seemed no longer as necessary for virtue. Hesiod taught that wealth could be gained through hard work, and "virtue and fame accompany wealth" ("Works and Days," 308ff.). Wealth and virtue, two sure examples of value, became closely associated, rarely if ever found apart, almost confused (see Adkins, 1960).

But by the end of the fifth century a *poor* man of no lineage nor glorious deeds drew a sharp line between virtue and possessions, saw *conflicts* between them, and took his countrymen to task for *preferring* wealth and power to virtue and knowledge. And he was made immortal by Plato, a man of knowledge but also of aristocratic birth and wealth. In his *Apology* (30ab) Plato has Socrates defiantly tell his fellow citizen:

> Good Sir, you are an Athenian, a citizen of the greatest city with the greatest reputation for both wisdom and power; are you not ashamed of your eagerness to possess as much wealth, reputation and honors as possible, while you do not care for nor give thought to wisdom or truth, or the best possible state of your soul? . . . I ask you to make your first and strongest concern not wealth but the soul – that it should be as virtuous as possible. For virtue does not come from wealth, but through virtue, wealth and everything else, private and public, become good for men.[1]

Here wisdom and virtue are sharply distinguished from all other goods and set above them as the source and condition of their value.

Wisdom had been prized in Homer's time, but it was the cunning intelligence of Odysseus and the sage advice of Nestor in practical enterprises. This high valuation of practical knowledge was reinforced by the development of the arts of agriculture, architecture, navigation, and medicine. Here the benefits of knowledge were evident. Healing the human body seemed to depend on how much the ancients knew about it; and safety at sea on knowledge of navigation.

Then the pursuit of knowledge and truth took new meaning in the philosophers before Socrates. The pre-Socratics devoted their lives to discovering the origin, composition, and structure of the cosmos. What is the physical world made of? How did it come to have the beautiful order we observe in the seasons and the stars, or the orderly sequence of growth in plants and animals? These are the questions of Anaximander and Empedocles, Anaxagoras and Democritus. The pursuit of even more abstract questions about change and permanence, time and space, by Heraclitus, Parmenides, and Zeno, became prized by philosophers and scientists. The pre-Socratics pursued theoretical knowledge in mathematics, astronomy, physics, and metaphysics, seemingly for its own sake, out of curiosity about our world.

In Plato's dialogues theoretical and practical knowledge became the highest goods humans can attain. In his ethical investigations about how we should live Plato has Socrates constantly rely on the crucial role of knowledge in the arts, the *technai*. And he brings virtue up to the value of wisdom by the Socratic doctrine that virtue is knowledge. In the middle and later dialogues Plato brings theoretical knowledge into this high plateau by his appreciation of the role of mathematics and astronomy.

Wisdom, virtue, knowledge, beauty, health and strength, wealth and power, honors and fame – all these are human goods, the Greeks would agree. But they are different kinds of goods, Socrates says; and we can be in conflict about them, since rarely if ever can we have them all. Which then should we choose over others? Perhaps those which contribute most to the best life? But which life is the best or the happiest?

On these questions Plato's Socrates was in profound disagreement with most of his contemporaries.

From the *Apology* to the *Gorgias*, the *Euthydemus* and the *Meno* Socrates holds firmly that wisdom and virtue are of such great benefit to individuals that those who have them can be happy no matter what other good things they lack; while if they lack the virtues they cannot be happy no matter what other good things they have. This is the basis for a Socratic principle of choice which Gregory Vlastos has called the Sovereignty of Virtue: that whenever one is faced with a choice between virtue and vice one should always choose the path of virtue, no matter what good things go with vice and bad things with virtue. Not only are wisdom and virtue themselves beneficial to their possessors, but are prior over all other goods. Not *morally* prior, a priority of the right over the good as in deontological theories, but in terms of benefit and happiness to the individual.[2] Virtue and wisdom are absolutely *essential* to, and *dominant* in, human happiness.[3]

This is a position so strong that it borders on paradox. It is understandable that Socrates' contemporaries disagreed with it, no less than the moderns. Our task in this chapter is to examine this disagreement, begining with the *Gorgias*.

1   All Goods and their Socratic Rankings

The *Gorgias* is perhaps the most comprehensive Socratic dialogue on goods and their order of importance. It discusses important goods championed by Gorgias, Polus, and Callicles, which Socrates tries to radically downgrade. Rhetoric, power, and freedom are sponsored by Gorgias and Polus as the greatest instrumental goods for success and happiness. Pleasure is championed by Callicles as the ultimate end of human life: he accepts the competitive virtues of courage and wisdom as instrumental goods for pleasure (Adkins, 1960); but he rejects the cooperative virtues, justice as "the good of another," and temperance as self-control, because it deprives us of the most intense pleasures. Socrates argues against rhetoric, power, and pleasure,[4] while freedom is left for Plato in the *Republic*.

On the positive side, Socrates gives his own systematic *sorting* of all goods, and a partial *ranking* of them, the virtues being highest and the goods of the sophists the lowest:

> Goods of the Soul: Wisdom, Justice, Temperance, Courage, Piety
> Goods of the Body: Health, Strength, Beauty
> Social Goods: Wealth, Reputation, Offices and Honors

This *sorting* of all goods, by soul, body, and society, became standard, from Aristotle (*NE*, Bk. I, ch. 8) to Hume and beyond. Hume uses it to determine the domain of justice. Justice is primarily concerned with social goods: unlike the goods of the mind, social goods are insecure and are of use to those who can take them from us; goods of the body cannot be so used, but our bodily injury can be advantageous to others. Hence we need regulations about such things as theft, property damage, and bodily injury (*Treatise of Human Nature*, Bk. III, part 2, section 2). Aristotle thought of the social goods as "goods of fortune," and his distributive justice is also primarily concerned with them (Cooper, 1985; Keyt and Miller, 1991).

Nowadays the reach of justice may be longer than even Hume supposed. Parts of the body which can now be transplanted can be of use as artificial instruments, and justice comes very much into donors and transplants (see Dennis [1995]). Psychic goods also can be insecure. Our knowledge can be stolen and be of advantage to others, as can be seen in the disputes over "intellectual rights" and patents. And the acquisition of knowledge can be subject to fortune and social control, as can be seen in disputes over access to and resources for education. Knowledge, and even character formation, may be social goods or require social goods, subject to social control and the vagaries of fortune. Even self-respect can come under the indirect control of social institutions (Rawls, 1971, pp. 440ff.). But even in this widening of the scope of justice, the Socratic classification is useful background.

Unlike the sorting, the Socratic *ranking* of the three kinds of goods was and remains very controversial. Contrary to most of their contemporaries, Plato and Aristotle adopted and developed the basic Socratic ranking with many additional arguments for it.

But how did the philosophers propose to settle these controversies about priorities among acknowledged goods?

The most general way was by appeal to what Gregory Vlastos has called the "Eudaemonistic Axiom": we all desire our own happiness as *the* ultimate end of all our rational acts (1991, p. 203, n. 14). Once staked out by Socrates, Vlastos says, this principle "becomes foundational for virtually all subsequent moralists of classical antiquity."[5] Here we seem to have an Archimedian point for resolving priority disputes. We try to rank all other goods by how far they contribute to our happiness. This seems theoretically simple and appealing.

However, no Socratic dialogue gives a definition of happiness. Worse yet, three different disputed conceptions of happiness seem to underlie the disputes about priorities. Gorgias and Polus seem to think of happiness as the satisfaction of our desires, no matter what these are: we are happy when we can do and have whatever we want; and they rank goods by how far they enable us to do that. Callicles thinks of the happy life as a life of pleasure and ranks the virtues and other goods accordingly. And Socrates thinks of happiness as the best state of the soul, analogous to bodily health, and ranks other goods by how far they contribute to this psychic state. With Gorgias and Polus the disagreement about happiness does not surface, but it becomes explicit with Callicles.

So priority disputes cannot be settled by appeal to happiness as our common ultimate end, so long as there are disagreements about what human happiness is. The Eudaimonistic Axiom may still be helpful for individuals in settling their priorities, but it will not settle interpersonal disputes about priorities, unless we can argue and reason not only about means to happiness but also about different conceptions of happiness. Let us look at how these issues pay out with the sophist and his pupils.

2   The Dispute with Gorgias: Is Rhetoric the Greatest Good?

The disagreements begin when Gorgias claims that the greatest good is the art of rhetoric, the ability to persuade others in the law courts and the assemblies of the city-states (452d, 453a). Apparently in support of this, he claims that this ability is the cause of the power to rule in one's city and of freedom from the power of others. Political power and social freedom are treated as great *instrumental* goods, because they enable us to do as we please and get what we want; and rhetoric is the greatest instrumental good because it enables us to have power and freedom. Rhetoric, power, and freedom, are treated as if they were Rawlsian *primary goods*: things it is rational to want no matter what else we want, since they are generally necessary or useful for attaining any desired ends. Thus, if happiness is the satisfaction of our desires, rhetoric, power, and freedom are the greatest instrumental goods because they enable us – they provide us with resources and opportunities – to get what we want, no matter what that is; more so than other goods.

Socrates challenges Gorgias by bringing in the claims of other arts and goods. Medicine, gymnastics, and moneymaking, might each claim that the object *it* pursues is the greatest good: health for medicine, beauty and strength for gymnastics, wealth for business. How can we tell which is correct? Gorgias replies that rhetoric is the greatest good because in *any* dispute before the democratic courts and the assemblies over health, beauty, and wealth, the rhetorician can easily win over the doctor, the trainer and the moneymaker, or anyone else (456–7). Rhetoric is the greatest instrumental good, because if you have it you can have power and freedom to do whatever you want; whereas if you have any of the other goods – health, good looks, and wealth – you don't necessarily have all the other things you want; a rhetorician could take them away from you or could persuade someone else to do it.

Gorgias' underlying idea may be that if happiness is the satisfaction of our desires, we rank instrumental goods by the power of their instrumentality – by how far they enable us to get or do the things we want; the greatest of them will be those which more than others get us the things we want. Rhetoric is the greatest good because it is the most *inclusive*,[6] with power and freedom next in line: if we command them we can have everything else we want, something not necessarily true of health, wealth, or good looks.

Socrates tries to show that Gorgias is mistaken by two lines of argument. First, he shames Gorgias into making justice a constraint on the use of the art of the rhetorician. Gorgias grants that in other arts, such as boxing, we would censure the use of the boxer's trained ability to harm others physically outside the ring; similarly, the art of the rhetorician does not entitle him to use it unfairly to destroy others' reputations or take their goods. Gorgias says reasonably enough that if this happens, it is the fault of the student, not necessarily the rhetorician who taught him the art. But he is too ashamed to admit that if a young man comes to him not knowing what is good and bad, fine and shameful, just and unjust, Gorgias will not teach him. But if the rhetorician does know and teach his pupil what is just and the pupil has this knowledge, then, on the analogy of other arts (carpentry, medicine, music), the pupil will do what is just (Irwin, 1979; Santas, 1979). If the pupil does something unjust, it is evidence that the rhetorician did not teach him justice, which, Gorgias has admitted, the rhetorician should do.

This argument shifts some of the burden of proving that rhetoric is the greatest instrumental good to the relation of justice to happiness; since now the most benefit Gorgias can claim for rhetoric is confined to its just uses. With Polus this becomes the focus of dispute, because Polus is not similarly shamed to make a similar admission (461). He wants to know why we should constrain our behavior by justice.

The second line of attack is that since the rhetorician can outargue the physician, for example, in front of a crowd on the very issues the physician is most competent, as Gorgias boasts of (456–7), it seems that the rhetorician is most effective in persuading people that are ignorant of the subject under debate; he would not win before an audience of physicians. Not only that, but apparently what he produces in the minds of his audience on such occasions might actually include *false* beliefs, since presumably the physician is much more likely to know the truth about health. The rhetorician flourishes when talking to ignorant people, and his power to pursuade is enhanced when it is not confined to producing *true* beliefs. So, if there is a distinction between truth and falsehood and between knowledge and belief, as Gorgias admits, since he agrees that unlike knowledge beliefs are sometimes false, rhetoric is not a branch of knowlege like geometry, nor a practical discipline like medicine or gymnastics. For *these* aim at knowledge or the good of the body, and such ends can only be reached by discovering, proving, and using truths and avoiding falsehoods. In these disciplines learning means coming to know something or at least acquiring true beliefs, whereas the persuasion rhetoric aims at can be accomplished even with inducing false beliefs.

The two lines of argument taken together indicate that even on the assumption of happiness as the satisfaction of desires, rhetoric is not necessarily the greatest instrumental good, if it is constrained by justice and truth. If it is not so constrained, we need to know why we should practice an art such as rhetoric which countenances falsehoods and is indifferent to justice. So far, Socrates has tried to cut down the scope of rhetoric's instrumental good through the constraints of truth and justice.

3 *The Dispute with Polus about Power, Desire, and Good*

But Polus boldly questions these constraints. In our pursuit of happiness, why should we stay within the boundaries of truth and justice? Will the practice of rhetoric bound by truth and justice get us more of what we want than rhetoric unbound? Polus presses these questions still within the conception of happiness as the satisfaction of desires: if rhetoric unbound gets us everything we want, or more of what we want, and so makes us happy, why should we not use it?

The discussion with Polus reveals an ambiguity in the Eudaimonistic Axiom, that we all desire our own happiness as the end of all our rational actions. Polus perhaps accepts this axiom because he might have the idea that our happiness *just is* the greatest possible satisfaction of our desires, *no matter what these happen to be.*[7] Gorgias' earlier glorification of rhetoric points in the same direction: power over others gives us freedom from the power of others, freedom to do as we please. And if we ask, why should we want that?, the answer may be that happiness just is doing as we please.

But Socrates does not accept this idea. Satisfying our desires, no matter what these are, is not necessarily something good for us. Our good is a constraint on our desires, not conversely. Things are not good for us because we want them.[8] We want them only if our belief that they are good for us is true. We don't "really want" them unless they *are* good for us.[9] And we can make mistakes about what is good for us, at least about what is good for us as a means. Thus our desires must be bounded by our good, and desires for things as means must also be bounded by true beliefs or knowledge of means to our good. Rhetoric, and the power and freedom it may bring us as means to our good, must consequently be bounded by our good and be a true means to it.

The corresponding problem for things we want as our ultimate good is postponed till the discussion with Callicles, since the possiblity of mistakes is not as evident for ultimate good, as it is for means to our good: for all we know, what we desire as ultimate end is what is ultimately good for us, no matter what we desire as ultimate end. As for justice, Socrates tries to convince Polus later that justice and the other virtues are far greater goods for us than rhetoric or power or freedom to do as we please, and so, once again virtue should be a constraint on all our conduct, for our own good.

But Socrates does not attack directly Polus' conception of happiness as the satisfaction of desires, no matter what these are. Rather he tries to show that at least in the choice of means knowledge or true belief is a necessary condition of successful choice, if success means getting or doing what is best for us.

Polus comes to the rescue of rhetoric by pointing out what he takes to be a fact: rhetoricians have "the greatest power" in their cities, "the power to put to death anyone they want, to deprive him of his property, or expel him from the city as they think" (466b). As his example of king Archelaus shows, Polus' point is that these people are happy, indeed the happiest, without the contraints of truth and justice; they can *do* anything they please and *have* everything they want – how could they be anything but happy? This reveals his assumption that happiness is the satisfaction of desires, no matter what these are.

To the claim that rhetoricians have the greatest power in their cities Socrates replies, "No, if you mean power in the sense of something good for him who has it" (466b). Polus replies that he does mean that, and Socrates begins to argue against him by claiming that "rhetoricians and despots alike have the least power in their cities . . . since (1) they do nothing that they want to do . . . though (2) they do whatever they think to be best [for themselves]."

Polus challenges Socrates to prove how these two propositions *can* be true together; only *possibility* is at issue *here*. Polus believes that if you do what you think best you do what you want (467b). Why should Polus believe this? Perhaps because he thinks that getting what you want *is* what is best for you, *and* he fails to make a distinction between what is best as means and what is best as ultimate end.

Socrates takes advantage of this failure by concentrating on cases where one does something which he believes is best *as a means* to one's good, where one clearly *can* make mistakes; and when one does make a mistake, he is not doing what he wants to since it is *not* best for him.

"If one does something for the sake of something, he does not wish that which he does but that for the sake of which he does it" (467d).[10] For example painful medicine is taken for the sake of health, and dangerous trading by sea is done for the sake of wealth. The idea being illustrated is clearly that of doing something as a means to something else. And about such means we can certainly make mistakes; so, our wanting things as means is constrained by truth about the relation of that means to our good.

Further, "there is [no] existent thing which is not either good or bad or between [intermediate] these – neither good nor bad . . . wisdom and health and wealth and everything else of that kind good, and their opposites bad . . . things neither good nor bad [are] such things as sometimes partake of the good, sometimes of the bad, and sometimes of neither – for example sitting, walking, running, and sailing, or again, stones and sticks and anything else of that sort" (467e–468a).

Finally, Polus agrees also that (1) we do not want bad things; (2) we want only good things; and (3) we do intermediates for the sake of good things, and not conversely. This last proposition is noncontroversial, given the other two, and from all three it seems to follow that desire should be constrained by good: we do not want things as means unless they benefit us.

Why does Polus readily agree without argument that we do not want bad things but only good things? In the *Meno*, Meno puts up a fight when these views are proposed by Socrates, and Socrates has to argue for them. Why does Plato have Polus agree without resistence when he knows that argument is needed? I have not seen this question discussed. One possible answer is that Meno and Polus have different underlying ideas about the relation between good and human desires. Meno may be thinking that we can work up sets of good things and sets of bad things independently of what particular human beings happen to want; then when we look at what human beings do want, we find that sometimes they want some of the things in the set of good things and sometimes some in the set of bad things. For example we observe that sometimes human beings eat fatty foods and we know that fatty foods are bad for them. Socrates brings Meno to heel by confining desiring bad things to desiring things for oneself (thus excluding desiring bad things for others); by confining bad things to things whose possession harms one and makes one unhappy (thus excluding moral evils such as injustice); and by relying on a corollary of the Eudaimonistic Axiom, that no one wants to be unhappy.

But Polus may have other ideas, as I have indicated: we don't want bad things, and we want only good things, because bad things just are things we don't want, and good things just are things we want. On this view, we cannot make an inventory of good things and of bad things independently of what human beings want and don't want; we decide what things are good and what bad on the basis of what human beings want and don't want. Socrates brings Polus to heel by the distinction between good as means and good as end. For Polus' view is plainly false for things good or bad as means, since people can and do make mistakes about what things are good or bad means to what they ultimately want. For example at one time people found smoking satisfying and thought it harmless; an inventory of good things based on what people wanted at that time would have included smoking. But people were wrong in thinking smoking harmless; so it would have been a mistake to include smoking among good things, even though lots of people at the time wanted it. So, even if we identify human good with what most or all humans ultimately want, we cannot determine what is good for humans as means on the basis of what humans want as means to their ultimate ends.

This is the line of argument Socrates pursues. On the assumption that the actions of the rhetoricians and the despots – the exercises of power Polus so admires – are intermediates, Socrates concludes that no one wants to put people to death, take their property, and expel them from the city "simply as such", but "we want to do them" if they benefit us and not otherwise. Thus *if* a despot *happens* to have a *mistaken* belief that doing these things will benefit him, then, even though in doing them he does what he thinks best (for himself), he is not doing what he wants, since what he wants is some good thing for himself and these things do not bring him any such good.

What does this argument show? It shows that it is *possible* to do what one thinks is best for oneself and yet not do what one wants to do.[11] It shows this by drawing a distinction between things we want for themselves, "simply as such," and those we want because of other things we want, and proceeding on the true assumption that we can make mistakes about what we want *as means*. In making choices, if we want effective means to our ends, we should constrain ourselves by truths in the choice of means. Nowadays, this constraint of truth on desire comes under the name of "information": if our choices are to be rational they must be informed.

But has Socrates shown that desire must also be constrained by good? Once more, the answer to this question depends on what view one has on the relation between human desire and human good. Polus' admission that we desire (only) good things for ourselves is simply assumed in this dialogue. But it is also ambiguous: it may be interpreted on a hypothesis of ultimate good (or happiness) as independent of desire, or of ultimate good as the satisfaction of desires. Taking the latter hypothesis, Polus can admit that we can make mistakes in our choice of means and still stay with happiness or ultimate good as the satisfaction of desires. He can proceed in a Humean way: he accepts the distinction between desiring things as means and desiring things as ends, and admits, in the present case, that the intermediate actions the rhetoricians and despots pursue should be pursued only if they serve the things these people desire as ends. He can admit the introduction of good as a constraint, but think of good as end as simply something we want as end; so the constraint of good on desire amounts to no more than the constraints of causal relations between means and ends.

Whether this notion of *ultimate good*, the notion of being desired as ultimate end, is itself constrained by truth, i.e. knowledge or true belief, depends on whether we can *reason at all* about things we desire as *ultimate* ends. On the Humean view we cannot, except for ironing out misunderstandings about what something we desire only as an end *is* or what its causal properties might be. The Humean view of practical reason as being purely instrumental also seems to go well with the conception of happiness and the good as the satisfaction of desires.

4 The Dispute with Polus about Justice and Happiness

Socrates now proceeds with a battery of three famous arguments designed to prove his own priorities among goods. He relies on the classification of goods into psychic, bodily, and social, and tries to show that the psychic goods, the virtues of justice, courage, temperance, piety, and wisdom are the greatest goods; the bodily goods next; and the social goods last. The opposites of these goods, the corresponding evils, receive a similar ranking: the vices are the greatest evils, the bodily next, and the social the least evils. Only the third of these arguments argues for this ranking, but premises from the other two are presupposed. This ranking is then taken to imply that the virtues are constraints on the pursuit of the other two classes of goods, or even that the pursuit of bodily and social goods should be for the sake of cultivating and maintaining the virtues.

Socrates' approach here is very indirect. He does not argue for the ranking by *measuring* these goods as he proposes in the *Protagoras*; nor by estimating roughly the *power of their instrumentality*, as Gorgias did earlier. Rather, he relies on whether his fellow Greeks praise or admire one or another of these goods more than they admire others, and whether they condemn or find shameful some evils more than others. From such comparative judgments, granted by Polus, *and* an analysis of such admiration and shame, he derives comparative judgments about the relative greatness of these goods and bads.[12]

Here is the third argument. In one's material resources poverty is a bad thing, in bodily resources, weakness, disease, and ugliness are bad things, and in the soul, injustice, ignorance, and cowardice. Of these, injustice is the most shameful. If so, it exceeds the others in pain or harm or both.[13] But being unjust, intemperate, cowardly, or ignorant does not exceed in pain being sick or poor. Hence the former set of bad things exceed being sick or poor in harm. What exceeds in harm exceeds in the same measure in badness. Hence of the three kinds of bad things the vices are the greatest "bads" (477be).[14]

Next a corresponding argument is made for the ranking of three instrumental goods: the arts of justice, medicine, and moneymaking, which produce the psychic good of justice, the bodily good of health, and the social good of wealth. Of these three arts justice is the greatest good, because justice is the most admired of the three; the most admired exceeds the others in pleasure or benefit or both, and justice does not cause more pleasure than the arts of medicine or moneymaking. Hence the art of justice causes greater benefit than the other two, and so is the greater good. (478bff.). And if it is the greater good by causing a greater benefit, that benefit, psychic justice, must be a greater benefit than health or wealth.

Finally, Socrates tells us who are happiest and unhappiest; *not* on the basis of who has the most things she or he wants, but who has the greatest goods and least bads. This shows clearly enough that unlike Gorgias and Polus, Socrates believes that happiness depends on good things, not on the satisfaction of desires (whatever these happen to be). "Happiest therefore is he who has no vice in his soul, since we found this to be the greatest of bad things. . . . Next after him, is he who is relieved of it . . . [by the art of justice]. The worst life is led by him who has the vice and is not relieved of it" (478e).

These ranking arguments have been much criticized. The inductively arrived at analyses of the admirable and the shameful is in terms of the benefits and pleasures, harms and pains, which various actions produce in *society at large*, to those who behold these actions or are affected by them; from this we cannot validly derive specific benefits/pleasures or harms/pains *to the agents* of the actions. We admire justice for the benefits and/or pleasures it brings, or the harms it helps avoid, to most people perhaps most of the time, not necessarily or always to the just person herself; similarly for the shame of injustice. So from the supposition that injustice is more shameful than poverty though not more painful, it does not follow that it is more harmful *to the unjust person*. But this is the very conclusion Socrates seeks to establish, as is shown by his ranking of happy and unhappy persons on the basis of the ranking of goods and bads they possess; if injustice is not necessarily the greatest bad *to the unjust person*, he need not be the most unhappy person. Socrates seeks to establish rankings or priorities among goods from the point of view of the individual (not of society), and so does the opposition.

Socrates may have been correct in the deepest assumption of his arguments: that the admiration (or shame) that a society bestows on certain actions reflects the belief that they are of some benefit (or harm) to human beings; and that this belief is not likely to be mistaken if it represents a judgment of many persons over many generations. Witness the universal admiration for the human arts and sciences to which Socrates so often appeals; or the universal admiration for acts of courage. But to account for this admiration we do not need the stronger assumption that it is always the agent of the admired action who is benefited by it, whether it be an act of courage or the discovery of the printing press.

5   The Dispute with Callicles about Good and Pleasure

Plato himself brings another criticism to these ranking arguments. He has Callicles attack the comparative judgments of admiration and shame which Polus agreed to and Socrates used. These, he says, are conventional, social constructs cultivated by the majority of the people who are individually weaker but collectively stronger than highly intelligent and brave individuals. In individual contests, these stronger persons can take and use for themselves the social goods of the weaker and inflict bodily harm on them. The weaker get together, become collectively stronger, impose constraints on such actions and call such constraints justice. This is justice by convention or law, not by nature. Further, the weaker cultivate in the younger generations the feelings of shame and condemnation of injustices (so defined), thus producing an internal, psychological sanction to the conduct they seek to banish. So understood, this conventional shame that an unjust person is trained to feel for her wrongdoing is not a reflection of a judgment that injustices are bad for the unjust persons who commit them; but rather that they are bad for weak persons who suffer injustice without the power to retaliate. So once more, Socrates' conclusions are unjustified, even if we conceed the comparative judgments of admiration and shame. Callicles has produced a non-Socratic explanation of societal admiration and shame, which concedes some connection to benefits and harms but still does not support the Socratic rankings.[15]

Callicles also claims that humans experience another kind of shame, which is natural, not a cultural construct; but this is the *shame of failure*, failure to get or achieve what we want, not the shame of wrongdoing. And this once more is of no help to the Socratic rankings.

Callicles then proceeds to do some very different rankings of his own. The happiest life is the pleasantest, we get pleasure when we satisfy our desires, and the intensity of the pleasure is proportional to the intensity of the desires.[16] On these assumptions he ranks the personal qualities of intelligence and courage above those of conventional justice and of temperance as self-control: intelligence enables us to discover the best means to pleasure and courage enables us to dare the risks and dangers of such choices; whereas conventional justice as the good of another and temperance as self-control deprives us of some of the most intense pleasures. The method of ranking here is similar to that used by Gorgias and Polus: we rank instrumental goods (the virtues here) by how far they enable us to attain our ultimate ends (maximal pleasures). Callicles too relies on the Eudaimonistic Axiom, but with happiness as pleasure. Socrates attacks the conception of happiness or the good as pleasure, but his arguments are inconclusive.[17]

The ranking arguments in the *Gorgias* are instructive since they introduce some ways to rank goods and bads, which any theory of good must do if it is to be choice guiding. None of these arguments is completely successful. One reason is the disagreements we noted about happiness or ultimate good, which spread into the ranking of instrumental goods. Another is the disagreement about what our admiration of the virtues presupposes. Both show up in the round with Callicles.

Finally, if Socrates is trying to prove the Sovereignty of Virtue, his arguments are unsuccessful even if we bypass these criticisms and grant the conclusions of all his three ranking arguments. First, his rankings are only partial, since within each of the three classes of goods there is no ranking: which is a greater good, justice or temperance? Beauty or strength? Wealth or honors? Then again, there are no measures or weights attached to the various goods: the ranking is purely ordinal, and we don't know by how much one good is greater than another. It is still possible that all the bodily and social goods taken together outweigh all the virtues together; if so, why should not Hercules choose the road to pleasure rather than the path of virtue? The partial ordinal rankings do not entail that the harm of injustice outweighs *all the goods combined* which the unjust person may succeed in attaining; or that justice in the soul outweighs *all the bad things combined* which a just person may meet. And yet this is what Socrates would have to prove in order to show that a person who has the virtues but lacks all other goods can be happy, while a person who lacks the virtues cannot be happy even if he or she has all other goods. The mere ordinal and partial *ranking* of the three classes of goods is not sufficient for the Sovereignty of Virtue, or for Socrates' rankings of happy and unhappy persons.

But in the transitional dialogues of the *Euthydemus* and the *Meno* Plato tries another ranking strategy, which might be thought sufficient. To this we now turn.

6   Conditional and Unconditional Goods

The arguments using this distinction, for the thesis that all goods depend for their value on wisdom and virtue, in the *Euthydemus*, 279ff., and the *Meno*, 87–9, have been neglected until very recently. Yet their importance for Socratic ethics may be considerable. They are the only arguments in Plato's dialogues capable of proving Sovereignty of Virtue: that whenever one has to choose between virtue and vice one should choose the path of virtue, no matter which social and bodily goods go with vice and which bad things with virtue. Also, the distinction between conditional and unconditional goods has been influential with such philosophers as Aristotle, Kant, and Moore. Moore disputes the arguments because they violate his principle of organic unities. Kant seems to use similar arguments and a similar distinction, but he arrives at a very different conclusion, that the only unconditional good is a good will while wisdom is another conditional good (1981, first section, 393–4). As John Cooper (1984) has remarked, these texts are crucial in the history of moral philosophy.

The argument in the *Euthydemus* (278e–279a) begins with easy agreements on two plausible Socratic and Greek cultural assumptions: that we all wish to do well or attain happiness,[18] and that we will be happy and do well if we possess good things. The first of these is a version of the Eudaimonistic Axiom. The second is easily and explicitly granted in *Symposium* (205a): "it is by the possession of good things that the happy are happy." Both may be popular views, innocent of the philosophical controversies about what things are good, their order of importance, and the various distinctions and relations among them.

These agreements suggest that *the way* to do well or become happy, Socrates' second question and the main concern of the passage, is by acquiring goods. But this at once raises priority questions. Socrates' contemporaries pursued primarily the social goods of wealth, offices, honors, and reputation, thinking that these goods would make them happy; whereas Socrates takes them to task for pursuing them exclusively or in preference to the goods of the soul, arguing that the latter is what makes us happy. Here and in the *Meno* Socrates *argues* for some sort of very strong priority of the virtues over all the other goods: the virtues are never outweighed by *any* combination of other goods.

It is not clear what sort of priority this is. Is it an absolute priority, admitting no trade-offs of any kind, like Rawls's *lexical* priority of the liberties over the goods of wealth and opportunity (1971, section 8, "The Priority Problem")? Such priority would certainly support the principle of the Sovereignty of Virtue, but what argument would establish it? In any case, though it is a priority of virtue over other goods, we must not confuse it with a Kantian *moral* priority, or Rawls's priority of the right over the good.[19] Socrates still argues for his priority on the ground of benefit and happiness for the virtuous individual; we should choose the path of virtue, no matter what other goods are included in the other options, because such choice and only such choice will make us happy. And this is certainly not a Kantian justification and allows for a legitimate non-Kantian motivation.

What are the goods by the possession of which allegedly we shall be happy? Socrates constructs an inventory of goods, beginning with wealth, adding health, good looks, noble birth, powers and honors – all undisputed social and bodily goods.[20] He ends with the goods of the soul, temperance, justice, bravery, and finally wisdom, remarking that someone might dispute these. We saw this dispute in the *Gorgias*, and we shall see it in the *Republic*: there was no opposition to the view that the social goods and the goods of the body benefit their possessor; but though the virtues were seen as perhaps always benefiting *somebody*, it was not necessarily or always the virtuous man.

This inventory of goods is by no means complete, either by Plato's standard or our own. Friendship is a great good in the *Lysis*, love in the *Symposium* and *Phaedrus;* and the opposition brings up freedom and pleasure in *Gorgias*. These missing goods are certainly endorsed by the moderns. But all the missing goods are discussed in the *Republic* and given some role in the happy life.

The argument in *Euthydemus* proceeds by making two distinctions used to modify the hypothesis that happiness consists in the possession of good things.

Possession and use: A person may possess but not use good things; and if she does not use the goods she possesses she will not necessarily benefit from them; and if she does not benefit she will not thereby be happy. For example, if one had food but did not eat it, or a carpenter had tools but did not use them, one would not be benefited by them.

Does the distinction apply to all goods? What is it to have and not use health? Or pleasure? Merely having these seems directly beneficial. If so, are these goods conditional on wisdom? And Socrates cites only uses, apparently not recognizing "exchange value," though the functional uses may be more fundamental.

In any case, the original hypothesis becomes modified: Happiness consists in the possession and *use* of goods.

Correct and incorrect use: However, using these goods is not sufficient for benefit and happiness, since they may be used correctly or incorrectly: when they are used incorrectly they can harm us even more than their opposites, so that we are better off with no use at all than with incorrect use. Wealth presumably is a prime example of this: it has so many uses – an "all purpose [primary] good" Rawls calls it (1988); wealth can be used powerfully to harm or benefit ourselves or others, and similarly with power, strength and good looks, and most other goods and instruments.

So, our hypothesis gets modified once more:

Happiness depends on the possession *and correct* use of good things.

But what is correct use of goods? In context, clearly correct use is use that produces benefit and happiness for the person who uses them. And how do we get to use such goods correctly? On the basis of a series of examples, Socrates argues that correct use depends on wisdom. Correct use of a carpenter's tools and materials, for example, depends on knowledge of carpentry; correct use of a ship, on knowledge of navigation; correct use of food on knowledge of its nutritional value. Socrates' examples come from the *technai*, the arts and sciences, in which some human good is the accepted goal, and we use materials, tools and instruments, to attain such a good: a house, safe passage at sea, health. Correct use depends on knowledge of how to use materials and tools to attain the good the *technē* aims at. Similarly, if we aim at our own happiness, correct use of the goods of the inventory will depend on wisdom, that is, knowledge of what uses will bring us benefit and happiness.

As a result, we have a final modification of the hypothesis:

Correct use of good things, the use that will bring us happiness, *depends on wisdom.*

So, none of the things ordinarily thought good are beneficial and bring us happiness unless they are *used and* used with *wisdom*. Wisdom is *the* condition of their goodness.

On the other hand, Socrates claims, wisdom is not like *these* other goods in this respect: among the goods of the inventory it is (the only thing) "good by itself"; it does not depend for its goodness on these other goods. Similarly, ignorance is (the only) thing *bad by itself* (281de).[21]

So, if we ultimately want to be happy, as we all do, then no matter what else we aim at, we *must* aim at acquiring wisdom before all else; without it other goods we possess are not necessarily of any benefit to us or make us happy.

Before assessing the soundness of this argument, let us consider its major significance: it has as a powerful consequence the Sovereignty of Virtue; at least when put together with a parallel argument in *Meno*, 87–9, which makes all the virtues, not just wisdom, unconditional goods and the condition of the value of all other goods.[22] If the virtues are the only unconditional goods *and* the condition of the goodness of all other goods, this principle follows at once: if people lack the virtues, then they will not be able to use any other goods correctly (except accidentally) and so will derive no benefit and so no happiness from them; *the other goods are valueless* to them – they can even be harmful – *without the virtues*. On the other hand, if one has the virtues she will have all the benefits they bring, by themselves and by enabling her to use bodily and social goods beneficially.

So unlike the ranking arguments in the *Gorgias* or any other ranking arguments in the dialogues, the arguments in *Euthydemus*, together with those of the *Meno*, are powerful enough to imply the Sovereignty of Virtue: for they bypass the need for knowing the measures and weights of various goods: if successful they show that the other goods, by themselves and without the virtues, *are of no benefit to their possessor*; so one could not possibly be happy without the virtues no matter what else she or he had. And one would be happier with the virtues, at least if she or he had a "base line" amount of the other goods, than with indefinitely large amounts of the other goods and no virtue.

These are powerful consequences. But is the argument sound?

To begin with, there is a problem about the unconditionality of wisdom: other goods being used wisely seems to presuppose that one has them to use, and so their possession is a condition of wise use. Wisdom without *any* other goods to use would seem to be as valueless as the other goods are without wisdom. This objection implies that wisdom is as conditional on other goods as they are on it. Mike Ferejohn (1984) identified this problem and suggested the following solution.

First, he distinguishes helpfully two related but different properties: invariable beneficence and value independence, as being the properties wisdom presumably has and the other goods lack.

Invariable beneficence is a property Socrates often attributes to the virtues, and he sometimes uses it in arguments against proposed definitions of the virtues: temperance is not identical with modesty because temperance is *always* beneficial and modesty is not; courage is not identical with endurance because courage is *always* beneficial and endurance is not (*Charmides*, 161; *Laches*, 192). In the present argument Socrates is arguing that the absence of wisdom in a life is harmful; while the addition of wisdom is invariably beneficial, at least given some "base line" amount of goods.

With value independence the situation is more complex. Ferejohn distinguishes a stronger and weaker notion: a thing is *self-sufficiently good* if and only if it "requires the presence of nothing else in order for it to produce benefit" or to be beneficial. This property wisdom does not seem to have since it requires *some* good or other to be used wisely, some "base line" amount of goods.[23] However, wisdom does not require any *particular* good, as the other goods require the particular good of wisdom, to produce benefit. A thing x has this weaker property of *value independence* if there is no *particular* object y such that x brings benefit only if y is present. Wealth does not have this value independence since there is a particular thing, wisdom, which must be present if wealth is to produce benefit. On the other hand, though some good or other must be present for wisdom to produce benefit, there is no one particular good which must be present.

It is not clear that Socrates distinguishes between being self-sufficiently good and being value independent. However, the distinction, besides being necessary for the soundness of the argument, answers another puzzle about it. If we do not allow the distinction and attribute to wisdom the stronger property of self-sufficiency, we are immediately faced with the question about the value of happiness itself. If wisdom is the *only* self-sufficient good, and happiness is a good (indeed the good), as Socrates certainly holds, it follows either that happiness is not a self-suffcent good, which seems paradoxical; or that wisdom and happiness are identical, which also seems paradoxical. If wisdom and happiness were identical, why would anyone need any other goods at all to use wisely and be happy?

But if Socrates is allowed the distinction, he can say that wisdom is value independent, and the condition of the goodness of all the other things in the original inventory, while happiness is a self-sufficient good, indeed a *complete* good, that is, a good such that nothing added to it would make it a greater good. And from the *Philebus* and the *NE*

(Bk. I, ch. 7) we know that Plato and Aristotle held just this view of happiness or the good.

Self-sufficiency is of course stronger than value independence, but not strong enough to be the same as the self-sufficiency of *the* good in the *Philebus*, and the self-sufficiency of the good in Aristotle (*NE*, Bk. I, ch. 7). In Aristotle we also have the notion of a "complete good," a good such that there is nothing the addition of which would make it a greater good. These two properties, Ferejohn's self-sufficieny and (the *Philebus* and Aristotle's) being a complete good, are the two properties Kant attributes to the good will and to deserved happiness; the first is the only unconditional good the second the only highest good (Korsgaard, 1983, pp. 178–81).

I have drawn quite a few distinctions among good things: some but not all are invariably good, some have value independence, some are self-sufficiently good, and one is a complete good. Goodness is complex as well as fragile.

The distinctions enable us to interpret the grand conclusion of the *Euthydemus* argument: none of the goods of the inventory besides wisdom have invariable beneficence or value independence, but depend for their beneficence on the presence of wisdom. Wisdom has both invariable beneficence and value independence; while happiness, for the sake of which all other goods are sought, is self-sufficently good and the complete good.

It is also not clear that Socrates distinguishes between invariable beneficence and value independence. However, he proceeds in a reasonable way from variable beneficence to value dependence: for each of the goods of the inventory besides wisdom he shows or implies that it is variably beneficent, that is, sometimes beneficial and sometimes not; he then seeks the condition(s) under which it is beneficial, and finds one and the same condition always, namely, the addition of wisdom. So from variable beneficence he infers value dependence, and then identifies the dependence to be always on wisdom. Wisdom, on the other hand, since its addition to any good always brings benefit, is invariably beneficent, and so apparently value independent.

7   Socrates and Kant: Wisdom or the Good Will?

Centuries later Kant seems to have reasoned in the same way, proceeding from variable beneficence to value dependence, though he reached a different conclusion. Kant tried to show that every good including knowledge, except a good will, is variably beneficent and so conditionally good (or good with qualification); he then identifies the condition of beneficence to be always one and the same, a good will. And since the addition of good will is something which renders the other goods always beneficial, the good will must be invariably beneficent and value independent. But when Kant argues also that the good will is good independently of any results it may bring, he seems to imply that the good will has also the stronger property of being self-sufficiently good. And finally he holds that the combination of virtue and happiness, or *deserved* happiness, is the comlete good (1981, first section, 393–4; Korsgaard, 1983).

How could Socrates and Kant reach such different results using similar distinctions and similar reasoning?

One reason may be the possibility that wisdom also can be used incorrectly, to bring about ill rather than good, a possibility Socrates seems to overlook altogether. And if so, wisdom too is variably beneficent, and so value dependent. In conscious opposition to the ancients, Kant has no difficulty supposing that "intelligence," "judgment," and "calm deliberation" can be misused and so are variably beneficent and dependent on the good will. Even some qualities of temperament can be so misused according to Kant, "however unconditionally they were esteemed by the ancients": courage and self-control can be exceedingly bad without a good will, he says, and gives the example of a scoundrel whose coolness makes him not only more dangerous but more abominable (1981, first section, 393–4). It is not entirely clear that Socrates' wisdom and Kant's judgment and calm deliberation refer to the same things; Kant may talking about judgment and deliberation concerning means, no matter what the ends, whereas Socrates' wisdom is about correct means to good ends. Nor is it clear that they mean the same things by courage and self-control; the "courage of a scoundrel" is not really courage, Socrates would say, since it is not always admirable or praiseworthy. Still a substantial question arises here: how are we to explain Socrates overlooking the possibility that wisdom too can be misused?

As far as I can see, there is only one convincing explanation: Socrates assumes one of his favorite doctrines, that we desire only good things, things that benefit and bring happiness to their possessor. If so, then we shall never missuse knowledge of what things are good for us, in the sense of using such knowledge to acquire bad things *for ourselves*. We know that Socrates explicitly argues for the view that we desire only good things, in the *Meno*, 77–8. And so the *Meno* contains two arguments, this and the argument later showing that the virtues are unconditional goods, both of which solve problems created by the argument of the *Euthydemus.*

We should note, though, that this solution in the *Meno* is not sufficient to show that we might not misuse knowledge of good and evil to harm *others*, to do injustice or *wrong*. This is the kind of misuse that Kant may have had in mind, as his example of the scoundrel suggests. But here too, we can understand the difference between Socrates and Kant. Socrates claims and argues in the *Gorgias* that doing wrong is always harmful to the wrongdoer – even more than to the wronged person: doing injustice brings unhappiness to the unjust agent, while virtue is sufficient for the virtuous person's happiness. If this is so and we have knowledge of it, as well as knowledge of what is good and bad for us, we shall not misuse this knowledge to do wrong, since we want to be happy and we know or believe that doing wrong would make us unhappy. For Socrates, whenever we use a good, say, power or wealth, to do wrong (a moral misuse, a use contrary to the virtues), we are also using that good also against ourselves, against our own happiness (a prudential misuse).

But Kant disagrees that virtue and only virtue brings happiness: a person with no touch of a good will can be happy, though not worthy of being happy. So for Kant there can be no knowledge that virtue and only virtue can bring happiness, and knowledge of what is good and bad for us can still be misused, i.e., used to do wrong, to act contrary to duty.[24] Indeed it is moral misuses of the goods of his inventory that Kant seems to have chiefly or exclusively in mind, in his argument that the good will is the condition of worth of all other goods, including even happiness. And the worth he has in mind is not any value whatsoever, since happiness has some value independently of the good will and without it, but *moral* worth, presumably, the worth of character, the worth of persons.

Happiness is conceived differently by Kant, independently of virtue, as the sum total of the satisfactions of our inclinations. And virtue and the good will are conceived independently of happiness.[25] In Kant we seem to have two kinds of "value," each defined or conceived independently of the other, a fundamental bifurcation of value, and perhaps of human reason as well. But we still have some conditionality of the one on the other, of the worth of happiness on the good will. And the two can still combine in some way in the complete good, deserved happiness, or a happy being with a good will.

8   The Conditional Value of All Goods on Virtue in the Meno

There is a second major problem in the *Euthydemus* argument, and has a solution in the *Meno*. In a little subargument, Socrates takes up courage and temperance and says that these too, as well as wealth, strength, and high position, can be more harmful without wisdom than not having them at all.[26] But he is completely silent on how courage and temperance can exist without wisdom, as wealth, strength, and high position certainly can. Nor does he argue or say that temperance, justice, and courage, are all variably beneficent and thus value dependent on wisdom, even though in his conclusion he apparently does include these virtues as being value dependent on wisdom. The reason for this silence is probably that Socrates holds that these virtues are invariably beneficent; and this is not something easily given up, since it is an axiomatic anchor of his refutations of the ordinary definitions of the virtues in the early dialogues: Socrates insists that nothing is a virtue unless it is invariably beneficent (*Laches*, 192; *Charmides*, 161).

In any case, without an explicit treatment of the relation between wisdom and the other virtues, the argument so far does not imply the Sovereignty of Virtue, only that of wisdom.

The solution comes in the *Meno*, 87–9, in an argument that parallels the *Euthydemus*, but with one crucial change. Here it is explicitly acknowledged that each virtue is invariably beneficent, but it is nevertheless argued that each is value dependent on wisdom. This is done by a thought experiment: by imagining what, say, courage would be if we were to take wisdom away from it. The answer given is that (i) what would be left would be *not courage* but a "sort of boldness," and (ii) that this boldness is variably beneficent, whereas (iii) courage itself is invariably beneficent. And from this the conclusion is drawn that the invariable beneficence of courage is due to that part of it which is wisdom, and so courage is value dependent on wisdom. The reason why courage is invariably beneficent is that it cannot be found apart from wisdom, and similarly with the other virtues; something which is not true of wealth, health, and the rest of bodily and social goods.[27] A fool can be wealthy, but no fool can be courageous.[28]

Socrates' thought experiment also shows that here at least the virtues consist in more than wisdom, since a part of courage is identified which is not wisdom, a certain daring. This is what makes possible the thought experiment by which Socrates decides that the good of courage is due to the element of wisdom in it. If courage were nothing but wisdom, there would be nothing left if we took away wisdom. This conception of the virtues as constituted by more than wisdom, in Plato's transitional dialogues, is further developed in the *Republic*, and in Aristotle.

9   Socrates and G. E. Moore on the Value of Knowledge

In this argument in the *Meno* Plato boldly goes beyond identifing what things are good and what invariably good; he goes inside an invariably good complex and tries to discover to what element its goodness is due, the source of its value. Moreover, he does this by a thought experiment in which he isolates one element of the complex from another and makes a judgment about it: he isolates the noncognitive element in courage, a certain daring, from the wisdom which is also part of courage, and judges *that* to be sometimes good and sometimes bad, whereas the whole complex, courage, is judged to be invariably (admirable and) good; so the invariable good of the whole complex, courage, Socrates infers, must reside in its other element, wisdom. In modern times, Sidgwick and Moore used similar isolation thought experiments to discover the source of value in valuable complexes.

Sidgwick appears to use such an isolation test to show that in valuable complexes such as enjoyments, one element, cognition of truth, has no intrinsic value. For example if we separate such cognition from any feeling normally attending it, such as pleasure, and from the object known, what is left is "an element of consciousness quite neutral with respect to desirablity" (1981, pp. 398ff.). Sidgwick of course wants to argue that it is the feeling, pleasure, which gives the whole its value.

Moore objects to this inference, relying on his principle of "organic unities" (1903, pp. 92ff.): "from the fact that no value resides in one part of a whole, considered by itself, we cannot infer that all the value belonging to the whole does reside in the other part, considered by itself" (1903, pp. 27–8; and Korsgaard, 1983, pp. 190–2). But this is an objection to Socrates' inference as well: for this is just what Socrates did in the *Meno*: no invariable value resides in daring considered by itself, so the invariable value of courage must reside in the other part, wisdom, which indeed is said to be "good by itself." But, Moore would claim, courage is an organic whole, and if his principle is correct, the inference is invalid.

Moore thinks that Sidgwick's, and presumably Socrates' mistake, lies in applying the method of isolation "only to one element in the wholes he is considering." "He [Sidgwick] does not ask," Moore continues, "If consciousness of pleasure existed absolutely by itself, ["and absolutely nothing else, should exist" (1903, p. 94; see also 187ff.)] would a sober judgement be able to attribute much value to it?" (1903, p. 93). Presumably, such sober judgment in this second test would confirm the principle of organic unities: we would have a very valuable complex, consisting of enjoyment and knowledge, each of which, considered by itself, had little or no value. Also presumably, had Socrates performed such a second isolation test with courage, isolating wisdom this time, he would have judged that wisdom too had no invariable goodness, was not good by itself. I call what Moore claims Sidgwick did a *partial* isolation test, since Sidwick applied it to only one of the elements of the complex; and what Moore proposed to complete the test, a *total* isolation test, since Moore proposed that the isolation test is applied to *each* elment of a complex.

Moore approves, and cites against Sidgwick, another isolation test we find in Plato, this time in the *Philebus*, 21a (1903, pp. 88ff.); perhaps because Socrates applied it to each element of the mixed life, pleasure apart from all knowlege, and knowledge apart from all pleasure, and got the same negative result in both cases: that no one would choose a life with one of these elements alone. The best human life is made up of both knowledge and pleasure; and the double isolation test shows that neither alone can account for the great value of this best human life, which is far greater in value than the sum of the values of its two parts, and not in any proportion to them. The results of the isolation tests of the *Philebus* are supposed to refute both hedonism (the good = pleasure) and the Socratic good of knowledge (the good = knowledge), the two theories also refuted in the *Republic*, as we shall see. At least in the *Philebus*, Moore thinks, Plato did not make Sidgwick' mistake or Socrates' mistake in the *Meno*.

In the elevating last chapter of *Principia Ethica*, after he gives his total isolation tests to all the elements of ideal goods, Moore concludes that his analysis

> affords some justification for the immense intrisic value commonly attributed to the mere knowledge of some truths, and which was expressly attributed to some kinds of knowledge by Plato and Aristotle. If the results of this section are correct, it appears that knowledge, though having little or no value by itself, is an absolutely essential constituent to the highest goods, and contributes immensely to their value. (1903, p. 199)

Like Sidgwick, Socrates in the *Meno* does not subscribe to G. E. Moore's principle of "organic unities"; at least his argument violates the principle.

Did Socrates then make a mistake? It is not clear. To begin with, how do we know that courage is "an organic unity"? What makes a complex an organic unity? When Moore broaches this question for the first time, he says:

> But a thing belonging to any of these three classes [things which have intrinsic value, things positively bad, and things which appear indifferent] may occur as part of a whole, which includes among its other parts other things belonging to the same and to the other two classes; and these wholes as such may have instrinsic value. (1903, p. 27)

It is to these wholes that his principle is at first and immediately applied: "the value of such a whole bears no regular proportion to the sum of the value of its parts."

To apply the principle to courage, then, it seems that we need to know that courage has intrinsic value and that its parts belong to one or another of these three classes.[29] But how do we know these things, or know them independently of the principle itself?

Aside from these questions, why should we suppose that the principle of organic unities (or "organic relations") is true? What is the argument for the principle? As far as I can tell, Moore gives illustrations of the principle (the first one on pp. 28–9), but no evidence other than the results of isolation tests themselves. That makes the isolation tests the fundamental points of agreement or disagreement.

Now Moore's isolation tests seem to me to have two big difficulties, one of coherence and another of completely uncertain judgments or intuitions. First, Moore's isolation test is total in two respects: it isolates *each* and *every* element of a complex, *and* it isolates each element from everything else in the universe, imagining that it "and absolutely noting else should exist." Is this coherent? What is it to imagine a universe in which a certain daring, either as an individual thing or as a kind of thing, and absolutely nothing else exists? Are there people in it with darings and no wisdom, or are there just darings? If the former there must be many other things in that universe, for example, objects and circumstances of daring. If not, I cannot imagine it; I have no idea what it means to have a universe with nothing whatsoever in it except darings. Similarly with wisdom and absolutely nothing else. Which did Moore mean? If we take Moore's language literally, since he was justly famous for his careful use of words, apparently he meant what he said: "and absolutely nothing else should exist."

Socrates' thought experiment in the *Meno* was not total in the second respect, as well as not total in the first. He was not asking us to think of a universe of daring(s) and absolutely nothing else. He was asking us to think of cases in which people displayed daring behavior, in circumstances of personal risk and danger, but did not have knowledge or wisdom of the risks, the costs, the aims, or their chances of success; and he made the judgment that without such wisdom the daring sometimes resulted in good and sometimes not, whereas the same daring with wisdom always resulted in good. Whether or not we agree with these judgments and the inference he drew from them, this is certainly coherent.

The second difficulty is the uncertainty of the judgments we make in the thought experiment. In thought experiments, as distinct from actual experiments, the question always arises about how much confidence we have in the judgments we make and about the sources of such confidence. The less radical isolation thought experiment Socrates performed bears enough similarity to experience to make sense of confirming or discon-firming the judgments by observation or experiment. But this question becomes the most difficult to answer in Moore's doubly total isolation test: because isolating something from everything else whatsoever removes it from our experience completely, and the corresponding judgments become completely cut off from any evidence.

Even in the far less radical isolation tests Socrates performs, consider-able uncertainty remains. Suppose we isolated wisdom from daring; Socrates would say that wisdom so considered by itself is always good; Moore would say that it has little or no value. How are we to tell who is correct? It would appear that we need to observe or produce actual rel-evant situations where the persons have wisdom but no daring and see what the relevant results are. Moore seems to assume that had Socrates performed such a test, he would have judged, at least if sober, that wisdom had little or no value by itself. Perhaps, perhaps not. The point is that even in the less radical thought experiments it is hard enough to tell who is correct; in Moore's total isolation thought experiments it seems impossi-ble. If only we could reliably measure value!

10 Goods, Wisdom, and Happiness

Some other problems with Socratic ethics come to a head in the *Euthy-demus*. Let us begin with the notion of the correct use of the goods: what counts as correct use of the bodily and social goods? The ultimate question the argument seeks to answer gives us the clue: how to become happy – to discover "the road to eudaimonia" as Ferejohn calls it; and the initial answer was, by acquiring good things. Once the distinctions are drawn, between possession and use and between correct aand incorrect use, correct use must mean use that benefits the possessor, and in turn, beneficial use must be use that contributes to the happiness of the possessor; for the whole motivation for these distinctions was to isolate the uses of these goods which contribute to happiness.

Now this understanding of correct use has an important consequence: it presupposes that happiness can be understood and characterized independently of the original inventory of good things. For the argument needs to use contribution to happiness to determine beneficial use of the original goods, and beneficial use to determine correct use of these goods. So, Socrates cannot rely on these goods – their possession or any use – to determine what happiness is, without going around in a circle. Do we have then a conception of happiness independent of these goods? None in the present argument, or in the rest of the dialogue.

This lack of an independent conception of happiness in the *Euthydemus* creates an immediate problem about the *content* of wisdom. What is the wisdom necessary for the correct use of the goods a wisdom of? If we take the criterion of correct use just proposed, it is knowledge of how to use the goods so as to bring benefit and thus happpiness to their possessor. To use the goods of the inventory correctly (except by accident) one would need to know (or truly believe) what happiness is *and* what use of these goods would contribute to happiness. To use wealth so as to contribute to happiness I would need to know what happiness is and what uses of wealth, among its many uses, would contribute to that happiness; just as to use wood correctly to build a house I would need to know what a house is and how to cut and fit wood so as to construct a house. Both pieces of information are necessary for correct use.

But since Socrates provides no conception of happiness independent of the inventory of good things in the *Euthydemus*, he cannot fill in the content of wisdom. Once Socrates has made the distinction between correct and incorrect use of goods, he can no longer say, as he does easily and without argument in the *Charmides* and the *Laches*, that the wisdom necessary and sufficient for happiness is knowledge of good and evil: for if by knowledge of good he means knowledge of what goods are in the inventory, that is not longer sufficient – we must also know their correct use. And if he means knowledge of correct use, then we need knowledge of happiness independently of the goods of the inventory.

It should be no surprise at all, then, that when Socrates takes the conversation in his own hands for the second and last time in the *Euthydemus* (288d–293a), returns to his previous themes and raises this question – what is the knowledge, possession of which would make us happy – he is unable to answer it. This second passage is a natural continuation of the previous argument which showed that wisdom is the only thing good by itself and the condition of the goodness of all other things; and now the question is, What is this wisdom of? Between 288e and 292e, over and over Socrates raises this question, goes over a number of answers – knowledge of gold, of moneymaking, of lyremaking, of speechmaking, of generalship, of the kingly art – and he rejects them all. For the same reason, it is also no surprise that in all this wealth of answers Socrates does not even take up the answer so readily given in the *Charmides*, namely, knowledge of good and evil.[30] Socrates' argument of the *Euthydemus* presupposes that there is some value *outside* the original inventory of good things *and* outside wisdom: there must be some thing(s) which is self-sufficiently good and is brought about by the wise use of the good things in the inventory. And what is that? The obvious answer is happiness. But what is happiness?

One possible solution to both problems, of an independent conception of happiness and of the content of wisdom, is to separate all the other goods from the virtues, make happiness consist (in part or in whole) in the virtues, and make the other goods conditional on the virtues. This is not done here, but it is apparently the solution proposed in the parallel argument in the *Meno* (87b–89a). Here, as we saw, the position of the *Euthydemus* is modified: the beneficence of all the *other* goods (social and bodily) is variable, depending on whether wisdom is present. But this is not true of the virtues themselves since they cannot exist separately from wisdom and thus cannot be misused; what can be misused and is variably beneficent is, for example, daring, not courage. The virtues are now in effect unconditional goods: each virtue as a whole has value independence, though it is trivially value dependent on itself, and one element in it (daring) is value dependent on another (wisdom).

The *Meno* modification solves the present problem by having a conception of happiness independent of *bodily* and *social* (even nonmoral psychic) goods,[31] all of which are conditional. Happiness can now consist of the virtues, or the virtues can be sufficient for it; while all the other goods, social and bodily are value dependent on virtue. This also solves the problem of the content of wisdom. Wisdom can now be knowledge of what this happiness is (i.e. virtue) and of the uses of conditional goods which promote this happiness.

This may well be the Socratic view of happiness and of the value of conditional goods, or at least Plato's solution to Socratic problems in these two "transitional" dialogues. It is the position, I believe, which Sidgwick identifies as the perfectionism of the ancients: the good is perfection (or rather excellence, a high approximation of perfection) and the main or only perfection is moral virtue (1981, part 1, ch. 1). It is what Thomas Hurka calls moralistic perfectionism (Hurka, 1993, intro., ch. 1).

But the theory now faces new problems. First, it can no longer be a teleological ethical theory without problems of circularity – a fundamental change difficult to understand. For now, though it has a conception of happiness independent of conditional goods, it has no conception of happiness independent of virtue, and so it violates the first condition of a teleological ethical theory, the independence of the good from the right.[32] Second, it faces immediately the fundamental objection that injustice sometimes seems to benefit the agent more than justice. And unless this objection can be successfully answered, then the virtues cannot be necessary for happiness. No wonder that in the *Republic* Plato tries so strenuously to prove that virtue and only virtue brings happiness.

11   Is All Value Conditional on Virtue?

There appear to be obvious counterexamples to the Socratic view we have reached. According to this view the sole value of food, for example, obtains only when food is used with virtue, directly or through another good such as health, since health itself has value only when it is used with virtue. And the same would be true of wealth, good looks, offices, reputations and honors: all of them would be correctly and beneficially used only when used with virtue. This seems at best dubious, and at worst false. The value of food lies in its nutritious qualities which promote life, health, and strength; and this value seems to be no less to a man who lacks virtue than to the courageous or the just. It may be replied that it is still true that the correct use of food depends on wisdom. But the wisdom in question is knowledge of the nutritional value of various foods; it seems false that the wisdom required for correct use of food is knowledge of virtue and of the use of food that promotes virtue. So this solution seems paradoxical; though it is consistent with what Socrates says about knowledge, virtue, and happiness, in the *Euthydemus* and the *Meno*, where this solution is most probable.

Aside from this objection, the Socratic argument ignores two other kinds of value the moderns recognize. One is "exchange value," recognized by Aristotle and much elaborated by Adam Smith (1937, Bk. I, ch. 4). Food can be eaten (its "value in use"), or it can be exchanged for another good, say, shoes. Division of labor depends on the ability and willingness to trade one kind of good for another, a uniquely human activity, and trade in turn creates "value in exchange," whether in older barter or the newer money economies. Smith points out that there is no direct proportion between utility (value in use) and exchange value: nothing is more useful than water, he says, but it had hardly any exchange value (in his time and area), whereas diamonds had hardly any value in use but have great exchange value.

The introduction of exchange value would complicate the Socratic argument. For one thing, all the goods of the inventory including wisdom would seem to have exchange value as well as value in use, except for the virtues of character (courage, justice, and temperance) and for happiness (and possibly pleasure). The exceptions hold not because people would be unwilling to trade other goods for virtue or happiness, but because these virtues and happiness cannot be exchanged at all. Wisdom, on the other hand, can have exchange value since being a kind of knowledge it can be taught for a fee (or sold, for that matter). Socrates was notoriously unwilling to teach for a fee, but that was part of his character, not part of the nature of knowledge. In modern societies knowledge can command a very high premium; witness the disputes about patents and "intellectual rights", and the exorbitant fees various "experts" can command. So it is not true that if a person had some knowledge but no other goods, this knowledge would not be of any value to her; she might be able to exchange it, without even losing it, for other goods she needs, as teachers do. But the same is true for any other good in the inventory: if a person had a lot of foodstuffs but no wisdom, she could exchange some foodstuffs for some wisdom. So far as exchange value is concerned, it would appear that wisdom and the other goods are on a par.

The other kind of value ignored by the Socratic argument is what we might call "opportunity value." The idea of opportunity value is found in Talcot Parsons, in Brian Barry and in early Rawls. Barry gives as "a first approximation" of a definition of one's interests: "an action or a policy is in a man's interests if it increases his opportunities to get what he wants"; and he quotes the sociologist Parsons, *The Structure of Social Action*: "Wealth and power . . . are potential means to any ultimate ends. . . ." The key words here are "potential" and "any." These notions seem similar to the notions by which Rawls's primary goods were originally defined: namely, instrumentality and generality: primary goods are things a rational person wants no matter what else he or she wants; for they are normally neces- sary or useful means to anything he or she wants (Barry, 1990, p. 176; Rawls, 1971, pp. 62, 92). The Rawlsian primary goods, rights and liber- ties, income and wealth, and positions of authority all have opportunity value: their value, or at least some of it, derives from the opportunities they afford us to do as we please; as we please within the confines of justice, for Rawls, since the right is prior to the good in his nonteleo- logical ethical theory.

Opportunity value does not seem to be Socratic. In the argument of the *Euthydemus* the value of the goods of the inventory seems to derive entirely from their correct use, i.e. their beneficial or happiness producing use. We also see this in the distinction between the useful and the bene- ficial Socrates draws in the *Hippias Major* (295–7), and his rejection of the useful as identical with the fine (or the admirable): the useful, whether displayed in ability or instrumentally, can be the cause of bad things as well as good, and so the fine cannot be identical with the useful, a reason which cannot be given against the beneficial since this is the cause of good only.

But in the notion of opportunity value there is no reference to bene- ficial use nor to any specific end. The opportunity value of the freedom to travel, for example, does not derive from some specific use(s) of this freedom which is "the correct use(s)" of travel; people might want to travel for any number of reasons. Nor does the opportunity value of the freedom of speech derive from the use of speech to say, for example, what is true; often we don't know what is true, and we would not want to restrict freedom of speech to cases where we know what is true. For Parsons, Barry, or Rawls such things as wealth and freedom have value because they afford us opportunities or resources to do as we please, no matter what that is.

We must note that for Rawls doing as we please has no value at all if it violates principles of right; but within these confines the good of a person depends on what she finally wants and on what she rationally wants given her final ends, rationality being "thinly" defined in terms of the counting principles and deliberative rationality (Rawls, 1971, pp. 399–424). But for Socrates such things as wealth and power have value only when they are used to bring benefit and happiness to their possessor; and any other value we attribute to them derives from that use.

If freedom or wealth or power have some opporunity value independently of their beneficial uses, then wisdom or knowledge of such beneficial uses is not a condition of their opportunity value. Wisdom and knowledge seem to lose some of their unique value.

Socrates might reply: if freedom and wealth and power have opportunity value independently of beneficial use, it still is instrumental value (a point conceded by Parsons and the early Rawls, e.g.), and instrumental value is derivative. So what does opportunity value derive from? The proponents of opportunity value presumably would answer: there is inherent or intrinsic value in the freedom to do as we please; the freedoms have value because they allow us to do as we please, and wealth and power have value because they give us the resources to do as we please.

Here we have reached a fundamental disagreement, hints of which we already saw in the *Gorgias* and which we shall see again in the *Republic*. The ability to do as we please has no value for Socrates unless doing as we please is good for us to begin with.

12 Was Plato Aware of These Socratic Problems?

Plato was aware of a potential circle in Socratic ethics, the view that all value depends on knowledge. In the *Republic*, Bk. VI (505b), where he takes up the question "What is the good?" Plato claims that those who say that the good is identical with knowledge are not able to say what this is knowledge of, and are finally compelled to say that it (the good) is knowledge of the good. But this, he correctly says, is absurd: this answer is given as if we already knew what the good was, whereas that is precisely the question we started with. "The good is knowledge of the good" is certainly circular and uninformative as an analysis of the good. The passage is interesting not only because of Plato's awareness of a *potential* circle, but also because Plato implies that those who said that the good is knowledge could actually point to no other answer to the question "Knowledge of what?" than "Knowledge of the good." If he is talking about the Socratic theory of the good, as he seems to be, he is saying that the silence of the *Euthydemus* on the content of wisdom could be broken by Socrates only with a circular answer.

Second, Plato knew and considered one way out of this and other Sidgwickean circles, but apparently he did not take it, nor did he attribute it to Socrates. This way out is the hedonism of the *Protagoras*. And this constitutes a powerful theoretical reason for attributing such hedonism to Socrates, as some influential scholars have done, even though we have strong textual evidence against it (see Zeyl [1980]; Gosling and Taylor [1982]; Irwin [1995]; and Rudebusch [1999]). If we say that the good or happiness is identical with pleasure, we can solve all our problems and fill all the gaps in Socratic ethics without circularity. Happiness is not composed of the virtues or any of the other goods in the inventory. Happiness is pleasure. Wisdom occupies a special place among goods other than pleasure, because it is knowledge of the sources of and means to pleasure and of the quantities of expected pleasures and pains;[33] and so it is the unique condition of the correct use (i.e. pleasure producing use) and so the value of all goods other than pleasure. The virtues are no longer parts of happiness but instrumental means to it: for if happiness is pleasure, it is made up of pleasures, and no one would hold that the virtues are identical with pleasures, literally, though of course virtuous activities can be pleasant. Notice that on this interpretation Socrates could still argue as he does: he could say that knowledge of pleasure and its sources and causes is value independent and the condition of the value of all the goods of the inventory; only pleasures themselves are self-sufficiently good, while a life of the greatest possible pleasures and the least possible pains is the complete good. Moreover, he could argue that this knowledge can never be at least prudentially misused if psychological hedonism is true. The whole view of the *Euthydemus* is consistent with hedonism and under that hypothesis would be free of all Sidgwickean circularities!

This might do for the *Protagoras*; and conceivably even for the *Euthydemus*, since the conspicuous absence of pleasure from the inventory of good things makes it at least logically possible to say that by happiness Socrates means pleasure. But this would certainly not do for the *Gorgias*, because of the arguments there against the identification of happiness or *the* good with pleasure (495–9). The *anti*hedonism here is very strong because Socrates holds that pleasure is not even *a* good in itself: he says that only some pleasures are good; others are bad; and he appears to argue that the value of the good pleasures comes from outside the pleasures themselves (499cd). This contradicts the *Protagoras* (355–6) view that pleasure is always good; and that when we call some pleasure bad we mean not that the pleasure itself is bad but that the cost of getting it is painful or that it has painful consequences, so that the totality is painful on balance. This interpretation of the badness of some pleasures is not allowed to Callicles; instead, his admission that some pleasures are bad is taken as his giving up the identity of good and pleasure. That some pleasures are bad is taken as conclusive proof that pleasure and the good are not identical. The same kind of thing happens in the *Republic*, 505, the passage we have just discussed. Here a second answer, as to what the good is, is taken up and refuted: that the good is (identical with) pleasure.[34] Plato says that the people who hold this admit that some pleasures are bad, and thus admit that the same things are both good and bad – presumably a contradiction. This is probably the shortest refutation of hedonism on record! Aside from its soundness, it seems to suggest an *anti*hedonistic view, not simply a *non*hedonistic view. If some pleasures are bad as such (or in themselves, which is how the admission has to be taken to generate a contradiction), not simply on account of their bad costs or consequences, then we cannot even say that pleasure is *a* good in itself (or, equivalently, that each and every pleasure is good in itself), along with other things good in themselves, the usual *non*hedonistic position. In antihedonistic views even the value of those pleasures which are good has to come to them from the outside.

Despite all their faults and though ultimately unsuccessful, the Socratic arguments in the *Euthydemus* and the *Meno* are great hunting grounds for understanding not only the Socratic conception of good, but also more generally the concept of the good. To see this, we need only remind ourselves that they contain the seeds of almost all the distinctions subsequent philosophers have made among different kinds of goods.

Notes

1   Vlastos (1991, p. 219) corrects a common mistranslation "virtue does not come from money" but "money comes from virtue", which contradicts Hesiod but is non-Socratic.

2   I agree with Terry Penner (1999) that there is no absolute distinction between the moral and the prudential in Socratic ethics, as there is in Kant, who has two basic values independent of each other, the good will and the satisfaction of inclination. In Plato there is only one basic value, goodness. My distinction between a "moral" and "prudential" paradox is compatible with this view. The point of the distinction was to highlight that additional premises are needed to derive the moral paradox, that no one does injustice knowingly. "Moral" need not mean moral *à la* Kant, but moral as in Aristotle's virtues of character.

3   For dominance see Irwin (1995), who uses it for the *Republic.*

4   Pleasure does not appear in Socrates' inventories of goods. That pleasure is not identical with *the* good would not explain this, since that still leaves it open that pleasure is *a* good. In the *Gorgias* and the *Republic* Plato claims that *some* pleasures are good and *some* bad. The value of the good pleasures is brought in from the outside. For a subtle recent discussion see Rudebusch (1999).

5   But with some exceptions, e.g. White (1986).

6   For the principle of inclusion, see Rawls (1971, section 63); the comparison is appropriate because Rawls too has a desire-satisfaction theory of goodness.

7   This clause is necessary to distingush Polus' view of happiness from that of Socrates. If we confine all desires to desires for our real good (excluding what appears good to us but is not), as Terry Penner does, Socrates may well agree that happiness is the satisfaction of those desires. See Penner's two spectacular articles on Socratic ethics (1991, 1994). But Polus does not so confine desires, at least at the outset. He may have the primitive notion that to be happy is to have whatever I happen to want.

8   The relation between good and human desires may be like the relation between piety and love in the *Euthyphro*: just as the gods' loving something does not make it pious, so desiring something, even by omniscient gods, does not make it good. And if this is so for gods who make no mistakes whether something is pious or good, so much more is it true of human desires and loves.

9   When we want an object and have no mistaken relevant beliefs about it we can say we really want it. When some of our relevant beliefs about it are false it might be that we don't "really" want it. But this is a complex notion: we want it because of the properties we believe it to have, and we don't want it because some of these beliefs are false and the object does not have some of these properties. Not wanting it can be understood in terms of counterfactuals: had we known we would not have wanted it. Also, if we get to know, we might no longer want it.

10 This may seem to violate the Kantian dictum that he who wants the end wants the necessary means to it. But 468c indicates that it is an overstatement: here Socrates draws inferences from the principle and the assumption that the rhetoricians' and despots' actions at issue are intermediates (means): he says explicitly that (i) we do not want these things simply as such (*haplos houtos*), and (ii) we *do* want to do them if they are beneficial (i.e. productive of good).

11 Penner (1991, pp. 174–202). The argument up to 468 shows no more than possibility. To show, further, that the power of rhetoricians *is* constrained by justice, Socrates has to show that using this power to expel people or put them to death is better for the agent only when these actions are just. This Socrates tries to do in the three famous *subsequent* arguments.

12 Here Socrates tries to prove that it is worse for one to do rather than suffer injustice; that if one does injustice it is better for him to receive just punishment rather than go unpunished; and that injustice in the soul is the greatest evil to its possessor and justice the greatest good. See Irwin (1979); Santas (1979, ch. 8); and Vlastos (1991, ch. 5, section 3).

13 This relies on definitions of the admirable and the shameful arrived at inductively in the first argument: the admirable is what is pleasant and/or beneficial, and the shameful what is painful and/or harmful. See Santas (1979, pp. 233ff.).

14 Penner (1991) uses "bads" for *kaka* to avoid the "moral" overtones of "evils."

15 In the *Republic*, Bk. II, Plato has Glaucon and Adeimantus, his brothers, produce another explanation yet: that the admiration for justice is for the benefits of the *reputation* of justice which is beneficial to the seeming just person, not admiration for justice itself, which is the good of another.

16 Because of this, it is not clear that Callicles distinguishes here between hedonistic and desire-satisfaction theories of good. In Plato and Aristotle, hedonism is explicitly expounded and criticized. But a desire-satisfaction conception of happiness and the good, in which the satisfaction of desires is not the same as pleasure but the more common-sense view of getting the things you want, is not explicitly formulated.

17 These and other arguments in Plato against hedonism are not examined here since they have already received a lot of attention. See, e.g., Gosling and Taylor (1982); Irwin (1979, 1995); Santas (1979); Vlastos (1991); Zeyl (1980); Kahn (1996); and Rudebusch (1999). The good or happiness as desire satisfaction, being less explicit in Plato, needs more attention and receives more in this book.

18 *Eu prattein* at 278e, and *eudaimonein* at 280b seem equivalent.

19 Rawls (1971, e.g. p. 31): "the principles of right, and so of justice, put limits to *which satisfactions have value*" (added emphasis).

20 For good fortune see Irwin (1992).

21 Socrates never says that *of all goods whatsoever* wisdom alone is good by itself, since this would include happiness and pose immediate problems. It is to the goods of the original inventory, not happiness itself, which the argument applies.

22 Vlastos believes that this principle Socrates derives from the identity of virtue with happiness in the *Crito* 48b4–48b10 (1991, pp. 213–14). That derivation, however, may be question begging, unlike the present argument.

23 It is difficult to imagine a life completely bereft of all goods other than wisdom. But even in such a life wisdom could be beneficial: one can exchange it for other goods, as the sophists did, and contemporary "experts" do even more.

24 In the *Euthydemus* Socrates proceeds as if they were arguing within an egoistic context, psychological and ethical, as if only the agent's happiness were

at issue. But since he was arguably not an *ethical* egoist, it is best to suppose that using knowledge of what is good to harm others would be an incorrect use. The problem created by this possibility is addressed in the *Gorgias*, with arguments that virtue and only virtue can bring happiness. If we know what is good and bad for ourselves and also know that only through virtue can we be happy, then we shall not misuse knowledge of good and bad, either to harm ourelves or to harm others. This solution is not available to Kant because he believes that one can have happiness without virtue.

25 Kant had another conception of happiness, as contentment, but this too is independent of the good will or the virtues of character. See, e.g., Watson (1984).

26 Aristotle apparently holds (Bk. III, ch. 6) that even courage can sometimes harm the courageous person and so it is not invariably beneficent. Whether he means courage without wisdom, the "natural virtue," is unclear. See Anagnostopoulos (1993, ch. 5).

27 Vlastos (1991, n. 84) favors a counterfactual solution, thinking that in the *Euthydemus* Socrates had the same view as in the *Meno*. But if he did, why did he not give the same analysis in the *Euthydemus* as he did in the *Meno*? In the latter a difficult point is made crystal clear, in the former it is passed over in silence.

28 At least for the philosophers. Common sense, ancient and modern, says that one can be a fool and courageous, or wise and cowardly.

29 Moore explains that by parts of such wholes he does not mean causal means to ends, where the means and ends are taken together as a whole (1903, p. 29).

30 *Charmides*, 289de, 290b, 291b, 292bc, and finally in 292e. No one seems to have noticed this remarkable difference between the two dialogues.

31 Nonmoral psychic goods could be such things as technical knowledge, imagination and talents, and pleasure.

32 Does Vlastos's interpretation of the Socratic relation of virtue to happiness (1991, ch. 8), provide a partial solution to this circularity problem? Vlastos holds that virtue is (necessary and) sufficient for happiness, not identical with it: bodily and social goods make up the rest of happiness. But the problem is that the correct use of *these* goods makes reference to the other part of happiness, the part occupied by virtue. So none of the Socratic happiness can be defined or explicated without reference to virtue. It is difficult to see how such a theory could be teleological without circularity.

33 Socrates' art of measurement in the *Protagoras* is still a dream. I believe that the art in question is crucial to a significant application of hedonism. Yet its difficulties are immense: we would have to be able to measure pleasures and aggregate them across times; for teleological hedonistic theories across persons as well; and the same for pains; and then we would have to aggregate plea-

sures *and* pains, to calculate the net of pleasure or pain. See Mirrlees (1988); Rawls (1971, p. 557).

34 *Republic*, 505b, is interesting also because it implies that those who took knowledge to be the good, presumably Socrates, were not hedonists – otherwise they could give as their noncircular answer "knowledge of pleasure."

3

The Good of Platonic Social Justice

The *Republic* makes fundamental advances in ethical theory beyond the Socratic dialogues. The most evident and discussed are the construction of definitions for the virtues, both social and individual, and the defense of justice. Even more fundamental, if less recognized, are the construction and application of two related theories of good: good as well functioning and good as perfect form. These theories underlie the construction and defense of the social and individual virtues. At the same time, two alternative theories of good, good as pleasure and good as the satisfaction of desire, are rejected. Plato supposes that these two theories of good underlie the alternative theories of justice, Thrasymachus' theory and the democratic theory of Glaucon; and in the case of democratic justice at least, Plato proceeds on the assumption that if he can refute the good as the satisfaction of desire he can refute democratic justice.

Plato does not define happiness in the *Republic*, even though his defense of justice is that it makes us happy or happier than injustice (Irwin, 1995). But he thinks that what human happiness is depends on what is good for us; and since he does have theories of good, we can reconstruct his views of happiness on the basis of his theories of good. Because of this and because he defines the virtues, the *Republic* fills the gaps left in the Socratic dialogues and avoids Sidgwickean circularities and paucity of practical content. The Socratic role of knowledge, as the condition of the valuable use of all social and bodily goods, is still held – indeed taken for granted. Though the good is not identical with knowledge, the Socratic role coheres well with both the functional and the metaphysical theories of the good, since what is good is within the province of reason to know. Because of all these advances, the important debate begun in the *Gorgias*, whether virtue makes us happy, can now be understood on a broader and deeper level.

In this chapter I begin with the great ethical questions of the *Republic*. Then I shall sketch Plato's functional theory of good and discuss its first important application: the construction of a just city or the theory of social justice. In the next chapter I discuss its second important application, the construction of justice as a virtue of persons. And in chapter 5 I discuss the theory of the form of the good.

1   The Great Questions of the Republic

At the end of Book I Socrates tells us what issues they have been debating and claims that the discussion failed because they did not follow the proper order of investigation:

> before finding the first object of our inquiry – what justice is – I let go of that and set out to consider something about it, namely whether it is a vice and ignorance or wisdom; and again, when the view was sprung upon us that injustice is more profitable than justice I could not refrain from turning to that from the other topic. So that for me the present outcome of the discussion is that I know nothing. For if I don't know what the just is, I shall hardly know whether it is a virtue or not, and whether its possessor is or is not happy. (Shorey transl.)

Here we have two of the great questions pursued in the rest of the work:[1]

1.   What is justice?
2.   Is one better off or happier being just rather than unjust?

In the order of investigation the first is prior to the second question, Socrates says. Why? Plato appears to hold a general principle from which this particular priority follows.[2] But in the *Republic* we can propose a more substantial and less disputed reason. In that work we find several answers to what justice is, for example those of Thrasymachus, Glaucon, and Plato himself, and all the systems criticized in Bk. VIII. One way to understand the priority is to say that the question about the benefits of justice will have to wait till a *true* answer is found about the nature of justice, and then the question of benefits will be about *that* justice. Perhaps this is the natural way for Plato to understand the relations between these two questions, since he is an ethical realist who thinks there is a form justice and a form good.

Another way, perhaps more comprehensive and illuminating, is to understand the first question in terms of a broad notion of adequacy which includes truth. A person who raises the question What is justice? will probably have before her several answers provided by several traditions, and she may have some new answers herself. This is exactly the situation Plato faced in the *Republic*, not unlike the situation John Rawls found,[3] or more recently Brian Barry (1989). Plato sketches traditional answers, by Cephalus and Polemarchus, Thrasymachus, Glaucon, and a new one by himself. These were not simply possible theoretical answers, but (except for his own perhaps) represented different actual systems of justice. Once this is understood, the first question can be stated so as to reflect the more comprehensive outlook which does not presuppose ethical realism, but can include it: Which of the several known or proposed systems of justice is the most adequate? Here adequacy can include truth, but need not be confined to it: the criteria of adequacy might be truth, stability, formal and procedural fairness, efficiency, rational prudence, or some combination thereof. The second question, then, can be thought of as arising about every available or known system of justice: For each of the known systems of justice, is one better off being just *under it* rather than unjust?

This second question presupposes some answers to the first, but the first need not be entirely independent of the second. Answers to the second question can function as *one* criterion for an answer to the first question, on the reasonable assumption that, other things equal, a system of justice in which *each* individual under it is better off being just than she is under any other system is the most adequate. This assumption of course introduces a wider comparison, among different systems of justice: not only between being just and unjust in any given system; but also between being just under all known systems of justice. This wider comparison is important on that reasonable assumption: other things equal, that system of justice is the most adequate in which each individual is best off being just rather than unjust. Even an ethical realist like Plato might allow for this more accommodating conception of the two questions: for he might hold that true justice is best for one, and so if one system of justice serves individuals better than any other known one, this may be at least a clue that it is true justice. Thus, even though it might reasonably be thought that an ethical realist does not decide among different conceptions of justice by making them objects of rational choice, as a constructivist such as Rawls does, there is a way of understanding Plato's discussion in the *Republic* in a similar way, though with a crucial qualification: rational choice would be defined in terms of an independent conception of goodness as an objective property, rather than the other way around, as in Rawls.[4] Here we must also remember that in this work Plato *does* after all put before us several systems of justice; and he is presumably inviting us to decide among them: presumably by deciding which of these is best for us.

Even within the more comprehensive way of understanding the relations between our two questions, a certain priority of the nature of justice over its benefits remains: we cannot just ask in the abstract, which is better for us, justice or injustice? For this question immediately invites another: under which system of justice? Once this is understood, I believe that it liberates the *Republic* from the burden which some commentators have come close to placing on Plato, mistakenly in any case in my opinion: to prove that under Glaucon's system of justice one would be better off or happier being just rather than unjust. This presupposes that the first question is already answered in favor of Glaucon and the second question is therefore about Glaucon's justice. But why should Plato have to "defend" a system of justice which he thinks is mistaken? The just man passing the so-called vulgar tests of justice, that is, refraining from commonly proscribed criminal acts, is not a sufficient reason for putting such a burden on Plato.[5] Common criminal acts, theft, property damage, bodily harm, and homicide, are proscribed by all systems of justice worth our attention. Plato's system proscribes these by his principle of social justice. But the problem of the benefits of justice, raised by the second question, lies in the first place and mainly elsewhere, namely, in the *content* of principles of justice and the laws made according to such principles, rather than in the benefits and costs of breaking laws. The problem of benefits lies in that part of justice commonly known as distributive justice, embodied in the institutions of society: how property, offices, rights, and opportunities are distributed *to begin with* by such institutions. These are the important differences, the different distributions of the burdens and benefits of social cooperation, between Glaucon's contractarian democratic justice, the partial justice of Thrasymachus, oligarchic justice, timocratic justice, tyrannical justice, and Platonic social justice. Beginning with Thrasymachus, Plato seems to recognize this broader and deeper scope of social justice, since he brings into the discussion constitutions and social and ecomonic institutions.

The question of the nature of justice is answered by Polemarchus and Thrasymachus in Bk. I, by Glaucon and Adeimantus in Bk. II, and by Plato in Bks. II, III, IV, and VIII. The question of the benefits of justice is answered negatively by Thrasymachus and Glaucon in Bks. I and II, and positively by Plato in Bks. IV, VIII, and IX.

Our comprehensive interpretation of the interplay between these two questions can be seen in the discussions of the second question by Thrasymachus and Glaucon. When Thrasymachus claims that injustice is better for one than justice, the benefits of which justice is he downgrading? His own justice, surely, defined as what is to the interest of the ruling party and embodied into laws which promote that interest.[6] The injustice he means is the breaking of *these* laws by the weaker;[7] and the persons for whom such injustice is better are not the ruling party but the subjects who are the weaker, provided they can get away with such disobedience through deception or revolution. Thus his defense of injustice is a defense of *his* injustice *from* the point of view of the weaker. But Plato has no interest in defending *that* justice. The fundamental problem with Thrasymachus' system of justice is that it is *partial by definition*: it favors the ruling party at the expense of the ruled. At the opening lines of Bk. IV Plato explicitly repudiates it: they have been sketching a city which is so organized as to serve the good of the city as a whole, not only that of the rulers, believing that justice would exist in such a city. In Bk. I the same question arises about Socrates' defense of justice: Which justice is he defending in the dispute about the benefits of justice? Thrasymachus' justice? Surely not. Which justice then? *He never says!* Thus his complaint at the end of that book, that they rushed to the question of benefits before they settled the question of the nature of justice, is fully justified. Imagine Rawls going into the question of the "congruence between justice and the good" before he told us what justice is! In fact he does not discuss this matter till the last chapter of the book; and surely what he seeks to show is the congruence between his two principles of justice (through the concept of the sense of justice) and the good of the individual. Readers and commentators discussing the dispute with Thrasymachus on the benefits of justice tend to forget Socrates' complaint at the end of Bk. I. But it is an absolutely fundamental point and overshadows that whole dispute.

When Glaucon resumes the discussion, he *begins* with the second question, what kind of good justice is, and he says that the system of justice *he* is about to expound answers it differently from Socrates who claims that justice is good in itself *and* for its results. But after noting this disagreement, Plato has Glaucon take up the nature of justice and expound a contractarian theory, apparently egalitarian.[8] And it is clear that when Glaucon returns to argue his claim that justice is good *only* for its results, he is talking about the justice he just expounded. It is a most remarkable fact about the *Republic* that after the speeches of Glaucon and Adeimantus, expounding views on the nature *and* benefits of justice, which Plato opposes on both scores, Plato does not criticize them;[9] instead Plato proceeds to construct another theory of justice. This signals a new constructive method, beyond the aporetic method of the early dialogues. But it is also Plato making sure that the fundamental mistake of Bk. I is never repeated: in the rest of the work he does not dispute the benefits of Glaucon's justice till he investigates the nature of justice and satisfies himself on that question first: it is not till the end of Bk. IV, and in Bks. VIII and IX that the benefits of justice are taken up again. And in these passages there is no doubt about which justice he is arguing the benefits of: in Bks. IV and IX he is arguing the benefits of *his* system of justice; and in Bk. VIII he is downgrading the benefits of systems of justice he disagrees with.

Our second question about the benefits of justice is sometimes stated in terms of good, sometimes in terms of happiness. Thus it clearly presupposes two other related questions:

3. What is (the) good?
4. What is happiness?

The first of these is taken up explicitly in Bk. VI, and answered on the basis of the theory of forms, as we shall see in chapter 5. But, I will argue here, it is also taken up much earlier and answered by a contexual functional definition at the end of Bk. I. And of course Plato says lots about goods. When we look at all the relevant passages, we shall find that in the *Republic* we have not only different theories of justice, but also different theories of good: a desire-satisfaction theory of good underlies Glaucon's theory of justice,[10] a hedonistic theory explicitly refuted;[11] and Plato's own theories of perfectionist-functional and formal good on which his theory of justice is founded.

Even aside from the fact that the second question of the benefits of justice raises issues about the good, it may be that the first question of the nature of justice cannot be answered without presupposing some theory of good. If the structure of an ethical theory is teleological, the right being conceived as what maximizes the good, clearly a theory of justice will presuppose some good or other to be maximized, some conception of good which can be defined independently of the right. But even if an ethical theory is not teleological, the theory of justice it contains may need to presuppose some account of good; for example, Jonh Rawls's nonteleological theory of justice presupposes the theory of primary goods whose distribution is regulated by the basic structure of society.

Somewhat similar considerations apply to the question What is happiness? Plato does not take up this question explicitly; but there are passages from which his view of happiness can be gathered, especially the beginning and end of Bk. IV, and Bks. VIII and IX. In addition, since he seems to suppose what human happiness is depends on what is good for human beings, different conceptions of happiness can be built up from different conceptions of the human good: happiness as a life of the greatest possible satisfaction of desires; happiness as a life of the greatest possible pleasures; and his own view of happiness as the development of human greater capabilities and the best possible performance of social and psychic human functions.

When we look at our four main questions so far, of the nature of justice, the benefits of justice, the conception of good, and the conception of happiness, we see that the situation in the *Republic* is far more complex than is usually realized. For Plato is faced not only with different systems of justice and the problem of choice among them, but also with different theories of good and different conceptions of happiness, and thus the problem of choice among *them*.[12] And he is perfectly aware of it, since he disputes not only certain conceptions of justice but also certain conceptions of good and of happiness.

Moreover, the second question of the benefits of justice is now far more complicated than it last looked: for it concerns not only the benefits of different systems of justice, but also different conceptions of benefits. People who disagree about the nature and benefits of justice may be disagreeing about the nature of justice or they may be disagreeing about the nature of benefits, or about both. To give but a brief, initial illustration of the second disagreement, it may be that the benefits of democratic justice which Plato so radically downgrades in Bk. VIII are far greater if we assume a conception of the good as the satisfaction of desire; for under that conception social and political freedoms to do as one pleases are a very great instrumental good, and the democratic conception promotes that freedom more widely and equally than any other system of justice including Plato's. But Plato, using his own conception of functional-perfectionist good for which he argued earlier in the work, downgrades the good of freedom radically, and thus downgrades the democratic conception of justice all the way down next to the worst. It is clear from this that the very first question, the most prior question of investigation among all our questions so far, is the one about the nature of good. And Plato indeed tells us this quite explicitly at the beginning of his discussion of the form of the good, at 506a.

Whether Plato is mistaken or not, either in his theories of justice or of good, he is well aware of the breadth and depth of the questions he is discussing. The *Republic* is a great book because it explores the complex and fundamental relations between justice and the good. It undertakes what people have called a defense of justice, against the larger and deeper background of both different theories of justice and different theories of good. It even shows awareness of different methods for discovering what justice is and the difference these make. It is a great book also because it offers new fundamental theories of justice and the good, which went much further than anything Plato's contemporaries had dreamt of.

To sum up so far: in the *Republic* we have different theories of justice, and Plato's first great question is, Which of these is true, or perhaps more adequate? We also have different theories of good and happiness, and his third great question is, Which of these is more adequate? And assuming correct answers to these two questions, the second great question is, Under which system of justice is the individual better off or happier being just rather than unjust?

In Bk. V a new question is raised:

5. How can justice be realized (471ff.)?

More exactly, How can the justice he has defined and defended as the most adequate for both cities and individuals be realized? The famous paradox of the philosopher-king is his answer, after he has distinguished between the perfectly just city or person and earthly approximations thereof. But this has to be supplemented by the discussion of the institutions which implement his social justice and engender his psychic justice: education (Bks. II, III, VII), property (III, V), family (III, V,) and the role of gender (V).

Finally, in Bks. V, VI, and VII another important question is implicitly raised:

6. Can we know what justice is, and if so how?

On Plato's view knowledge of justice depends on knowledge of the good, a reasonable proposition given the priority of the nature of good over the nature of justice. The priority of knowledge of the good over knowledge of justice shows up in the justification of the full definition of just city and the just person: in both cases a certain structure and order is said to be just on the ground that it promotes the good of the whole

complex, as we would expect in a teleological theory. The more fundamental question is then about knowledge of the good, and this is the question Plato explicitly raises and takes pains to discuss (505ff.).[13]

An answer to this question is also presupposed by Plato's answer to the
previous question of the possible realization of justice: for the philosopher-
king is defined as one who must have knowledge of good, not simply
opinion; so a philosopher-king is possible only if knowledge of the good
is possible. Given all this, and given the dependence of justice on the good,
the question of knowledge of the good is indeed the most fundamental
epistemological question of the *Republic*. Plato's comments (Bk. VI, 504–5)
about the importance of knowledge of the form of the good, though
seemingly hyperbolic, are indeed well taken for his theory.

The distinction between knowledge and belief, the theory of forms,
and the theory of the form of the good, are all used by Plato in the middle
books to answer the question of knowledge of the good. I discuss them
in chapter 5 below.

If these are the great issues debated in the *Republic* and they are related
in the ways we have sketched, it is clear that good is the most fundamental
concept in Plato's ethics and politics. His whole theory depends on his
view of what the good is and whether anyone can know it. It is surprising that until very recently the theories of good in the *Republic* have been
relatively neglected and not clearly understood; a situation the reverse of
that existing in studies of Aristotle's ethics whose theory of good has been
much discussed and his theory of justice neglected.[14] In this and the next
two chapters we shall try to better understand Plato's theories of good,
within the larger context I have just sketched.

2   The Functional-Perfectionist Theory of Good

The theory is sketched in Bk. I, and it is immediately applied to individuals to convince Thrasymachus that we would be happier being just rather
than unjust.[15] Far more important and less commonly recognized, the
functional theory is the theoretical foundation upon which Plato builds
his ideals of the completely good city and the completely good person
and the definitions of justice and the other virtues. His defense of justice
and the rejection of other systems of justice also uses this theory.[16]

Here I shall sketch the theory, look at its immediate Socratic application (in Bk. I,) find it unsuccessful for good Platonic reasons, and discuss
some of its ambiguities and problems. In the next two sections we shall

examine its more elaborate Platonic application to the city to work up the theory of social justice and the other social virtues.

Let us look at the main parts of the theory. After getting agreement on the *assumption* that

1.   Some things have a function; Socrates offers a *definition* of function (*ergon*):[17]

2.   "the work of a horse or anything else is that which one can do only with it or best with it" (352e). Restated as: "that is the work of a thing which it only or it better than anything else can perform" (353a, Shorey transl.).[18]

Subsequent statements make it clear that Socrates also *assumes* that

3.   Things with a function may perform their function well or poorly.

Socrates gets agreement on another assumption:

4.   There is a virtue for everything that has a function (353b).

Next, it is also agreed that

5.   A thing performs its function well by its own proper virtue, badly by its vice (353c).

We can extract an assumption or definition of good of a kind from the immediate application of the theory:

6.   A thing with a function is a good of its kind if it carries out well the function of things of that kind.[19]

From the same immediate application of the theory it seems that Socrates also assumes that

7.   Functioning well and the virtue which enables a thing to function well are the good or part of the good of that thing.

As we shall see, this assumption is necessary both for the immediate application of the argument against Thrasymachus, and for Plato's subsequent defense of justice in the rest of the work.

Socrates proceeds to an immediate use of the theory, to prove that justice (or virtue) and only justice brings happiness. The argument proceeds by an application of the abstract or formal theory of functional good and virtue to the case of a human, i.e. the argument takes the theory as (a set of) premise(s), adds material propositions about human beings, and draws inferences:

The functions of the human soul are to live, deliberate, plan, and guide living.[20] A good soul will do these things well, a bad soul badly.[21] Justice (perhaps in the broadest sense of virtue) is the virtue of the soul, injustice its vice (assumption). Therefore, a just soul will deliberate well, plan life well and live well, an unjust soul poorly.[22] Therefore, the just person will live well, the unjust badly. A person who lives well will be blessed and happy, an unjust person unhappy.[23] Therefore, the just will be happy, the unjust unhappy.

The argument has been usually judged unsound because of the ambiguity of *eu pratein*, doing or living well: this may mean living a virtuous life, or it may mean prospering or succeeding in whatever one wants and tries to do; justice enables one to live virtuously; but happiness has to do also with prospering and succeeding, and the argument does not show that justice enables us to do *that*.[24]

This may be correct, but the argument has a more fundamental problem: it suffers from the fact that it does not contain a particular conception of justice. We may concede that justice is a human virtue, and that virtues are qualities that enable things to perform their own functions well; but this still leaves open what qualities or traits of character constitute the various human virtues. So, when the distinction is made between living virtuously and succeeding or prospering, since the argument does not tell us what justice is – and there have already been several answers to that question in Bk. I – we cannot tell whether justice will enable us to live rightly or to prosper or both. If, for example, justice is what Thrasymachus says it is, it enables the stronger party to prosper or advance its interests; but it does not necessarily enable it to live rightly, as for example Socrates conceives living rightly in the *Crito* and even in the *Republic*, Bk. I, since for Socrates it is never right to harm another human being. But if justice is what Socrates says it is in these dialogues,[25] it may enable us to live rightly, but not necessarily prosper, at least not as Thrasymachus or Glaucon understand prospering. The immediate application of the functional theory by Socrates has the main problems we encountered in Socratic ethics: the unargued assumption that living well and living happily are the same, no definition of either conception, and no definition of justice.

We see once again how fundamentally correct Socrates is when at the end of the argument he says that he cannot know whether justice makes us happy, or even whether it is a virtue, until he knows what justice is. He could have easily added: until he knows also what happiness is, since, he and Thrasymachus have different conceptions of prospering and happiness, further complicating their disagreement.

But it is essential to notice that in his aporetic conclusion at the end of Bk. I, Socrates does not retract anything from the formal functional theory itself. He complains only about the application he makes of it: in particular about their failure to find out what justice is; he voices no complaint about the formal theory itself. When the functional theory is applied later in Bks. II to V, we shall find the defects of the first application remedied. And we shall find plenty of evidence in later books that the functional theory of good is used to build up definitions of social and individual justice, to sketch an ideal society, and even to lay the foundations for a conception of happiness.

To return to the abstract theory itself, we note first that there is no commitment to the idea that everything has a function, so there may be important limits to the scope of the theory; if there are things which can be good but have no function, the functional theory cannot account for their goodness. This turns out to be an important point when we consider the metaphysical theory of the form of the good. Platonic forms have no functions in the relevant sense.[26]

Socrates illustrates various parts of the theory with examples: the eyes and the ears to illustrate the first part of the definition of function, what I shall call *exclusive* function, since seeing is assigned as the function of the eyes because it can be done *only* with the eyes (and similarly with hearing and the ears). A knife and a pruning knife illustrate the second part of the definition, what I shall call *optimal* function, since cutting vines is assigned to the pruning knife because it can do it "better" than a plain knife. The eyes and the ears are used again to illustrate the introduction to virtue and its relation to functioning well.[27]

The theory has several ambiguities and faces several problems and objections. We shall look briefly at some of them hoping for a better understanding of the theory.

The Greek *ergon* is product–process ambiguous, much as "work" and "function" are in English. In the *Republic* the definition of *ergon* appears to favor process or activity. And the same is true in Aristotle's corresponding famous function argument.[28]

Ergon, "function," and "work" can refer to any of several uses. We can assign as a thing's function what it was *designed* to do, for a computer or a pump – this is the standard way of assigning functions to artifacts. Or we could assign a thing's *predominant or standard use* as its function, independently of what it was made for, as antique chairs were made for sitting but are now used for decoration; or the *special use* some person makes independently of standard use or designing purpose, as a vase made to hold flowers is now used as a doorstop (see Santas, 1974; Wright, 1973).

But in the *Republic* Socrates selects none of these notions of function for his definition. Rather he defines function on the basis of a thing's capabilities – exclusive or optimal – what only things of a given kind can do, or what things of a given kind can do "best." But there are connections between his definition and common notions of function applied to artifacts and organs. In the case of artifacts the concept of optimal function is natural, since in designing artifacts we try to construct them so as to be optimal (i.e. better or best instruments) for the work we have in mind. In the case of organs the notion of exclusive function is natural, since we discover the function of organs by figuring out what work is peculiar to them. In Plato's division of the psyche and in his analogy between justice and health we shall see that he was using the notion of function he found in medicine. Aristotle uses it extensively in his biology.

As defined here, function makes no *essential* reference to human desires, purposes, or interests, a crucial point often misunderstood. This is very clear for exclusive function. The heart has a function(s) which can be discovered independently of human interests or desires; and it has that function no matter what humans desire or take an interest in; and the same is true of the roots of plants. Socrates gives criteria for a thing's *ergon* which may not correspond to some of our notions of function; things made for a purpose, artifacts, are clearly only a subset of things with Platonic functions. The significance of this for our study is that since we have definitions of good of a kind and of the good of a thing based on the *defined* notion of function, we clearly have a theory of good different from the conception of the good as the satisfaction of desire or relative to human interests, as in the theories of Rawls (1971, pp. 399ff.) and Perry (1926). Plato's theory of good is "objective," in *this* respect similar to the theories of good of G. E. Moore and W. D. Ross: ontologically objective in that goodness inheres in the objects, in the performing of their function, not *in* the subjects making the judgment, or in some relation of a sentient subject to an object, such as desiring or taking an interest (Korsgaard, 1983, 1996).

Why does Plato single out two capabilities to define function? The defined notion is both narrower and broader than the many common uses: narrower in that it excludes arbitrary purpose (a flower vase being used for a doorstop); broader in that it includes the functions of organs of animals and plants, as in the practice of ancient medicine. I think Plato's definition is framed so as to include the important notions of function and to suit his views of the relation between form and function. Perhaps he thinks that there is a closer connection between a thing's form and its capabilities, than there is between its form and the purpose it was made for or its predominant use; because an engineer, say, can make mistakes about what the best structure is for the purpose she has in mind, and the predominant use we make of something is subject to the same possible fault as well as arbitrariness of use. Plato's definition may provide a more objective basis for a definition of good. In any case, Plato wants to secure some connection between form and function, since he has another theory of good, based on form rather than function, and the two theories must coincide,[29] at least in the *Republic*. He starts with the functional theory because it is closer to our evaluative practices in everyday life and in the arts, but he shapes the notion of function so that the theory of good he builds on it comes into line with his metaphysical theory of the form of the good. He wants a connection between form and function that is close to what we find in nature, particularly in organisms and their parts.

It should be observed, though, that once we get away from the notion of function as what a thing was made for or its standard use, and we employ the Platonic definition instead, it may be far more difficult to discover a thing's function. We may have to investigate an indefinite number of comparisons before we can determine what a thing's function is, either the exclusive or the optimal. The examples Socrates considers are easy for obvious reasons. But suppose we had to determine the function of dolphins or plane trees, or branches of trees, or leaves or livers[30]: we would have to find out something which only dolphins can do among all(?) animals or can do better than all(?) other animals, and similarly with plane trees and what not. The question marks indicate the problem: the comparison classes seem to be indefinitely large, and unless we can limit them the problem is hardly manageable. And since judgments of being a good so and so presuppose determination of function, the problem spreads to such judgments as well. But a solution is possible. Aristotle, for example, was able to determine the exclusive function of a human with impressive ease (*NE*, Bk. I, ch. 7); though he was taking advantage of his classification of plants and animals which was the result of enormous labor.

Another problem is that any individual falls under several kinds – how do we pick the kind relative to which we assign a function to that individual? Some theory of natural kinds may be presupposed. Plato starts with kinds of things – a horse, a knife, an eye, an ear – and inquires of them what is their function as these kinds of things. He starts with kinds and so he bypasses our question.

Plato allows that some things, for example persons and cities, can have many virtues; so would they not also have many corresponding functions? We shall see that the city is allowed many functions and has several virtues; for example, defense is *one* of the functions of the city, and social courage is the virtue that enables it to perform that function well. Contrary to what is sometimes supposed, on the ground of Plato's assigning *one* social function to each citizen, the theory allows multiple functions and virtues for the same kind of thing, cities and individuals.

Plurality of functions can also pose problems. A thing may be exclusively capable of doing many things. Which of them are its functions? For example among many other actions a person can steal, and presumably only persons can steal (animals only by analogy), so this satisfies the first disjunct of the definition; and there are many other things only persons can do, such as trading goods. Why is not stealing an exclusive function of humankind? Some further restriction in the choice of capabilities may be presupposed: for example in the case of persons, inborn or native capabilities, as distinct from culture-based capabilities; in Aristotle the restriction may come from his essentialism. It is unclear that Plato ever thought of this problem.

But we may note that the definition of good of a kind in terms of exclusive or optimal function is morally neutral: if stealing is someone's optimal or exclusive function, he or she is a good thief if he or she steals well. To account for the judgment that stealing is wrong (and the ability to steal well not a human virtue) Plato would need to introduce his theory of social and individual human virtues.

The notion of optimal function is ambiguous, because the comparison is syntactically ambiguous: it can mean doing something better than anything else an object can do, or better than any other (kind of) object can do the same thing. Though the examples Socrates uses, and perhaps the second statement of the definition, favor the second interpretation, the ambiguity turns out to be important in Bk. II, and we shall come back to it. Using the examples of a knife and a hammer, the first comparison is between using a knife to cut bread and using that knife to hammer nails; presumably, the knife can cut better than it can hammer, so cutting is its optimal function. The second comparison is different: we compare using a knife to hammer nails with a hammer to hammer nails; presumably the hammer can hammer better than the knife can, so hammering is the optimal function of the hammer, not of the knife. We shall shortly see the importance of the ambiguity of optimal function.

The basic notion of functioning well, used in the definition of good and of virtue, also involves a comparison, and it should not be confused with either of the above comparisons. The present comparison is within the class of things with the same function. Thus a knife performs its function well if and only if it performs it at least as well as an average knife.[31] Thus the comparison here is with the performance of other knives with the same function. Since good of a kind and the virtue of a kind are defined by reference to functioning well, this comparison is also implicit in these notions.

In sum, we have three difference comparison classes: the two involved in assigning optimal function, and the third involved in determining well functioning. It is crucial that these not be confused with one another. Such confusions can result in some common criticisms of the functional theory, for example that the theory cannot distinguish between a carpenter and a bad carpenter. This is not so. A bad carpenter can still be a carpenter, in that carpentry can be her optimal function: she can do carpentry better than she can do anything else; or she can do carpentry better than most people, though not better than most carpenters. Here the comparison is to other things the person can do or to herself and other persons doing carpentry; only the first two comparisons are involved here. But she can still be a bad carpenter in the sense that she does not do carpentry as well as the average carpenter, and this involves our third comparison. The confusion, however, is easy to fall into because some comparisons are closely related and can even overlap: one comparison to find out whether this person is, say, a runner at all, the other how good he is among runners, having determined that he is a runner to begin with; or, one comparison to find out what inborn ability(ies) a person has, the other how great that ability is once it has been developed.

We can understand the introduction of good in the theory as a contextual definition of good of a kind[32]: a thing is good of its kind if it performs well the function of things of that kind. This is parallel in structure to modern definitions of a good so and so, for example those of Ross and Rawls: all of these evaluate something of a given kind relative to the "function(s)" of that kind of thing. However, Rawls's definition at least, is crucially different because he is not using the Platonic notion of function, but the notion of desire or human interest taken in an object of a certain kind, or its standard use, which Rawls and Korsgaard take to be based on the interest humans have in the object.

Once the definition of good of a kind is added to the theory, however, we may have problems of circularity. Given Plato's definition of function, would not a definition of good in terms of it be circular? Not with the notion of exclusive function, for this is not a normative notion. But what about optimal function which uses the idea of doing something "better"? There is no circle if "better" means "more efficiently," though this case may be limited to things good as means. However, more generally, there is no vicious circle if better functioning is understood in purely quantitative terms. For example, a thermometer measures the temperature of a room "better" than a person feeling the air, that is, more accurately and more consistently.

A circularity problem may also arise with the definition of a *good* so and so as one that performs its function *well*. After all, "well" is just the adverbial form of "good." So this definition seems to use a normative notion, the adverbial form of the term "good" to define the adjectival form; if so it avoids the naturalistic fallacy, and it is not a naturalistic theory of good,[33] but all this at the expense of vicious and uninformative circularity. There is no vicious circle, however, if functioning well can be given a purely quantitative interpretation: in general it can mean more *reliably*, more *easily*, more *efficiently* than the average or mean performance; in specific cases, it can mean more sharply for knives, more rapidly for pumps, more clearly for eyes, and so on. Whether this can be done as generally as the definition demands is more difficult to determine. And the theory may have different degrees of success in medicine or biology than in the productive and fine arts and sciences. An ophthalmologist may have no such philosophical problems if he thinks that good eyes are eyes that see well, since he in fact has purely quantitative tests for seeing well; he is not plagued either by circularity or the naturalist fallacy. But a painter or an engineer may have more problems with functional definitions of a good painting or a good bridge. The theory does not necessarily fare equally well with both notions of function and when applied to both nature and artifice.

The introduction of virtue in the theory can be understood as a partial definition of virtue in terms of functioning well. It is a definition of virtue for anything whatsoever with a function, not just humans; and even in the case of humans it includes nonmoral activities such as building or sculpting; so, clearly the notion of virtue defined is far broader than our notion of "moral" virtues or the virtues of character. Here we must not be misled by the immediate application of the theory by Socrates, which is to a moral virtue, justice.

The definition of virtue may be partial since a thing's virtue may include only a subset of the things that enable it to perform its function well and the definition does not specify this subset. For example a racehorse cannot run well unless it has a fairly smooth road, but we would not include such a road as part of the horse's virtues. Even among the thing's properties, as distinct from necessary external conditions, we may need to select a subset for its virtues, for example having legs enables a racing horse to run well but is not part of its virtues, as speed and stamina are.

The final proposition of the theory, that functioning well and the virtue that enables a thing to do so are part of the good of that thing, is an implicit premise necessary for the immediate application of the theory.[34] It gives a partial explication of the notion of *the good of something*, as distinct from the related notion of being *good of a kind*, directly in terms of functioning well and indirectly in terms of virtue. The direct explication is extremely plausible: for what sorts of things would we ever deny that functioning well is good for them? Certainly not for plants or animals or their parts; physical well functioning is a criterion of health, for example, and health is good for animals and plants. As far as I can tell, this explication is taken for granted and never argued for by Plato. Even the indirect explication, of the good of virtue, is plausible. It was not controversial in the case of the "competitive virtues," such as wisdom: wisdom enables us to plan and deliberate well and that is good for us. It was controversial for the "cooperative virtues," such as justice; and so its application to justice has to be argued for, as Plato indeed does.

3   The Application of the Functional Theory of Good to the City

After the speeches of Glaucon and Adeimantus, Socrates undertakes a new search for the nature and defense of justice. Having remarked that there is justice in an individual and in a city, and that it would be easier to look for justice in the city first,[35] he begins as follows:

> I think a city comes to be, I said, because no one of us is self-sufficient, but needs many things. Do you think a city is founded on any other principle? On no other. As they need many things, people make use of one another for many purposes. They gather many associates and helpers and live in one place, and to this settlement we give the name of city. Is that not so? It is. And they share with one another, both giving and taking, in so far as they do, because they think this better for themselves? Quite so. Come then, I said, let us create a city from the beginning of our discussion. And it is our needs, it seems, that will create it. (369bc, Shorey transl.)

Plato does not explain why he starts in this particular way in his search for justice in the city. But if we assume the functional theory, he is making exactly the right start. For on that theory, to discover the justice (and other virtues) of a city, one has to determine first the function(s) of a city; then one has to find or to imagine a city that performs these functions well (or best if one wants to make sure that it has all the virtues appropriate to a city and is the best possible city); finally, one has to determine the social conditions that are responsible for the city performing its functions best – for example its economic and political structures and its educational institutions. The justice of the city, as one of the virtues that enables the city to perform its functions well, will be found among these conditions. In general, when applied to discover the virtue(s) of anything with a function, the functional theory prescribes this three-step procedure: find the functions of that thing, isolate its performing these functions well, and find the conditions that enable it to do so. And this is essentially what Socrates does in Bks. II–IV, on the reasonable assumption that justice is one of the virtues of a city.

The functional theory guides the search for justice and the other virtues of a city. This is a very different methodology, in the search for justice, than the methodologies used earlier to support other theories of justice. Near the end of his life, Cephalus relies on his experience for the two rules of justice he comes up with, telling the truth and keeping promises. Polemarchus relies on the wisdom of the poets, the moral educators of the Greeks. Thrasymachus proceeds as an empirical political scientist: on the assumption that the justice of any city is to be found in (or, is identical with) its system of laws, he defines justice on the basis of what he thinks is a general observable fact about all such systems, that they are created to promote the interests of their rulers. Glaucon uses a contractarian methodology: he assumes certain facts about humans (they are rational creatures) and their environment in nature (moderate scarcity of the things they want and consequent conflicts among them), and relates how such creatures would reason to a system of laws: each gives up equally the freedom to harm others in return for the equal security of not being harmed by them, a rational decision made on the ground that each would be better off than in a state of nature, though not best off – something beyond their reach. The functional three-step methodology Plato uses is different from all these. The *Republic* discusses not only different systems of justice but also suggests different methodologies for discovering and justifying different systems. And methodologies make a difference to what results are reached. The contractarian methodology would never lead, for example, to Thrasymachus' system of justice.[36] We see the same lessons in John Rawls.[37]

It may be doubted that the passage I quoted represents the first step of the application of the functional theory to the city; and indeed the passage I have just quoted does not use the term *ergon* (work, function).[38] But subsequent crucial passages use the term constantly: for the work various citizens should do (369e); in the first elaboration of the principle of social justice (370b twice); again in a discussion of the same principle (374b); to refer to the guardian's work (374e); to refer to the craftsmen's "own work" (421c); to express a short form of the principle of social justice, "one man to one work" (423d). It is truly remarkable that the application of the functional theory after the first book has been rarely explicitly recognized, even though Plato has taken the trouble to define the concept of *ergon* and uses the term for it constantly in his construction and defense of justice.

We can also see the functional theory clearly at work if we go all the way to a passage in Book IV, which marks the end of the first two steps and the beginning of the last, the definitions of the city virtues:

> Well, son of Ariston, I said, your city might now be said to be established. The next step is for you to look . . . and see where justice resides in it, and where injustice, what the difference is between them, and which of the two of them the man who intends to be happy should possess. . . . I hope to find it in this way, I said. I think our city, if it has been correctly founded, is completely good. Necessarily so, he said. Clearly then it is wise, brave, moderate, and just. Clearly. (427e, Shorey transl., modified by author)

The functional theory of good provides a clear rationale for this passage. Having identified the functions of the city in our first passage, Socrates and Glaucon have tried to imagine a city which performs these functions as well as possible (in their joint judgments). If they made no mistakes, they have constructed a city which is completely good; since on the functional theory something is completely good if it performs its function(s) as well as possible. And since it does *that* by the virtues appropriate to it, a completely good city will have all the virtues appropriate to a city. And now they can try to discover what these are in their city.

But we have to remember that the *Republic* is such a rich work; it is written in such an informal dialogue style, and it has so many ins and outs, that its underlying logic, which in the first half of the work is the functional theory, is sometimes difficult to discern clearly. Here we must stay with the fundamentals and not let contingent particulars throw us off the track, however important these particulars may be. We must also remember that the substantive conclusions Plato reaches in the *Republic*, in ethics and political philosophy, are the result not only of the functional theory but also of many empirical assumptions he makes about human beings and their cities. The functional theory itself is abstract and formal; it is applied by putting it together with relevant factual information about the functions of particular kinds of things, about the conditions under which they perform their functions best, and appropriate conclusions are drawn. These empirical propositions are what I have called contingent particulars: the assumption that human beings are born with substantially different talents and abilities; what qualities or talents are needed to perform functions best; the education needed to enable soldiers or artisans or rulers to develop their inborn capacities best. These are immensely important. The point is that they are contingent empirical propositions, and here Plato could be making all sorts of factual errors – not unexpectedly in any case since the empirical disciplines had not even been born. The functional theory is not necessarily discredited if the substantive conclusions Plato reaches are mistaken, since these mistakes may be due to mistakes he makes about empirical propositions. Put together with different facts, perfectionist theories can lead to different ethics and politics. Thomas Hurka's *Perfectionism* illustrates the point beautifully.[39]

Our main interest is in Plato's functional theory of good and its *main* applications. So I shall skip much detail, however interesting, and keep to the main track. In any case the contingent particulars have been frequently discussed.

Let us return to the second step of the functional procedure: the difficult task of discovering an economic, social, and political organization or structure for a city, which would enable the city to perform its function(s), the satisfaction of the needs of the individual who make it up, as well as possible.

Plato begins with the main *economic* needs of food, shelter, and clothing, and tries to discover how best to satisfy these. Later he expands the model to include the needs for defense and ruling. Here he imagines a very simple case of the three economic needs and, say, three citizens, and puts forward two fundamentally different ways of satisfying these needs:

Model A	**Model B**
Citizen 1 farms, builds, and sews	Citizen 1 farms
Citizen 2 farms, builds, and sews	Citizen 2 builds
Citizen 3 farms, builds, and sews	Citizen 3 sews

Asked to express a preference, Glaucon says that Model B would be "easier." The difference between the two models is clearly division of labor,

and the gains in productivity or efficiency it brings, so Glaucon's preference is understandable.

Next, Socrates introduces a new factor, that people differ in native or
inborn (naturally given) abilities or talents relative to the social tasks to be
performed, which suggests a new model:

Model C

The citizen naturally best suited to farming is assigned to farming;
the citizen naturally best suited to sewing is assigned to sewing; the
citizen naturally best suited to building is assigned to building.

Model C differs importantly from B: in C the division of labor takes into
account inborn ability or talent in matching citizens and social functions.

Socrates now works up an argument which would justify a preference
for Model C over A or B: People differ in native or inborn abilities or
talents; the production of food, shelter, and clothing requires technique
and so training or education; the production of each of these goods also
requires a lot of time and so takes scheduling and leisure from other things.
In view of these facts, more and better of these goods would be produced,
and easier too, if each citizen were to do that for which she is best suited
by her inborn nature and subsequent appropriate education, rather than if
each citizen were to produce all goods herself or were to specialize
without regard to native ability.

Next, the economic model is expanded to include the needs of a city
and its citizens for defense and ruling. With all the economic needs lumped
together, the population expanded to realistic levels, and the new needs
introduced we have the final model:

Model C1

The citizens best suited for farming, sewing, building, and so on are
severally assigned to these. The citizens best suited for defending are
assigned to defense. The citizens best suited for ruling are assigned to
ruling.[40]

An argument similar to that given for the economic model C will reach
a broader conclusion favoring the model C1: namely, a city will perform
best its functions of producing economic goods, of defending, and of
ruling, if each citizen is assigned one of these functions on the basis of
what she or he can do best, given inborn ability and subsequent appropriate education.

In Bk. IV this generalization is elevated into Plato's principle of social justice. Two fundamental questions arise about it: is it the best way to satisfy the needs of human beings – the original reason for cities? And, is it a principle of social justice?

On the first issue, one problem arises from the ambiguity of optimal functions. This notion is used in Plato's principle, which could be restated as: the city is to be so organized that each citizen is assigned to perform his or her optimal social function. But, as we saw in the definition of function, optimal function is ambiguous: it can be either the work someone can do better than other things she or he can do, or the work someone can do better than other people can do that same work. If so, application of Plato's principle poses the following problem. Suppose we have the same three citizens and social tasks as in the earlier simple economic model. The ambiguity of optimal functions allows two kinds of comparisons which may or not match:

Best–Case Scenario

Citizen 1 does farming better than sewing or building, *and*
Citizen 1 does farming better than Citizens 2 or 3 do farming.
Similar matchings for 2 and 3 would give us the best-case senario for maximizing the production of things needed *and* for each citizen doing what she or he is best at.

Worst–Case Scenario

Citizen 1 does farming better than sewing or building, *but*
Citizens 2 or 3 do farming better than 1 does farming.
Similar conflicts for Citizens 2 and 3.

In the best-case scenario the principle of division of labour by educated talent assigns Citizen 1 to farming by both comparative criteria; and similar assignments are made for Citizens 2 and 3. Here social good, maximizing total production of things needed, and perfectionist individual good, developing and exercising one's greater abilities or talents, coincide.

But in the worst-case scenario, the two comparative criteria conflict. And this is an important conflict: it drives a wedge between social and individual good. It would be better for Citizen 1 to assign her to farming, since it exercizes and develops her greater abilities and talents. But for maximizing total production of things needed, it would be better if we instead assigned Citizens 2 or 3 to farming. The problem is pressing for Plato because he wishes to construct a social system in which the good of social justice and individual perfectionist good coincide. This is a crucial part of his defense of *social* justice, perhaps his whole defense.

How does Plato solve this problem? Well, it is not even clear that he is aware of it. When he applies the notion of optimal function to the construction of the ideal city his comparisons always seem to be of one citizen with another with respect to the same social function, rather than one function with another of the same citizen.[41] And this makes some sort of sense, since in the construction of the ideal city he is primarily guided by what will maximize the good of the city as a whole. When it comes to solutions, we know that he tries to solve similar matching problems, such as ensuring a supply of very intelligent people for his guardians, by restricting marriage and procreation, resorting to eugenics (Bk. V). So presumably he might try this here also; social engineering based on eugenics, as in Huxley's *Brave New World*, presumably a *dis*topia in criticism of Plato. In any case, a solution would be difficult, especially in large societies. It would require something like perfect information and genetic engineering to solve it. But it is a problem which all societies can have, not just Plato's. The differences between theories of justice would be in the solutions they allow.

The ambiguity of optimal functions hides another problem, besides matching the two kinds of optimal function. Plato seems to simply assume that one is better off doing what one does best *among the various social tasks one can do* (among vocations or careers). But though this is certainly an important human good, a person might conceivably, and even often, be better off doing one of the things he or she can do less well. The most obvious examples are occupations of very low social esteem and/or compensation, things that society needs but no one particularly wants to do even if that is the thing one can do best. Collecting trash, cleaning streets, domestic service – these are obvious examples. A person may be better off building houses, even though he or she is not as good at it as at cleaning houses, though of course society may be better off if he or she cleans houses.

Other advantages and problems for Plato's principle can be seen by comparing Model B, according to which a city is organized by the principle of division of labor, and Model C1, according to which it is organized by the princple of division of labor on the basis of talent. Important differences between the two principles can be appreciated by looking at Adam Smith's *The Wealth of Nations*, whose first three chapters contain a masterful discussion of division of labor and its advantages. In a famous passage about the pin factory Smith says:

One man draws out the wire, another straits it, a third cuts it a fourth points it. . . . I have seen a small manufactory of this kind where ten men only were employed . . . they could when they exerted themselves make among them about twelve pounds of pins a day. . . . These ten persons, therefore, could make among them upwards of forty eight thousand pins in a day. . . . But if they had all wrought separately and independently . . . they could certainly not each of them make twenty, perhaps not one pin a day. (1937, p. 4)

What is being illustrated here is division of labor and its advantages, not division of labor on the basis of talent; since the division of labor in the pin factory is so minute and the tasks so simple that differences in abilities or talents are pretty irrelevant. By using such division of labor many more pins are produced than without division, given the same materials, tools, and labor.

This division of labor seems clearly to be a principle of efficiency or productivity; by its application more goods and services will be produced, with the same materials, machinery, and labor. But it says nothing about how the greater goods or services are to be distributed among the citizens. There may be a presumption in the background that the more productive workers are the greater can be their compensation; or more generally, the greater the amount of total goods produced by society the better for everyone – the bigger the whole pie the bigger the individual shares can be. Even so, division of labor by itself seems silent on *how* the greater quantities of goods or services produced by its application are to be distributed: whether, for example, everyone is to be benefited, or benefited equally, or in some proportion to, say, contribution. The principle is in fact compatible with all theories of justice in the *Republic*.

Now the division of labor *by talent* is also silent on how the goods and services produced by *its* application are to be distributed.[42] However, it does by itself and directly distribute something: it requires that social vocations or careers be matched to educated talents. In this part of it, the matching of social labors to talents, the principle can be thought of as a distributive principle; it goes beyond the division of labor, which it includes and which is a maximizing principle, maximizing the total production of social goods and services. Plato assumes that it is better for an individual to do that social labor for which she is best suited by inborn ability and appropriate education than to do other social labors for which she is less suited: the education will help her develop her greater capabilities[43] and the social labor will enable her to exercise them. If we suppose that generally she would perform such matched social tasks better than she would do others (other things equal), then the functional theory explicitly says that doing so is part of her good. By matching citizens' abilities and social labors, Plato's principle of social justice promotes *that* individual good of citizens equally. Not absolutely equally, since it does not distribute the very same thing to every one (e.g. assigning everyone to defense), but proportionately so, the same job for the same talent and education. And since division of labor by talent includes division of labor, its application promotes also greater total good or the good of the city as a whole. Division of labor by talent, it seems, promotes total social good and the good of each citizen equally. We shall see these implications clearly when Socrates applies the principle to the role of gender in society.

The meaningful application of division of labor by talent, however, does presuppose that the division of labor is not so minute that talent becomes irrelevant. Minute division of labor has heavy human costs (as well as great gains in productivity), which may not obtain in grosser divisions of labor to which talent is relevant. In assembly lines of modern factories, ability and talent become pretty irrelevant, the jobs dull human potentialities instead of developing them, and the results can be boredom and alienation. Assembly lines neither require nor encourage the development of talent and ability, the kind of perfectionist good Plato and Aristotle prized.

Plato did not have to face the problems created by minute division of labor. The divisions he knew were far grosser, along the lines of the arts, crafts, and sciences: the division between a carpenter, a shoemaker, an architect, or a sculptor, not between places in an assembly line. And the divisions along the *technai* — the arts, crafts, and sciences — make talent or ability relevant and encourage its development. So Plato had the luxury of being in a position to design a social system of division of occupations, vocations, and careers, which appears to maximize both total social good *and* the development and exercise of individual talents and abilities equally for all the citizens — something presumably good for each individual. His principle of division of labor by native ability or talent is designed to capture these two goods, aggregate social good and the good of each individual citizen. Because of this it has more of a claim to being a principle of justice, not merely a principle of efficiency as the division of labor is. Later we shall see that Plato, by showing the implications of his principle for the distribution of wealth and property and for the role of gender in society, enhances the connection between his principle of division of labor by talent and common notions of social justice.

So far, we have been comparing division of labor and division of labor by talent, and Plato certainly makes this comparison. There is another important comparison, however, which Plato fails to make till later. The principle that labor be divided and social tasks be assigned on the basis of talents may be compared with the traditional modern principle of "careers *open* to talents," which Rawls calls the principle of formal equality of opportunity (1971, ch. 2, pp. 65ff.). This holds that all social positions shall be *legally open* to all citizens, so that each has an equal legal opportunity to pursue a career of her or his choice. But as it becomes subsequently clear, Plato's principle of social justice *requires* each citizen to do what she or he is best suited to (optimal social function). Nowhere is this clearer than in the famous passage on the interchanges of functions as being the cause of the greatest harm to the city (*Republic*, 434): the greatest harm would come to the city if the citizens were allowed to change social functions and perform functions for which they are not suited by talent and education; especially if those suited to be soldiers were to take over the function of ruling; and the greatest harm to the city, it is readily agreed, constitutes injustice.

The problem here is that it cannot simply be taken for granted that a city or its citizens would be better off if the citizens were required to match careers to talents than if they were given the freedom, and perhaps incentives, to do so. For one thing, Adam Smith (or someone similarly minded) might say, in a situation of free choice of occupations, competition, and incentives, social occupations will tend in the long run to be distributed on the basis of ability, and so both total social good and individual good will be promoted. To these benefits Adam Smith no doubt would add the value of freedom of choice of occupations and lifestyles – presumably an individual good which promotes autonomy and the development of rational agency. The value of such freedom has to be put in the balance and weighed before we can pronounce Model C1 the victor over all known alternatives. We find no argument for this in the *Republic* till Plato's criticism of democracy; and even there, as we shall see, he changes the issue from social freedom to psychic freedom of desires.

4   The Definitions of the Social Virtues

In Book IV Plato begins the last step of the application of the functional theory to the city: the search for the definition of justice and the other virtues. The functional theory can be used to understand the logic of this step and the passage I quoted earlier (427e).

Socrates and his companions begin by identifying the functions of the city, and they try to construct a city which will perform these functions as well as possible (better than any alternatively organized city they can think of). If they make no mistakes of reasoning or of fact, then, according to the functional theory, this city is completely good. A completely good city has all the virtues appropriate to a city, since, according to the functional theory, the virtues appropriate to a city are "qualities" it has that enable it to perform its functions well. These virtues are social courage, social wisdom, social temperance, and social justice.[44] Hence the city they have constructed is courageous, wise, temperate, and just (427e, 434e).

The task now is to discover the good that each of these four virtues contributes to the city and define that virtue so as to account for this good. Plato finds it easy to define social courage and social wisdom, for there was no disagreement about them (except for his very strong notion of wisdom as infallible knowledge of the good); but he goes through laborious pains in constructing definitions of temperance and justice.

It is agreed that a city is thought to be well counseled not by the presence of the various arts and sciences in it, such as agriculture or architecture, each of which thinks and takes care of a *part* of the city; but by deliberating well about the whole city and what is best for it as a whole in its internal and international relations (428). It is this knowledge which makes the city wise. Wisdom is thus at least a necessary condition for achieving what is good for the city as a whole (e.g. war or peace). It is wisdom about the whole city and the good of the city as a whole, but it resides in part of the city, the rulers, since they are entrusted with guiding the whole city and making choices on behalf of the city as a whole. Here, as in the case of the other virtues, we must observe the distinction between the object of a virtue, and in what that virtue resides; the object of social wisdom is the good of the city as a whole, but it resides in a part of the city, the class of rulers.[45] It is *social* wisdom primarily because its object is the good of the city as a whole, as distinct from *individual* wisdom whose object is the good of the whole individual.

The good which courage contributes was also easy to identify, because there was no disagreement that it was good for the city as a whole to defend itself successfully; and that the quality which contributes most to the success of such defense is courage in the city's defenders. A city is brave if its soldiers are brave and the city's soldiers fight for something which is good for the whole city.[46] So what we need to do is to identify the elements which make up courage so as to account for this power it has. Plato finds that one element is cognitive: true belief about what the city as a whole should fear and not fear, the weighing of social goods and evils, what is worth fighting for, what risks are worth taking, and the like; in this the soldiers are to be guided by the rulers.[47] The other, a noncognitive element, is high spirit which enables the soldiers to act in accordance with these beliefs in situations of danger and risk to life. If this is correct, then the city will defend itself best only if the citizens assigned to defend it have these particular qualities which make up social courage: inborn high spirit and appropriate education, including education in true beliefs about what the city as a whole should fear, and experience of dangerous situations which test these beliefs. Citizens who are born with high spirit and have received such education will be able to defend their city better than any other citizens and (in the best case scenario) better than they themselves can perform other social functions (429–30).

About temperance there was wide disagreement among the ancients. Plato appeals to common-sense notions implicit in the virtue applied to individuals[48]: "master of oneself," "self-control," and "harmony" or "lack of inner conflict." He thinks that the first notion, to be coherent, must imply some division in the self;[49] and also that one of these parts is better and this better part is master of a worse, since temperance is a virtue.[50] The second notion involved in temperance, harmony, also presupposes parts, and it must mean that these parts are in harmony. Assuming that when temperance is applied to the city it must mean the same thing,[51] he concludes that city temperance obtains when the best part of the city (those citizens whose optimal function is to rule the city) is master of the other parts *and* all these parts are in agreement about who should rule and who should be ruled (431e–432b). Here we most note that the latter part of this statement is ambiguous: it may be interpreted formally, that the classes agree on who should rule and be ruled, no matter who that is; or it may refer to an agreement with the specific content that those of high intelligence and appropriate education should rule and the others be ruled. On the former interpretation, the good of temperance consists in the harmony it secures between rulers and ruled, no matter who they are; on the latter the good of temperance includes also the good secured by the most intelligent and educated ruling the city. The context favors the latter interptetation, a point to which we shall return.

Plato also points out that unlike social wisdom and social courage, temperance resides in the whole city, not just in parts of it, since all three parts need to agree on who among them should rule. Social temperance is doubly social: its good is the good of the whole city *and* it resides in the whole city.

At last the definition of social justice is constructed, in accordance with the functional theory, and on the assumption that it is the remaining virtue of the city.

Socrates claims social justice is to be found in the founding principle of their city: a city is just if and only if it is so organized that each of the citizens is assigned to that social task for which she or he is best suited by nature and appropriate education; or, in the slogan "each does his own" (433a). This, however, is only the *formal* part (principle) of Platonic justice, since it is compatible with different social assignments for different citizens and thus can have different contents. An "oligarch," for example, might agree with it but argue that a wealthy man is best suited by nature and experience to rule the city. To understand Plato's full conception of social justice, we need to add the following *material* parts or content, which we can gather from our discussion of how he applies the functional theory to the city. To fully appreciate the logic of the functional theory, we can arrange the definition as the conclusion of an argument, whose first premise is the formal principle of justice just stated.

The main social tasks are governing, defending, and provisioning the city. Therefore, a city is just when it is so organized that those best suited to govern (to be called "rulers" – an optimal functional name for Plato), are assigned to govern; those naturally best suited to defend the city (guardians) are assigned to defend, and those best suited to provision it (artisans) are assigned to that.[52] Those best suited to govern are people of inborn high intelligence and appropriate education; those best suited to defend the city are persons of inborn high spirit and appropriate education; and those best suited to provision the city are persons of inborn abilities and education for arts and trades. Therefore, a city is just when it is so organized that those of high intelligence and appropriate education are assigned to rule the city, those of high spirit and appropriate education are assigned to defend it, and those of inborn abilities and appropriate education in the arts and trades are assigned to provision the city.

This last statement, which is the conclusion of the formal principle and the material premises, is the *full definition* of Platonic justice. Usually only the formal part is given, sometimes even by Plato himself, as the definition of social justice. But this can be misleading, and it leads to unnecessary controversies. The full definition, together with its derivation from the formal and material premises, has many advantages. The different elements in it, some formal and some empirical, are made explicit and their place in Plato's theory of justice is clear; disagreements with this definition can be clarified and handled more easily: one may disagree with one or another of these elements or with all of them. A timocrat, for example, may agree with the formal principle, but disagree that those best suited to rule are people of high inborn intelligence; he would argue that those with inborn high spirit and appropriate military experience are more suited to rule. A democrat, on the other hand, might disagree with the formal principle itself; he can claim that the formal principle by itself, since it *requires* matching social careers to talents, deprives him of freedom to choose a vocation, which is itself an important good.

The full definition can be useful also in clarifying the vexed doctrine of unity of virtue. For example, it makes a difference to the relations among the virtues, whether temperance makes reference only to the formal principle of justice, or also to the matchings of parts and functions required by the full definition of Platonic justice. If temperance is agreement merely on formal Platonic justice, then it is compatible with Platonic injustices, for example, with timocracy or oligarchy;[53] an oligarch may agree with the formal principle of justice but claim that the wealthy are best suited to rule; *and* the ruled in an oligarchy might also agree to this claim, in which case such an oligarchy will be temperate. But if Platonic temperance is agreement among all the parties on the full definition of justice, which includes the Platonic matchings of particular inborn talents with particular social functions, then temperance is not compatible with Platonic injustices; since Platonically unjust matchings (say, wealthy persons with ruling) would violate the agreement. I take the discussion of social temperance to show that the agreement refers to the full definition of justice, and so social temperance does not obtain in Platonically unjust societies. However, a society can be Platonically just (full definition) without being Platonically temperate: the city might be Platonically organized, and even all citizens might in fact be actually performing their Platonic functions, but some may well disagree that this is the best way to organize the city and so disagree with the matchings.

What about the rest of the unity of the social virtues? Does a city having Platonic justice (full definition) entail its having wisdom or courage? And if it has wisdom or courage, will it necessarily also be just? No, because what justice secures is that the function of ruling is performed by those whose optimal function it is, i.e. persons of high intelligence and appropriate education; it does not necessarily secure that they perform it well; they might perform it more or less well or even poorly. We must not conflate the notions of performing one's optimal function and of performing that function well. Thus even the full definition of justice does not entail that a just city will also be a wise city. For similar reasons justice does not by itself secure courage.

However, Plato might include the wisdom of the rulers in their appropriate education, so that appropriately educated rulers have the virtue of wisdom; and true beliefs in the soldiers is included in their education; and skills for the artisans. If we make these additional assumptions, then a Platonically just society will have the rest of the virtues.

On the other hand, if a society is Platonically courageous or wise, it will not necessarily also be just; it might be only partially just; we can imagine a society which is so organized that it requires those best suited to defend the city to do that, but allows choice of other occupations, in which case it might be brave but not just.

We can thus resolve at least part of the controversy whether Plato in the *Republic* holds to the unity of the *social* virtues, and we can also see what this doctrine amounts to and what are its grounds. All this is made possible not only by the distinction between formal and material parts of justice and temperance, and the distinction between optimal function and functioning well, but also by the fact that Plato defines the virtues. In the Socratic dialogues, by contrast, we are not in this position, because Socrates, in both the *Laches* and the *Protagoras*, fails to define all the virtues; at most he defines courage and wisdom, and so the controversy about the unity of the virtues is difficult even to understand, not to say resolve. But the *Republic* is a constructive work, and the full definitions of the virtues helps us better understand the relations among them.

The isomorphism between the social and the individual virtues, which I shall formulate and discuss in the next chapter, will enable us to give a similar resolution to the problem of the unity of individual virtues. Personal temperance has formal and material parts, and personal justice has formal and material parts. The full definition of temperance (in which reason, spirit, and appetite all agree that reason should rule), is incompatible with Platonic injustice. And if the particular matchings justice requires between parts of the soul and psychic functions are based on the complete education of the psychic parts as well as their optimal natural capabilities, then in a just person reason will have at least true beliefs about the good, and spirit will have been educated to be able to carry out the commands of reason. So here too, in analogy to the social virtues, if a person is temperate she will also be just, and if just then also wise and courageous. A corresponding unity of virtues for the person is not surprising. If anything, we would expect more of a unity of the virtues for persons than we would for cities, since a person is more of a unity than a city.

5   *The Role and Scope of Platonic Social Justice*

Now suppose we granted that the city would perform its functions better if citizens were assigned their optimal functions, rather than given free choice of occupation, or assigned by division of labor irrespective of talent, or were each doing all tasks. Why should we suppose that this is a principle of social justice? Why, for example, might it not be just a principle of efficiency or productivity, like division of labor without regard to talent? This is to ask whether Plato's principle plays "the role of justice,"[54] which marks whether a principle is one of justice, as distinct from whether it is a correct principle of justice. Plato must be aware of possible objections here, since he takes pains to argue that it is justice he has defined.

His first argument is that the matching of citizens to their optimal social functions makes possible and preserves the other social virtues and the good they promote. The good of courage, defending the city well, is advanced most by assigning defense to the citizens who are born high spirited and appropriately educated, those who can have most the virtue for that function. The good of wisdom, ruling the city well, is advanced most by assigning the task of ruling to the most intelligent, since they are most capable of attaining wisdom through appropriate education, knowledge of the good of the city as a whole. How justice makes temperance and its good possible is less clear. How does justice promote the primary good of social temperance, civil harmony and the avoidance of civil strife? Justice provides the standard upon which assignments of rulers and ruled are made, but how does it promote agreement on this? Perhaps Plato thinks that the matchings his justice requires are so reasonable or rational, compared to the alternatives, that citizens are more likely to agree to them than to any of the alternatives; the matchings oligarchic justice, for example, requires would not be agreed to by the poor; or those of timocracy by the intellectuals. But what of democratic justice, which allows freedom to choose any career or vocation? Would not all citizens be likely to agree to this, since it gives them greater equal freedom and a voice in what is their own good?

A second argument is that the contribution which social justice makes to the goodness of the city rivals those of courage, wisdom, and temprance; it would be difficult to decide which of these most of all makes the city good; and justice must be the name of the principle which rivals these virtues in making the city good (433d). This argument may rely on two unstated premises: that a virtue makes a thing good of its kind, a proposition of the functional theory; and that justice is the remaining social virtue.

Plato's third argument is based on what judges aim at – that no one shall have what belongs to others or be deprived of his or her own. Since his principle also aims at this, and what judges aim at is justice, his principle must be a principle of justice. Here he is trying to connect his definition with judicial notions of justice. This seems to be a weak argument. What Plato's principle of justice requires is the optimal matching of social tasks and talent; and this has to be the Platonic interpretation of the catch phrase "to do one's own." But one would be hard put, to say the least, to find evidence that judges or juries in ancient Greece, or elsewhere for that matter, saw to it that citizens performed their optimal social functions and required the citizens to revert to them if they did what they were not suited for.[55]

Fourth, there is the argument from harm to the city as a whole: interchange of functions, between those best suited to be artisans or soldiers and those best suited to be rulers, constitutes the *greatest* harm to the city as a whole. What causes the greatest harm to the city as a whole is injustice (434bc), and if this is injustice, then the principle which such interchanges violate must be a principle of justice. The argument can be understood within a nonegoistic teleological ethical theory: if the right is what maximizes the good of the whole society, and justice is part of the right, injustice will do maximal harm to the whole society. So if interchanges do maximal harm to the whole society, they will be injustice, and their opposite justice.

Finally, a substantial argument can be constructed from what Plato says about wealth and poverty: it is argued that extremes of poverty and wealth hinder excellent performance of function; poverty because of want of adequate means (materials and instruments), wealth because it saps incentives and diverts motivations (421dff.). This is a principal reason why the rulers and guardians are deprived of *private* property,[56] while artisans are allowed enough to do their job well. So the functional principle of Platonic social justice does regulate the distribution of wealth and property and thus it does qualify as a principle of justice, though *indirectly* through the effects on the performance of functions.

The regulation of property and wealth is, as in Hume and Rawls, one of the *roles* of social justice. But it must be noted that, unlike Platonic justice, principles of justice in Hume and Rawls are more directly concerned with the distribution of property; in Hume rules of property seem to be the main object of justice. In Rawls the difference principle regulates the distribution of income and wealth, by placing constraints on inequalities in its distribution. Though there are thus differences in *what* is being distributed, at least directly, there is overlap and all these principles can qualify as principles of justice.

But the differences in their scope, objects, and content are most interesting. Through the basic structure and its institutions, Rawls's principles of justice regulate the distribution of the "primary goods," of rights and liberties, income and wealth, positions of authority and opportunities (and indirectly of self-respect). These are the fruits of social cooperation, and they are conceived as major goods for individuals: what it is rational for individuals to want, no matter what their ultimate ends are, since these are major means generally necessary or useful to any ends they may have. But ends themselves are not in any way regulated within the limits of justice. In Rawls's theory, individuals have the freedom to develop and pursue their own comprehensive conception of the good, which includes choice of ultimate ends and intrinsic goods, within the constraints of justice. By relying only on primary goods, Rawls's theory seems to avoid the traditional and seemingly unresolvable controversies about the ultimate ends of life and about intrinsic goods; though it may also be argued that if justice regulates only primary goods it leaves some considerable room for injustices (see Nussbaum and Sen, 1992). Equally important, by leaving the choice of ultimate ends to individuals (within the constraints of justice), Rawls's justice allows great freedom of lifestyles and allows the development of autonomy.

Plato's principle of justice, on the other hand, when taken together with all its implications for careers, social freedom, property, family, and the role of gender, regulates far more of the individual's life, including ultimate ends and comprehensive good. Writing at the beginning of the study of ethics, Plato felt confident enough about the good, at least in the *Republic*, to bring the ends of life, ultimate and intrinsic goods, within the scope of justice. As Vlastos has pointed out, Plato's justice reaches almost everywhere in the life of individuals, especially his soldiers and rulers, and the distinction between the public and private realm is almost abolished.

Twenty-four centuries later, having witnessed the controversies about ultimate ends and intrinsic goods as well as the value of individual liberty,
Rawls adopted a desire satisfaction theory of good, which is very toler-
ant about the good of the individual, as Thomas Nagel pointed out
(Daniels, 1974); and a theory of justice which is very liberal about individual good, unlike the theories of the ancients, as Rawls himself recognizes (1982).

6   The Good of Platonic Social Justice

What is the good which Platonic social justice promotes? The application
of the functional theory to the city, which we have tracked, gives us Plato's
answer. By requiring division of social labor and the optimal matching of
social labors to inborn abilities appropriately educated, the principle of
social justice contributes essentially to the the better performance of the
functions of ruling, defending, and provisioning the city: these things are
done better than individuals could do for themselves and by themselves,
better than without division of labor, and better than with division but
no matching to talents. The remaining virtues contribute to performing
social functions best, temperance providing social harmony, courage good
defense, and social wisdom good government. Plato's defense of *social*
justice is presumably that his justice better secures these things, which
undoubtedly are good things for the city and its citizens.

But since the virtue is social justice, some further questions arise: Is
Plato's social justice good for *all* the citizens? *Equally* good? With respect
to *all the good* things of life?

Perhaps the most revealing passage for an answer to these questions is
Socrates' reply to an objection made by Adeimantus in the opening lines
of Book IV. Socrates had proposed that the upper two classes should not
have private property and wealth or private wives and children, because
these things would divide them and would distract them from optimal
performance of their jobs.[57] Adeimantus points out that this might make
the rulers and soldiers unhappy, since they are being deprived of all the
things usually thought to make people happy: land and grand houses,
wives and children, money for travel, entertainment and mistresses. These
people rule the city, but they enjoy none of "the good things of life."
Wouldn't they be unhappy?

Socrates' answer falls into two parts. First, their aim has been all along
not to make any one class of people in the city as happy as possible, but

to make the city as a whole as happy as possible. For only in such a city, they think, are they likely to find social justice, the first object of their search. Here he is thinking of social justice as something which maximizes the good of the city as a whole; not only the good of the rulers, as the egoistic theory of Thrasymachus does.[58] He is rejecting as being unjust what Aristotle calls deviant constitutions,[59] and affirming a nonegoistic and teleological nature of social justice, as maximizing the good of the city as a whole.

The second part of Socrates' answer challenges the conception of good and happiness underlying the objection, that happiness consists in the satisfaction of desires; or in the possession of the goods of power, riches, and pleasures, which are the things people show by their behavior to be the things they want. This is the view of good and happiness on which Glaucon's theory of justice is built.[60]

Plato agrees that what human happiness is depends on what is good for human beings, but disagrees that what is good for human beings depends on their desires, as shown by what people ordinarily pursue as their good. Socrates says that he would not be surprised if the guardians were the happiest they could be, even though they were deprived of the goods people ordinarily sought. But in any case, he says, they must be apportioned "a happiness that is appropriate to guardians"; and the same for the other classes: "the helpers and the guardians are to be constrained and persuaded to do what will make them the best craftsmen in their own work [*ergon*] . . ." [61] To be the best "craftsmen" they can be at their own work is their happiness as citizens.[62] Now plainly this happiness is not the satisfaction of desires, whatever they happen to be; nor the enjoyment of the usual good things of life; for these are not peculiar to any one class of human beings or citizens; but a happiness which is relative to optimal social function, a functional good. It is the good of doing well what one is best at, among the various social tasks, careers, or vocations in society; a good that requires the developing and exercising of one's greater social capabilities. And there is general agreement that this is an important human good.[63]

This is a good which Platonic social justice secures equally for all its citizens. Not absolutely equally in the sense of securing the very same occupation for all citizens, but proportionately equal: to all citizens the occupation in proportion to their inborn ability and appropriate education. The occupations are different, but the good is the same, doing well what one is best at.

And here we may note that this theory clearly implies that education and resources for it should also be distributed similarly equally, in proportion to inborn capability and the demands of the occupation which matches that capability. Those with greater inborn ability for mathematics should have an education appropriate to developing that ability and to the practice of that science; and similarly for those with greater inborn ability for architecture or building.

7   The Application of Platonic Social Justice to Gender

There is no better illustration in the *Republic* of the main points I have been making about Plato's principle of social justice than Socrates' application of it to gender.

In Bk. V Socrates faces the question whether men and women should have similar educations and similar pursuits, "whether female human nature is capable of sharing with the male all tasks or none at all, or some but not others" (453a).

The question arises for two reasons.

First, Plato's principle of *social* justice has no part which would exclude women from its scope.[64] This is also true of his principle of individual justice: an individual is just when reason rules his or her soul, spirit helps to carry out the commands of reason, and appetite obeys. Here there is no hint and not even any plausibility – unlike the social case – to the view that women's souls are essentially different from men's: either in the tripartite division of the psyche (434–40), or in the normative assignment of psychic labor, which is individual justice (441–2).

Second, the view of Plato's contemporaries was that men and women should have different pursuits – and in fact did have different pursuits: men's responsibilities were the affairs of the city, women's the affairs of the home. We can see this in Plato's *Meno* (71–2): Meno defines different virtues for men and women on the assumption of different pursuits; the virtue of a woman is what enables her to conduct the household well, of man the management of the city.

The conjunction of these two circumstances – the open scope of Plato's principle of social justice and current opinion and practice about the role of women – gives rise to Socrates' question about women's pursuits and education; to omit this question would have been a serious incompleteness in Plato's theory of social justice and the ideal constitution.

Socrates begins with the question whether women and men should have similar educations. He proposes the sound principle that persons should have similar educations if they have similar pursuits in life and different educations if different pursuits. This need not be understood except in the sense in which it is true: Architects should have similar (higher) educations, physicians and architects different (higher) educations, because architecture and medicine are different pursuits and so require different knowledge.

Thus the question of education depends on the question of pursuits. Should then men and women have the same or different pursuits? The pursuits in question are social tasks, and in particular, in Bk.V, the tasks of defending and ruling the city; *the* tasks, it may be noted, which were then practiced by men exclusively, and even nowadays are carried out predominantly by men.

Plato approaches this question from the opposition, and an opposition using his very principle of social justice: According to you, Socrates and Glaucon, a city is just if it is so organized that each person is assigned to that social task for which s/he is best suited by nature; men and women are different by nature; therefore, in your just society men and women should perform different social tasks (453b).

Plato correctly perceives that the answer to this argument depends, first, on what *in fact* are the natural differences between men and women, and, second, on whether these are *relevant* differences to the determination of division of labor by natural talents and abilities.

Plato finds that there are only two natural differences between men and women, considered as groups: first, men beget and women bear children (454e); and second, men are *by and large* (not always) physically stronger than women.

Next, he points out that not all natural differences between persons are relevant to the determination of what their social pursuits should be: for example, some men grow naturally bald, others do not, but it would be absurd to assign the first to defense and the second to ruling on that basis: "we did not posit likeness and difference in nature in every respect . . . but only those that were pertinent to the pursuits themselves. . . . We meant, for example, that a man and a woman who had a physician's soul have the same nature . . . and that a man physician and a man carpenter have different natures" (454d, Shorey transl., modified by author).

The pertinent differences, on the basis of which persons are assigned different social pursuits, are differences in ability, relative to the social tasks, as shown by differences in learning. The differences between a man who is naturally gifted for mathematics and another who is not, are that the one learns mathematics easily, the other with difficulty; the one with slight instruction can discover much for himself, the other after much instruction and drill could at most only remember what he learned (455b).

Now the two natural differences conceded between men and women are not of this kind, except possibly that the differences in physical strength will indeed be relevant to pursuits requiring great physical strength and stamina; though even this difference, unlike the first one, is not universal between the sexes: some women are physically stronger than some men.

At the same time, Socrates points out, the three main natural differences on which Plato relied all along to assign ruling, defense, and provisioning the city, namely, high intelligence, high spirit, and ability for production and trade, are not distributed in any consistent way between men and women. Some women are more intelligent than some men, some are braver than some men, and some are better producers and traders; while other men are better than some women in one or another of these ways.

"Then there is no pursuit of the administrators of a state that belongs to a woman because she is a woman or to a man because he is a man. But the natural capacities are distributed alike among both creatures, and woman naturally share in all pursuits and men in all . . ." (455de).

Therefore, given the principle of social justice, and given *these facts*, it follows that in a Platonically just society men and women will be assigned to the same social tasks and pursuits, all on exactly the same basis. It will be just that some men and some women be rulers, some men and some women be soldiers, and some men and some women be producers and traders. And since men and women should share the same pursuits, and those who share the same pursuits should share the same education, men and women of the same pursuits should have the same education, and men and women of different pursuits should have different educations; just as men who share different pursuits should have different educations, and women who share the same pusuits should have the same educations.

This is Plato's argument for the equality of women in society. It is a deduction constructed with his *principle* of social justice and his perception of *relevant facts* about men and women. The principle itself picks out what facts are relevant, natural abilities and talents properly educated, and social functions. The beauty of this deduction is that it is based entirely on Plato's principle of social justice and what we now know are true propositions about the distribution of intelligence and talents among men and women. It shows us clearly what Plato's social justice can do when put together with truths about the world.

We must, however, enter an important qualification to Plato's egalitarianism about women.

In "Was Plato a Feminist?" (1989) Gregory Vlastos gives a balanced and judicious answer to his question. He defines feminism by reference to a recently proposed constitutional amendment (which did not in fact pass): "Equality of rights under the law shall not be denied or abridged by the U.S. or any State on account of sex." He then understands his question to be whether such equality of rights is consonant with Plato's "ideas, sentiments, and proposals for social policy." He answers that in the *Republic*, Bk. V, Plato was "unambiguously feminist"; that "political rights" would be "the same for women as for men among Plato's Guardians"; though, Vlastos points out, elsewhere the story is at best mixed; "in his personal attitudes to women Plato is virulently anti-feminist."

The qualification is that Plato's theory of social justice in the *Republic* does not seem to be a *rights based* theory at all, or a theory that *generates rights*. Plato's principle of social justice is not grounded on any other principle about rights of persons as, say, Locke's theory of civil government is based on a principle attributing rights to human beings in a state of nature. When we look at Plato's *justification* of his principle, we find him talking about human *needs*, how they can be best satisfied, and about satisfying or promoting the good of the city as a whole rather than some part of it.[65] These appear to be teleological justifications of the principle of social justice, like those of, say, J. S. Mill, not like those of Locke or Rawls. Further, Plato's principle of social justice itself makes no reference, explicit or implicit, to any rights of persons. When we look at the *content* of the principle, we see nothing said or implied about rights; it is all about social tasks and natural human abilities and talents.

As one might well expect if this is true, the questions about women's pursuits and education in Bk. V are not *in fact* posed in terms of rights, any more than questions about careers and education for men are ever posed in terms of rights. We might tease rights, or perhaps freedoms, out of Glaucon's theory (in Bk. II) or the theory of democracy Plato expounds (in Bk. VIII). Glaucon's contract theory of justice might generate rights, and Athenian democracy seemed to guarantee political rights to citizens, such as participation in the Assembly, and freedoms such as the freedom of speech. But these theories Plato criticizes. And his criticism of democracy is precisely that it allows for the freedom to do as one pleases, includ-

ing the freedom of choice of career, in utter disregard to his own principle of social justice. The freedom to choose a career, a social task in the
ideal city, is a freedom his priciple of justice denies. We saw a similar point
earlier in the contrast between the principle of "Careers (legally) *open* to
talents" and Plato's principle of justice: the former might create rights by
prohibiting laws which would exclude any persons or groups of persons
from pursuing some career; Plato's principle *requires* matching careers to
talents.

So, it may be too much to say that "political rights" would be "the
same for women as for men among Plato's Guardians." It may be more
accurate to say that no one, man or woman equally, has political rights in
Plato's ideal city, at least not "liberty rights," since no one has a right to
refuse doing that for which she or he is best suited, or a right to do something other than what she or he is best suited for.[66]

However, if we lay aside the question of rights, and look at what Plato
actually does when he faces the issue of the place of women in the ideal
city, we see clearly that his theory of social justice *does not discriminate*
between men and women; that is, it *does not discriminate on the basis of
gender* when assignments of offices and other social tasks are made. And
this *was* revolutionary for Plato's time. But it is not enough to guarantee
or generate rights: he could have the most oppressive laws, allowing no
rights and no freedoms, without such laws discriminating on the basis of
gender; men and women might be oppressed absolutely equally. We can
even put the matter negatively in terms of rights: in Plato's ideal city there
are no rights that men have which women do not have; but this may be
because no citizen has any rights or freedoms to begin with. The amendment which Vlastos cited was not empty in this way because there are
other parts of the US Constitution, for example the first ten Amendments
(the "Bill of Rights"), which explicitly guarantee certain rights to citizens.
But there are no such rights in Plato's ideal city; and when we do find
any hint of such rights or at least freedoms in the *Republic*, in his discussion of Athenian democracy, Plato opposes them.

In her lively discussion of this issue Julia Annas (1981) argues that Plato
was not a feminist. She recognizes his proposals as revolutionary, but she
points out that there is no evidence that Plato was motivated by sympa-
thy for the plight of women in ancient male-chauvinistic societies, or by
indignation at the thought that their rights and their dignity as human
beings were not recognized – things that might be said of John Stuart
Mill, for example. So Annas too appears to see the issue of feminism in
terms of rights, but her answer, for the *Republic* at least, is the opposite of

Vlastos's: Plato was not a feminist. And here I am in agreement, given the qualification about rights made earlier.

But how then are we to account for Plato's revolutionary proposals about women? Annas suggests that he saw women as

> a huge untapped pool of resources; here are half the citizens sitting at home wasting effort doing identical trivial jobs. The state will benefit if women do public, not private jobs (if this does not flout nature as it does not). Benefit to the state is the sole, frequently repeated ground for the proposals (456c, 457a,b,c, 452d–e). (1981, p. 183)

As I set it out, Plato's argument for the equality of women makes no appeal to the benefit of the state; though the justification of Plato's principle of social justice, which used as a premise in the equality argument, may be by appeal to the good of the city as a whole. We can think of the matter as a two stage procedure: the principle itself may be justified teleologically, but the argument for the equality of women uses that principle itself, not the justification; and that is sufficent, together with the relevant facts I cited, for the conclusion. Even if eventually we were to bring in the teleological justification, we must consider what "benefit to the state" might mean in the ideal city of the *Republic*: the original ground for the principle of social justice was that if adopted it would result in a greater and better satisfaction of the needs for provisioning, defending, and ruling (369–72). These are needs of the citizens, not some entity other than the citizens.[67] Appeals to the good of the city as a whole are appeals to the good of all the citizens, including women, as distinct from appeals to the good of some of the citizens only. For example, an appeal to the good of the city as a whole is made when Socrates responds to Adeimantus' objection that he has made the guardians unhappy by depriving them of private property and all the usual good things of life. He says that they did not set out to construct a city which would make any one class exceptionally happy, as the just city of Thrasymachus is constructed to make the rulers happy, but a city which promotes "the greatest possible happiness of the city as a whole" (*Republic*, 420b). This phrase does not refer to anything else than the better satisfaction of the needs of the citizens of the city, including women; it just refers to them without favor of one person or group over others. So even if we supposed a direct teleological argument for the equality of women, it would not discriminate in its application to men and women. Finally, we must remember that part of Plato's defense of *social* justice is that it is *better for individuals* to do that for which they are best suited by nature and appropriate education. He thinks that doing that social task for which one is best suited presupposes developing and exercising one's greater social capabilities, and that is a great human good, for men and women. He would not be surprised, Socrates says, if the guardians, though deprived of private property and wealth, were nevertheless happy (*Republic*, 420bc). Their happiness as citizens will derive from doing well that which they do best, "to be the best craftsmen in their own proper work" (*Republic*, 421c).

If we construct Plato's argument for the equality of women as I have, without a direct teleological appeal to the good of the city as a whole, what then is the explanation for Plato's revolutionary proposals? I have a two part answer: one part relates to Plato's concept of justice, the formal part of social justice, the other to his unusual perception of the pertinent facts, men's and women's abilities.

We know already from the *Meno* that Plato thought that virtue is the same for all human beings; Socrates explicitly denies that there is one virtue for men and another for women, as Meno had explicitly stated in *his* definition of virtue (the virtue of men is to manage the affairs of the city well, of women the affairs of the household). And since justice is one of the virtues, this has to apply to justice: there is one and the same justice for men and women. And we know that this is true in the *Republic*. In Book IV Plato tells us explicitly that justice is one and the same for all (435). This is very much supported by his theory of forms, explicit in the *Republic*, which holds that there is exactly one form justice. So, if cities and citizens can be just, they are so by participation in the same form; similarly, if men and women are just, *they* are so by participation in the same form. And since women can be just or unjust, the same principle of justice must a apply to them as well as to men.

This explanation is partial because it does not cover the factual part of the argument; it does not account for the fact that Plato stretched the evidence in favor of women. How did he know, or why did he think that women had talents for soldiering and ruling?

Here his metaphysical views about the human soul may have been an advantage. According to him, human souls can exist disembodied and can occupy several human bodies successively;[68] and this would naturally incline him to the view that human souls are not gendered. Gender is an attribute of bodies, not souls. Moreover, the inborn abilities or talents, which his theory of justice matches to social labors, are attributes of souls, not of bodies.[69] And if souls are not gendered, there is no reason to believe that their attributes, such as intelligence, talents and abilities, are distributed on the basis of gender. So, when Plato applies his principle of social justice, which matches inborn intelligence and talents and abilities with social labors, to women, he supplies factual premises according to which high intelligence and various talents are distributed without regard to gender. With respect to such attributes the "natural lottery" is gender neutral.

Similar results may be expected in the case of individual justice. If human souls are not gendered, the tripartite analysis of the human soul is not gendered, or is gender neutral. And psychic justice, which requires the matching of psychic labors to parts of the soul on the basis of what these parts can do best, is also not gender sensitive, or is gender neutral.

Finally, side by side with the evidence which Vlastos fairly cites for his verdict that Plato, in his less theoretical moments, was also "virulently anti-feminist," we have evidence that goes along with the theoretical explanation we have provided. Plato, we are told, allowed women to enter the Academy, the first institution of higher learning to do so, thousands of years ahead of the universities of Europe. And in the *Symposium* we have striking evidence that Plato thought women could have the highest human intelligence. He has a woman, Diotima, instruct Socrates in the theory of Platonic eros. What is remarkable here is not so much that a women tells Socrates about eros, but that Plato has a woman instruct Socrates in the theory of forms, in which his own theory of eros is embedded. Indeed, one of the most remarkable statements about Platonic forms in the whole corpus is put in the mouth of Diotima, with Socrates listening to her mystified but with open-mouthed admiration. The form beauty, *she* says, is the highest object of love; and unlike everything else beautiful, it is completely beautiful in all respects, the most beautiful thing there is or could be, existing alone by itself for all eternity. So Plato must have thought that at least one woman could be a philosopher and understand the theory of forms, a mark of the highest intelligence in the *Republic*. And if he thought one women could be that intelligent, why not others? Even a single contrary token is enough to break down the prejudice of a stereotype.

Plato was no feminist, if we think of feminism in terms of rights. But he was a revolutionary about gender all the same. We can put the revolution in a nutshell. If Plato were living today, and had the same theory of justice as he had then, and he had the same access to relevant facts that we do, and he were president of a university devoted to educating citizens in the arts and sciences, in government, the army, and business, he would be assigning men and women to education and employment without prejudice against women. And this not because of any federal mandate, but because of his meritocratic theory of justice and his metaphysical belief that human souls are not gendered. According to the tradition, this is pretty much what he did as president of the Academy.

8 Conclusion

In this chapter I began with Plato's major questions about justice and the good of the individual. I sketched Plato's functional theory of good and tracked his application of it to the city, to discover social justice and other social virtues. We saw the functional theory guiding Plato's discovery of both the principle of social justice and the concept of the happiness of citizens. Social justice aims at promoting the good of the city as a whole; it does that by dividing social labors or functions and by assigning optimal social functions to all the citizens equally. Performing one's optimal social function is doing the social work one is best at, and this requires the development and exercise of one's greater social capabilities. Since this is an important human good, and what human happiness is depends on what is good for human beings, social justice also promotes that part of the happiness of all the citizens equally.

Since Plato thinks of the defense of justice, including social justice, as being a defense from the point of view of the good of the individual, showing that his principle of social justice promotes the good of individual citizens, and promotes it equally, is part of his defense of justice. It is only part of his defense even from his point of view, since justice applies to individuals as well as to cities, and he must also show that psychic justice also is good for the just person. But it is also partial from a modern point of view, because Plato radically downgrades, indeed dismisses, such goods as individual liberty and private property and wealth. Plato's justice does not promote these things, indeed deprives individuals of them; and if they are important goods for individuals, as they are important primary goods in Rawls's theory, for example, then Plato's defense of justice is incomplete, even if completely successful in his own terms. I shall discuss psychic justice and its good in the next chapter and and there we shall return to Plato's treatment of the good of individual freedom.

Notes

1   The question whether justice is a virtue, is not argued again. Plato may think
    it settled by arguments in Bk. I, 348ff. Or he thinks his own theory answers

it: whether justice is a virtue depends on what justice is; if a virtue is something which enables one to function well, justice would have to satisfy this condition to be a virtue. In his own theory it does.

2   The *Meno* implies that unless we know what something is we cannot tell what qualities it has; e.g. unless we know what virtue is we cannot tell whether it can be taught. See, e.g. Benson (1992).

3   Rawls, 1971. All the traditional theories among which the persons in the original position are to choose. See ch. 3, section 21.

4   In ch. 7 of *A Theory of Justice*, Rawls defines goodness in terms of rationality, namely the "counting principles" of effectiveness, greater likelihood, inclusiveness, and deliberative rationality. I take Plato to proceed in the reverse direction, explicating rationality in terms of goodness; as, e.g. Socrates begins to do in the *Protagoras*, 352ff., when he explicates rational choice by such rules as: of two goods the greater one is always to be preferred (contra Hume, who claims that this cannot be a rule of reason). Both procedures of course have to avoid circularities.

5   This issue was ably revived in the mid-twentieth century by David Sachs (1963), and much discussed subsequently.

6   Thrasymachus' identification of the justice of a given society with its laws is an essential part of his view, because he needs it as a premise in his argument *in support of* his definition of justice. See further Penner (1988).

7   Such injustice would include the vulgar and commonly thought injustices of Thrasymachus' second speech. But they would also include breaking tax laws, commercial and industrial laws, civil laws, etc.; and *these* can be significantly different in different systems of justice, democratic, oligarchic, and so on. It is a mistake to focus exclusively on criminal laws and suppose that injustice consists in breaking these. The most important injustices people fight about concern the content of constitutions and laws about political rights, freedoms, economic policies of distribution of income and wealth, and opportunities.

8   Glaucon refers to the contract as the principle of equality (359c); and his contractarian method, which makes justice an object of rational choice by rational parties in a state of nature, results in egalitarianism: *all* the parties in that state are parties to the contract, and the contract limits each person's freedom to harm others *equally* in return for *equal* security from being harmed by others. This method is very different from that of Thrasymachus, who operates like an empirical political scientist doing comparative government, generalizing from what he takes to be facts about various regimes, democratic, oligarchic or tyrannical. He and Glaucon differ *on the nature* of justice, though they may have in common the defense of injustice. When Glaucon says he is going to take up the *logos* of Thrasymachus, he means the defense of injustice, not the nature of justice. Thrasymachus includes democracies in his theory, but he, like Aristotle, may think of democracies as arising

from revolution against the rich, rather than as a result of contract. There is no hint of a contractarian method in his approach.

9   Plato may be criticizing Glaucon's view indirectly, ironically by the hyperbolic way he has Glaucon present his perfectly unjust persons and the goods they pursue. In Plato's eyes Glaucon's justice has a built in failing: it would encourage the strong and intelligent few to become a combination of free riders and hypocrites, and Glaucon's system of justice would have a built-in tendency to instability. But all this is at best implicit.

10 According to Glaucon, we find out what things are good and what happiness is by finding out what people want and go after under idealized conditions such as wearing the ring of Gyges, which frees persons from the usual social constraints, so we can tell what they really want.

11 Bk. VI, 505c, contains a very fast, three-line refutation of hedonism! And Bk. IX has an account of good and bad pleasures.

12 These different choices may not be on the same level, for us or for Plato. Plato believes that goodness is objective – he is a realist about goodness. So that the choice among theories of goodness would be like a choice among different theories of health: some one of them, if any, is true and the others false, and the problem is to discover the true one. But the choice among different systems of justice may be a matter of rational preference, even for Plato. Plato's realism about the form Justice seems to count against this. But *Republic* reads as if Plato expects us to determine which system of justice is correct by making a rational choice about which system would be best for us or which would make us happier. The two approaches can be reconciled if rationality is subservient to truth and goodness, as I think it is for Plato: he does not explicate goodness in terms of rational choice, as Rawls does, but the other way around.

13 As we shall see in chapter 5 below, Plato explicitly says in Bk. VI (504cd, 506ab) that unless we have knowledge of the good we shall not completely understand the virtues; the earlier definitions of the virtues are not secure unless knowledge of the good can be secured.

14 Till David Keyt first published his classic article in *Topoi* (1984), substantially expanded in Keyt and Miller (1991).

15 There are signs of a functional theory in Meno's first definition of virtue in the *Meno*: he proceeds by assigning functions to persons in their various roles and occupations (men, women, slaves, children) and then saying that their virtue consists in performing these functions well. Meno's definition indicates that functional evaluations were common in the culture, as they are in ours. But the *Republic* is the first place where function is defined and the theory is explicitly stated and used.

16 There is resistence to recognizing the functional theory sketched in Bk. I as a theory used in the rest of the work; perhaps because some think Bk. I is a separate Socratic aporetic dialogue and the work really begins with Bk. II.

This is a big mistake, in my view, contrary to all the evidence in the work itself, a mistake preventing us from understanding the unity and coherence of the work. Plato has Socrates *define ergon* in Bk. I, and uses the concept crucially in the rest of the work. In view of this and the importance Plato attributes to definitions, it is remarkable that commentators still hesitate to appreciate the importance of the functional theory to the rest of the work. In this and the next chapter I show the importance of the functional theory constructively, by showing how it is used to work up the theories of social and psychic justice and the rest of the virtues and the defense of justice.

17   I sometimes follow Shorey who translates *ergon* as work. "Work" is a good translation of *ergon* in general; both, e.g. are product/process ambiguous. But Plato's definition picks some of the work that a thing of a certain kind can do and assigns that as its function. So, "its own proper work" is closer to the defined notion.

18   *Ergon*, function is relative to a kind: See Anagnostopoulos (1980). A thing has a function as a thing of a certain kind. The definition can be reformulated as: The function of a thing of a given kind is what only things of that kind can do or can do best. Proposition 6, which might be taken as a contextual definition of good of a kind, reflects the attributive nature of the notion of function; and so does the notion of a thing's own proper virtue.

19   This is a generalization from Socrates' application of the theory to the human soul at 353e: having assigned ruling as the function of the soul, he says, "A good soul will rule well, a bad one poorly."

20   Derived from one disjunct of the definition of function, and the assumption that only by the human soul can human beings live, deliberate, plan, and so on, and so that is the (exclusive) function the human soul.

21   From the previous statement and proposition 6 of the functional theory.

22   From the previous statement and proposition 5 of the theory.

23   From the previous statement and proposition 7 of the theory.

24   This criticism is found in nearly every commentary on the passage. Socrates could reply that since the human function is planning and deliberating about what to do, doing these things well *is* prospering or succeeding. Perhaps, but justice does not necessarily enable us to deliberate and plan well in all the things relevant to prospering or flourishing, e.g. in activities which sometimes might be neutral with respect to justice. Not even all the virtues of character together have such a large scope (covering *all* choices).

25   In the *Crito* and *Republic*, Bk. I, Socrates does not give a definition of justice, but in both he claims that justice is incompatible with harming others, something that is no part of Thrasymachean justice. This is sufficient for the point I am making here.

26   If functioning is spread out in time. See chapter 5 below.

27   Plato may have a "pluralist" theory of functions, since he has exclusive and optimal functions, which do not reduce each to the other. See Preston (1998).

Her "system functions" and "proper functions" do not necessarily correspond to Plato's exclusive and optimal functions; especially since her proper functions are embedded in the theory of evolution, and Plato was a "creationist" at least in the *Timaeus*; but Plato probably uses system functions for complexes such as cities and persons.

28   The ambiguity is explicitly noted by Aristotle in *Eudemian Ethics*, Bk. II, ch. 1.

29   Coincide in that when the two theories are combined with the same facts they result in the same judgments about what things are good.

30   It was not till the middle of the twentieth century that the function of leaves, photosynthesis, was discovered, and its author got a Nobel prize for it.

31   On using the notion of an average as a standard, see the definitions of a good so and so by Rawls (1971, pp. 399ff.); and Ross (1930, p. 67).

32   What is being defined is not good simpliciter, but a good so and so. Similarly Rawls and Ross define a good so and so.

33   In *The Nature of Morality*, G. Harman sketches a functional theory as an example of a "naturalistic" theory of good. How naturalistic Plato's theory is depends on how he construes the notion of functioning well, the fundamental normative notion. If it can be construed in purely quantitative terms, the theory of good may be naturalistic.

34   From the proposition that justice enables human beings to perform human functions well Socrates concludes that justice makes us happy.

35   The isomorphism between social and psychic justice is discussed extensively in the next chapter.

36   If a human being knew he would not be a member of the ruling party he would not consent to a contract whose basic principle was the justice of Thrasymachus, if he is rational; if he did not know whether he would be a member of the ruling party, it would not be rational to take the risk, if he had alternatives such as Glaucon's basic principle according to which each person gives up the same freedoms equally for an equal assurance of security. For a different view, see Irwin (1995).

37   Rawls (1971, pp. 183ff.) notes that the classical utilitarians knew that the principle of classical utility (which maximizes total rather than average utility) would never be chosen using the contractarian methodology.

38   Plato uses *chreia* which much later at *Republic*, 601c–602a, is linked with *aretē* in a way which coheres well with the functional theory. The main idea of the passage is clear enough: if the needs of the citizens are what accounts for the coming into being of a city, the functions of the city will be to satisfy these needs. People not being individually self-sufficient could show what the function(s) of cities are either in the exclusive or optimal sense; if people could survive or flourish only in cities, it is an exclusive function; if they can survive or flourish without cities but have an even better life in the cities, it is an optimal function.

39   E.g. Hurka argues convincingly that at least his version of perfectionism is
      compatible with our egalitarian intuitions.
40   Best suited by inborn ability and subsequent appropriate education. Plato's
      principle of social justice matches careers to educated talent or ability. This
      is meant all along.
41   This is clear in the initial argument for Model C; the same interpretation
      of optimal function is favored by the examples he gives when he defines
      function.
42   Plato might assume that the good of defending the city well is equally dis-
      tributed, and similarly with the good of governing. For the distribution of pro-
      visions, he has proposals about extremes of wealth and poverty (Bks. III, IV),
      and private property (Bks. III,V). These result from the principle and what he
      takes to be some general facts about human beings (e.g. private property tends
      to divide them, preoccupation with wealth tends to detract from performance
      of public functions).
43   Greater than one's other capabilities or greater than other men's – the ambi-
      guity of optimal function, which may be endemic to perfectionist theories,
      and can be seen clearly in athletic competitions: to find out what one is best
      at; or to find out whether one is the best. Happiness could derive from doing
      either of these or both well.
44   Only for justice do we find evidence as to how Plato would argue for this
      premise: The concept "justice" applies to cities (368e); justice is a virtue;
      therefore, justice is a virtue of cities. Analogous first premises for the other
      virtues are not as plausible; e.g. the concept of wisdom applies to cities. Nor
      is there an argument that these four are *all* the virtues of cities; nor why a
      social virtue is not assigned to the artisans.
45   An ancient democrat would argue that to ensure that the rulers make choices
      on behalf of the city as a whole, the rulers must be *all* the citizens, through
      such institutions as the Assembly, and rotation in office and lot; because you
      cannot trust any minority, such as Plato's rulers, to put first the interests of
      the whole city. Plato agrees with this in part, since he proposes radical insti-
      tutions to ensure that the rulers and soldiers of his ideal city put the inter-
      ests of the whole city first: e.g. the abolition of private property for these
      two classes.
46   It is *social* courage because its objects are the good of the city as a whole
      rather than the good of an individual or a family.
47   An interesting parallel here with constitutional democracies, in which the
      military should be subject to civilian authority.
48   Unlike his procedure so far, Plato proceeds from temperance as a virtue of
      individuals to it as a virtue of cities, indicating how difficult it must have
      been to think of temperance as a virtue of cities.
49   Presumably, "master of" applies uproblematically to at least two persons; but
      how can it apply to one person? The natural idea is to suppose that here a

division of the person into parts is presupposed. Freud divides the self on similar grounds, for example, to make sense of the notion of talking to oneself, or the illusion of hearing voices.

50 If being master of oneself is a virtue it enables one to function well; but why would one part being master of another enable one to function well unless the part in control were better than the other? Even if something being in control is better than no control at all, some order is better than anarchy; which element is in control will make a big difference to whether a particular order is good on balance and how good it is.

51 Here Plato proceeds from what temperance is as a virtue of individuals to what temperance is as a virtue of cities, obviously on the assumption that the two are isomorphic.

52 For Plato the composition of the social classes is not hereditary, nor based on wealth, but on inborn ability and subsequent education; meritocratic, if we define merit by these two factors.

53 But not democracy, because democracy seems to reject the Platonic *formal* principle of justice.

54 The "role of justice" is to regulate, through the basic structure of society the distribution of the benefits and burdens of social cooperation. See Rawls (1971, pp. 4, 5, 65ff.). Plato may not have had this idea; still, he takes pains to establish that the founding principle of his ideal city *is* a principle of justice.

55 Vlastos (1981, p. 121) points out that Plato adds the judicial "to *have* one's own" to his formula "to *do* one's own." The judicial formula is relevant mostly to property disputes; *by itself* Plato's principle of social justice says nothing about property; though Plato connects it with property by empirical assumptions.

56 The other major ground for depriving the rulers and guardians of private property is that having such property would be a cause of conflicts and of disunity within the ruling classes (Bk.V). Aristotle's *Politics*, Bk. II, and Irwin, 1991.

57 We can say these are Socrates' grounds for these extreme proposals, if we combine the end of Bk. III and the first half of Bk.V where these proposals about property and family are taken up again and further detailed and justified.

58 See Rawls (1971, p. 124ff.) on three versions of ethical egoism: first person dictatorship (every one is to serve my interests, I being the ruler), free rider (everyone is to act justly except myself, if I choose not to), and general egoism (all are permitted to advance their interests as they please). Thrasymachus' view is as a species of first person dictatorship, even extended to democracy.

59 See *Politics*, Bk. III. Having gathered and studied over 150 constitutions, Aristotle was in a good position to dispute Thrasymachus' empirical generalization (that in all systems of justice, laws are made to favor the rulers),

which is one of the two reasons for his definition of justice (the other being that justice is identical with legality).

60   In Glaucon's story, the idealized condition of having the power to do whatever one wants and avoid retaliation, is supposed to show what people really think is good and what happiness is: having everything they ever wanted without anyone else having the power to prevent them from getting these things or take these things from them once they have them. Adeimantus' objection presupposes the theory of individual goods and happiness present in Glaucon's view.

61   421c, which is one of the revealing passages in which the term *ergon* (function) is explicitly used in the statement of social justice.

62   Not their *whole* happiness; for that they must also function well psychically, cognitively, and emotionally.

63   Rawls, e.g. opposes perfectionism as a political principle and does not endorse a perfectionist theory of good; but he recognizes that developing and exercising our human faculties is an important human good; and he tries to bring it within the scope of his desire satisfaction theory of good through what he calls the "Aristotelian Principle" (1971, pp. 424ff.) See also chapter 7 below.

64   Indeed in 433d he explicitly applies the principle to *all human beings*.

65   See *Republic*, Bk. II, 370, the first justification of the principle of social justice; and Socrates' response to Adeimantus in Bk. IV.

66   I leave aside the question whether Plato or the ancient Greeks even had a *concept of rights*. See Miller (1994, ch. 4).

67   The latter is what Popper thought (1966). For corrections to Popper's extreme interpretations, see Vlastos (1977); and Taylor (1997).

68   In the *Phaedo* and the *Phaedrus*, souls can exist disembodied and can migrate from body to body and even transmigrate to animal bodies. Disemobodied souls are also assumed by the theory of recollection in the *Meno*. How could disembodied souls be gendered? David Keyt brought this point initially to my attention. See also N. D. Smith's illuminating discussion (1983); the different treatments of women by Plato and Aristotle correlate significantly with their different theories of soul. See Sorabji (1996).

69   "We meant, for example, that a man and a woman who had a physician's soul have the same nature . . ." (454d).

4

The Good of Justice in our Souls

In the last chapter I sketched Plato's functional theory of good and tracked Plato's application of it to construct a completely good city and to define its virtues. We saw that his defense of this highly cooperative social ideal is that it promotes most the good of all the citizens; and that this good is the development and exercise of the citizens' greater social capabilities, a functional and perfectionist human good.

In this chapter we look into Plato's ideal of completely good person and his defense of it. The functional theory of good is again the formal backbone of the construction of this personal ideal and its defense, though not as explicitly. The theory is at work in Plato's isomorphism between social and psychic justice; in his analysis of the human psyche; in his definitions of the psychic virtues; in his defense of psychic justice by the analogy between psychic justice and health; and in his criticism of psychic freedom.

1   The Isomorphism Between Social and Psychic Justice

Plato does not use the three step functional procedure, as he did in the case of the city, to discover the virtues of the individual, the psychic virtues. If he had done that, he would have determined functions of the soul, he would have tried to imagine a soul that performed these functions as well as possible, and then he would have sought to discover the qualities that enabled the soul to so function well, the virtues of the individual.

Instead, to construct the definition of psychic justice, he relies on (1) the full definition of social justice he constructed earlier, and the unusual idea that (2) a just city and a just man do not differ at all with respect to justice. Consequently, given his full definition of social justice, he sees as his main task to discover, by an argument independent of his definition of social justice, whether the human soul has the complexity required by these two premises: psychic parts which correspond in a relevant sense to his three natural divisions of the city. Once he has done that, he deduces his definition of a just person from (1), (2), and (3) his analysis of the psyche. As might well be expected from this procedure, he ends up with an unusual definition of a just person, as one whose soul is so organized that each psychic part is performing its optimal psychic function, what it can do best.

I will speak of (2) as the assumption of *isomorphism* between social and psychic justice, since it turns out to be an identity of the structure or form of just cities and just souls. This isomorphism is complex, unusual, and dominates Plato's search for psychic justice and its defense; it has been the subject of a great deal of discussion and controversy (see, e.g., Annas [1981]; Cross and Woozley [1964]; and White [1979]).

It is useful to begin by exhibiting its complexity in the form of the argument by which Plato derives the definition of a just person. The argument divides naturally into four stages: the full definition of social justice already at hand, the assumption of isomorphism and its application to justice, the analysis of the psyche into psychic parts, and the just matching of psychic labors to these psychic parts.

Stage One:

1.　A city is just when each of the natural kinds of people in it performs its own (its optimal) social function (433, 435b).

2.　The main social functions are ruling, defending, and provisioning the city (369bff., 374ff., 428dff.).

3.　There are three natural kinds of persons in the city, persons of inborn high intelligence, persons of inborn high spirit, and those of inborn abilities for arts and trades (415, 435).

4.　The optimal social function of persons of high intelligence is ruling the city; those of high spirit defending the city; and those of abilities in arts and crafts provisioning the city (434).

5.　Therefore, a city is just when it is so organized that those of high intelligence are assigned to rule, those of high spirit to defend, and those of artisan abilities to provision the city (from 1–4, 433).

Stage Two:

6.　If things, whether large or small, are [correctly] called [by] the same [name], they will be alike in the respect in which they are called the same (435a).

7. We [sometimes correctly] call cities and persons [by the same name] just (435a).

8. Therefore, a just person and a just city will not differ at all with respect to the kind justice (from 6 and 7; 435ab).

9. Therefore, a person is just when each of the natural psychic kinds (parts) in his or her psyche performs its own (its optimal) psychic function (from 1 and 8, 435ac, 441e).

Stage Three:

10. There are three natural psychic kinds (parts) in the human soul: reason, spirit, and appetite (by an independent argument, 436–41).

11. The human soul has three functions, to rule oneself, to defend oneself, and to provide for one's bodily needs (from 1, 2, 8; 441e, 442).

Stage Four:

12. Reason is the psychic part which corresponds to the social class of citizens of high intelligence, spirit to the class of high spirited citizens, and appetite to the class of citizens with abilities for the productive arts and trades (440, 441).[1]

13. Therefore, the optimal function of reason is to rule the person, of spirit to defend, and of appetite to provide for bodily needs (from 4, 8, 10, 11, 12; 441e).

14. Therefore, a soul is just when it is so organized that reason is assigned to rule the person, spirit to defend it, and appetite to provide for one's bodily needs (from 9 and 12, 441e–442a).[2]

From this argument we can see that the asumption of isomorphism is an extremely strong and demanding way to understand the relation between a just person and a just city-state. How strong it is can be seen from the fact that it is an isomorphism not only between the two abstract principles of justice (premises 1 and 9), but also between the two full definitions: this demands a division of the soul into exactly three parts, a one to one correspondence between the two sets of parts (premise 12), a one to one correspondence between the two sets of functions (premise 13), and of course corresponding optimal matchings between the two sets of parts and functions (premises 5 and 14). That Plato understands the relation in this demanding way is shown not only by the argument I have just set out, but also by his analogy to the large and small inscriptions

(368d), which correspond to city and soul justice. To give another analogy yet, his inscription analogy is like the relation between a page of a book in small print and an enlarged photo copy of it; here we have not only identity of structure but also (type) identity of letters, words, sentences, and even content.[3] Plato's inscription analogy is even stronger than the isomorphism I exhibited!

This is not the only way to explain or understand the relation between just persons and just cities. We may agree that applying the term "justice" to both persons and cities is not accidental; it is not like applying the English word "bank" to a financial institution and the left side of the river Seine. However, the justice of persons and cities may be related nonaccidentally in at least two other ways, far less demanding than Plato's.

One way is to suppose that a just city is a city composed of just persons. This relation gives explanatory primacy to the concept of a just person: we first define just persons and then define a city, not as Plato does, but as a city composed of just persons as defined. Perhaps Gregory Vlastos at one time attributed this relation to Plato.[4] But this is not Plato's view: defining a just city as one composed of just persons does not demand that the city be isomorphic to, have the same structure as, the souls of the just persons composing it. It is also difficult to see how this can be a correct or fruitful way to understand a just city or a just society, since it would seem to render the nature of its institutions, its constitution or its economic system, for example, irrelevant to its justice.

The other non-Platonic way of relating the justice of society to the justice of individuals is to suppose that a just individual is one who subscribes to the principles by which a society is just. Here the justice of society is given explanatory primacy over the justice of individuals: we first define a just society and then define a just individual as one who has a strong and normally effective desire to act in accordance with the principles which make a society just. This is the way Rawls proceeds (1971, e.g. pp. 1, 7–17, 436), going back to an anti-Platonic tradition that begins with Aristotle; in fact it goes back to the *Republic*, since this is the way the justice of persons would be related to the justice of society in Thrasymachus' and Glaucon's theories.[5] This is by far the dominant tradition, that justice is primarily and essentially a social virtue; unlike perhaps such other virtues as wisdom, courage, and even temperance, which may be more plausibly thought to be primarily and essentially virtues of individuals.

Perhaps the greatest advantage of the Aristotelian–Rawlsian way of relating the justice of persons to the justice of societies is that it assures us of a coherent and unified theory of justice; there is only one standard of justice, the justice of society, and a just person is one who subscribes to that standard. But in Plato's theory there are two standards of justice, one of cities and one of persons. And the isomorphism has no built-in assurance that a person who is just according to the definition of a Platonically just person will also be just according to the definition of a Platonically just city, or conversely. In short, there is no built-in assurance that a just citizen in Plato's ideal city will be also a just person, or conversely. Not surprisingly therefore, we have notorious disputes whether citizens who are socially just, according to the theory, are or can be also just as individuals.[6]

It is not easy to see why Plato has this demanding relation of isomorphism between the justice of persons and the justice of cities, and why he lets it dominate his discussion of the virtues, not only in Bk. IV of course, but equally in Bk. VIII, the discussion of unjust cities and persons.

One explanation is that he holds this view because of his metaphysics and philosophy of language. The metaphysics of course is the theory of forms, which implies that there is only one form justice and that all things just are just by participating in that one form. The related linguistic principle is premise 6: if things are called by the same name they are alike in the respect in which they are called the same; with its immediate application to the case of just cities and just persons.

This explanation may be correct: it is because he believed in the theory of forms and the related linguistic principle that Plato believed in the isomorphic relation between just cities and just persons; once he defined a just city structurally and functionally he saw no choice but to define a just person isomorphically to the just city. Or conversely, since the isomorphism is perfectly symmetrical; though Plato proceeds from the just city to the just person (also in Bk. VIII, from unjust cities to unjust persons), this may be only his order of discovery or exposition; he might actually be modeling a just city after a just person.[7]

But this explanation certainly does not show that isomorphism is the correct or most fruitful way to conceive the relation between just cities and just persons. As we saw, the isomorphism, demanding as it is, still fails to ensure that the two standards of justice it employs would or could be satisfied together. Moreover, Plato's reasons for the isomorphism are not adequate. For one thing, the linguistic principle is false of natural languages, including English and Greek. There are many counterexamples to it in English and Greek: for example "sharp" as in "sharp knives" and "sharp notes," and *aischron* in Greek, according to Plato's Callicles (*Gorgias*, 482). Aristotle certainly rejected it. For another, even Plato is unable to

apply the principle consistently even to justice, within the *Republic*: at 443e
he says that actions are just (*dikaiai*) in so far as they produce and preserve
a just (*dikaia*) psyche; so just actions are defined by a causal relation to a
just soul, not by just actions being isomorphic to a just soul.

Aside from justification, though, we can see a philosophical motivation
for the isomorphism and a strategy behind Plato's order of exposition. We
see this if we realize that the isomorphism uses symmetrically the same
functional theory of good for the discovery and defense of justice in
society and justice in individual souls. This enables Plato to project a publicly observable social structure on to the mystery of the human soul: if
the justice of the city consists in division of social labor which matches
optimally inborn abilities of the city's parts (citizens) to the city's functions, the justice of the person will consist in division of psychic labor
which matches optimally psychic parts to the person's functions. Here the
isomorphism can be viewed as a heuristic principle, to help us understand
the functionings of the human soul and discover its virtues. But it provides also a philosophical strategy for the defense of justice. As we saw,
Plato's defense of his conception of *social* justice is that it promotes *most*
the good or happiness of the city as a whole.[8] This is a recognizable version
of a fundamental principle of teleological ethical theories, that the right
is what maximizes the good. Now if the same functional theory of good
and the isomorphism are used to construct psychic justice, then we can
have a corresponding defense of *psychic* justice: this structure promotes
most the good of the person as a whole. Thus the isomorphism, the
common functional theory of good, and the proceeding from social to
psychic justice, give Plato a heuristic device for understanding justice in
our souls, and some leverage in the defense of psychic justice: the same
theory of functional good and the same teleological principle are applied
to cities and persons. And a reasonable and recognizable defense of a conception of social justice, that it promotes most the good of the society as
a whole, is used as leverage for a similar defense of an analogous conception of psychic justice.

All this coheres well with the challenge Plato put in the mouth of
Glaucon in Bk. II: to show that *justice in our souls* is good for each one of
us. The Rawlsian–Aristotelian conception of the relation of individual to
social justice does not work out as well for defending justice, at least not
for teleological theories. Though Plato rejected Thrasymachus' conception
of social justice, and affirmed that social justice is a virtue that promotes
the good of the city as a whole, still his social justice is meritocratic and
even elitist and open to objections: that it does not distribute good things

equally or not equally enough, not even Platonic goods, among the citizens; for example it does not give equal opportunities to all citizens to have the experience of ruling the city – something which Athenian democracy, for example, claimed to do. If Plato had held that to be a just person is to have a strong and normally effective desire to act in accordance to his social justice, then the good of psychic justice would be infected by the inequalities of his social justice. The inequalities of his social justice of course do apply to citizens. But his isomorphic conception of individual justice enables him to claim a functional good for just souls. Psychic justice too distributes certain things unequally (for example ruling and defending), but these are inequalities *within* a person and can still be good for the whole person, while among persons psychic justice is the same for all.[9] Given that he allowed Glaucon's demanding way of conceiving the defense of justice – that justice in our souls is best for us – Plato had a powerful motivation for the isomorphism.

2   *Plato's Pioneering Analysis of the Psyche*

In any case, Plato is stuck with isomorphism. The deduction of his full definition of a just person from his full definition of a just city displays this isomorphism fully and at work. And it raises some fundamental questions, the most important of which Plato sees immediately and takes up first.

Does the human psyche have in it different natural psychic kinds, three in number, and the "same" three as the three natural social kinds in the city?

Further, does the human psyche have psychic functions which correspond to the main social functions of ruling, defending, and provisioning the city?

Finally, if the psyche has these three natural psychic kinds and if it does have these three psychic functions, which psychic activity is the optimal function of which psychic kind? Are we to answer this question simply on the basis of the isomorphism, or can we give independent and confirming arguments that it is best for reason to rule and the passions to obey?

One reason Plato gives for supposing that there are three psychic kinds corresponding to the three natural kinds in the city is that the city "kinds and dispositions" could only come from individuals; therefore, the same kinds must exist in individuals (435c). For example Thrace is said to be high spirited and this can only come from (some of) its citizens being high spirited; similarly with Egypt's being money loving, or Athens being a lover of knowledge; spirit, love of money, and love of knowledge must exist in individuals.[10]

Even if accepted, though, this does not show that there are three *different kinds* or *parts* (faculties or powers) in the soul corresponding to the psychic activities of thinking, getting angry, and desiring material things; since, as Socrates himself says (436a), we may be doing all these things with the whole soul. But this argument is useful because it shows that Plato takes the division of psychic *activities* into these three kinds, whose existence Plato takes to be evident, to be more fundamental, causally at least, than the divisions of the city. If a city such as Athens is a lover of learning this can only be because it has citizens (a majority or a dominant class) whose souls are dominated by love of learning; similarly with cities that are noted for their high spirit or love of commerce.[11]

The issue of the division of the soul is whether corresponding to the three kinds of psychic activities there are corresponding distinct "kinds," presumably psychic faculties or powers for these activities.

The division of the psyche into kinds or parts or powers is made on the basis of a principle of contradiction or contrariety,[12] an unspoken assumption that psychic activities imply psychic powers, faculties for such activities, and evidence of psychic conflicts within the following pairs of psychic activities: (1) between desiring something and not desiring it due to reasoning,[13] from which the nonidentity of the "kinds" (or powers) of reasoning and desiring is inferred; (2) between desiring something and being angry at one's desiring it, from which the nonidentity of the powers of desiring and being angry is inferred; and (3) between being angry at something and calculating that it is best not to act on one's anger, from which the nonidentity of the powers of reason and of anger is inferred. The argument thus construed has three stages: first, it assumes that individual psychic activities can be collected and divided naturally (individudals are born with them) into three kinds, desiring, getting angry, and caclulating;[14] then examples are given of evident conflicts among such activities; and finally, from these conflicts, the principle of contrariety, and the unspoken assumption that psychic activities of a given kind imply psychic faculties of parts of that kind, the nonidentity of three powers is inferred, each power being named after the kind of activity:

> naming that by which it reasons (calculates) the reasoning (calculating), that with which it (erotically) loves, hungers, thirsts, and feels the flutter and titil-

lation of other appetites, the arational and appetitive, companion of various
repletions and pleasures . . . and that by which we feel anger, spirit [literally:
angry-kind]. (439de, Shorey transl.)[15]

Unlike psychic activities themselves, which are hard enough to understand clearly, psyches and psychic parts and faculties are not things we can
publicly inspect, not even, according to Hume, introspect. By comparison
to the human body and its parts or the city and its parts, they are ghostly
entities at best. As might well be expected, Plato's first and pioneering psy-
choanalysis has been the subject of much dispute, both textually in many
commentators, and philosophically beginning with Aristotle. Two almost
universal interpretive tendencies are worth highlighting, both because of
their significance in the philosophy of mind and moral psychology, and
because the first needs explanation and the second I find dubious.

One is the tendency to think that the conflicts between appetites and
reason in Plato are really conflicts between appetites and the desires of
reason (see Penner [1971]; Cooper [1999]; and Irwin [1995, ch. 13]). There
may be two reasons for this. Plato speaks explicitly of desires and pleasures of reason in Bk. IX (580de); and of course we need to understand
and account for this important text. Then, there may be a modern,
Humean assumption at work that reason itself cannot conflict with the
passions, of which appetite and anger are clear examples; so the conflict
between appetite and reason Plato must have in mind is a conflict between
appetite and what he thinks is a desire of reason, and the conflict is
between two passions after all.

Now there is some evidence against this tendency in Plato's original
argument for partition in Bk. IV. The original conflict is clearly presented
as desiring and not desiring, wishing and not wishing; not between two
different kinds of desires, for example appetite for drink and wish (rational desire) not to drink.[16] What is more, Plato's conclusion from this conflict is that the two distinct parts we must postulate are appetite and reason,
not appetite and reasoning desire (or rational wish). Finally, for what it is
worth, Hume himself took "the ancients" to be postulating a conflict
between the passions and reason, not between two different kinds of
passions.[17]

If one maintains that Plato's conflict is between appetite and a desire
of reason, at the very least one needs to supply a bridge from this conflict to the conclusion that the two distinct parts are appetite and reason.
The usual link is the proposition that a desire of reason is a desire reason
has because it knows or believes that the thing it desires is good. As Penner

(nor 1971) points out, Plato here accepts the Socratic view that all desire is for the good but restricts it to the faculty of reason: all *desires of reason* are for the good. On this view, reason *by itself*, with no assistance from passion, generates desires. And now the challenge is to understand this: is it a conclusion from more primitive premises, or a primitive premise, or a self-evident axiom? It is also a challenge to understand whether Hume opposes *this* view: it supplies a desire to oppose appetite, thus seeming to satisfy Hume's insistence that only passion can oppose passion; but the desire is generated by reason without aid from the passions, implying that reason by its own psychic resources can oppose passion.[18] Presumably Hume would say that reason by itself cannot generate desire – any desire.

Now Bk. VIII is explicit and unambiguous in its insistence that reason has its own desires and pleasures (579–80); but even earlier, in his discussion of the form of the good Plato told us explicitly that every soul pursues the good as the end of all her actions (505e), and this pursuing would seem to be a seeking of reason. To understand the *Republic* it is imperative that we understand Plato's conception of the desire for the good in this work. We need to understand and reconcile these passages with the division of the soul in Bk. IV, in which reason appears to be a calculating and reasoning faculty and Plato seems to claim a conflict between that and appetite.

One explanation may be Plato's new understanding of the Socratic Eudaimonistic Axiom: that we all desire our own happiness as the ultimate end of all our voluntary or rational actions. In the Socratic dialogues this is taken for granted, as self-evident, or something which no one would deny; though we saw disputes of what happiness is. Now it may be that if we put this axiom together with Plato's new division of the soul, we can begin to understand how he might think that this desire for happiness is a desire of reason. Only reason can figure out what happiness is or can be; so if everyone has an innate desire for happiness, it must be a desire of reason. At any rate, since he strips the objects of appetite of everything except the bare minumum for identifying appetite (as thirst, hunger, or sexual desire), it is difficult to see how he can hold that the end, happiness, is an object of the inborn capacity of the appetitive part of the soul; or even that this capacity can learn what happiness is, at least if learning is cognitive, rather than habituation. This explanation is not entirely satisfactory because of the gap, in the *Republic*, between human happiness and the form of the good; the form of the good is cosmic, far wider than human happiness.

A second explanation for Plato's thinking that reason has its own desires seems closer to the *Republic* and the teachings of Bks. V–IX. In these books we learn that reason can enjoy performing its operations of learning, reasoning, and calculating, *and* that reason loves learning and the objects and results of learning, truth and knowledge. Plato may be using here implicitly Rawls's "Aristotelian principle," a version of which we certainly shall find in Aristotle: that we enjoy the development and exercise of our human powers and faculties, at least when successful, and because of this enjoyment we desire to continue and repeat such activities; moreover, the more we develop and the better we exercise our faculties the more we enjoy them; and the more we enjoy them the more we want to exercise them, at least successfully. Since reason is one of our faculties and it has its own distinctive activities, it enjoys these activities, at least when they are successful, and the enjoyment gives rise to a desire to continue exercising them or to exercise them again. The evident enjoyment of success-ful mathematical reasoning was no doubt an evident example. So by the successful practicing of its activities reason can generate enjoying them and enjoying them can generate desires of reason for these activities, their objects and results. And even Hume would admit that enjoyment, at least its prospect, can generate desire (1955, Bk. II, part 1, section 1).

Thus Plato starts his account of the soul with psychic activites; suc-cessful psychic activities are enjoyed, and such enjoyment generates desires to continue or repeat the activities. It is natural to attribute these plea-sures and desires to the psychic kind or part which is the source of the activities. Later, in Bks. VIII and IX, another dimension is explicitly added to the psychic division: a characteristic value is correlated with each kind of activity and its pursuit is attributed to the corresponding part. For example reason reasons and calculates; when it does so successfully it enjoys doing so, and consequently desires to repeat the activity; in turn it comes to value the activity, its objects, truth or reality, and its result, knowledge.

The second interpretive tendency in trying to understand Plato's divi-sion of the soul is to attribute some rationality to the kinds appetite and anger. Irwin has done this most persuasively, and probably as well as can be done, navigating expertly between the anthropomorphic danger of ending up with three persons within a person and the Aristotelian danger of ending up with infinite divisions of the psyche (1995, ch. 13; see also Annas [1981]). There are two major pieces of evidence for this tendency. In Bk. IV Plato says that psychic temperance consists in harmony or agree-ment among the three parts that reason should rule; this seems to presuppose that anger and appetite have beliefs about what is good for them, and thus have some rationality. He actually says that they believe this together (442d), but there is disagreement about whether he is speaking literally or metaphorically.[19] And in Bk.VIII he seems to say that the desire for wealth, the dominant motivation of the oligarchic person, has appetite as its source, since he clearly holds that in such a person the appetitive part rules; but this desire for wealth is clearly a result of the oligarchic person's calculation that wealth is the best general instrument for the satisfaction of appetites; so if the desire for wealth is appetitive, then perhaps appetite can calculate and reason.

Now I doubt seriously that Plato attributes reasoning to the appetite or even to spirit; and it is not clear that such a attribution would even be coherent.[20] I shall strive to develop an interpretation in which he does not need to attribute any rationality to appetite in order to have conflicts between reason and appetite, or in order to have his theory of psychic justice and the classification and rankings of unjust persons in Bk.VIII.

I shall take Plato's functional theory of good to be an assumption in the partition of the psyche. Similarly with the isomorphism, which motivates and demands the partition. These two assumptions together imply that the parts of the soul are natural or inborn, that they have functions, and that we can see how justice in the soul can be understood using these parts and their functions. I shall also assume a related principle Plato enunciates and uses later (477c) to distinguish psychic powers or faculties: by their objects and functions, what these powers operate on (their objects), and what they accomplish (their functions) (Santas, 1974). He gives as evident applications of this principle the *powers* of hearing and seeing: they are to be distinguished by their objects (sounds for hearing, colors and shapes for seeing) and their functions (the psychic *activity* of hearing, and that of seeing). It will be recalled that Socrates gave the seeing of the eyes and the hearing of the ears as examples of *exclusive functions*, back in Bk. I: the ears have the power of hearing and they are the only (kinds of) objects that have it; and now, we are told, that power, in turn, is to be specified by the objects it exercises itself on and the result it accomplishes.

I believe that these two ideas, of exclusive functions and characteristic objects, are the main principles at work for individuating the parts of the soul;[21] the partition itself, as based on psychic conflict and the principle of contrariety, is not sufficient for understanding the nature of each part. We must remember that Plato needs not only a partition of the soul, but also psychic parts that are naturally suited for the roles his theory of justice requires.

We see the reliance on objects in the discussion of the appetites thirst and hunger: we are told that the object of thirst is drink (liquids), the object of hunger food, rather than hot or cold or good drink (or hot or cold or good food). To be sure, as Penner and others have pointed out, one target of this argumentation is the Socratic view that all our desires are for the good. But the object of thirst is stripped not only of goodness but of heat, cold – and what else? Where does this abstracting stop? The answer is that every cognition, everything about objects of drinking that is the result of cognitive learning is taken away; only what is needed to identify the appetite as thirst is to remain, and that is the stopping point of the abstracting. And similarly with hunger, and presumably sexual appetite. Of course, the vast majority of our appetites are not just for drink, food, or sex, but, far more specifically, for water or wine, for pasta or fish; but their specificity is the result of learning, a function of reason: and that is the more general point of the abstraction exercise, to discover the nature of appetite itself apart from the contributions cognitive learning makes. In Bk. IV, Plato is trying to figure out the nature of appetite, as distinct from other kinds of psychic activities; and so he abstracts from, mentally takes away from, appetite, other psychic activities that attach to it, notably all learning and cognition about the objects of our appetites. The natural, inborn, unlearned power of appetite operates on the generic objects of food, drink, and sex; these are its most evident objects; we understand what this power is by reference to these objects and the activities which satisfy or extinguish the appetites.

I believe we also see Plato's conception of exclusive function at work in the partition argument. In the conclusion of the argument, the parts or powers of the psyche are each named after what they do: the part that gets angry is called the angry-kind; the part that calculates, the calculating; and the part that appetites, the appetitive; this is naming things by their characteristic functions, whether exclusive or optimal, a common linguistic practice in many natural languages.[22] But Plato adds that appetite is "arational" or "noncalculating". Now what this clearly implies is not that both appetite and reason can calculate but reason can do it better, but that appetite cannot or at least does not calculate at all; which is pretty consistent with the conception of the generic objects of appetite, which have been stripped of any learning. So calculating is the exclusive function of reason; presumably, similarly only the angry-kind can become and be angry, or it is only by it that one becomes angry. And what is the exclusive function of appetite? Presumably the activity of appetiting, psychically moving toward something; in different terms, Anscombe's masterful phrase seems apt here: "the primitive sign of wanting is trying to get." In Plato, perhaps literally: a motion of the soul toward an object (Penner, 1971).

Once more we must remember that in the argument for the partition of the psyche Plato is trying to determine the *natural* or *inborn* parts of the soul, in a parallel with the natural division of the city by inborn abilities. And so, in trying to determine the nature of appetite, for example, he *abstracts from learning* (or education) about objects, which most of our desires are mixed with. Similarly with spirit and reason.[23] The division of the psyche into these three powers is natural in this sense: it is a division of primary, inborn, *unlearned* (uneducated) psychic powers. Plato is claiming that we are born with psyches that already have a division of psychic labor in them, a division he conceives in terms of exclusive functions and characteristic objects. This division is in this sense natural, not cultural, nor normative. There is an analogue here to the conception of the human body, about which ancient medicine had already discovered an inborn division of labor, for organs, for example: witness Socrates' earlier assignment of *exclusive* functions to the eyes and ears. This bodily division also is natural, not cultural, nor normative.

But this psychic division in Bk. IV does not imply that these three inborn psychic activities never interact nor are combined with each other, combinations which generate mixed or derivative psychic states, as a result of experience, habituation, and education. The discussions of just and unjust persons appeal to or presuppose these natural non-normative divisions of the soul; but their definitions use other divisions by optimal functions; and they sometimes use notions of appetite or desire that are mixtures rather than pure appetites. Thus the desire for wealth, which is used in Bk. VIII to characterize the oligarchic person is clearly a mixture of pure appetites and learning. We must be careful how we use this passage to understand the argument for partition, as evidence for what the partition is and for what goes into each part: it is not evidence that the desire for wealth is an appetite, nor that appetite can reason. The argument by which Plato strips the objects of hunger or thirst of everything except liquids or food would certainly not permit wealth as an object of appetite. When Plato partitions the soul he does not mean that the different basic and pure psychic activites are not combined to perform complex psychic functions such as desiring wealth. He does not need to ascribe reasoning to appetite, because the person has reason as well as appetite and can learn to use her reason to find out how to satisfy her appetites. Nor does Plato need to ascribe some rationality to appetite in order to pronounce the oligarchic person Platonically unjust: he is unjust because he uses his reason only and purely instrumentally to calculate that wealth is the best general means for appetite satisfaction.

3 Psychic Justice and the Good of it

Plato concludes the argument for the division of the soul with a reminder of the basic isomorphism: "we are fairly agreed that the same kinds equal in number are to be found in the state and in the soul of each one of us" (441c). The kinds in the state are the citizens of high intelligence, of high spirit, and of talents for production and trade. Since social justice consists in the matching of the three natural parts of the city optimally to the three functions of ruling, defending, and provisioning the city, psychic justice must consist in the matching optimally of the three corresponding natural psychic parts to the psychic functions of ruling, defending and provisioning oneself. Similarly with temperance. And somewhat similarly with courage and wisdom.[24]

It is essential here not to conflate the natural social and psychic divisions with the social and psychic states which are the virtues. The division of the city into persons of high intelligence, high spirit and productive talent is natural for Plato because it is division by inborn abilities and talents; it is a division made by the "natural lottery," in Rawls's phrase. Similarly, his division of the soul is natural since it is division by the inborn capabilities of the psychic parts. On the other hand, the virtues themselves, both social and psychic, are not natural in this sense: we are not born with the psychic virtues, nor do Platonically just cities come into being as seasons do or as plants grow. Plato's conception of the social virtues uses the distributions of talent and abilities by the natural lottery, and in that sense they have a base in nature. But these virtues are human constructions, the result of legislation; they are not completely determined by the natural lottery, since we can have different legislative constructions with the same distributions of the natural lottery, as with timocratic or democratic states. As Rawls remarks, the distributions of the natural lottery are neither just or unjust; what society does with them, can be; witness what societies can do with the natural distributions of gender or color. Or what Plato himself did with the natural distribution of gender.

Similarly, Plato uses the natural divisions of the psyche as a base for the construction of the virtues; but the virtues themselves are human constructions, the result of education, and are not completely determined by the natural lottery. And Plato is clearly aware of this, since he knows that education can shape a soul so as to be Platonically just or oligarchic or timocratic. His virtues are ideals, not just the product of nature without human intervention.

From this alone we can see clearly that Plato needs strong reasons for the central claims he makes in Bk. IV about justice and social and individual good. For social justice, we saw that he makes two central claims: the justice of a city consists in the optimal matchings of innate talents and abilities to the three important functions of a city; and this matching, together with the other social virtues, is the best way to organize a city, best for the parts and best for the whole city.

Similarly, according to the isomorphism, the justice of a person consists in the optimal matching of the natural parts of her psyche to the three important functions of psyche; and this way of organizing a psyche is best for the parts of a psyche and for the psyche as a whole.

Now as we saw in the deductive argument set out earlier, Plato can use his central claims about social justice and the isomorphism to justify his central claims about psychic justice. But as we also saw the isomorphism is a very disputed way to connect social and individual justice. And in any case it is doubtful that the isomorphism can work out as neatly as Plato seems to suppose, as we shall soon see.

For these reasons, one would like to find Platonic grounds independent of the isomorphism for the central claims Plato makes about his psychic justice: for example for the anti-Humean claim that reason ought to rule the other parts of the soul, or that a person is virtuous when reason rules; and that it is best for a person when reason so rules. Plato cannot take his anti-Humean view of reason and passion for granted. His discussion of Callicles in the *Gorgias*, and his discussion in Bk. VIII of the *Republic*, show clearly enough that he was aware of the view that spirit or appetite can dominate and reason be used purely instrumentally; and that some think that this is virtue and this psychic organization is best for one.

I think perhaps we can see some of the central reasons for Plato's claims, if we think of the functional theory of good as applying to the psyche as well as to the city; and if we ourselves use the isomorphism heuristically, not as Plato uses it to discover the virtues, but as our guide to Plato's deeper reasons for his claims. Proceeding in this way, we can see at least two strong arguments for Plato's claims, one proceeding from his conception of appetite, and another from his conception of reason.

Let us start with a well-known difficulty about appetite. The optimal function of the citizens with talents for production and trade is to provision the city, to provide it with the economic goods of food, shelter, clothing, and so on. According to the isomorphism the part of the soul that corresponds to the artisans is appetite; accordingly, the optimal function of appetite is to provision the person – presumably provide for her bodily needs. But surely appetite cannot do that at all – appetite for food cannot provide me with food! What can Plato be thinking of? I think we have to be satisfied with a more limited correspondence between the optimal social function of the artisans to provision the city and the psychic optimal function of the appetitive part. And we have to go back to the nature of appetite as Plato thinks of it in the division of the soul. Here we might see what the limited correspondence is; and independently of the isomorphism argument, why Plato thinks the appetites should be ruled by reason. The isomorphism argument does not tell us that; we have to reconstruct the reasons indirectly and isomorphically, from his reasons for assigning ruling to persons of high intelligence and being ruled (by implication) to persons of artisan abilities. In the case of social justice his reasons are pretty evident: the city will performs its functions better if, in modern language, careers are matched to talents, than if they are not; this benefits both the city as a whole (the social functions will be performed better) and its citizens individually (they will be doing what they are best at). But is this correspondingly true of the person? The isomorphism itself implies that this is true, but it does not offer us independent reasons that apply specifically to reason and appetite.

It is essential to remember once more that in the original division of the soul Plato thinks of appetites as separated and in abstraction from learning about objects; thirst, for example, he considers as simply the appetite for drink, not cold or hot, sweet or bitter, good or bad drink; the latter would be mixed with learning, a cognitive function and a function of reason. "For drink" is necessary for identifying the appetite as thirst and so identified the appetite is not mixed with learning.[25] Most appetites we are acquainted with are of course mixed with learning. In Bks. VI and VIII where Plato is discussing various types of injustice he is usually talking about such mixed or learned appetites. As noted earlier, the desire for money, for example the dominant desire of the oligarchic type of person, is such a mixed desire; Plato locates it in the appetitive part of the soul on the ground that "money is the principal means of satisfying appetites of this kind" (Bk. IX, 580); this proposition of course is a bit of learning about the relation of money to the satisfacion of the appetites for food, drink, and sex – appetites which originally and correctly Plato put in the appetitive part of the soul. But if we want to find out what appetite *simply as such* is and what it does, we must abstract from such learning. And this is how Plato thinks of it, I submit, when he comes to think of what is the optimal psychic function of appetite: its optimal function, given what it is, pure and unmixed with other parts of the soul.

Given this, I suggest that Plato is thinking of appetite, simply as such, as a kind of psychic signal system for bodily needs, or a system which brings to consciousness signs of the kinds of things the body needs, and motivates seeking them: thirst for drink, hunger for food, sexual impulse for sexual release, and other such. Appetite cannot *provide* for bodily needs, but it can signal such needs and *motivate* providing for them. However, simply as such a psychic signal system, that is, without the help of learning, appetite is not accurate or specific enough about what particular objects the body needs, nor what quantities of them, nor how frequently they are needed. With respect to these questions, therefore, appetite should be guided by learning or wisdom or at least true belief, all of which are cognitive functions or virtues of reason: the person needs reason's learning to tell her what and how much to drink when thirsty, how much and what to eat when hungry, what would keep the body warm, and so on.[26] The exclusive function of appetite as such is to signal bodily needs and to motivate the activities required for their satisfaction. This is all it *can* do toward providing for the body's needs; this is its exclusive function. But because of its essential lack of accuracy appetite cannot by itself do even *these* things *well*, i.e. signal and motivate correctly, unless it is guided by learning and reason. For example appetite may keep wanting sweets long after the body's need for sweets has beeen satisfied; and on the daily need for vitamin C, appetite is almost totally blind. We can appreciate the force of this argument by imagining beings like us but with a completely accurate appetitive signal system, a pre-established harmony between what they need or what is good for them and what they have appetites for: what substances, in what amounts, with what frequency. In such beings appetite would not need to be ruled by learning and reason, and some branches of ancient medicine, such as diatetics, would not be necessary. But of course we are not such beings. So we can see from below, as it were, from the nature of our appetites, in abstraction from learning, that the optimal function of appetite is to be ruled by reason on all questions of what will satisfy bodily needs.

This argument *is* independent of the isomorphism; it proceeds from the nature of appetite, what it can do and what it cannot do by itself and what it can do best: it can signal and motivate bodily needs; but it is not by itself the best instrument for their satisfaction; it becomes the best instrument when obedient to reason and its discoveries, such as the sciences of medicine and chemistry. Therefore, the psyche is best organized, best for the parts and for the whole psyche, only when appetite is obedient to reason on what will satisfy bodily needs. And if the right is what produces the most good, for persons as well as for societies, appetite being obedient to reason will be part of the virtue of a person.

The argument from above, why reason should rule, might be somewhat different: it begins with the nature of reason, but the complete argument relies also on theories of good Plato believes correct and his view that goodness is an object of reason. The argument is based on the exclusive functions of the three psychic powers, as conceived in the partition argument, *and* what is required for assigning optimally to the various parts of the soul the psychic functions of ruling, defending, and provisioning. The argument might run as follows for assigning ruling to reason.

To rule oneself one needs to make decisions about what to do; to do that one needs to reason and calculate about alternative courses of action and their comparative good.[27] But only reason can do these things, appetite and spirit cannot do them at all. Therefore, ruling oneself is the optimal function of reason, not of appetite or spirit.[28] Here such psychic activities as thinking about possibilities, about causal connections, and making judgments about good, are said to be necessary for ruling oneself, and from this and the premise that such thinking is an exclusive function of reason, it is inferred that ruling oneself is the optimal function of reason. We know from Bk. VIII that Plato thinks spirit and appetite *can* rule a person, for example in the timocratic and democratic persons; so ruling is not an exclusive function of reason. The argument produces reasons why spirit and appetite cannot rule as well as reason can, because of what is required for ruling oneself; so ruling is assigned to reason as *its* optimal function. Of course reason will rule *well* only if it has attained the virtue of reason, wisdom, knowledge of the good, or at least true belief about it; and this too is something that only reason can have.

4   Plato and Hume on Reason or Passion as the Rule of Life

This argument is strong, but it does have some controversial premises, which Hume would dispute and thus dispute the conclusion. The comparison with Hume is natural and instructive here, since Hume, in a well-known passage of his *Treatise of Human Nature*, sets himself in explicit opposition to moral theories, "ancient and modern," which maintain that reason and the passions can conflict and that in such conflicts the person

should follow the counsel of reason, right conduct being conduct prescribed by reason. Hume appears to accept some of the terms of the debate
which Plato set: of several "elements" or at least activities in the soul, the
idea that some of them might conflict with each other, and the idea that
one or another of these might rule or be ruled. But he disputes that reason
and the passions (of which desire is one) can conflict and that reason
should rule. Reason cannot oppose preferring "the destruction of the
whole world to the scratching of my finger"; it cannot even oppose a
preference for "my own acknowledged lesser good to my greater."
And Hume certainly disputes that reason is or ought to be our ruler:
"reason is and ought to be the slave of the passions" (1955, Bk. II, part 3,
section 3)

In support of these striking propositions, Hume argues that reason by
itself cannot move us to action, that some passion must always be part of
the motive. Reason does play a role in motivation, but it is only to judge
whether the objects of our passions exist and to dicsover efficient *means*
to the satisfaction of our passions or the consequences of satisfying them.
Its operations are also value neutral, except purely instrumentally; reason
cannot set ends of human action; only the passions, perhaps the calm passions, can do that. Plato's appetites and spirit are passions and these, contrary to what Plato says, are and ought to be the rulers, and reason their
"slave," that is, their instrument. Calculating possibilities and their causal
networks *are* things that only reason can do; but setting ends or what is
ultimately good only the passions can do. To secure their satisfactions, the
passions need and can allow the logical and purely instrumental powers
of reason; but they and only they set the ultimate ends of life, and in that
sense they are the ultimate rulers. Plato's timocratic, oligarchic, democratic, and even tyrranical personalities of Bk. VIII are anti-Platonic, Humean
personalities, though they might not be ideal even for Hume since they
might not be using instrumental reason well enough, or they might be
giving precedence to the violent over the calm passions.

This disagreement between Plato and Hume is not easy to understand,
let alone adjudicate. For one thing, Hume does not appear to think of the
passions, such as desires and preferences, in isolation from or in abstraction from learning about objects. He seems to separate the cognitive
psychic functions, the functions of learning and reasoning and judging,
from "the sentiments" and "the passions"; indeed his views of the relations
between "reason" and the "passions" presupposes some sort of separation
of the two. But his examples seem to confuse them. He talks as if, for
example, the desire or preference to destroy the whole world is a desire

with no reason mixed into it; reason might come in only to do such things as judge whether it is possible to destroy the whole world, what might be means to it and what the consequences. But, as Plato and the rest of us might ask, what on earth does desire by itself know about the whole world? It takes an enormous amount of learning about the world to have such a desire, not to speak of having the *concept* of "the whole world." The same goes for preferring (presumably desiring one thing more than another), another learned passion. Hume's examples of passions are all mixtures of learning and passions. But all these striking propositions of his presuppose some separation of reason and the passions: somehow, we are to think of reason without the passions and the passions without reason. And the same holds for Plato in his original division of the psyche in Bk. IV and his talk of what part of the soul should rule what.

But it is not easy to "separate" the passions from learning, not even to know what is meant by such separation. The philosophers apparently do such separating by abstracting in a thought experiment: they hold before their minds something, the desire for some hot tea, let us say; they take away from it the heat and the tea, and what is left, they think, is a kind of desire without learning (or the smallest possible learning), namely thirst. What is left *as the object of desire* is *liquids* (or taking liquids), since this much is necessary for *identifying* this kind of desire as thirst. In a second stage of high abstraction, we might think that if we held before our minds thirst, hunger, and desire for sex, and we could do a similar abstracting (take away the objects liquids, solid food, and intercourse), we might reach the very nature of, say, physiological desire separate from all learning. Something like this is what I take Plato to have done.

But it is more difficult to know what separation Hume had in mind, since he was neither a logical realist like Plato or Aristotle nor a conceptualist like Locke, and presumably did not believe in "abstract ideas." Whatever separating Hume may have done was still "armchair separating" or "armchair psychologizing." For the psychologizing part we can go to someone like Freud. We need not suppose that Hume was Freudian or pre-Freudian. Freud is a good example here because he also, like Plato and Hume, divided the psyche; *however*, the separation was not by abstraction in thought experiments, as in Plato or Locke, but a real separation reached by going back to earlier and earlier periods in an individual's life when there was less and less learning present. In analysis, by the techniques of hypnosis, free association, and the interpretation of dreams, Freud was trying to uncover (memories of) earlier and earlier experiences, desires, and impulses, all the way to the infantile. The source or seat of such infantile desires and impulses he called the Id, and explicitly said that the Id knows of no time, contradiction, or rationality. So here we have another notion of desire without reason: inborn impulse, uninformed and arational. Perhaps this is close to the kind of separation Hume had in mind.

Now supposing we could separate the passions from reason, either in the Platonic way or the Humean–Freudian way, we would have a fundamental question for Hume: Why should we trust our "immaculate passions" more than learning to tell us what to do? This is similar to the question we asked of Plato earlier: Why should we trust learning more than our immaculate passions to tell us what to do?

Hume's answer appears to be that reason *cannot* judge what is ultimately or intrinsically good or what should be the ends of life. Here he is denying one of the fundamental propositions of Plato's *Republic*, one of the crucial premises in Plato's argument for the conclusion that reason should be the master, not the slave, of the passions.

But it is not clear what this disagreement between Plato and Hume is about. It might be a disagreement in their estimates about the scope of the powers of human reason.[29] Or it might instead be a disagreement about goodness: they have different theories of good (and perhaps different theories of value judgments). If Hume is correct in his view that value judgments and moral distinctions are the objects of sentiment, not reason, except purely instrumentally, then he is correct about what element of the soul ought to rule, assuming we accept a psychic division and the metaphor of ruling. But if Plato is correct either in his functional theory of good, or his later metaphysical theory of the form of the good, it follows that reason ought to rule: because on either of Plato's two theories of good, reason and only reason can judge what is good or bad, either instrumentally or ultimately. Only reason can find out what the exclusive or optimal function of something is, whether it performs that function well, and what enables it to do so; as *in fact* reason performs these tasks in biology, medicine, and the productive arts. Hume might not dispute that only reason can do these things, but he would dispute that knowing them would tell us what is good, except instrumentally. Plato would further say that only reason can know what forms are and can determine how far something approximates forms. Here Hume might dispute that we can know these things at all, but in any case he would dispute that knowing them would tell us what is good intrinsically or ultimately.

On Plato's theories of good, if we accept the reasonable premise that to rule ourselves, or at least to rule ourselves well, we need to determine what is good and bad for ourselves, instrumentally *and* ultimately, it follows that reason ought to rule, since only reason can determine these things. To rule is the optimal function of reason, because determining what is good or bad for ourselves is the exclusive function of reason. And this last proposition clearly depends on what good is. If what is ultimately good is a matter of what we feel or ultimately feel, then we need only consult our feelings on ultimate good, and make them the ultimate guide to action, as in Hume and, I believe, Rawls.[30] But if what is good depends on what function a thing has and how it performs that function, or on what form it resembles and how far it resembles it, then we must consult our reason and make it the guide to action. Once more we can see that the nature of good is the most fundamental issue in Plato's ethics and political philosophy.

5   The Defense of Psychic Justice as Analogous to Health

At the very end of Bk. IV, Socrates returns to Glaucon's challenge, to show that justice in our souls is better for us, better *in itself*, aside from rewards and punishments; and he tries to show this by an analogy between *psychic* justice and health.

Now Plato had tried out this kind of analogy before, most notably in the *Gorgias* (464–6, 504, 517, 520, 521). Here Socrates says that body and soul each have a good condition, which are health and (he claims) justice and temperance, respectively. He then draws up a rather elaborate analogy between the arts of the body, gymnastics and medicine, and (what he claims are) the arts of the psyche, legislation and (corrective) justice: as gymnastics is to the body so legislation is to the psyche, and as medicine is to the body so (corrective) justice is to the psyche. Gymnastics and med- icine aim at producing or restoring the good condition of the body, health; legislation and corrective justice aim at producing or restoring the good condition of the soul, justice and temperance. These analogies have been found unconvincing for many reasons, one of which is that in the *Gorgias* soul justice is undefined and opaque.

The big difference in the *Republic* is that Plato has now defined justice, and his analogy is between psychic justice *as he has defined it* and health. He has also elaborated and used a theory of good on which he based his theory of justice. So we now know what he means by justice in our souls and what he might mean by the claim that this justice is better for us. There can be no better context for understanding and assessing this analogy than his theory of justice and his theory of good.

Let us see how Socrates draws the analogy:

> "Doing justice and doing injustice . . . do not differ at all from the healthful and the diseaseful: the former are in the soul as the latter are in the body. Doing just acts engenders justice [in the soul of the agent] and doing unjust injustice. But to produce health is to establish the elements of the body in the relation of dominating and being dominated by one another according to nature, while to cause disease is to bring it about that one rules or is ruled by another contrary to nature. Likewise, to engender justice [in the soul] is to establish the elements of the soul in the relation of ruling and being ruled according to nature, while [to cause] injustice is to cause one to rule or be ruled by another contrary to nature. Virtue then is a kind of health . . . and vice disease . . . (444cd, author's transl.)

He also claims just actions are to psychic justice as healthful actions are to health: both are actions that produce and maintain the corresponding psychic and bodily states, and analogously for injustice and disease. He then uses the analogy to argue that since health is the good of the body, and justice is to the psyche as health is to the body, justice must be the good of the psyche; and thus it is good for us to be just, or at least better for us to be just rather than unjust.

Despite the fact that Plato has now defined justice, this argument also has not generated much conviction among readers or commentators of the *Republic*; their reactions have been very much unlike Plato's Glaucon, who immediately concedes that injustice in our souls makes life even less worth living than a ruined body, even if we could do as we pleased.

One reason may be Plato's analogical, isomorphic relation of psychic to social justice: as we saw, this does not ensure that a person who has psychic justice will be socially just, act justly toward others, which Aristotle tells us is essential to both general and particular justice.[31] Plato's definition of psychic justice may in this respect bring that justice closer to health, since we think the health of a person can be defined by how well his or her body and its parts function, independently of relation to other persons. But this only reinforces our reaction that Plato's psychic justice isn't justice; it looks more like what we nowadays might call mental health. So even if there is the analogy Plato claims between *his* justice and health, it does not show what he claims it shows – that it is good or better for us to be just in the sense of being disposed to act justly toward others, to be just by the standard of social justice. So Plato can't win: either there is no analogy from which to draw his inference; or if there is, it does not show that we are better off being just but something else, that we are better off being mentally healthy. Now, though this difficulty affects the health analogy, we cannot expect any interpretation of that analogy to solve it, because it is a difficulty whose cause is the *other* analogy, between social and psychic justice.

Further, an important similarity the analogy claims is puzzling. We think of health as a natural condition of the body, at least up to a certain age, and of the deterioration of health in old age also as natural, a biologic rhythm of the body. But we think of justice as something we have to be instructed and habituated in, an artificial virtue; while the fall from justice, if it occurs, has no particular association with old age or any rhythm of psychobiological normality. But in our passage Plato says explicitly that both justice and health are "according to nature" and both injustice and disease "contrary to nature."

Further yet, Plato has not defined health; he has given us far more information about his conception of justice than he has about his idea of bodily health. The analogy directs us to think of psychic justice as being like health; but given the relative amounts of information he gives about the two, we are more likely to take his justice as a guide to how he thinks about health. And indeed I am going to do this, but only as a heuristic device to guide interpretation; I take what the analogy prima facie directs us to do to be the fundamental comparison: Plato means to say that justice is like health; but of course only as what he knows or thinks health is.

Now if his theory of justice is based on his theory of functional good and virtue and he thinks there is a close analogy between psychic justice and health, perhaps he thinks of health functionally as well. This assumption is very much confirmed by the long discusion of the human body in the *Timaeus*. Here the parts and organs of the body are conceived functionally or teleologically: each part and organ is there to do some particular work (teleological), or at least has some particular work to do (functional),[32] which is its exclusive or optimal function. When all the parts and organs are performing their functions and doing so well, the organism is healthy; when some are prevented from performing their functions, by excessive food intake or violence, for example, we have illness and disease. The functional theory of good seems very much implicit, or taken for granted, in this conception of health. The examples of functions for eyes and ears Plato gives to illustrate his definition of exclusive function in the *Republic* coheres well with this interpretation.

If the functional theory of good is implicit in both his conceptions of health and psychic justice, his analogy becomes more understandable: the good of justice and health is the same good, functioning well, applied to the human body and soul and their parts. And Plato's claim that both justice and health are according to nature, and injustice and disease are contrary to nature, also becomes more understandable. According to the functional theory psychic justice is both a natural and an artificial entity: the just matching of psychic parts to psychic functions is *based on* an *inborn* psychic division of labor, the exclusive functions of reason, spirit, and appetite, and in that sense it is natural; but the actual matching of reason to ruling, spirit to defense, and appetite to obeying reason, is the result of legislation and education, and so it is artificial. Similarly, we are born with bodies that already have a physical division of labor, with eyes and ears and stomachs and hearts and brains having and doing their exclusive work, and this division is certainly natural. But well functioning and health also require learning; we have to learn to see well, the brain has to develop by use; and any of the bodily systems can malfunction and might require human intervention. The ancient arts of gymnastics and medicine were devoted to promoting, maintaining, and restoring health. For example, one of the three branches of ancient medicine, diatetics, had rules and regimens, for attaining this end; and these can be thought of as parallel to the laws of justice, as Socrates in fact thinks of them in the *Gorgias*.[33] In so far as health is the result of such medical practices, it is an artificial entity. So both justice and health are natural and artificial entities, the results of nature and human art.

The larger idea of nature and artifice that underlie these conceptions is nonevolutionary and teleological, as the *Timaeus* makes clear. Organisms themselves are the work of divine art. According to Plato, we are divine artifacts. What we take as natural is really the work of the Divine Craftsman imposing the order and goodness of the forms on matter. *Our* division between the natural and the artificial is a division between the regularity and order we find in the world independently of human intervention *and* the results of our human intervention: industry, science, and art. But for Plato it is a division between divine creation and human creation; with the important qualification that divine creation was limited in its results by the nature of matter – the results of even divine creation were good but not perfectly so. Justice as Plato defines it is the result of divine creativity and human intervention; and so is health, he thinks. He observes the order of nature and postulates divine creativity according to forms to explain it. The evidence for human intervention for both justice and health is easier to find, in the arts of legislation and medicine.

But the analogy can be pressed too far. Our distinction between the formal and material parts of justice reveals an important ambiguity in the health analogy. A crucial sentence can be taken in two ways: "to produce health is to establish the elements of the body in the relation of dominating and being dominated by one another according to nature, while to cause disease . . . contrary to nature." Are we to take this very abstractly, as matching the *formal* principle of psychic justice? If so, health would be conceived as the bodily condition in which every part or organ of the body, whatever these are, is carrying out its function (exclusive or optimal) and, presumably, doing so well. Health would be the condition of the body that enables it, the whole body and its parts, to function well. In this abstract interpretation there is not necessarily any exact correspondence between the parts and functions of the body and those of the psyche, as there is between the parts and functions of the city and those of the soul when both city and soul are Platonically just. The fuller interpretation of the analogy, using both formal and material elements, would require three parts of the body and three corresponding functions, as the analogy between social and psychic justice does; so that we would have a continuous full analogy or isomorphism: between a tripartite just city and a tripartite just soul and between a tripartite just soul and a tripartite healthy body.

Which analogy did Plato have in mind? It is at best difficult to say, but I favor the more abstract interpretation. When we look at the long discussion of the human body in the *Timaeus*, we might make a case that the head, the heart, and the stomach are physical analogues to, or sources of, or organs for, reason, spirit, and appetite. And we might try to work up corresponding functions which would enable us to order these by the relations of dominating and being dominated, according or contrary to nature. But there are so many more parts and organs found in the body and discussed in the *Timaeus* that it would take a lot of pure phantasy and probably falsehoods to work up the concrete analogical interpretation for all of these. How can we group all the parts and organs into three parts? How can we group all the functions of these into three kinds of functions?

The further characterization in the analogy, of dominating or ruling and being dominated, might be problematic for this conception of health. But perhaps it can be thought of as a relation among the parts that simply results from each part and organ doing its proper function; it is perhaps a supervening relation of the optimal matching of parts or organs to exclusive or optimal functions; it may be a weak analogue to reason ruling over appetite in the choice of food, drink, and sex; but there is still some analogue – reason's ruling *is* doing its proper (optimal) work.

The analogy in the *Republic* can be read in this more formal and abstract way, I believe, and still serve its purpose. The fundamental ideas in Plato's theory of justice are not the ideas of ruling over, but those of exclusive and optimal functions and natural division of labor, found in nature and in art. With respect to these ideas we do have a continuous analogy from a just city to a just soul to a health body. All three (city, psyche, body) are conceived functionally or telelogically, as complexes with naturally divided parts which are naturally suited, or adapted as we would now say, for some function or other, exclusive or optimal, needed by the complex. And they all share the idea that when the parts are doing the functions for which are naturally suited, the whole complex functions well and is in its best state, justice and virtue for cities and persons, health for organisms.

6   The Criticism of the Democratic Individual

Plato's discussion of the democratic constitution and the democratic individual is in many ways the most interesting of his discussions of unjust constitutions and unjust individuals. For one thing, modern audiences especially are likely to take his criticism of democracy as a sure indication that his own ideal city is totalitarian in the worst way, even though he ranks his ideal as the polar opposite of tyranny.[34] For another, while his description of democracy is essentially correct, his description of the democratic individual is puzzling and hardly recognizable. Finally, though his criticism of democracy is at least understandable from the point of view of his own theory of social justice, his criticism of the democratic person is as puzzling as his characterization of it.

Our discussion of Plato's construction of justice enables us to light on the two puzzles about the democratic individual. His puzzling description of such an individual is due to his view that a democratic indiviudal is someone whose soul is isomorphic to the democratic city; Plato carries the isomorphic relation over to his discussion of species of injustice. The puzzle here is parallel to his puzzling definition of a just individual, and the solution is similar. Having paid a lot of attention to the isomorphism between a just city and a just person, we are now in a better position to understand this assumption as applied to democracy; though its application to democracy throws new doubts on it. Further, Plato's criticism of the democratic individual can be understood better once we see that he attributes to the democratic individual a theory of good as the satisfaction of desire, a theory contrary to his own functional theory; he is criticizing what he takes to be a democratic version of the desire satisfaction theory. We can understand this better now because we took to heart the idea that all theories of justice presuppose some theory of good and used it to understand better Plato's theory of justice.

As with justice in Bks. II–V, Plato proceeds from the democratic city to the democratic person on the assumption of isomorphism.

Plato says that democracy comes into being when everyone in the city is granted an "equal share in both citizenship and in offices and for the most part these offices are assigned by lot" (557a, Shorey transl.). Let us call this the principle of democratic equality. The institution that satisfied this principle most fully was the Assembly: every citizen was a member of it, every member had exactly one vote, and being the most egalitarian of all institutions the Assembly was the supreme political authority. Other institutions, such as the Council and the Jury Courts, could not be as egalitarian, since not all citizens could be members all the time; but they were made to approximate equality by such devices as rotation in office and selection to them from all citizens by lot. Through rotation in office each citizen, over an average lifetime, could be a member of the Council and the Jury Courts as often (equally in this sense) as every other citizen; and through selection by lot every citizen had an equal probability of being selected. Plato mentions both of these egalitarian devices in his description of the democratic city.

The second principle by which Plato defines democracy is freedom: he lists freedom of speech, freedom to do as a person pleases with her or his life, and freedom to choose any vocation or career including the freedom to move from any career into politics. All citizens have all these freedoms equally.

This definition of democracy and democratic justice, by the principles of equal political shares and equal maximum liberties, is essentially accurate. It agrees with our other sources on Athenian democracy;[35] and it is even essentially accurate for modern democracies.[36]

But what is Plato's criticism of the democratic city? We find his fundamental criticism in the heavily ironic statement with which he ends his description of the democratic city: it is, he says, "a delightful form of government, anarchic and motley, assigning a kind of equality to equals and unequals alike" (558c, Shorey transl.).

Presumably, democracy is anarchic in the sense that no one has *archē*, authority, over anyone else, since all are equal in holding citizenship and office, though it allows rotational authority in the Council and the Courts. It is motley in the sense that all types of persons are found in it, since everyone is allowed to do and live as she or he pleases – it embodies the famous and anti-Platonic idea of happy versatility of which Pericles boasted. Most importantly, democracy distributes ruling equally to those who are equal and unequals alike. But in what? Clearly, in what they are naturally best suited, and subsequently educated, to do: as Plato says explicitly (558b), the democratic city violates Plato's fundamental principle of justice, *both* the formal principle and the specific matchings of careers to talents.[37]

Here Plato gives no arguments independent of his own theory of justice against the democratic city; this seems to beg the question at issue. But we must remember that he gives arguments for his own principle of social justice; and he probably assumes that his arguments *for* his principle of social justice are at the same time arguments against the democratic principle of equality. If we have reasons to believe the city is performing its functions best when each person is assigned that social task for which she or he is best suited, then we have reasons to believe that the city is not performing its tasks as well when each person is allowed to do whatever she or he pleases.

True. But Plato's reasons are not sufficient for this conclusion about the democratic city. As pointed out in the last chapter, it may be that in a democratic city, under certain conditions of information and incentives the long-run tendency will be for jobs, vocations, and careers to be occupied by the people with the most talent for them. This may be an assumption behind the famous principle of "Careers *open* to talents." This principle is of course related to Plato's principle of social justice; the difference being that the latter *requires*, as a matter of justice, that careers be *matched* to talents. If careers tend to match talents in a democracy, most of the functional benefits which Platonic justice confers might obtain. Equally important, what is lost may well be more than compensated by the social and political freedom of choice democracy allows and the benefits such freedom of choice confers on character development and personal autonomy. To make his case against democracy Plato would have to argue also against the value of this freedom to the individual. Is one always better off with no choice but doing what she or he does best, rather than being allowed the freedom to choose what to do, even at the cost of making mistaken choices?

I believe that in his attack on the democratic type of person Plato does indeed attack the value of social and political freedom. But the attack is implicit and indirect, since what he attacks here is the internal, psychic freedom of desires, rather than the social and political freedom in the democratic city. The social and political freedom is freedom from social and political constraints; the inner freedom of desires is freedom from internal constraints – in Platonic language the constraints of reason and spirit. I believe that Plato supposes that if he can criticize effectively the psychic freedom of desires he will thereby also have criticized a person's sociopolitical freedom to do and live as he or she pleases. The central idea here is that the value of the freedom to do as one pleases depends on the value of doing as one pleases. If doing as one pleases has no value as such (simply as doing what one pleases, no matter what that is), then the freedom to do as one pleases has no value – it is at best a species of the useful, not the beneficial.[38]

Plato characterizes the democratic person by reference to two conditions, which result from applications of the political principles of equality and freedom to the human psyche, and so parallel the two conditions by which Plato correctly characterized the democratic city.[39]

We see one condition by contrast to the other three types of unjust persons. The oligarchic person, for example, has a dominant desire to accumulate wealth, and he makes all his other desires subordinate or subservient to it; he also thinks that wealth is the good and makes all other goods subordinate or subservient to it. And similarly with the timocratic and the tyrannical persons. All these persons may be mistaken, as Plato holds, in thinking that wealth or honor or power is the good and in making reason nothing but an instrument for gaining these ends; but all the same these priorities do bring some order and instrumental rationality into their lives. By contrast, the democratic person has no dominant end or (stable) dominant desire by which to bring order into his desires and make choices accordingly; nor does he think that any one (or subset) of the things he desires is *the* good. Consequently, lacking the kind of priorities reason can set in Plato's just person, and the kind of priorities the other unjust persons have, the democratic person adopts the political principle of equality to her desires, regards them all as equal and equally worthy of satisfaction.[40]

The second condition is that the democratic person does not observe the distinction between "necessary" and "unnecessary" appetites and pleasures, which Plato draws as follows: necessary appetites are those which cannot be got rid of by training and education, those which are necessary for survival, and those whose satisfaction promotes a person's own good; for example the desire for bread is one, the satisfaction of which is necessary for survival, while the desire for lean and fat-free food is one, the satisfaction of which promotes the goods of health and strength

(558d–559e). Unnecessary appetites are those that exceed what is necessary for survival, those that can be got rid of by training or education, and those that are harmful to the body and the soul (559bc).[41] The democratic person refuses to distinguish between good and bad desires and to restrain any of them on such grounds. She is thereby deprived of another way of bringing order into her life, the way Plato's just person brings order into his life, namely, by ordering his desires on the basis of criteria external to desires themselves, such as the goodness of their objects independently of their being desired.

All this Plato sums up:

> he establishes and maintains all his pleasures on a footing of equality forsooth, and so lives turning over the guard house of his soul to each as it happens along until it is sated, as if it had been drawn by lot for that office, and then in turn to another, disdaining none but fostering them all equally . . . and does not admit or accept that some pleasures arise from good desires and others from those that are base, and that we ought to practice and esteem the one and control and subdue the other . . . and avers that they are all alike and to be equally esteemed . . . and lives out his life in this fashion indulging the appetite of the day . . ." (561bc, Shorey transl.)

A remarkable description of the democratic personality, conceived as isomorphic to the democratic city: corresponding to citizens we have desires and pleasures: corresponding to the freedom of citizens (from political and social constraints) to do as they like we have the freedom of desires (from internal constraints) to be sated; and corresponding to the equality of political authority among citizens we have the equality of desires, with the political devices of rotation in office and even selection by lot applied to the desires themselves!

Though our texts here are not as clear as in the case of justice, we can think of the psychic equality of desires as corresponding to the political equality of citizens, and the psychic refusal to restrain any of them as corresponding to the political refusal to restrain the freedom of citizens (except by the similar freedom of other citizens).[42]

Thus we can set out the democratic isomorphism argument, by which Plato infers his characterization of the democratic person from his characterization of the democratic city, as follows:

1. (a) If things are called [correctly] by the same name, they will be alike in the respect in which they are called the same. (b) We call

cities and persons democratic. Therefore, (c) democratic cities and persons do not differ at all with respect to being democratic.

2.   A democratic city is a city in which (a) all citizens have equal political shares, and (b) all citizens have equal [maximum possible] freedoms to do and live as they please.

[3.   The principle of equal political shares is implemented through (a) all citizens being members of the Assembly with one vote each, (b) rotation in office and (c) selection by lot in the Council and the Jury Courts. The principle of equal maximum freedoms is implemented through the fewest possible political contraints [laws] on freedom to do as one pleases.]

4.   Desires in a democratic person correspond to citizens in a democratic city.

5.   Therefore, a democratic person is a person in whom (a) all desires have equal shares in ruling, and (b) all desires have equal freedom to be satisfied (from 1c and 2ab).

[6.   Therefore, the democratic person is a person in whom (a) each desire has one vote [equal claim to satisfaction], (b) desires take turns [rotation] for satisfaction, and (c) desires are selected for satisfaction by lot (from 1c, and 3abc).][43]

In the passage we last quoted we can see that Plato comes very close to applying the democratic egalitarian devices of rotation in office and election by lot, to the psyche of the democratic person, presumably to bring some order into it and make choices possible.

These must be Plato's principal reasons for calling such a person democratic.

Here we can perhaps see that Plato's definition of a democratic person is not totally mistaken. We may still have a difficult time seeing why a democratic person has to apply the principles of political equality and freedom of citizens to his psyche; why a democratic person is not simply a person who subscribes to the principles of political equality and freedom of citizens, as, let us say, the Socrates of the *Crito* seems to be, surely no democrat of the psyche. But we can at least see why Plato's democratic person might prefer to live in a democracy. Such a person would prefer a democratic constitution to any of the others Plato discusses in the *Republic*, because it gives him greater political freedom to do as he pleases: in a democracy he has fewer external (political) constraints on his attempts to satisfy his desires, and he has at least as much political freedom to do so as anyone else. In Plato's ideal city, and in timocracies, oligarchies, and tyrannies, Plato's democratic person would have no such freedom (or equality); unless he were a philosopher-king, which he could not be, or happened to be a general in charge, a wealthy person, or a tyrant. In addition, a democracy seems to prize the very values he applies to his own soul, freedom and equality; whereas in an oligarchy, for example, he would be in disagreement with the dominant value of that society, wealth.

If we assume the isomorphism, as Plato does, we can see that there would be reciprocal relations between a democratic city and a democratic person: a democratic person would have to be pretty exactly what Plato says he or she is. And if such a person is as Plato defines him or her, then we can see why such a person would prefer a democratic constitution.

This resolves the first puzzle, not in the sense that it makes Plato's definition of a democratic person correct, but in that it makes it understandable to us, by revealing its basis. We are more familiar with a similar puzzle about Plato's definition of a just person, from the Grote–Sachs objection to that definition, now a century and a half old; I think it presents a similar puzzle and it may have a similar resolution.[44]

What is Plato's criticism of this democratic person? Plato does not say explicitly enough; but the two conditions he imposes on the type (psychic equality of desires and freedom of desires from the psychic constraints of reason and spirit), and the heavy irony of the passage we quoted suggest the following.

In general, he thinks that the democratic personality has severe problems with order and rationality. Since such a person has no dominant end or dominant desire, she or he is deprived of the timocratic, oligarchic, and even tyrannical ways of making choices, by appeal to dominant ends. Moreover, since she or he makes no distinction between necessary and unnecessary appetites, on the basis of criteria of goodness external to desires and pleasures, she or he is deprived of an alternative, presumably Platonic, way of ordering and ranking desires and thus making rational choices. Apparently, the Platonic democratic person holds the view that something is good if and only if it is the satisfaction of a desire or a means to it – this for all desires equally. Plato is burdening the democratic person with a version of a desire satisfaction theory of good and then criticizes that theory.

More concretely, one problem is that since the democratic person has no dominant desire but treats them all alike, she or he has no rational way

for making choices when desires *conflict* with each other and cannot all be
satisfied at once, perhaps not even successively. Examples of conflicts of
desires abound: say, a person wants to smoke and also wants to stay healthy,
she wants to take a vacation and finish her book. In such conflicts, how
is the person to choose? The objection takes it as a *fact* that our desires
sometimes do conflict, and suggests that the theory of democracy, when
applied to the psyche, has no way of guiding choices in such cases. So at
best, the theory is *incomplete*; and if such conflicts are frequent, as they
appear to be, the theory may be devastatingly incomplete. I shall call this
the conflict of desires problem.[45]

A second problem is that some desires are for things *known* to be
bad for us: for example, if we happen to have no desire for food we may
hasten our death; if we have desires for fatty foods, their satisfaction may
be bad for our health. The desires for smoking, for fatty foods, for avoiding school, are all desires for things known to be bad for us. And if this
is so, it is a mistake to treat all desires as equal. I call this the bad desires
problem.

Plato himself, as far as I can tell, suggests no reply on behalf of his
democratic person to the bad desires objection: the distinction between
necessary and unnecessary appetites, based as it seems to be on a theory
of good external to desire, would provide a solution, but it amounts to
abandoning the freedom of desires from internal constraints and their
equality.

To the conflict of desires problem Plato does suggest a solution (in the
passage quoted), and with heavy irony implies that it is very much mistaken. The solution is for the person, when faced with conflict of desires,
to adopt *for his psyche* the democratic *political* devices for solving conflicts
among citizens: to the conflicts in his own psyche he applies the devices
of rotation in office and selection by lot. When his desires conflict, he tries
to satisfy them in turn. And further, if there is a conflict about which
desire to satisfy *first*, he uses selection by lot. The lucky desire is satisfied
first, the unlucky second, and so on.

Plato seems to think that the adoption of rotation and selection by lot
is a reductio ad absurdum of the application of the theory of democracy
to a person's psyche. He is probably right in supposing that it is absurd to
treat all desires as equal, as these two devices do. After all, it is clear enough
that desires differ extrinsically with respect to their objects, such as survival, health, food, pleasure, knowledge, wealth, honor, and so on. And they
differ inherently with respect to their intensities, durations, and cycles of

recurrence. The desire for food occurs with periodic regularity, it can be very intense, and its generic object (food) is necessary for survival and health. None of this is true of the desires to go to the theater, attend the Assembly, or travel abroad. As a general strategy, to rotate the satisfaction of these four desires over a four day period is simply irrational if not outright mad. And to select by lot which of these is to be satisfied first, second, or third is even worse.

But now we are faced with the second part of our second puzzle: we may have made sense of Plato's criticism of *his* democratic person; but if a democratic person is one who subscribes to the political principles of the equality and freedom of citizens, and not necessarily one who applies these principles to her or his very psyche, what is Plato criticizing? The obvious answer is, of course, that he is criticizing the democratic person as he conceives that person. But *what* about the person is he criticizing?

My suggestion is that he is criticizing a version of a desire satisfaction theory of the human good.

One piece of evidence is that Plato seems to correlate every constitution with some theory of the good of the individual, and seems to attribute such a theory to the corresponding person. In an oligarchy, for example, wealth is the dominant value, institutionalized by putting a high property qualification for office; wealth is also the dominant value of the oligarchic person, it is the good, correlated with his or her dominant desire to accumulate wealth. Similarly, honor is the dominant value of timocracy and dominant value of the timocratic person; power for tyrannies and the tyrant. The same is true, I think, for Plato's theory of the ideal city and the ideal person: his political theory of justice and the other social virtues is correlated – based on I would say – with his theories of functional and formal good and reason's unique ability to discover them. If we now ask, what theory of the human good Plato correlates with the political theory of democracy, a very plausible answer is that it is the good as desire satisfaction: because in the relevant passages the satisfaction of desire is precisely what Plato's democratic person prizes and goes after.[46]

A second piece of evidence is that Plato takes away from his democratic person the distinction he draws between necessary and unnecessary appetites, though he seems to allow that distinction to all his other types of character, though they might draw it differently from Plato. If we interpret this distinction as importing criteria for the goodness of a desire from outside desires, then what we seem to have left seems to be a person who seems to think that her good is the satisfaction of her desires and tries to make her choices accordingly.

A third piece of evidence is that the chief objections Plato has to the way of life of his democratic person, what I called the conflict of desires and the bad desires problems, are indeed among the chief problems that any theory of the good as desire satisfaction faces.

If the suggestion is correct, we can look on Plato's criticisms of the democratic person as criticisms of theories of the good as the satisfaction of desire, and even ask how sound they are.

Now to begin with, a desire-satisfaction theory need not adopt the democratic political devices of rotation in office and selection by lot to solve the psychic problem of which conflicting desires to satisfy. These political devices seem rational when applied to the city and irrational when applied to the psyche, but a desire-satisfaction theory has no commitment to such irrationalities. A person who holds a desire-satisfaction theory of good need not be a democrat in Plato's sense. And if he is a democrat in the normal sense (one who subscribes to the principles of freedom and equality of citizens), he does not have to adopt rotation in office and selection by lot in order to make choices in his life. So Plato's criticisms of psychic rotation and psychic selection are not sound criticisms of all versions of a desire-satisfaction theory of the good or of a person who is a democrat in the normal sense.

Moreover, the problem of bad desires which Plato brings up against the desire-satisfaction theory, is indeed severe *if* the theory is that a person's good consists in the satisfaction of her *actual* desires, the desires she happens to have at any given time and over a lifetime. But this is a *naive* version of the desire satisfaction theory of human good.

The moderns who favor desire-satisfaction theories, from John Rawls to Richard Brandt to Jon Elster and John Broome, all admit that *actual* desire-satisfaction theories of good are false: because, they admit, it is a widespread and well-known fact that human beings sometimes desire things which are known to be bad for them (if we admit weakness of will, known *by the subjects themselves* to be bad for them). The desire to smoke is a well-known example.

The moderns propose a different solution to these problems: they define the good not as the satisfaction of actual desires, but of desires a person *would* have under certain conditions, the satisfaction of *hypothetical* desires.

Thus Rawls tells us not that the good is the satisfaction of desire, but that it is the satisfaction of *rational* desire. Rationality, in turn, he explicates by a series of conditions: the counting principles and deliberative rationality.[47]

Here are Broome's conditions: A person's good consists in the satisfaction of all the desires (preferences) she *would have* if she were *well informed and rational* (Broome, 1966, p. 133).

This definition is supposed to overcome the objections to the view that the good is the satisfaction of desires. Broome treats this theory as overcoming the bad desires objection and even the conflict of desires objection. Presumably, being well informed answers the bad desires objection; and being rational answers the conflict of desires objection, since rationality requires at least consistency.

This is not the place to examine whether these theories do successfully resolve these problems, a huge task which, in any case, requires a lot more than I know. But it is not clear to me that they do, and in any case there is certainly disagreement about it.

It is not clear, for example, how information about facts would enable us to decide that some of the things we desire are bad for us. Suppose we desire to smoke and we learn that smoking will cause an early death. How can this affect our choices on the modern theory? Presumably it will affect our choice only if we want to avoid an early death. But now we have reduced the problem of bad desires to a problem of conflicts of desires: we want to smoke and we want to avoid an early death, but how do we decide which desire to satisfy?[48] Elster, for one, has argued that rationality, what he calls "thin rationality" – that is to say, *consistency* and *information* – does not exclude known immoral desires or desires for things bad for us: one can have consistent immoral desires and make no factual errors; and consistent desires for things bad for us. Elster mentions voluntary suicide, homicide, and genocide as all being consistent with rationality as consistency and information (1985, pp. 15ff.).

Again, how is rationality supposed to resolve conflict of desires? Rationality requires consistency of preferences, for example, transitivity of preferences; so that we have no conflicting or inconsistent preferences. Presumably, this is supposed to answer the conflict of desires objection. But if conflicts occur in our *actual* desires or preferences, how are we supposed to eliminate the conflict and become consistent? By eliminating which desires, which preferences? If we admit consistency into the desire-satisfaction theory, it is not clear how *to reach* consistency, how to decide which of the actual conflicting desires to eliminate or satisfy.[49]

Now one might suppose that Plato would agree with the idealized version of the desire-satisfaction theory: in his terms, he might agree that the satisfaction of desire is good if it is guided by reason. But though true, this is misleading, because he has a different notion of the powers and functions of reason from the moderns, as well as different theories of the good, the functional and formal theory, both now out of favor. Plato believes that human reason is capable of knowing what is good in itself; it is capable of knowing functional good and ultimately the forms and the form of the good. So rationality includes the capacity to know ultimate human good. It is not simply instrumental rationality or simply formal rationality, or a conjunction of the two.

That is why, for Plato, not only the democratic person, but also the timocratic, the oligarchic, and the tyrannical, are all both unjust and unhappy: they all share the characteristic of putting reason to a purely instrumental use: to discover means to victory, to honor, wealth, or power. Only Plato's ideally just person assigns reason to its correct functions: to discover what is ultimately good, as well as correct means to it; and for that reason to deserve the role of ruling the soul.

But the moderns seem to use a much thinner notion of rationality,[50] formal and instrumental rationality, which does not include the capacity to know things good in themselves or intrinsic goods or ultimate goods. So there remains a very substantial disagreement between Plato and the moderns on rationality; and consequenly on their idealized versions of desire satisfaction. On Plato's view, desire – desire which is not itself the result of reasoning – has nothing to say about what is good, either ultimately or instrumentally; these are reason's functions. This is certainly true of appetite; while the so-called desires of reason are reason's tendencies toward the good, or desires based entirely on reason and reasoning, not desires in the modern sense.

On the modern view, reason only operates on desires, given from outside reason, to make them rational: that is, consistent, a formal cognitive and value-neutral function; and, with the help of the senses, well informed about their objects (and their causes and effects), an empirical cognitive and value-neutral function. That is all. But the problems Plato raised for his version of a democratic person, the problems of bad desires and of conflicts of desires, keep intruding into the modern versions of desire satisfaction theories of the human good, which use this limited notion of reason. Whatever the present state of affairs with respect to these problems, Plato may have been the first to recognize and articulate them, admittedly in a roundabout way.

7   *Which is Prior, Social or Psychic Justice?*

Why does Plato have an essentially correct definition of a democratic city and such an incorrect definition of a democratic person? I believe that for democracy, even more than for justice,[51] the isomorphism misleads Plato. In both cases Plato proceeds from city virtues to the personal virtues on the assumption of isomorphism. But the social and political freedoms and equalities of democracy apply to whole persons, and they are one reasonable way of settling conflicting claims to offices and rights among persons. Plato seems to take these concepts of sociopolitical freedoms and equalities and apply them to parts of the psyche, to form the concept of a democratic psyche, which he then criticizes as incoherent. This seems to treat parts of the psyche as if they were persons, and to treat intrapersonal, inner conflicts, as if they were interpersonal conflicts (Annas, 1981, ch. 5). But the social and political democratic freedoms and equalities a person may commit herself to, do not logically require that she apply these principles to her soul and its parts, as Plato seems to think.

However, there are passages in the *Republic* which indicate that Plato is really doing the reverse, modeling the completely good city after the completely good soul. If so, the theories of good he uses and the theories he rejects may be even more fundamental than we have seen so far.

The primacy of the individual over the social virtues is suggested in Bk. IV (443c), where Plato says that the justice of the city is an image (*eidōlon*) of real justice, which is the internal justice of the individual soul; also at 435, where he says that some "forms and characters" we find in cities can only come from individuals; and even at 368, when he starts with city justice because it is bigger and easier to make out, thus suggesting that this is only the order of discovery or exposition.

But the most direct and revealing passage is in Bk. V (462c): "That city then is best ordered in which the greatest number use the expressions 'mine' and 'not mine' of the same things and in the same way. – Much the best. And the city whose condition is most like that of the individual man" (author's transl.). How sweeping this passage is can be seen if we remember that the "same things" to which these expressions are to apply are not only property and wealth, and not only children and parents and husbands and wives, but also beliefs about what is good and bad and feelings of love and hate, hope and fear. In context, Plato is saying that a city is best governed when the greatest number in it (all if possible) share property and wealth, parents and children, husbands and wives, brothers and sisters; they all believe the same things are good, they all love the same things and all hate the same things. Only in this way, he thinks, will the social unity of a city approximate the natural unity of a person, and only such a city will be best ordered and the best city. The overriding concern here is not some metaphysical notion of unity, but the avoidance of unresolvable political conflict and instability.[52]

So even though Plato first defined justice in the city and then derived the definition of justice in the soul from city justice and the assumption of isomorphism, and he did the same for all the "unjust" constitutions and persons of Bk. VIII, this is only his order of discovery or exposition.

He may hold that *causally* a good city comes from good men, and the virtues and vices of a city come from and reflect the virtues and vices of its citizens. Though Plato realizes that through education constitutions and cultures put their stamp on the younger generations raised under them, nevertheless such constitutions and cultures are themselves the results, through custom and legislation, of previous adult generations. Bk. VIII depicts these causal interplays between older and younger generations and between constitutions and character.

But there may be even more to it than this: for Plato still holds to the isomorphism; and from a purely logical point of view, the deductions can go the other way, from the virtues of the individual and the good of the individual to those of the city. The passage I have just quoted from Bk. V (462c) seems to be saying that this is the definitional, not only the causal, priority. That is, in a deductive Euclidean system, the definitions of the individual virtues would appear at the beginning and the definitions of the social virtues would appear as theorems, deduced from the individual definitions and the axiom of isomorphism. Maximizing the good of the city as a whole, which is what Plato told us was his aim in constructing an ideal city, would be modeled after maximizing the good of a person as a whole over a lifetime, the latter being the self-evident principle. They are parallel principles of (practical) rationality. And they are realized by putting into effect one and the same principle, which Plato may have thought was his major discovery, the theory of optimal functions applied to complexes, or equivalently the theory of division of labor based on inborn, natural, appropriately educated abilities. When each part of the whole, city or body or soul, is doing its own proper work (optimal function), the work for which it is naturally suited and appropriately educated, this promotes most the good of the whole *and* the good of each part. This is what Socrates' reply to Adeimantus (419–21) is telling us, this is what the isomorphism is telling us, and this is what his analogy between virtue and health is telling us: each part of a complex, city, body, or soul, has its own parts, and each part has its own proper function, based on its natural abilities and also has its own proper good; when each part is doing its own work, it finds its own good in doing that work well and by doing that it promotes most the good of the whole as well. In all three cases the isomorphism among them and the functional theory of good common to all require that the good of the parts of a city bear to the good of the city as a whole the same relation as the good of the parts of a person, body or soul, bear to the good of the person as a whole. Whether we are talking about eyes or ears, persons of high intelligence or talent for achitecture, reason, or appetite, the principle is the same: when each is doing its own proper work, it finds its own proper good in doing that work well, contributes maximally to the good of the whole, and there is no conflict between *this* good of the parts and the good of the whole.[53]

If, in addition to the isomorphism and the functional theory, Plato was modeling the good of the city and its parts after the good of the person, body or soul and their parts, he must have thought that the principle was more evidently true in these cases; and for the body at least, ancient medicine seems to have indeed supported this view. Moreover, his anthropomorphic language, often noted by commentators, for parts of the soul may reflect *not* the thought that parts of the soul are little persons, as is often supposed. It may reflect the opposite thought, that citizens are like parts of the soul, in the sense that the good of citizens bears to the good of the whole city the same relation as the good of parts of a person bears to the whole person. And this profound thought may be profoundly mistaken. At least here we are reminded of what may be John Rawls's deepest criticism of teleological ethical theories, that they do not take seriously the distinction between persons.[54]

It is Platonic justice so interpreted, as modeling social justice after soul justice, which Brian Barry criticizes, or rather dismisses in one sentence: "In the *Republic* Plato discussed two main theories of justice. One is his own, a hierarchical notion according to which a just society is one modeled on a well-ordered soul. For reasons which will become clear . . . I totally reject the presuppositions of this theory and shall say no more about it" (1989, pp. 5–6). We have seen that there is some evidence for attributing this view to Plato. It should be noted, though, that as we have construed the isomorphism, this modeling does not require that Plato think the city is an organism or "an organic unity." It only requires that a city be organized according to division of labor by natural talent and appropriate education, and that the good of citizens be understood functionally, rather than hedonically or as the satisfaction of desires. The principle of division of labor by capability can clearly be applied to groups and artifacts. Plato need no more suppose that a city is an organism than a machine is an organism.

Moreover, the fact remains that Plato deduces soul justice from city justice and the assumption of isomorphism, not vice versa. This is of some importance. The isomorphism itself is logically symmetrical; logically, the deductions can go either way, from social to soul justice, or from soul to city justice. But epistemologically, or from the point of view of justification, the way in which Plato actually proceeds makes a difference to Barry's criticism: for in fact Plato gives arguments, some of which I have discussed, for his principle of social justice, independently of the isomorphism; as well as some arguments for his principle of soul justice independent of the isomorphism. So his view of social justice cannot be dismissed, as Barry dismisses it, since he gives arguments for it which do not rely on an appeal to soul justice.

Which is the real Platonic view? It may be that Plato was unable to make up his mind which was more fundamental, city or soul justice. When he elaborates the isomorphism for the first time in Bk. IV (434de), right after the construction of the definition of city justice, Socrates says

> Let us not yet affirm it [the definition of city justice] quite fixedly . . . but if this form when applied to the individual man, is accepted there also as a definition of justice, we will then concede the point. . . . But if something different manifests itself in the individual, we will return again to the state and test it there and it may be that, by examining them side by side and rubbing them against one another, as it were from the fire-sticks we may cause the sparks of justice to fly forth, and when it is thus revealed confirm it in our own minds. (Shorey transl.)

Here he seems to be more sure of the isomorphism, that the two definitions must agree in some sense, than he is of any priority of the one over the other.

8   The Structure of Plato's Ethical Theory

Having expounded Plato's theory of functional good and virtue in the *Republic* in some detail, we may be in a favorable position to review some puzzling questions about Plato's ethical theory, some of which I broached in chapter 1. Is Plato's theory of justice teleolgical? If so, is it circular? Or does it have the structure of a virtue ethics? As we saw, Sidgwick answers the first two questions affirmatively, while more recent commentators answer them negatively but give an affirmative answer to the third question.

When we look at the functional theory of good and its applications to the city and the soul, which of its main concepts – function, functioning well, good, virtue – is the most fundamental? In the formal theory itself we have seen that function is the most fundamental notion, for it is used to explicate all the other notions; and functioning well is the most fundamental value concept, since it is used to explicate good of a kind, the virtue of a kind, and the good of a kind. All this seems to be true of the applications Socrates makes of the theory.

The relation between virtue and good may be more complex and difficult to discern. In the initial functional theory itself and its immediate application, a thing is *good of its kind* if and only if it has the *virtue* appropriate to that kind; but it is not clear whether there is any priority in explication or definition here, though both are explicated in terms of functioning well. At the same time, in the formal theory and all its applications, it seems taken for granted that functioning well is *good for* the thing that functions well; and since virtue is something which enables things to function well, it follows that virtue is good for the virtuous thing.

This is confirmed by the analogy between health in the body and justice in the soul, which once accepted makes it "obvious" that justice in the soul is good for the just person: health is good for a person since it enables her to function well physically; so if justice is like health (justice is to the soul what health is to the body), it enables the soul to function well psychically and so "obviously" is good for it.

All this tends to show that Plato explicates virtue in terms of good. Moreover, there is no reference back to virtue in the various applications of the concept of functioning well or in the concept of the good of a thing. Plato never appeals to the social virtues to explicate the functioning well of the city or the good of the city; on the contrary, the virtues of the city are sought only after the well functioning and the good of the city as a whole have been explained. Similarly, in the formulation of the soul virtues, the isomorphism and independent arguments based on the nature of reason and desire are the fundamental notions; and these are understood without reference back to virtue. Finally, wisdom, both social and individual, is explicated in terms of the good of the city as a whole and the good of the individual as a whole, and wisdom is not appealed back in the explication of these notions. There is not even the appearance of a circle here, as there is in Aristotle.

In addition, there is a famous passage in which Plato explicitly affirms *some* priority of the good over virtue: in Bk. VI (506a) he says that the guardians will not understand adequately the just and the honorable (and the earlier definitions of the virtues) unless they know the good and understand how these things are good. This epistemological priority would seem to imply a priority in explication. On *this* point Sidgwick was correct, that is, in attributing a priority in explication of good over virtue to the ancients. A priority in explication of good over virtue, if accompanied by a theory of good which does not make reference back to virtue, would provide something lacking in the Socratic dialogues, and it would avoid circularity between good and virtue within the whole theory. We have found no evidence of any *such* circularity in the functional theory or in its applications the city and soul. The virtues are explicated in terms of functioning well, and not conversely.

But the definitional priority of good over virtue would not by itself entail a teleological ethical theory; in addition a maximizing principle is needed. Rawls's theory illustrates the difference; his principles of justice contain reference to primary goods, and not conversely; but he denies the maximizing principle. John Stuart Mill's utilitarianism satisfies both conditions, the priority of the good over the right and the maximizing principle.

Now when we come to the applications of the functional theory, we see that Plato's principle of social justice appears to be a maximizing principle, at any rate, if we look at its initial justification in Bk. II, and the reply to Adeimantus in the opening of Bk. IV. So his theory of social justice does indeed appear to be a teleological ethical theory, but with a theory of functional good, rather than hedonic good or good as desire satisfaction.

But for his principle of individual justice he does not give a similar justification. Perhaps for justice as a virtue of persons, Plato has a virtue ethics: a structure which is neither teleological nor deontological, and in which the concept of virtue applies primarily to persons and is not derivative from rules or principles of conduct. In such an ethics the virtues are understood independently of principles or rules of conduct, while rules or principles for conduct are derived from the notion of virtue as applied to persons.[55]

Now there is indeed a remarkable passage in the *Republic* which suggests that Plato had a virtue ethics. At 443e–444a, right after he has defined the virtues of individuals, he says that the man who has attained order (i.e. justice) and harmony (i.e. temperance) in his soul will

> then and only then turn to practice . . . in the getting of wealth or the tendance of the body or in political action or private business, in all such doing believing and naming the just and honorable action to be that which preserves and helps to produce this condition of soul, and wisdom the science that presides over such conduct . . . and the unjust action to be that which tends to overthrow this spiritual constitution. . . . (Shorey transl.)

Plato's earlier definition of justice in the soul makes no reference to some prior notion of right conduct, indeed no reference to conduct at all. So here we do indeed seem to have an essential condition of a virtue ethics satisfied: just conduct is explicated in terms of (its effects on) character, not conversely.

Unfortunately, from the point of view of clarity, this is not decisive, since Plato of course also has a concept of social justice, which is applied to the city and which has implications for conduct; and, as we have seen, psychic justice is derived from social justice and the assumption of isomorphism. So the Platonic case is complicated. It looks as if Plato has a teleological structure for social justice and a virtue ethics structure for justice as a virtue of persons.

Is this coherent? Coherence requires at least that the two "justices" be in harmony. Plato will have to hold that a Platonically just person living in a Platonically just society will conform to the principles of social justice of that society, and will never have conflict between the conduct which social justice requires, performing the social task for which she or he is best suited, and the conduct required by internal psychic justice, actions which promote and maintain the just order of the soul (in which each part of the soul performing its optimal function). The conflict that arose within Socrates in the *Apology*, between what admittedly just laws required – that court verdicts and orders be obeyed – and what Socrates thought he should do to preserve the justice of his soul – continue philosophizing even if the court ordered him to stop – would never have arisen had Socrates been living in a Platonically just society; or so Plato would have to hold.

But what assurance is there in the Platonic theory that such a conflict would never arise? It is doubtful that the isomorphism argument, by which

Plato derives soul justice from city justice, and the only argument by which Plato substantially connects the two justices, gives any such assurance. The formal principle of justice which soul justice and city justice share – that each of the three parts does that for which it is best suited – is too abstract to assure that the conduct which city justice requires will always coincide with the conduct soul justice requires. Even if we go to the two "full definitions" of justice, there seems to be no clear way of obtaining such coincidence. How does the social justice requirement, that I do that social work for which I am best suited, imply the requirement of soul justice, that I choose the actions which promote and maintain the rule of reason in my soul? On the other hand, no one has produced a proof that a conflict between the two full-blooded definitions of justice, and what they require, might obtain. The verdict both for Plato's view and for his objectors is "not proven."

Notes

1   There is discussion below of this premise.
2   The isomorphism between just city and just person, as expounded here, does not specify fully the relation between a just city and a just person. The full definition of a just city together with the isomorphism certainly does not entail that a just city is made up of just persons. We might then ask the more modest question: What is the relation between a person being socially just and individually just? To answer, we have to go to the passage where Plato tells us that a person who has justice in his soul will pronounce those actions just which tend to produce and preserve that just state of soul, and unjust those which destroy it. We can then say clearly that internal consistency of Plato's theory of justice, social and individual, demands at least that the kinds of behavior which social justice requires (namely performing one's own optimal social function) does not conflict with the kinds of actions individual justice requires (actions that preserve psychic justice) – the two "justices" cannot have conflicting requirements with respect to conduct. But why Plato thought this consistency requirment would be satisfied no one has succeeded in making clear.
3   Plato's inscription analogy and the photocopy analogy are very strong cases of isomorphism, since we have identity of structures and type identity of parts or elements (letters, syllables, and words) and thus identity of content. The isomorphism between social and psychic justice cannot be this strong, since we don't have type identity of parts. Psychic parts are not identical in type with social classes but only smaller! But there are many varieties of isomor-

phism; e.g. between a house and the architect's plans for it, only identity of structure; or an architect's idea of a house and the house built on that idea, which may be an identity of structure, but also allows for causal relations between the two. In Bk.VIII, it becomes clear that Plato has also causal connections going between various types of characters, just or unjust, and the corresponding types of cities.

4   Vlastos, 1977. For criticism, Cooper (1999).

5   Quite explicit in Thrasymachus: persons are just in so far as they (are disposed to and) act according to the laws of their societies; and these laws are just if obedience to them promotes the interests of the ruling party.

6   See Cooper (1999) on whether the soldiers who are doing their proper function and even doing it well, thus being presumably just citizens, are, or even can be, Patonically just persons. One may wonder whether Plato's theory of justice is coherent, if he has two standards of justice both of which some persons cannot satisfy. But I argue below that artisans and the soldiers need not have knowledge, as distinct from belief, about what is best. It would certainly be an extraordinary view of justice according to which in an ideally just society the majority of citizens would not be just persons because they lacked the ability to understand the theory of good on which justice depends. It would take very strong evidence to convict Plato of this paradox.

7   This is a widespread interpretation, by no means clearly mistaken. John Cooper's remarks (1999) suggest it, and Brian Barry (1989) assumes it.

8   That is, more than the known alternatives, which as we saw in the last chapter are the other models of organization for the city that Plato considered.

9   In his classic article (1999) John Cooper argues forcefully that in Bk. IV Plato's justice requires wisdom, and that from Bks. VI, VII, and VIII it seems clear that this wisdom must include knowledge of the form of the good; so that Platonic justice, at least psychic justice, requires knowledge of the form of the good – true belief is not sufficient, as Vlastos has argued. If Cooper's interpretation is accurate, Plato's theory of justice has a fatal flaw, if it is also true, as Plato held, that very few very intelligent human beings can have the inborn ability to reach knowledge of the form of the good. At any rate, it is a fatal flaw if ought presupposes can: what justice requires is something that I ought to do (or be); but if it is beyond my human ability to do it, how can I be morally or legally required to do it, and be held responsible and be blamed and punished for not doing it? Though Cooper produces some strong textual evidence for his interpretation (e.g. 441e4–6), it is still rather uncharitable; and Cooper himself softens it a bit by the qualification "strictly speaking." I seriously doubt that Plato thought that the vast majority of citizens in his completely good city could not be just. I think his texts leave substantial room for a more plausible interpretation. For one thing, he certainly thinks that all the citizens in his ideal city can be socially just, as Cooper agrees; Platonic social justice requires knowledge of the form of the

good only of the rulers; it is sufficient for other citizens to have true beliefs about what is best for the city as a whole. For most theories of justice this would be quite sufficient for being a just person, since they define justice as a virtue of persons not by the isomorphic relation, but by a strong and normally effective desire to act according to the principles of social justice. The problem Cooper brings up arises because of Plato's isomorphic conception of social and individual justice. Secondly, Cooper's interpretation may conflate somewhat the assignment of optimal functions to various parts of the soul, which is what psychic justice requires, with the performing well of these functions, which is principally due to other virtues. Psychic justice assigns ruling to reason and defense to spirit; however, it is not by the virtue of justice that a person defends herself well but by the virtue of courage; similarly, it is not by the virtue of justice but by the virtue of wisdom that a person rules herself well. So even though assigning optimal functions to parts may be a necessary condition of well functioning, and even make well functioning of the parts more likely, it is by other virtues that the parts perform their optimal functions well. Perhaps persons can be Platonically psychically just without being wise; Plato's definition of justice by itself does not entail wisdom, or courage. Moreover, we know from the *Meno* that Plato is aware of the practical value of true belief; as a guide to action it does as well as knowledge; though true belief without a causal account is less stable than knowledge. So why cannot citizens of Plato's ideal city be psychically just with true belief about their good, though they will be less stably just than the rulers who have knowledge of the good? Finally, if we are to rely on Plato's "metaphysical epistemology," as Nick White calls it (1979), should we not allow Plato that even though one has knowledge of the good one cannot have knowledge of "earthly matters" anyway?

10 A controversial passage. Williams (1997) claims that there is a part–whole principle at work here which contradicts the isomorphism, creating a central incoherence in the *Republic*. For corrections see Taylor, and Lear, both in Kraut (1997). Aside from questions of scope, it is doubtful that the present passage employs a part–whole principle at all; it seems rather to give a causal explanation of the characterization of a city as high spirited or money loving; it is in line with causal explanations Plato gives, for say, a city being timocratic in Bk. IV. We must also be careful not to conflate any analogy Plato may claim between the city and the soul with the isomorphism between a just person and a just city. Aside from the fact that we have different entities in the two cases (city, soul; just city, just person), the isomorphism is really a case of two things participating in one and the same form, two just things participating in the form Justice (see, e.g. 434d); but the city–soul analogy is not that but an analogy, a proportion between three natural parts of a city and three natural parts of a soul. Williams's criticisms seem based on a very uncharitable interpretation with respect to all these points.

11   I have stated the causal connection here so that it coheres with the isomorphism, though the latter is structural. This coheres well with Bk. VIII, where we get causal connections between unjust individuals and unjust constitutions (Lear, 1993). We must be careful not to confuse causal connections between, say, timocratic cities and timocratic individuals with the isomorphic relations between them. The isomorphism is structural and gives the formal cause of cities and individuals being timocratic; the causal connections give the efficient causes of individuals or cities becoming timocratic. Lear claims that Plato's efficient cause accounts underwrite or support the isomorphic claims, but it is by no means clear that the causal accounts are strong enough to do that, as distinct, say, from merely supporting the view that a timocratic person is one who subscribes to a timocratic constitution.

12   The principle of contrariety is the relevant principle to use because inner psychic conflict is the fundamental fact on which partitions of the psyche are based, as can be amply seen in Freud; though Hume partitions at least psychic activities into reason and passion even though he holds that the two cannot conflict with each other. Irwin (1995) is right in his persistent efforts to isolate the sort of conflict which is relevant to partition. At times it looks as if Plato has in mind something like contradiction rather than contrariety: thus 437bd, we have desiring opposed to not desiring, wanting to not wanting, and wishing and not wishing. As Penner pointed out (1971), Plato boldly maintained that one can desire and not desire the same thing at the same time, and proposed partition of the soul to account for this. Plato talks as if the oppositions themselves are movements towards and away from the same object, and his analogies of the archer and the spin top are indeed cases of physical movements. As Fred Miller (1994) has reminded us Plato held that the psyche is capable of movements, so psychic approaches and repulsions can be literally movements toward and away from a given thing. See Samuel Scolnicov (1978).

13   Plato says that the conflict is between desiring, wanting, wishing, and not desiring, not wanting, and not wishing, respectively; and at 439d that these rejections and repulsions are from reason. And from the latter and the principle of contrariety, he infers that the conflict is between desire and reason.

14   John Cooper (1999) has made the most persuasive attempt to find a principle of unity for each kind, what all members of each kind have in common by which Plato characterizes them as being desires of appetite, being angry, or having desires of reason. He is especially persuasive on the motivation of spirit.

15   Two small changes in Shorey's translation: "other appetites" for his "other desires," to keep the naming of each power after the name of the activities; and "arational" for Shorey's "irrational," because it is more accurate and serves the argument better: appetite as such is not for the good, but neither is it necessarily for something bad. Plato need not argue that all appetites are

always contrary to reason, which "irrational" implies; it is sufficient for his present and later purposes to consider appetite in abstraction from any learning or reason.

16　Not desiring to drink, I assume, is not equivalent to a desire not to drink. In the latter case we seem to have desires, in the former we need not. Plato thought that a refusal to satisfy appetite is due to reason, as Freud thought that delay or postponement of gratification is due to the ego.

17　*Treatise*, Bk. II, part 3, section 3. Hume has no problem allowing conflicts between the violent and the calm passions; what he attributes to the ancients is not *this* conflict; though he might have supposed that the ancients confused this conflict with a conflict between passion and reason, by confusing the calm passions with reason.

18　According to Hume reason is so indifferent to value, that it is not even opposed to a preference to one's own acknowledged lesser good; it has not preference for the greater good. Plato opposed this very explicitly in the *Protagoras*: of two goods or two pleasures the greater is always to be preferred – this is like an axiom of practical reason. Even writers who hold a desire satisfaction theory of good disagree with Hume on this.

19　See, e.g. White (1979). Another important ambiguity is whether Plato thinks that appetite and spirit come to agree that reason should rule through habituation or instruction (cognitive learning). If the former, as his theory of elementary education in the earlier books would indicate (gymnastics and "music"), temperance need not be interpreted as presupposing or requiring that appetite and spirit have any rationality or any cognitive powers. This would be an Aristotelian interpretation.

20　See this question raised near the end, in Kahn (1987).

21　Plato uses a similar principle to define eros in the *Symposium*, 204e–205 (Santas, 1988, pp. 31–2). Freud also uses object and aim, and somatic source to individuate instincts (in *The Three Essays on the Theory of Sexuality*, part 1). In the *Timaeus* Plato himself tries to find somatic parts or organs for his three psychic parts. Thus, object, aim, and somatic source are well-established principles for differentiating and individuating psychic activites and powers.

22　A pump is named after pumping, a shield after shielding, the power of sight is named after seeing.

23　Several writers think that in Bks. VII and IX Plato expands the functions of reason, appetite, and spirit, and this is a more accurate reflection of his view than the argument for the division of the soul in Bk. IV (Annas, 1981, pp. 122–55; Cooper, 1984; Irwin, 1995; Kahn, 1987). I think that to understand the differences between Bks. IV and VIII about psychic activities and parts we need not revise the argument for partition in Bk. IV; we need only assume that reason, appetite, and spirit, can work together in an individual to produce mixed or combined psychic activities, such as a desire for wealth. The oli-

garchic person is not a person in whom an inborn, unlearned appetite dominates, but one in whom (1) a learned desire for wealth dominates, and (2)
that desire is the result of reason calculating that money is the most powerful means for appetite satisfaction. The desire for money is rational (I confine
myself to Humean instrumental rationality); to suppose this does not require
either that this is a desire of reason alone or of appetite alone. To make good
sense of Plato's psychic divisions and his normative moral psychology we
need not attribute to him the seemingly incoherent view that appetite thinks.
In Kahn, the charge of incoherence comes up explicitly, and, in my view, is
not by any means adequately answered.

24   Psychic temperance can be as isomorphic to social temperance as psychic
justice is to social justice. For wisdom and courage the isomorphism is less
appropriate. Wisdom, whether of one's own good or the good of the city,
would seem to be primarily a virtue of persons; cities have wisdom by virtue
of some of their citizens having wisdom about the good of the city. Perhaps
similarly with courage.

25   When we so abstract desire from learning we reach the modern psycholo-
gists' distinctions between primary and secondary drives or "unlearned" and
"learned" drives; or biological and cultural desires.

26   In the *Charmides*, Plato says that the object of appetites is pleasure. The
argument here would be very similar: there is not enough correlation
between the things that give us bodily pleasures and what is good for out
bodies (e.g. sweets). So, once more, appetites need regulation by learning and
reason.

27   The concept of reason ruling is ambiguous as between a value model or a
strength model. Reason might be ruling in a person, in that it is the instrument that calculates what to do in any choice situation (the value model of
human action); but it might or might not be effective in enforcing its decision (the strength model). Plato seems to think that the two go together
sometimes as a just person who is also temperate with spirit helping reason
to carry out its decisions. See Kraut (1973); and Irwin (1995).

28   There is another ambiguity in ruling: setting ends or only discoving means
to ends. Spirit and appetite can set ends, in that the person is brought up to
have or comes to have the satisfaction of appetite or the aims of spirit (victory
and honor) as the end of his life; reason here is confined to calculating the
means to such ends. In Hume the calm passions set ends, reason finds means
to them, and in that sense they rule and reason is their "slave."

29   This appears to be Frede's view (1986).

30   Rawls, 1971, section 64 on Deliberative Rationality, especially p. 416; see also
the "blades of grass" case on p. 432. For a comparison between Plato and
Rawls on goodness and rationality see Santas (1986).

31   *NE*, Bk. V; and Irwin, 1995, pp. 256ff.

32 The teleology assumed here can be strong: each part or organ comes into being or exists for the sake of its function. Or weaker: each part or organ serves a particular function, aside from how it came to exist. Since Plato has a divine craftsman creating the order of the material universe, he may have the stronger teleology, which is not compatible with evolution.

33 Both social and psychic justice may require *nomoi*, artificial laws and regulations, and learning, but these are based on *physis*; as diatetics, one of the three branches in ancient medicine concerned with the regulations of nutrition, was artificial but based on *physis* – the needs of the body.

34 See Popper (1966); Vlastos (1977); and Taylor (1997). I agree with Taylor's distinctions among three different kinds of totalitarianism and his attribution to Plato of the paternalistic kind. I do not agree with his interpretations of Platonic happiness as "psychic harmony, the integration of the personality under the control of the intellect, itself directed by knowledge of the Forms" (p. 40). As I have argued, psychic harmony is the virtue of temperance, while the matching of reason to ruling, spirit to defending, and appetite obeying reason on bodily needs is psychic justice. I think Platonic individual happiness is the psychic well functioning which immediately results from psychic justice and temperance and other psychic virtues. I think Taylor's definition or description is too strong, including as it does knowledge of the forms, thus resulting in the problem of Plato's ideal city excluding the artisans and soldiers from happiness, on the empirical assumption that they are not capable of knowledge of the forms and the form of the good. Plato has no definition of happiness from which this paradox can be derived. There is also textual evidence to the contrary: the opening paragraphs of Bk. IV, in which Socrates claims that the just city aims at the happiness of all three classes, not exclusively that of the rulers as in Thrasymachus' view; if the soldiers and the artisans cannot be happy, Plato's view would collapse into that of Thrasymachus, and Socrates' answer to Adeimantus would be false.

35 Aristotle's *Politics* and *Athenian Constitution* provide us with essentially the same view.

36 Rawls's first principle of justice, pretty universal to modern democracies, essentially captures the two principles by which Plato defines democracy.

37 Aristotle thinks of the dispute among democrats, oligarchs, and aristocrats differently: even democrats agree to his principle of proportional equality; they disagree with oligarchs and aristocrats on what worth is – they say it is freedom (*Politics*, Bk. V; and Keyt, 1991, p. 25). I believe Plato thinks that democrats disagree not only with his specific matching of careers to talents (full definition of justice), but with his formal and fundamental principle that a city is just when it is so organized that citizens are assigned to social tasks for which they are best suited by nature and education.

38   *Hippias Major:* the useful is what is efficient as a means to a given purpose, no matter what that purpose is; the beneficial is the productive cause of the good. Taylor (1997) points out that Plato needs to criticize autonomy, but he fails to do so, does not even show an awareness of the need. He needs to, but I think he does criticize some important versions of autonomy in his criticism of the democratic person; in Taylor's terms he is criticizing part of the democratic ideology, the theory of the good as desire satisfaction which usually goes together with democratic theories of justice.

39   Plato also gives accounts of how a just city can turn into a timocratic one, a timocratic into an olicharcic, and so on; and he does the same for the corresponding characters. He speaks of the "origin and nature" of each. I abstract here from Plato's discussion of the origin of the democratic city and person from the oligarchic ones, except in so far as these accounts help us to understand his conception of the nature of the democratic city and person.

40   Plato's description of how a democratic type emerges is obviously a contingent matter. It is difficult to say how Plato viewed this psychologizing, and the corresponding historicizing for cities about the change of constitutions and types from the best to the worst. He writes as if this sequence is a historical and/or psychological sequence; taking the various constitutions and personality types as realistic possibilities, aside from historical and psychological development, may be sufficient for our discussion.

41   It is not clear whether Plato has two or three classes of necessary appetites (see White [1979]). I take the distinction to import criteria from outside desire for distinguishing between good and bad desires.

42   What corresponds to citizens? The desires of the appetitive part, or the "desires" of spirit and reason as well? Plato has his democratic man occasionally indulge in philosophy, presumably prompted by a desire of reason, to which presumably he gives equal time. This suggests that the democratic person is someone who gives equal time to all his desires, no mattter what they are and in what they originate. If all of a person's desires, including those of spirit and reason, were put on a footing of equality, this would violate Platonic psychic justice.

43   Points 3 and 6 in brackets are added detail, indicating a fuller argument, taking seriously the application of the political devices or rotation in office and selection by lot to the human psyche.

44   Some writers try to resolve it without recourse to the isomorphism with Plato's city justice (perhaps Irwin [1995]; perhaps Vlastos [1977]). I think that to meet Glaucon's challenge we have to go from Plato's psychic justice *through* Plato's social justice; Plato needs and deserves, even at pain of mistakes, all the resources of his theory, including his theory of social justice and the isomorphism.

45   Plato presents us with vivid descriptions of such conflicts in his democratic person (in, e.g. 560ff.).

46 It might be that the theory of the good that Plato attributes to his democratic person is hedonism, rather than a desire-satisfaction theory. I think the objections he makes have a much better target in desire-satisfaction theories than in hedonistic ones.

47 Rawls, 1971, ch. 6, sections 63 and 64. Rawls admits that the counting principles and even deliberative rationality are not sufficient for making rational choices in all cases.

48 Nor will the receiving of the information itself lead to the extinction of one of the desires, even if we could decide which is bad for us to satisfy, if weakness of will occurs; even when we know the better we can still desire the worse.

49 There are arguments that inconsistency, lack of transitivity of preferences, e.g. is bad for one. What do these arguments show? They might be taken to show that consistency is good in itself, but then they bring in value from outside desire satisfaction. Or they might be taken to show that consistency is a necessary means to maximizing the satisfaction of desires. But they still leave us with the problem of how to bring about consistency: by eliminating which actual desires, which preferences?

50 Rawls (1971, section 60 [the opening section of ch. 7]); and Elster, *Sour Grapes*, on notions of "thin" practical rationality. Roughly speaking, thin notions are required by the idea that if we explicate goodness in terms of desire and rationality, we cannot turn around and explicate rationality in terms of goodness. That would be a vicious circle.

51 The isomorphism of the just person to the just city might have misled Plato into mistaking rational prudence for justice. This is a more radical difficulty than the David Sachs problem, since it is more internal to Plato's theory. If we could show that a Platonically just person would also act justly according to the standard of Platonic social justice, we would be solving the Sachs problem, since Platonic social justice proscribes the usual criminal acts by which Glaucon's justice is characterized.

52 A parallel concern about social unity is in Rawls (1982). The concept of primary goods is constructed and used so as to assure social unity, or agreement on justice, in the face of disagreements about final ends, or ultimate good.

53 Plato is here disputing some fundamental features of theories of justice such those of Glaucon, Hume, and Rawls. According to these theories the need for justice arises because of the "circumstances of justice" people find themselves in, moderate scarcity in the goods they go after and their self-seeking nature. Because of this, people find themselves in legitimate conflicts with each other, legitimate in the sense that each is pursuing his or her own good as he or she sees it, which is surely rational, if any thing is. And the role of justice is not to eliminate such conflicts but to provide principles by which people can agree to adjudicate their conflicts. Plato disputes this whole fun-

166   *The Good of Justice in our Souls*

damental picture by disputing the theories of individual good that seem to underlie it: his functional good is cooperative and complementary, not competitive, for bodies, souls, or cities and their parts.

54   Rawls, 1971, pp. 24, 183–90. It should be noted, though, that this criticism applies only to nonegoistic teleological ethical theories. In ethical egoism the maximizing principle would aim at maximizing the good of a *person* (the agent) as a whole, not society as a whole. So the alleged mistake is not in the teleological character of the theory per se.

55   See the sketch of recent theories of virtue ethics in chapter 8 below.

5

Plato's Metaphysical Theory of the Form of the Good

Unable to solve the difficulties Plato makes his escape in a cloud of metaphor. *Grote*

Looking into the orb of light he [Plato] sees nothing but he is warmed and elevated. *Jowett*

This and the next half page belong, I think, to transcendental rhetoric. *Shorey*

If things are deprived of all good whatsoever, they will not exist at all. *St. Augustine*

We have seen that Plato builds up his theory of the virtues using the functional theory of good in the *Republic*, Bks. II–V. Even the defense of Platonic justice and the attack on other constitutions in Bks. VIII and IX use the functional theory. But in the middle books of the *Republic*, beginning with the paradox of the philosopher-king, Plato expounds another theory of good, the metaphysical theory of the form of the good. And even though Socrates says modestly that he does not know this form, Plato has him make the most extravagant, exalted, and elevating claims about it:

1. [a]The greatest thing to learn is the idea of the Good, [b] by virtue of which just things and all the rest become useful and beneficial. (505b)
2. And if we do not know it [the Good], then, even if without knowledge of this we should know all other things . . . it would avail us nothing, just as no possession either is of any avail without possession of the Good. (505b)
3. That, then, which every soul pursues and for its sake does all that it does, with an intuition of its reality, but yet baffled and unable to apprehend its nature adequately, or to attain any stable belief about it as about other things, and for that reason failing of any possible benefit from other things – in a matter of this quality and moment, can we, I ask you, allow a like blindness

and obscurity in those best citizens to whose hand we are to entrust all things? (506bc)

4.   . . . the Form of the Good gives the objects of reason their truth and to reason its knowledge of them . . . the Form of the Good is the cause of truth and knowledge, and truth and knowledge are like the Form of the Good but they are not identical with it. (509a)

5.   . . . the objects of knowledge receive not only their being known from the presence of the Good, but also their being and essence comes from it, though the Good is not essence but still transcends essence in dignity and surpassing power. (509b, Shorey transl.)

In Shorey's translation, Plato's next two charming lines read, "And Glaucon very ludicrously said, 'Heaven save us, hyperbole can no further go'."

The three great similes which surround these remarkable claims put the form of the good at the very top of the pyramid of the Divided Line, they make it the Sun of all there is, and the ultimate reality a fortunate escapee from the Cave might finally behold. An endless source of fascination to philosophers, artists, and men of letters, the similes have received plenty of attention.

Not so with Plato's direct claims about the form of the good. These claims have been found so obscure that in the last century and a half a whole series of eminent commentators, from Grote to Jowett to Shorey to Popper to Crombie, have told us that there is nothing to them – just visions and metaphors, clouds and smoke (Shorey, 1894; Popper, 1966, p. 146; Crombie, 1963, vol. 1, pp. 103–33; Annas, 1999).

Plato's remarks have not always been so regarded. Aristotle thought he understood Plato's theory, at least enough to criticize it elaborately and reject it in two of his ethical works(*NE*, Bk. I, ch. 6; and *EE*, Bk. I, ch. 8). St. Augustine tried to weave it into his theology.[1] Indeed its influence has been as great a footnote in the history of philosophy as anything Plato wrote.

Both these traditions are understandable. Not only is what Plato says about the form of the good obscure, but the theory appears explicitly nowhere else in the Platonic corpus; even in the *Republic* it has no evident use, no clear connection to the functional theory of good, no obvious relation to the virtues. Extremely abstract and formal, it sits there in the middle of the *Republic*, in lofty isolation, seemingly doing nothing. No wonder Aristotle thought the form of the good useless, and Popper labeled the theory an "empty formalism (1966, p. 103).

Yet, the fine work that has been done on Plato's metaphysics in the twentieth century affords us a chance to understand the theory better and to show that we have here a substantial theory of good which deserves our attention.[2] Some Neoplatonists and Augustine may have been closer in understanding Plato's view than the moderns.

In this chapter I expound the theory and show the role in plays in Plato's ethics. I begin with a sketch of the ethical, epistemological, and metaphysical contexts in which the theory is set.

1   Opinion, Knowledge, and Platonic Forms

When Glaucon raises the fundamental question, whether their "completely good city" can be realized, Socrates responds that the simplest way to bring about an *approximation* of it is by a "philosopher-king." There will be no end to the troubles of our cities, he says, until there is a union of knowledge and political power, until "philosophers"[3] become "kings" or kings become philosophers.

The paradox of the philosopher-king is already implicit in the *full* definition of the just city, since it implies that only those who have wisdom of what is good for the city as a whole should be rulers of the city.[4] But since wisdom is knowledge of some sort, this implication raises at once three questions. Is knowledge distinct from opinion, and if so how? Is such knowledge possible to human beings? Even if it is possible in general, is such knowledge of *good* possible?

The theories of forms and the form of the good are supposed to make possible affirmative answers to these questions – this is their role and their potential use in the *Republic*. And affirmative answers are essential to Plato's ethics and politics in this work. If there is no significant distinction between knowledge and opinion, Plato's definitions of justice and wisdom collapse into triviality. The claim of reason to rule the soul is a lot weaker if reason has nothing but opinions about the good of the person; the claim of people of knowledge to rule the city is baseless if knowledge and opinion are the same, since every person can have opinions about the good of the city.

Here we see clearly that in the *Republic* Plato's ethics and politics can hardly be separated from his epistemology and metaphysics, by his own lights. It may be possible to base Plato's ethics on his functional theory of good, and to have a theory of practical reason which makes sense of Plato's insistence that reason ought to rule the soul, without recourse to the theory of forms and the form of the good and a demand that knowledge be infallible – perhaps a theory like Aristotle's. But it is far more difficult to make sense of Plato's insistence, in his political philosophy, that people of knowledge ought to rule the city, without recourse to his epistemology and metaphysics; since the absolute power of people of knowledge would appear difficult to justify without the possibility of exact and certain knowledge. In any case, Plato clearly thought that his theory of the virtues, which we saw was based on his functional theory, was not secure without the theory of the form of the good and the epistemology and metaphysics it presupposes. He *tells* us so in the opening passages of the theory of the form of the good (504).

Here then we clearly have the beginning of a tradition from which John Rawls (1987) tries to break away, when he tries to free ethics and political theory from the epistemological and metaphysical controversies of philosophy; a breakaway (we shall see in chapter 6) that Aristotle himself began – at least from Plato's prolific metaphysics of separate forms and a separate or universal good.

But Plato makes his ethics and politics depend on his epistemology and his epistemology on his metaphysics. The latter move comes when he argues that distinguishing between knowledge and opinion requires distinguishing between two kinds of objects: between forms such as beauty itself, justice itself, and good itself, and their sensible participants, beautiful tones, colors and shapes, just cities, and good men. He claims that a philosopher is one who approaches and apprehends the forms themselves and never confuses them with their sensible participants, whereas spectacle-lovers mistake resemblances of beauty for beauty itself (they think the resemblances are all the beauty there is), resemblances of justice for justice itself. It is philosophers who have knowledge, spectacle-lovers only opinion. When the spectacle-lovers protest, he proposes to convince them by a long, difficult, and much discussed argument.[5]

The argument uses three main principles. First, it treats knowledge and opinion not as mental states but as faculties or powers which produce mental states. Then using an uncontroversial distinction drawn in the *Gorgias*, 454, that knowledge never contains error or falsehood, whereas opinion sometimes does, he concludes that the faculty of knowledge produces only mental states that are free of falsehood, while the faculty of opinion sometimes produces mental states that contain falsehoods. This is a difference in what these faculties accomplish, their results or functions.

A second principle is that faculties or powers are distinguished by their functions and their objects: the powers are the same if they have the same functions and objects, and different otherwise. Since the faculties of knowledge and opinion have different functions or resutls, they are different faculties.

But the question now arises, how is it possible for this marvelous human faculty of knowledge to produce mental states that are always free of falsehood or error? How is it possible for knowledge to be "infallible"? In response, Plato brings in a third principle – *the* principle which connects his epistemology and metaphysics: that which "entirely is" is "entirely knowable",[6] that which "in no way is" (Parmenidian nonbeing) is entirely unknowable; and that which "is and is not" is the object of a faculty between knowledge and ignorance, which he claims is opinion (*Republic*, 477ab).

So the objects of knowledge "entirely are", those of opinion "are and are not," and it is this ontological difference which makes the former possible objects of knowledge and the latter only objects of belief.

As is well known, Plato assigns the physical world to what is and is not, and the forms to that which entirely is. Here we face two notoriously difficult questions of metaphysics, epistemology, and Platonic scholarship. What is it for some things to "entirely be" and for others to "both be and not be"? And why should Plato suppose that only the former sort of objects, the forms, are knowable, and the latter, the sensibles that participate in forms, only objects of belief?

In trying to answer these questions here, it is essential to recall that in the *Republic* the ethics and political theory drive the epistemology; the epistemology in turn drives the metaphysics. And the ethics, especially the definition of wisdom as knowledge of good, demands that we must go all the way to the metaphysics of the good.

Our strategy here is to understand Plato's view of the "defects" of the physical world that render it unknowable, and then search for the ontological features of forms which render them knowable. We then look for a reason for Plato's supposing that the form of the good is responsible for the features of the forms which render them knowable. The reason will be that these features are the same as those that make the forms the most valuable objects of their kind, and hence that the good must be the source of their value.

2   The Imperfections of the Sensible World: To Be and Not to Be?

Shakespeare's question is readily understandable and profound, Plato's might not even be coherent. Yet it is central to his view of the world and man's place in it: "to be and not to be" is Plato's formulaic summary of his theory of the sensible world, the world we know through our senses, the world of space and time, *the* world of modern science. Understanding this formula is crucial to understanding Plato's pessimism about the physical world and the predicaments of human knowledge. But it is also crucial to understanding his theory of perfectionist goodness: the physical world is full of imperfections; and if we can determine these imperfections, then we can also discover what properties of a thing of a given kind, if fully developed, would make it perfect of its kind – the best thing of that kind. No wonder a long series of distinguished writers have tried to understand Plato's formula and to make it coherent (e.g. Vlastos [1965, 1966]; Malcolm [1992]; Code [1993]).

As a result of their efforts, we have four interpretations of the imperfections of the physical world. There are the "existential" and the "predicative" interpretations of the formula. Then under the predicative view there are the "approximation" and the "relativity" interpretations. The approximation view in turn has two divisions: sensible participants have all the defining attributes of their form but to a lesser degree (Wedberg); or, they have some but not all of the attributes of the form (Vlastos–Code). The following chart exhibits these views.

To Be and Not to Be

To Exist and Not to Exist	To Be F And Not To Be F
To Be F But Not Absolutely F	To Be F But Not Perfectly F
To Be F But Not Wholly F	To Be F But Less F than the F

A brief explanation is in order. First, there has been controversy about Plato's use of the verb to be: does Plato mean that the forms exist whereas their sensible participants both exist and do not exist (the existential view); or does he mean that a form is entirely whatever it is whereas its sensible participant is and is not entirely what it is (the predicative view)? Since Vlastos (1983), the predicative interpretation seems to have won the day; but we shall see that there is still something left in the existential view that is compatible with the predicative view.

Second, given the predicative interpretation, does Plato mean (by the statement that a form entirely is whereas its sensible participants are and are not) that the form is perfectly what it is (the F itself is perfectly F) whereas the participants are not perfectly but only approximately so (the approximation view)? Or, does he mean that the form is what it is absolutely (without qualification) whereas the sensible participants are so relative to one thing and not so relative to another (the relativity view) (Patterson, 1985, pp. 165ff.; Malcolm, 1991, pp. 106ff.; Wedberg, 1955, chs. 2, 4, 5; Nahamas, 1975; White, 1979; Annas, 1981)? In turn, by being not perfectly but approximately F, does he mean that the sensible participant does not have all the defining properties of the form (Code, 1993), or that it has all the defining properties but to a lesser degree than the form (Wedberg, 1955, chs. 3 and 4)?

Though most commentators take sides, it can be fairly said, especially on the basis of recent and detailed reviews of the primary texts by Patterson (1985) and Malcolm (1991), that we have some evidence in Plato for all four interpretations. Given the immense scope, or apparently complete generality of Plato's theory of forms,[7] this is hardly suprising. According to our texts, there are mathematical forms (triangle, five), natural-kind forms (man, ox), ethical and aesthetic forms (justice, good, beauty), forms of very general notions (same, different), and forms for artifacts (bed, city) (see Wedberg's review [1955, ch. 3]). Is it surprising then that no single model of the relation of forms to participants will fit all of them? Or that Plato never defines participation or resemblance, and that these can mean different things?

A second, nearly universal theme in the secondary literature, with the notable exception of Malcolm (1991) and perhaps Wedberg (1955), is that the four main interpretations are incompatible with each other; that Plato must mean one or another of these things by his formula, but not all of them. It would be more accurate perhaps to call this an assumption, for no one, so far as I know, has argued for it.

But why should we assume this? As far as I can tell, and in the absence of proof to the contrary, it seems possible for Plato to hold that all the forms are whatever they are perfectly *and* absolutely, while their sensible participants *fail to be both* perfectly and absolutely so; the participants of some forms may be only relatively so and so, the participants of other forms approximately so and so. Indeed this is the approach Malcolm takes: for geometrical forms he uses the approximation interpretation – sensible drawn circles are only approximately circular (they are circular but not perfectly so); for the number forms, for which the approximation interpretation is difficult, he uses the relativity interpretation – one city can be many citizens. This seems also to be Wedberg's view, though he does not explicitly argue (or even say) that Plato can have both views;

rather, in his chapter on Plato's views of geometry he uses the approximation view, and in his chapter on Plato's view of arithmetic he uses the relativity view.

The more usual approach (embodying the incompatibility assumption) can be seen in an illuminating paper by Alan Code (1993), analyzing the views of Gregory Vlastos. Code identifies "two different conceptions of what it is to be (non-existentially) real in Gregory's [Vlastos's] discussion of degrees of reality in Plato" (p. 6). First, "The Form is *essentially* F in the sense that it has all the attributes specified in the definition of what it is to be F." A sensible participant can fail to be essentially F if it has some but not all of the attributes specified in the definition; it will then be partially but not completely F. This is illustrated by Vlastos's example of real and fake flowers; real flowers have all the attributes specified in the definition of flower, fake flowers have only the color, shape, and size of real flowers; Code calls this failure imperfection. Second, "The Form is *purely* F in that (i) it is essentially F, and (ii) it does not in any respect, time, place or relational environment possess those features specified in the definition of a contrary Form."[8] A sensible participant is impurely F "in the sense that it has all the defining properties of an F but also has the defining properties of the contrary characteristic" (p. 7). Here Code cites Vlastos's example of twenty-four carat vs. eighteen carat gold: the former is essentially gold and has none of the characteristics of non-gold and so it is purely gold, while the latter has all of the characteristics of gold and also characteristics of nongold (some of it is all gold and some of it is copper).[9]

Code's imperfection exemplifies one clear version of the approximation view; his impurity, the relativity view. And he attributes both of them to Vlastos's interpretation of Plato. His exposition of Vlastos is clear-headed and illuminating; it affords us an opportunity to unearth some underlying assumptions, raise some questions, and hopefully gain a more adequate understanding of Plato.

First, it is a peculiarity of Code's interpretation of Vlastos that in the definition of purity Code includes perfection. It is not clear to me why he does so. When Code, earlier in the paper, explicates Vlastos's interpretive strategy, of trying to understand the notion of a form being completely real by inferring to what is required by the epistemological requirement of "cognitive reliability," he sums up Vlastos's view thus: "It is only the Form that is *completely F and in no way not F*, and hence only the Form that is cognitively dependable for one seeking the knowledge of what it is to be F" (p. 6, my italics). This in my opinion is a correct interpetation of Vlastos, and also a correct statement of what Plato requires of forms so that they can be objects of knowledge. But in this quoted statement the italicized phrase states two separate and independent conditions, and they correspond to Code's perfection and a *weaker* notion of purity – a purity which does not include perfections, but is simply the exclusion of contrary or complementary characteristics. As far as I can see, there is no good epistemological reason, in either Plato or Vlastos, for. *including the first of these two conditions* (perfection) *in the second* (purity), as Code does. We shall soon return to this point.

But even if we accept Code's definition of purity, it does not follow from it that impurity must presuppose perfection. Whatever may be the case about Vlastos's examples, it is a peculiarity of Code's explication of impurity that it specifies only one, and excludes the other, of two possible failures of purity, *as purity is defined by him.* He explicates impurity so that impurity presupposes perfection, and this certainly does not follow from his definition of purity. His definition of purity includes perfection (it is a conjunction of perfectly F and in no way not F), and so one failure of purity would be imperfection, the other failure a mixture with contrary characteristics (or not being F). And surely we can have both of *these* failures in a sensible, that is, there is no incompatility here. Vlastos's fake flowers might be an example of both failures: they have some but not all of the definining properties of flowers, such as color, shape, and size, and so they are imperfect flowers; but they also have nonflower properties, for example they are made of silk and they don't wither, and so they are "impure" (in a weaker notion of impure which does not include perfection). The same would be true of the puppet-horse of Plato's cave, and even more so of the shadows it casts.

Of course it is understandable that Code works up his explication of impurity on the basis of Vlastos' example of impure gold – since impure gold is "real gold [perfect gold] mixed with something which is not gold at all [copper]" (p. 8). But Vlastos may have been wrong in his choice of example, or the example may simply be misleading. Vlastos's example of impure gold is not a sufficient reason for including perfection in impurity. But Code gives a second, more theoretical reason for his interpretation of Vlastos's impurity – Vlastos's view that Plato's forms are formal causes of their sensible participants: the view that "what makes it the case that a sensible F is an F is that it meets the logical conditions for being an F (PA, pp. 90–91). It is because the definition of what it is to be F is satisfied by a particular sensible that the word 'F' may be correctly applied to it" (Code, 1993, p. 11). And of course if this is so, then sensible Fs cannot be imperfect Fs, as the notion of imperfection has been defined by Code.

However, here one may concede Vlastos's formal cause requirement, but still have imperfection attributed to sensible participants in the other sense of imperfection, explained by Wedberg and others: a sensible F may have all the defining properties of an F but may have them to a lesser degree than the F itself.[10] Indeed, this is another interpretation of the approximation view: a sensible F may approximate the form F in the sense that it has some but not all the defining properties of F, as is the case with artificial flowers; *or* it may have all the defining properties but (at least one of them) to a lesser degree, as a man can be rational but less rational than, say, Socrates.

Of course, if it is a requirement for all forms that they are formal causes of their participants in Vlastos's sense, then we cannot also have the same sensible participants being imperfect in Code's sense. Theoretically, though, we could have, say, real flowers being perfect in Code's sense, though imperfect in Wedberg's, and artificial flowers, pictures, and images of flowers imperfect in both senses; indeed all works of the visual arts, at least representative art where what is depicted can be identified as belonging to some kind, can be imperfect in both senses. Presumably the sensible world is full of imperfections of all kinds.

Code's notion of perfection is clear enough, but it is not entirely clear to me that it is the notion Vlastos had in mind; it is even less clear that it is a notion that should be attributed to Plato. It seems a puzzling notion of perfection. For one thing, a rectangle has some but not all of the essential properties of a square (four right angles but not four equal sides); is a rectangle then an imperfect square? And also, by parity of reasoning, a square an imperfect rectangle? Aside from this, if sensible participants are as perfect as the forms they participate in, as they are in Code's interpretation of Vlastos, this kind of perfection is idle and drops out of the interpretation of degrees of reality: it will have no bearing at all on the forms being more real than their sensible participants, since they all are equally perfect. Finally, we might challenge the underlying assumption Vlastos seems to make about the semantic principle underlying formal causation: if it is correct to call a puppet-horse a horse and artificial flowers flowers (as he apparently assumes and Code attributes to him), even though they certainly do not have all the defining attributes of horses and flowers, why is it necessary for a correct application of the term "horse" or "flower" to real flowers and horses, that they have all the defining attributes of the forms horse and flower?

I have a third difficulty with Code's interpretation. Code points out that these two ways of failing to be real, being imperfectly F and being impurely F, are incompatible with each other, since being impurely F, as explicated by Code, presupposes being perfectly F. And he goes on to claim that this incompatibility introduces a confusion and an incoherence in Vlastos's account of Plato's middle period metaphysics: "However, I have argued that something that is less real in the first sense [impurity] cannot be less real in the second [imperfection], and hence Gregory has given Plato an inconsistent view about the relations between Forms and sensibles" (1993, p. 11)

And again:

> The middle period Plato that Gregory [Vlastos] found in the text combined the attributes of purity and perfection to explain the cognitive reliability of Forms, and denied both purity and perfection of the sensible in his explanation of their cognitive unreliablity. Hidden in this denial is a confusion, the sensible realm cannot be both impure and imperfect. (1993, p. 12)

Code's definitions of purity and perfection are clear, and result in clear-headed interpretations of the formula the F itself is F. But his conclusion that there is a confusion, that "the sensible world cannot be both impure and imperfect" does not follow. All that follows from his definitions is that *one and the same sensible participant* of a given form cannot be both impure and imperfect; it is not excluded that one participant might be imperfect and another impure. And it certainly does not follow that it cannot be the case that the sensible participants of some forms are impure and the participants of some other forms imperfect. The sensible world can be both impure and imperfect − at least in the sense of this being compatible with Code's definitions − in that some parts of the sensible world can be impure and other parts imperfect. For example in the domain of geometrical forms their sensible participants can be imperfect; in the domain of arithmetical forms their sensible participants can be impure. A drawn circle does not have all the properties of a circle − it is in touch with the straight everywhere − and so it can be imperfect; while Athens is perfectly one city it is also two warring parties, and so is impurely one.

Code might ultimately be right in his interpretation of Vlastos, and Code's Vlastos may be correct in *his* interpretation of Plato. But we don't know this unless some unstated and certainly unargued assumption is successfully argued for. I say "some," because though it is clear that Code's conclusion does not follow, it is not so clear what premise needs to be added to make it follow. If we agree, as I am inclined to do, that Plato's forms – all of them – are perfect *and* pure, it certainly does not follow that all sensible participants have to be both impure and imperfect, and so there is no incompatibility. All that follows is that sensible participants must be impure *or* imperfect. So, there is some assumption, nearly universally held by Plato's commentators, that the relation of forms to sensible participants must be somehow homogeneous or somehow the same for all the forms. Apparently this is the assumption Code makes when he says, "Gregory has given Plato an inconsistent view about the relation of Forms to sensibles." On Code's definitions and his explication of impurity, this is so; but only on some such assumption as that "the relation of Forms to sensibles" must be the same for all forms. An assumption that Vlastos himself may have made. But why does the relation of form to participant have to be the same for all forms and their participants? I have never seen a proof that this must so. In any case, in the subsequent discussion we shall not observe this assumption.

Until some such assumption surfaces and is successfully argued for, an inclusive rather than exclusive approach is plainly in order, at least where theoretically possible; an approach such as Malcolm's (1991) interpretation of geometrical forms using the approximation model, and of number forms using the relativity; or the apparently similar approach of Wedberg. I shall follow their example.

Using the inclusive approach, we can sum up so far. (1) All the Forms are *perfect* in both senses: the form F has all the defining features of what it is to be F *and* has them to the highest possible degree. Sensible Fs are imperfect either in not having all the defining features (images, reflections, works of art) *or* having all the defining features but at least one of them to a lesser degree than the form (the imperfect rationality of Socrates, the imperfect roundness of the wheels of Hector's chariot). (2) All the forms are *pure*: the form F is not not-F in any respect, time, place, or relational environment; sensible Fs are not F in some respect, at some time, place, or in relation to something or someone (a beautiful statue may be ugly in the back, a beautiful maiden ugly later, at another place, in comparison to a goddess, or ugly to Socrates).

3   Forms as the Best Objects of their Kind to Know

With all this in mind, let us come now to our second, epistemological question: why should Plato suppose that to be and not to be, in any one of the ways we just surveyed, renders an object not knowable, whereas to entirely be renders it knowable?

The most plausible answer is that he saw imperfection and impurity as sources of possible error in sensible objects. If we are trying to discover what a certain kind of thing is, what justice, what a triangle is, or what a human is, an imperfect and/or impure physical object of that kind could lead us astray. If it is imperfect we may not succeed in identifying from it all the defining properties of the kind; if it is impure we may include properties which are due to impurity but are not part of the defining properties. Both kinds of errors are familiar from the ways Socrates' interlocutors go wrong in Plato's early dialogues; usually working from sensible instances, they offer definitions sometimes too narrow, at other times too broad. Now if imperfection and impurity are sources of possible error, then objects having any one of these properties would be unfit for the faculty of knowledge to operate on, if that faculty is to produce cognitive states always free of error. If, on the other hand, the forms are free of all these defects, and these defects are *all* the possible sources of error *in objects*, then the forms are fit objects of knowledge.

There is, however, another possible source of error in objects according to Plato, namely, change and mutability. Even if the forms are perfect and pure, they are still not "cognitively reliable" if they are subject to change. I believe that Jaakko Hintikka has given us the most plausible answer as to why Plato (and Aristotle) thought this.[11]

The forms so conceived *exhibit* their essential properties (something not true of forms conceived as properties), since they are what they are perfectly, purely, and always. The form line *is* length without breadth, perfectly, purely, and always: it exhibits its Euclidean definition which Sir Thomas Heath tells us was the Platonic definition (1956, p. 158); and so what a line is, its true definition and the beginning of knowledge in geometry, can be discovered by direct mental inspection, without inference, of the form line. Unlike sensible lines, which have all sorts of misleading and accidental imperfections and impurities, such as breadth, color, and length, all of which are possible sources of error in determining what a line is, the form is *nothing but* length without breadth – it is pure and perfect. How, then, could the faculty of knowledge, operating directly on such objects, make any possible errors while inspecting them? This may be why in the famous *Symposium* passage (211ab), after listing all the ontological attributes of the form beauty, Plato lists the epistemological one last: "not . . . being beautiful for some, ugly for others."

Putting all our results together, we can say that for Plato the existence of perfect, pure, and unchanging objects are necessary conditions for the human faculty of knowledge to operate infallibly. But they are not sufficient, at least not for humans. The limits and imperfections of the human mind make that impossible. Only few can attain to such knowledge, and they must be properly directed and educated away from sensible objects and toward abstact entities. Above all, they must be so educated that they never confuse sensibles and forms, something, we shall see that a human might not attain till she beheld the form of the good. The higher studies of mathematics and the other sciences described in *Republic*, Bk. VII, are intended to promote this end (Mourelatos, 1980). But given such an educated mind, it is the nature of the objects that makes knowledge possible, including the logical beginnings of human knowledge, which must be knowledge without inference of what something really is.

Before going to the nature of the good, we may reasonably ask whether the properties required of the forms if they are to be knowable might not be the same as the properties required of the forms if they are to be objects of value. Vlastos apparently thought that they would not be the same. He investigated the properties required for knowledge, suggesting that the value properties would be a different matter; about the latter he only ventured a few suggestive remarks, hinting that Plato's mystical streak might be at work here (Vlastos, 1983). I cannot agree. The conditions for knowablity and the form of the good are intimately connected, because the crucial question Plato is trying to answer is whether there can be knowledge of good, the very challenge Protagorean relativism and subjectivism pose. It should be an open question whether the properties of forms so far identified as necessary for knowability might be the same as those required for the forms being objects of value, desirable and lovable as well as knowable. I shall argue below that they are the same properties. And this will provide a basis in Plato for the long and deep Neoplatonic tradition which identifies reality and goodness.

4   Forms as the Best Objects of their Kind and the Form of the Good as their Essence

Let us now return to Plato's extravagant and obscure claims about the good. We might try to understand Plato's claims in the first three passages (see p. 159) as simply applications of the theory of forms and its epistemology to the case of the form of the good. Thus in the first passage Plato implies that it is by participation in the form the good that just things are useful and beneficial. This may be an instance of a general metaphysical proposition asserted by Plato's theory of forms: i.e. it is by virtue of participation in the form F that anything is F; so, it is by participation in the form of the good that anything is good (Vlastos, 1969). In the same vein, the second passage implies that unless we know the good we cannot know that anything is good. And this too is an instance of a general epistemological proposition that Plato puts together with his metaphysics: that we cannot know that anything is F unless we know the form F (Santas, 1979, pp. 311–12). If so, we can understand why Plato claims that the rulers of his ideal city must know the form of the good: unless they know this they will not be in a position to know or understand what a good city or a good man is, or what is good about the social and individual virtues. And this, together with a proposition of the third passage, that we do everything for the sake of the good, may be thought sufficient to understand Plato's paradox of the philosopher-king: there will be no cessation of troubles in our cities and states till there is a union of knowledge of the good and political power.

So far, this interpretation treats the form of the good as on a par with every other form. The only primacy it has derives from the proposition that we do everything for the sake of the good, which is not true of the other forms.

But this simple interpretation will not do for the rest of Plato's claims about the good. To begin with, the opening sentence of the third passage, that the good is something "which every soul pursues and for its sake does all that it does," is perfectly intelligible if the good of the individual is identified with her happiness, as Socrates and Aristotle supposed; but if the good is a form the statement is baffling. What is it to pursue a Platonic form and do everything for its sake? (We shall see Aristotle's perplexity about this in the next chapter.)

Further, why should learning the form of the good be the greatest lesson, i.e. the ultimate aim of the highest education, a point confirmed by the similes of the Divided Line and the allegory of the Cave, in which the form of the good is at the very top?

Further yet, what does Plato mean by claiming (in passage four) that "the form of the good gives the objects of reason [i.e. the forms] their truth and to reason its knowledge of them?"

Above all, in the most extravagant and obscure of all Platonic claims (passage five), what does he mean by saying of "the objects of knowledge [i.e. the forms]" that "their being and essence comes from it [i.e. the form of the good], though the good is not essence but still transcends essence in dignity and surpassing power?"

Hyperbole could certainly no further go!

I seek answers to these questions in the categorial differences I reviewed in the last two sections between forms and their sensible participants, between the forms being *always perfectly and purely* what they are, *and* their sensible participants being imperfect, impure, or changing. In these differences we shall find "the being and essence of the forms," and the explanation of the form of the good being the "cause" of the form's being and essence.

There are two distinctions implicit in these categorial differences: (1) between Platonic forms as *ideal exemplars* with self-predication and forms as *properties*; and (2) between *proper* and *ideal* attributes of forms (Vlastos, 1983; Owen, 1968; Keyt, 1971; Malcolm, 1991). We can made sense of Plato's claims about the good if we assume that in the *Republic* he thought of forms as ideal exemplars complete with self-predication, rather than as properties; and that the distinction between ideal and proper attributes of forms can be drawn and consistently applied to Plato's theory of forms.

The first distinction and the self-predication assumption is implicit in the *predicative* interpretation of the statement that a form "entirely is": if the form F itself is perfectly F, then the form is an ideal exemplar, rather than a property; the form itself has all the defining properties of that form and has them to the highest degree. The form line, for instance, is a perfect line rather than the property of being a line; the form circle a perfect circle, rather the property of being circular (with forms as properties self-predication makes no sense at all). Similarly, the form beauty is thought of not as the property of being beautiful, but rather as something itself beautiful; indeed the most beautiful thing of all. The *Republic*, the *Symposium*, and the *Timaeus*[12] are dialogues in which Plato seems to have thought of the forms in this way, as ideal exemplars with self-predication (Vlastos, 1954, 1983; Wedberg, 1955; Malcolm, 1991).

The second assumption, that the distinction between ideal and proper attributes of forms can be applied to Plato's theory, enables us to see clearly what makes the forms *ideal* exemplars. The distinction was drawn explicitly by Aristotle (*Topics*, 137b3–13), and has been discussed by Keyt (1971), Vlastos (1983), Owen (1968), and Malcolm (1991). Roughly speaking, an ideal attribute of a form is one that a form has by virtue of being a form, or *qua* form, or because it is a form. Thus being eternal is an ideal attribute of the form beauty since the form beauty is eternal because it is a form. On the other hand, a proper attribute of a form is one the form has because of the particular form it is; thus being circular is a proper attribute of the form circle since the form has it because it is the form circle. The distinction between proper and ideal attributes of forms is implicit in the ontological differences I have reviewed between forms and their sensible particulars: being F and the definitional attibutes of what it is to be F are proper attributes of the form F and they can be shared by sensible participants; being perfectly, purely F, and always F are ideal attributes of the form, not shared by its sensible participants.

We can see the distinctions in *Symposium* 21ab, a crucial passage often noted by commentators: here, at the very top of the famous Ladder of Eros, Plato gives a remarkable characterization of the highest object of love, the form beauty. First, he tells us that unlike the many sensible beautiful things (1) the form beauty always exists, it is neither generated nor destroyed, it does not increase nor decrease, and it exists by itself. These are clearly ideal attributes of the form. Further, unlike sensible beautiful things the form beauty itself is not beautiful in one respect and ugly in another, nor beautiful at one time and not another, nor beautiful in comparison to one thing and not beautiful in comparison to another, nor appearing beautiful to some and ugly to others. By implication, Plato is claiming that (2) the form beauty is beautiful in all respects, at all times, in comparison to all things, and to all who apprehend it. These too are ideal attributes of the form, and we can see how our previous discussion helps us to interpret them: for example if the form beauty is perfectly beautiful, i.e. it has all the definitional features of Beauty and has them in the highest possible degree, then it is beautiful no matter compared to what; if it is purely beautiful as well, then it is beautiful in all respects; and if it is perfectly, purely, and always beautiful, it is difficult to see how it can appear ugly to anyone who apprehends it. Presumably, the last is an epistemological attribute consequent on the previous ontological attributes.[13]

Accordingly we have the following three sorts of attributes:

P: [The form beauty] is beautiful.
I: [The form beauty] is everlasting [or, eternal], ungenerated, and unchanging.
II: [The form beauty] is beautiful in all respects, always beautiful, beautiful no matter compared to what [and beautiful to all who apprehend it].

A pleasing side effect of distinguishing these three sorts of attributes is that we can resolve the controversy whether Plato's formula "is and is not" is to be given a predicative ("is and is not F") or an existential interpretation ("exists and does not exist").[14] Plato can mean both: the nonexistential, predicative interpretation can be cast in terms of the ideal attributes of sort II; the existential interpretation in terms of attributes of sort I. The form beauty, unlike the beautiful Alcebiades, is perfectly, purely, and always beautiful (ideal attributes II); and also, the form beauty always exists (ideal attributes I), unlike the beautiful Alcebiades who exists at some time and not at other times.

The relations among the three sorts of attributes are well worth our attention. Some sort II ideal attributes are entailed by the corresponding attributes of the other two sorts: being always beautiful is a logical consequence of the form's being beautiful (a proper attribute) and unchanging (an ideal attribute of sort I). We also note that sort II ideal attributes imply proper attributes of set P: if the form beauty is always beautiful then it certainly is beautiful. On the other hand, the clearly ideal attributes of sort I do not by themselves imply attributes of either of the other two sorts: the form beauty being everlasting does not entail being beautiful or always beautiful. This makes for a crucial difference between attributes of sort I, and those of sorts II and P: the forms as properties require at most attributes of sort I, whereas the forms as ideal exemplars seem to require all three. Thus the forms as ideal exemplars imply a greater ontological commitment than forms as properties, including a commitment to the notoriously difficult notion of self-predication. At the same time, as we shall shortly see, the forms as ideal exemplars seem to provide just what is needed in objects in order to make it possible to have some knowledge without inference and with assurance of freedom from error; they also provide what is needed to make the forms standards of value.

The ideal attributes I and II of the forms are perfect candidates for what Plato means by "the being and essence" of the forms in the last and most difficult of his notorious remarks about the form of the good: for it is these attributes that make something a form and distinguish it from sensibles. Moreover it is these attributes that make the forms knowable, and the lack of such attributes that makes sensible unknowable: for the ideal attributes of set I make the forms stable and unchanging objects, while the ideal attributes of set II make the forms undeceptive. Not only do the forms not change, but they also appear the same no matter who apprehends them, no matter when or where. For each form is perfectly what it is and nothing but what it always is (pure); it does not fall short and it has no accidental nor contingent features to confuse us with, as sensibles do; it is perfectly and purely exemplified.

But what do the ideal attributes of forms have to do with the form of the good? And why should the form of the good, rather than some other form, be "the cause" of the forms' essence?

When we bring the theory of forms under our assumptions, conceive of the forms as ideal exemplars with the two sets of ideal attributes and self-predication, we can see how the forms, other than the form of the good, can be thought of as perfect specimens, or the best objects of their kind. When we think of the form Circle, for example, under these assumptions, no better circle can be conceived (something not true of the form thought as a property). Moreover, it is plausible to think that a form is a perfect specimen and the best object of its kind by virtue of its ideal attributes. The form circle, for example, is the best circle there is or can be, and it is its ideal attributes that make it so: the fact that it is completely circular, circular no matter compared to what, always circular, and circular to all who apprehend it; while it is precisely the lack of one or another of these attributes that makes sensible circles imperfect circles "in contact with the straight everywhere" (Wedberg, 1955, pp. 49–50). Similarly, the form man is the best man there is or can be, the form justice the most just thing there is, the form beauty the most beautiful thing there is, and they are all so in virtue of their ideal attributes.

Now if the forms, other than the form of the good, are the best objects of their kind (or have superlative goodness of kind) then according to the theory of forms (the one-over-many principle),[15] there must be a single form by virtue of which they all have this attribute; and in view of the fact that this attribute is bestness of kind, that form must be the form of the good. Thus, on this interpretation, the form of the good belongs exactly where Plato places it in our fourth and fifth passages, and in the three great similes, the Sun, the Line, and the Cave. According to these passages and the three similes, the form of the good is the "cause" of the being and essence of the forms and of their knowability; and according to our interpretation, the forms are the best objects of their kind and the best objects of their kind to know. And since they are so by virtue of their ideal attributes and by participating in the form of the good, it seems to follow that they have their ideal attributes by virtue of participating in the form of the good. The causation in question here is formal causation. Aside from Vlastos's (1969) convincing arguments that in general forms are formal causes, we note that the form of the good is here said to be the cause of other forms: since forms are immaterial and unchanging entities, material, efficient, and final causes are inappropriate. This leaves open the possibility, though, that the form of the good can be the final cause of human actions and activities, as indeed Plato has it be (506CB).

The goodness of kind of sensible objects can also be accounted for by the present interpretation of the form of the good. To be a circle a sensible must participate in or resemble the form circle. This is participation or resemblance in the proper attributes of the form, i.e. the defining features of the form. To be a good circle (to some degree) a drawn circle must participate in or resemble (to some degree) the ideal attributes of the form circle, for example, have a high approximation of the highest degree of circularity of the form. And since the form circle has its ideal attributes by virtue of participating in the form of the good, the drawn circle indirectly participates or resembles the form of the good. Thus a good drawn circle obtains its goodness by participating in or resembling the form of the good, but only indirectly, by participating in or resembling the ideal attributes of the kind or form it belongs to (the form circle). A thing may of course belong to more than one form, as one can be both a man and a carpenter. But participating in the ideal attributes of one form does not entail participation in the ideal attributes of another; being a good man does not entail being a good carpenter and conversely.

Finally, the form of the good must be conceived very abstractly. If the form of the good is the formal cause of all the other forms having their ideal attributes, it would seem that the form of the good is constituted by the very ideality common to all the other forms, by virtue of which they are the best and most real objects of their kind. Or, if we can push the distinction this far, we can say that the ideal attributes of all the other forms are the proper attributes of the form of the good. But this ideality must be conceived very abstractly, supergenerally, as it were, since it cannot contain the proper attributes of forms. The common ideality is not ideality or goodness of kind, as is the case for the other forms, whose goodness is indeed superlative but also partial, the goodness of kind. The form of the good is not superlatively good something or other, it is superlatively good, period. Moreover, the other forms are not in a sense self-sufficient: they are the best objects of their kind by virtue of participating in the form of the good. But the good itself is presumably what it is by virtue of itself. The form of the good is truly *the form of forms*, at the very top of everything there is, the top of the Divided Line and the allegory of the Cave: the most real, the best, and the most knowable of all things. It is the Sun of abstract entities, what gives the other forms their reality and goodness, and to the sensible world by reflection its more shadowy existence and lesser good.

We have here a daring vision of the identity of goodness and reality. For everything that belongs to some kind, to be completely real is to have the ideal attributes of that kind; and to be completely good of a kind is exactly the same thing, to have the ideal attributes of that kind. And what makes each thing of a kind completely real and completely good is participation in the form of the good. Despite its lack of clear exposition in the *Republic*, this daring Platonic vision has been extremely influential both to its believers and its critics. To the critics we will soon turn. But a measure of its influence on the believers can be seen in St. Augustine's thought that "if things are deprived of all good whatsoever, they will not exist at all" (Augustine, 1960; McDonald, 1991).

5 Function, Form, and Goodness

In the last chapter we saw that in the *Republic* Plato has a functional theory of good upon which he builds his theory of justice and the other virtues. In this chapter we have seen that in the same work Plato also has a metaphysical theory of good, which he does not put to any use but claims that it is prior and more fundamental than all the other theories in the *Republic*. Our first question is whether the two theories are in substantial agreement, our second how they are related, our third why Plato did not use the metaphysical theory to begin with.

Let me clarify the first question. The two theories of good are formal: they tell us what makes things good and how to find out what things are good, but not by themselves what things are good. But presumably when each theory is put together with appropriate factual propositions it will yield information about what things are good. Evidently then, the two theories are in substantial agreement if, when conjoined with the same factual propositions they yield the same conclusions about what things are good. Moreover, if Plato's ethical theory is teleological, the virtues being qualities which maximize the good, the two theories should yield the same account of the virtues when put together with the same propositions about societies and human beings.

Are the two theories of good then in substantial agreement? It is one of the most puzzling things about the *Republic* that Plato does not discuss or even raise this question, even though he must assume that the two theories are in substantial agreement, on pain of the *Republic* being an incoherent work. He certainly does not apply the metaphysical theory of the good, as he did the functional theory, to determine the social and individual virtues and the good of humans and society. It is this "failure" that gives rise to Popper's charge that the metaphysical theory of the form of the good is an "empty formalism," and Aristotle's charge that it is useless. And it is this "failure" that makes it look as if the *Republic* is two separate and unrelated books, one containing political–ethical theories and the other epistemology and metaphysics. How is the philosopher-king to discover, using his knowledge of the good and the other forms, the just man and the just city and the good of each? And why did Plato suppose, as he must have, that by so doing the philosopher-king would arrive at the same results which Socrates reached earlier by applying the functional theory of good?

The most plausible hypothesis is that Plato thought the two theories in obvious agreement and not in need of argument. But how so? His commentators have certainly not found it obvious, from Aristotle to the present day.

One difficulty in seeing any connection between the two theories of good is that each is stated independently and without reference to the other. Neither in the statement of the functional theory nor in its application, before or after the statement of the metaphysical theory, is there any reference to the form of the good. And the theory of the form of the good is stated without any reference to function, for reasons we shall see directly below.

A second difficulty is that there is an obvious way of connecting the two theories, which is clearly incorrect: that is to suppose that the forms are functional paradigms, objects which carry out their functions perfectly. This cannot be Plato's thought, for the forms have no functions in the relevant sense. The forms are "at rest," they don't perform any activities, they don't do anything, and they may not even be in time. The form eye does not see, the form knife does not cut, the form man does not deliberate, the form city does not protect anyone, and nobody can sleep in the perfect bed, not even the perfect man. We cannot therefore suppose that the forms are perfect specimens, and the paradigms of goodness of kind, because they function perfectly. These absurdities cannot plausibly be attributed to Plato. In addition, this way of relating the two theories would make the functional theory the more fundamental of the two, whereas Plato seems to have held the reverse. The forms are the best objects of their kind because of what they are, not because of what they do. Their goodness is not "spread out in time," we might say, as is the functional goodness of sensible participants. The seeming chasm between the two theories of good seems to be a direct consequence of the chasm which separates forms and their sensible participants, the chasm of time, space, and change, the chasm between being and becoming.

But this gap is not unbridgeable, it is bridged by the relations between forms and sensibles. In the middle books of the *Republic* these relations seem to be ontological dependence and resemblance, the two relations illustrated over and over by the three great similes, the Sun, the Line, and the Cave. Thus, though the forms have no functions, all sensibles with functions "have form" in the sense that they resemble or participate in forms. This is an obvious truth in Plato's theory, part and parcel of the postulation of forms and the relations of forms to sensibles introduced in Bk. IV. It is here that we must seek the agreement between the two theories of good and the priority of the metaphysical theory. And now that we have come this far, only one possibility seems to satisfy both conditions, i.e. agreement between the two theories and the priority of the metaphysical over the functional theory. Plato must be assuming (1) that what function a sensible has "depends on what it is," i.e. what form(s) it resembles; and (2) how well it carries out its function(s) depends on how far it resembles its form. The first of these assumptions must have been obvious to him indeed. After all, whatever a sensible is, whatever structure, organization, or characteristics it has, it has by virtue of resembling some form(s). So, whatever activity or work only a sensible of a given kind can do, or can do more efficiently that sensibles of another kind can do, must depend, if it depends on anything at all, on one or another of these: the structure, organization, or characteristics it has. And that it does so depend also seems obvious from examples: by changing the shape of the edge of a knife, from sharp to flat, we can affect its cutting; by changing the shape of a wheel we can affect its rotation; by changing the structure of an eye we can affect its seeing. How Plato conceived of this relation is not entirely clear; the relation between form and function was not elaborated till later in Aristotle's biological works. We can perhaps say that Plato would not be inclined to identify what a sensible is with its function, or to construct functional definitions of sensibles, as Aristotle sometimes did. The separation of forms from sensibles and the fact that forms have no functions would prevent him from doing that. Beyond that, perhaps the most we can say is that he thought of the relation between what a sensible is (its structure or form) and its function as some sort of causal relation, perhaps analogous to the relation between a thing's virtue and its functioning well: just as the virtues enable things to function well, so what a sensible is enables it to have a given function.

Assumption (2) is also a natural one for Plato to make, in view of assumption (1) and the proposition, also part of the theory of forms, that sensibles resemble forms more or less but never completely. Indeed, (2) seems to follow from (1) and this proposition. If, for example, what enables a sensible wheel to peform its characteristic work, rotating, is its circular shape, and the sensible wheel is more or less circular but never completely so, it seems to follow that the more circular it is, i.e. the more it resembles the form circle, the better it will rotate. Just as what work a sensible can do depends on what it is, i.e. what form it resembles, so how well it does that work depends on how much it resembles this form.

If Plato made these two assumptions, we can see why he thought that the two theories of good in the *Republic* are in agreement, and also why he thought the theory of the form of the good is the more fundamental. If these two assumptions hold, in principle one could judge the goodness of sensibles in either of two ways and be assured that he would get the same result: either by knowing the form a sensible resembles and determining how far it resembles it relative to other participants in the same form; or by knowing the function of that sensible and determining how well it carries out that function relative to other things with the same function. Moreover, on these assumptions the theory of the form of the good is the more fundamental in this sense: though a sensible can show or exhibit its goodness in the efficient performance of its function, this is really a result of what it is and how far it is what it is, i.e., what form it resembles and how far it resembles it. It is the degree of resemblance to the forms that makes it good, the degree of resemblance to the things that are perfectly good; and these in turn are perfectly good of their kind by virtue of participating in the form of the good.

But if this is so, isn't Plato's procedure in the *Republic* rather strange? If the theory of the form of the good is more fundamental, why did he not start in Bk. II with this theory and proceed in the way he recommends the philosopher-king to do? Look at the forms city and man and construct the closest possible approximations or resemblances of them? Actually, Plato seems to describe such an undertaking in the *Timaeus*. The divine craftsman, being unenvious and good, wishes to fashion a sensible world which is as good as possible, that is, as good as presumably matter, time, and space allow. To do so he looks to the forms and using them as paradigms he fashions sensibles which resemble them as much as possible. The theory of the form of the good seems to be presupposed in this creative act. The forms are thought of as the best objects of their kind; why else would the divine craftsman want to imitate them in order to create the best possible sensibles? But the divine craftsman can do this because he has complete knowledge of the forms and of the form of the good, knowledge which is clearly prior and independent of perception of sensible participants. Socrates in the *Republic*, though he describes how the philosopher-king can, through dialectic, assent to the form of the good, does not pretend to have any such knowledge; he has only opinions about the form of the good. Humans approach the forms by being "reminded" of them through the perception of their sensible participants.

So perhaps we can see why Plato starts the *Republic* with the functional theory of good and builds up the theory of the social and individual virtues on the basis of it. The functional theory deals with sensibles, and it is closer to our evaluative practices in medicine and the other arts and crafts. We judge the good condition of organisms by how well they and their organs function, and the goodness of the products of the arts by how well they do what they were made to do. And Plato has framed his definition of function in terms of exclusive or optimal capacities, rather than desires or interests we take in objects (since he rejects a desire-satisfaction theory of good), so that judgments of functional goodness will accord with judgments of perfectionist goodness made on the basis of forms and the theory of the form of the good eventually introduced. At least so he thinks, I have argued, given the usual assumptions of the theory of forms and the plausible truth that what a sensible can do depends on what it is. If he is correct, the *Republic* is indeed a coherent work, and the agreement between the two theories of good unites his ethics and politics with his epistemology and metaphysics.

In the *Republic*, the theory of the form of the good is so formal and abstract and it is so removed from any evident application that it seems empty, and the complaints of Aristotle, Popper, and others are understandable. To these criticisms we shall soon turn. But if Plato's metaphysical theory of good can be united with his functional theory, as Plato seems to have thought, it can emerge as the first great perfectionist theory of goodness. Aristotle perhaps had a more plausible theory because he rejected the separation of forms from sensibles, and perhaps because he was more sensitive to the claims of desire and pleasure to play a role in the good life. But if we allow for the modifications resulting from the rejection of separation of forms from sensibles, we shall find that Aristotle followed in Plato's perfectionist footsteps.

Notes

1   See, e.g., his discussion of good and evil in *The Confessions*, Bk. VII, chs. 12, 13.

2   I first began work on this topic in 1977: see Santas (1980), reprinted in Anton and Press, 1983, and in Fine (1999); and Santas (1984). This chapter uses work not available in 1977, including Burnyeat (1988); Patterson (1985); Malcolm (1991); and Code (1993).

3   Philosophers here are persons of knowledge; as is clear from Bks. V, VI, and VII, Plato's philosophers have to study all the sciences and branches of knowledge, not just the special discipline known in contemporary times as philosophy.

4   The full definition of justice would have this implication if the criterion for assigning persons to ruling includes a complete education for ruling, which would include the "greatest lesson" – knowledge of the good.

5   *Republic*, 477a–479; for discussion see, e.g., Hintikka (1974); Penner (1987); Fine (1999); and Santas (1974, 1990).

6   The parallel for knowledge of propositions would be: to be knowable a proposition must be "entirely true"; or better, "always true," or "necessarily true."

7   Wedberg's classic review of the scope of the theory (in ch. 2) is still valid.

8   Code correctly amends the last clause on Vlastos's behalf to "not being F" rather than the contrary of F.

9   One might object that these examples can only be analogies, for on Plato's view sensible flowers are not real flowers but sensible participants of the form flower, and so they themselves are both flowers and not flowers, while fake flowers are twice removed from reality. But I set this aside.

10   Wedberg, 1955, pp. 50–1, and Appendices A and C. "when a physical object is said to partake of a Euclidean Idea, this can imply merely that the object has some inferior degree of a determinable quality of which the idea represents the highest degree. A wheel, say, will partake of the Idea of the Circle merely in the sense that it exhibits a certain inferior degree of the quality roundness, whereof the Idea of the Circle as defined in geometry represents the highest degree" (Wedberg, 1955, p. 50).

11   Hintikka, 1967. Briefly, Hintikka showed that there was a tendency among ancient Greek thinkers to think of temporally indefinite sentences as typical vehicles of communication, which, like Quine's "occasion sentences" can change truth values, unlike Quine's "eternal sentences." When such sentences are about changing objects they can change in truth value; when they are about unchanging objects they cannot. Thus, given the Platonic assumption that forms are unchanging and everlasting, it follows that whatever is true of a Platonic form is always true; whereas whatever is true of sensible participants, which change, will sometime or other become false. Hintikka also

showed that there was a tendency among ancient Greek thinkers "to think of knowledge in terms of some sort of direct acquaintance with the objects of knowledge, e.g., in terms of seeing or witnessing them." And Plato does indeed seem to think in the *Republic*, in the discussion of dialectic (511), of the faculty of knowledge as a kind of "mind's eye" which "sees," inspects, and examines nonsensible, intelligible objects (see also White [1976, pp. 91–3]). If we put together these two tendencies, we can see how the existence of objects immune to change is a necessary condition for the faculty of knowledge to perform its function successfully, producing only mental states which are free from error; given that human beings, unlike the gods, do not have the power of continuous mental inspection of objects.

12 In 1980 I argued that in the *Timaeus* the creation of the world by the divine craftsman presupposes the theory of the form of the good, in so far as it presupposes that the forms are the best objects of their kind.

13 In the *Republic* itself (477a, 478d, 478e, 479ac), Plato repeats and amplifies his statement that forms "entirely are" whereas sensible objects "both are and are not" in ways consistent with the *Symposium* passage.

14 Vlastos (1983) argued for the predicative interpretation and against the existential interpretation of Cross and Woozley, obviously assuming that the two interpretations are incompatible.

15 *Republic* 596a: "We are in the habit, I take it, of positing a single idea or form in the case of the various multiplicities to which we give the same name."

6

Aristotle's Criticism of Plato's Form of the Good

In the *Republic* Plato departed from the Socratic method and began a new tradition in moral philosophy. In the early dialogues Socrates cross-examined the ethical views of others and proposed his own theories of virtue and happiness without very strong metaphysical assumptions. But in the *Republic* Plato proposed a bold new theory of the form of the good, which he made a foundation for his ethical theory, and which rested squarely on his theory of forms and the strong epistemology that goes with it (White, 1992). Thus in Plato's early and middle dialogues we already have two contrasting traditions in the history of ethics: ethics with and ethics without Platonic metaphysics; and what sometimes goes with these two traditions, ethics as an exact science and ethics as a rational discipline of what is true for the most part.

While working out his own theory of the good, Aristotle pauses, both in the *Nicomachean Ethics* (*NE*), Bk. I, ch. 6, and the *Eudemian Ethics* (*EE*), Bk. I, ch. 8, to criticize severely Plato's theory of the form of the good and the epistemology that goes with it. He breaks decisively with Plato's theory of a transcendent (separate form of) good, even with the concept of a universal immanent good, and the idea of ethics as an exact science. The most important concept in ethics is not the form of the good – there is no such form – but the good for a person, something attainable. Neither can ethics be an exact science like mathematics; it is a rational discipline which deals with what is true for the most part – more like medicine or biology (Anagnostopoulos, 1993). With some notable exceptions such as Spinoza, the moderns favor the idea that ethics is not an exact science, though Rawls, who seems to hold this view, still speaks of a "moral geometry"; they also favor the idea that ethics should be as free as possible of metaphysical controversies. But the debate is far from over, as can be seen from Rawls's article "Justice as Fairness: Political, not Metaphysical" (1985), which disavows the metaphysical assumptions his critics attribute to him and tries to free ethics and social normative theory from philosophy's metaphysical and epistemological controversies (see also McCabe, 2000).

Aristotle does not always expound sufficiently the theory he is criticizing, though he does so more than recent commentators.[1] It is not clear he recognizes the complexity of Plato's theory, beyond attributing to Plato the view that the good "is something common, universal and single" (*NE*, 1096a28); he might assume his audience is familiar with it. Sometimes he writes as if the form of the good is on a par with any other Platonic form, the form by participation in which things are good. But there are also signs he recognizes the greater complexity of the theory: for example he attributes to Plato the view that good can be predicated of every thing there is (in every category), which would make the good abstract enough to be at the top of the Divided Line, and in this sense universal; and he denies that lasting longer makes anything better, which hints at Plato's view that being eternal is a good-making characteristic. There is also some evidence that in his criticism he takes the forms to be ideal exemplars, something required by the theory of the form of the good. So even though he does not bring in explicitly the distinction between proper and ideal attributes, which he himself makes elsewhere, there is evidence that the theory he had in mind for criticism is close to the theory of the *Republic* I expounded earlier. Equally significant, the heavy and detailed criticisms he makes of Plato's form of the good shows convincingly that he thought there *was* a theory that could be understood sufficiently to be criticized, contrary to the modern prevailing view that Plato had only a dim vision whose obscurity he tried to cloak in impressive artistic similes, metaphors, and allegories.

In *EE* (Bk. I, ch. 8) Aristotle gives us more of an introduction to the theory he criticizes by telling us how "the Platonists" may have argued for it. The Platonists say that the best of all things is the good itself;[2] and that the good itself is that which is first among goods and the cause (by its presence) of all other things being good. But, they continue, (only?) the form of the good has the last two properties: being the first among goods, since if the form of the good did not exist nothing else good would exist; and being the cause of all good things, since it is by participation or similarity to the form of the good that things are good. Hence the good itself is identical with the form of the good.

The *NE* and *EE* also make it clear that Aristotle distinguished between the good being a transcendent, separate Platonic form and the good being an immanent universal common to all good things; and he attacked both theories. Moreover, he may be criticizing not only Plato's theory in the

Republic, but also "Platonists" more generally, including Pythagorean Platonists who may have thought that numbers are good and that the form of the good is identical with unity.

We are in an advantageous position to understand and assess Aristotle's criticisms against Plato, I trust, since we have worked out a version of Plato's theory of the form of the good in the *Republic*, which allows us to consider the accuracy as well as the soundness of the criticisms.

1   *Aristotle's Arguments from Priority*

Aristotle begins in *NE*, Bk. I, ch. 6, with a fairly technical argument. Those who introduced the theory of the form of the good, he claims, did not postulate forms for groups of things within which they recognized priority and posteriority. This is the reason why they did not postulate a form common to all numbers. But good is said in the categories of substance, quality, relation, and so on; and substance is prior to quality or quantity, and hence there is prior and posterior in the class of goods. Therefore, they should not postulate a form for good.

Now the theory of the categories is a premise to this argument, used to show that among good things there is prior and posterior. And the priority in question is priority in nature: items in all the other categories would not exist unless primary substances existed. But the *Categories* is certainly an anti-Platonic work, and not neutral ground for an argument against the form of the good.[3] The Platonists did not recognize the priority of Aristotelian substances over items in the other categories and would not arrange goods according to such priority.

In *EE*, Bk. I, ch. 8, however, we have a similar argument which does not rely on the theory of the categories, and which also illuminates the remark about no common form for numbers. Here Aristotle argues that there is not any good which is first among all goods and also common to all goods and separate from them, as the Platonists claim; because in things in which there is a prior and a posterior there is not anything which is common to them and separate from them. In turn, this is so because, if there were a separate element common to all members of the series (formed by a prior and a posterior among goods), it would be prior to the first element of the series (and thus the first element would not be the first element); and *this* in turn is so because, if the separate and common element were destroyed (or did not exist), the first element would be destroyed (or would not exist).

Consider, for example, the double as the first element of the series of multiples.[4] If we postulate multiplicity as a separate form common to all the multiples, this form would be prior to the double and *it* would then be the first element in the series, since if multiplicity did not exist the double would not exist either; but the double *is* the first element in the series of multiples. Hence we cannot postulate multiplicity as a separate form for the series of multiples. This argument clearly has the form of a reductio: reduction to absurdity or falsehood and consequent denial of the hypothesis.

This argument, unlike the previous one in *NE*, pretends to be a purely internal criticism: it tries to prove an inconsistency between two propositions both of which are attributed to the Platonists: that the good itself is first among goods and that the form of the good is common to all goods and separate from them. And it gives an argument why this is so, without simply assuming that the Platonists did not postulate forms for classes within which they recognized a prior and posterior, and without assuming the priority of substance over other categories. Hence this argument does not have the faults we found in the previous one.

However, it seems to equivocate on the notion of priority, at least in the example.[5] The double is the first element in the series of multiples because it is the smallest multiple (priority in quantity); not because if the double did not exist the next multiple would not exist (priority in nature), even though the latter may be true. Therefore, if multiplicity were a separate form common to all multiples, it would not follow that it would then be the first in the series of multiples and the double would be the second. The alleged fact, that if the separate multiplicity did not exist the double would not exist, would certainly not imply that multiplicity is a smaller multiple than the double! But this last ground would be the only relevant ground for putting the separate form multiplicity as the first element in the series of multiples, and then claiming that this is false since the double is indeed the first element in that series. It is possible for the double as the smallest multiple to be the first multiple in the series of multiples and also for multiplicity to be a separate Platonic form without which no multiple of the series would exist.

Similarly, if the form of the good is that by which all goods are good and separate from them, it follows that if it did not exist none of the other goods would exist; but it does not in turn follow that the form of the good would then take the place of the first good in the series of all goods arranged from the greatest good to the smallest in, say, quantity.

Unfortunately it is not clear what series of goods Aristotle had in mind supposed to parallel the series of multiples of which the double is the smallest and first multiple. This series of multiples is presumably formed, without Platonic or anti-Platonic assumptions, by taking the class of multiples, beginning with the smallest multiple, the double, and adding units successively to obtain greater and greater multiples. And it has a prior and posterior in it, given the way it is formed: the prior is the smaller, and the prosterior the greater, multiple in succession. All this would be also admitted without Platonic or anti-Platonic assumptions.

Suppose then that, without Platonic or anti-Platonic assumptions, we take the class of all good things (*not* including the form of the good in this initial class) and arrange them in some order of priority and posteriority parallel to the class of multiples. For example if all goods are commensurable we can arrange them from the greatest to the smallest in quantity, as we might arrange the wealth of all wealthy people; or, if some goods are more inclusive than others, perhaps we can arrange them from the most to the least inclusive, as Aristotle might arrange good lives from those that include all the things good in themselves to those that include fewer; or if goods make life worth living, perhaps we can arrange them from those that make life most worthwhile to those that make it least so; or if some goods are preferable to others, we can arrange them all from the most to the least preferred.

Now the same problem for Aristotle's argument seems present in all these series: if a Platonist held that all these good things, however they may be arranged into such priorities, are good by participation in a common and separate form good, it would follow that if this form did not exist none of these goods would exist; but it would not follow in turn from this that such a form would then be prior to the highest of these goods in quantity, or inclusiveness, or worthwhileness, or preferability; because all these priorities are different from, and are not implied by, the natural priority which the form would have.

It has been suggested that the argument relies on two assumptions we find in Plato's dialogues: "the Idea [Platonic form] is viewed . . . as a supreme instance possessing in fullness that which particulars strive with different degrees of success to obtain, and as a separate universal" (Allan, 1963–4, p. 284). The main merit of this suggestion is that it supplies from within Plato's theory the premise needed to form a series of goods that might include the form of the good as its first member without equivocation on priority.[6]

If we apply the first assumption to the form of good, then the form of the good exemplifies goodness to the highest possible degree, and so it is the best of all goods; and it would also be a separate universal goodness.[7] Let us consider how the argument would next proceed. We form again an initial class of all goods without the form of the good; then we arrange them from the best to the least good, in one or another of the ways already mentioned; the Platonists would now add to this class the form of the good since it itself also is a good; and they would also allow, according to the present suggestion, that in this new set the form of the good, and not the best good of the initial class, would be the first member of the series, since the form of the good is the perfect exemplar of goodness and so a greater (or "better") good than any other good.

This argument might avoid equivocation on priority, but it does not seem very accurate to Aristotle's text, and in any case it fails as a reductio. It is not accurate because it does not use the premise that if the form of the good did not exist no other good would exist, as in the text, but instead the premise that the form of the good is the perfect exemplar of goodness. More importantly, it fails as a reductio, because there is no evident absurdity nor falsehood in its conclusion, as there is in the conclusion of the argument about the double, namely, that the form multiplicity would be a smaller multiple than the double.

However, it might be thought that the argument is now a reductio by generating an infinite regress: if the form of the good is added to the initial set as a good and the best good, then, by the Platonic principle of the one over many, there must be a form good separate from any and all members of the new set, by virtue of which all the members of that set are good. Thus we have a second form good, and by application of the same principle over the new set a third form, and so on. Thus we have a "third man" type of regress, perhaps. But even if we allow that this new form of good is a second form good, and thus allow the generation of the regress, it does not follow that this new form good would now be better than all the other goods in that set, and that thus *it* would be the first member, rather than the initial form good. The most that would follow is that both forms good are the best goods, and we would have a maximal class of best goods (the set in which these two are equally good, but each better than any good outside this set). In any case, the argument so conceived is simply a version of the third man argument using the form good as a sample, rather the the form large or the form woman. It is far removed from our text and not directed particularly against the theory of the form of the good.

Finally, even if we set all other objections aside, Aristotle's argument does not touch Plato's theory of the form of the good in the *Republic* as I have interpreted it. The criticism would seem to be directed against a naive view in which the form of the good is on a par with every other form, as the form by participation in which all good things are good; in this naive theory we would have a direct comparison with respect to goodness between the form of the good and all the other goods, and in such a comparison the form of the good is said to be the best, better than any other good. But in the sophisticated theory of the *Republic* I expounded in the last chapter, no such direct comparison can be made. In that theory the form of the good is the form by virtue of which all the other forms are the best objects of their kind; in that theory the form of the good being the best good can only mean that it is good absolutely, rather than a good so and so. The form of the good is that by virtue of which, say, the form line is the best line there is or can be, and similarly with the form woman, the form city, and so on. In the set of all lines the form line would indeed be the best line; but this is a harmless result. We cannot now add the form of the good to the set of all lines and pronounce the form the best of all members in this set; the form of the good is not a better line than the form line or any other line, since it is not a line at all! Even less so can we add the form good to the sets of all lines, all good human beings and all good cities, and so on, and then infer that the form good is the best of all these things. Nothing in the known Platonic corpus authorizes such an inference, and it is highly doubtful that the resulting view is coherent.

But there may have been "Platonists" who had the naive version of the theory, against which the arguments in the text do apply, though even there unsuccessfully.

2   *Breaking up Goodness: Aristotle's Argument from Homonymy*

Aristotle's second important argument, in *NE*, Bk. I, ch. 6, is that there is no single universal good nor a separate Platonic form good, because good "is said in many ways," in as many ways as being is said and as there are categories. Here Aristotle is arguing not only against Plato's view that there is a *transcendent* ("separate") form good "by which all things are useful and beneficial", but also against a more modest view, that there is an *immanent* attribute good present in all good things.

This argument has received a lot of attention,[8] and its major propositions have been disputed, for example by G. H. von Wright and G. E. Moore, in a controversy that echoes Aristotle's fight with Plato.[9]

Aristotle argues as follows:

> Further, since good is said in as many ways as being[10] (for it is predicated both in the category of substance, as of god and of reason, and in quality, i.e. of the virtues, and in quantity, i.e. of that which is moderate, and in relation, i.e. of the useful, and in time, i.e. of the right opportunity, and in place, i.e. of the right locality and the like), clearly it cannot be something universally present in all cases and single; for then it could not be predicated in all the categories but in one only. (1096a23–9, Ross transl.)

This argument has two apparent faults. First, it relies on Aristotle's own theory of categories rather cryptically: from the premise that good can be predicated of items in the several categories Aristotle directly infers that "it is said in many ways"; and from the latter that good cannot be some single thing universally present in all good things. But Aristotle does not tell us why he thinks either inference is valid.[11] Second, the theory of the categories is clearly anti-Platonic and seems to beg the question against all Platonic interpretations of very abstract and universal terms such as goodness and being. It is worth asking whether the argument could be freed from these two faults.[12]

The argument can be freed from these faults if, first, Aristotle can show that good (or rather *to agathon*) is said in many ways without appeal to the categories, something that von Wright tries to do, for example;[13] and if, in turn, Aristotle can show that we can validly infer from good being said in many ways that good cannot be one and the same property in all good things.

Aristotle can try to do so by using his definition of homonymy as a major premise:

> When things have only a name in common and the definition of being which corresponds to the name is different, they are called homonymous. Thus, for example, both man and a picture are animals. These have only a name in common and the definition of being which corresponds to the name is different; for if one is to say what being an animal is for each of them, one will give two distinct definitions. When things have the name in common and the definition of being which corresponds to the name is the same, they are called

synonymous. Thus, for example, both a man and an ox are animals. Each of these is called by a common name, an animal, and the definition of being is also the same; for if one is to give the definition of each – what being an animal is for each of them – one will give the same definition. (*Categories*, 1a1–6; Ackrill transl.)

Though this is the opening passage of the *Categories*, it does not depend on the anti-Platonic theory of categories contained in that work.[14]

Now in *Topics*, Bk. I, ch. 15, Aristotle relies on this definition of homonymy and uses it to show the homonymy of good without appeal to categories:

One should examine also the genera of the predications corresponding to the word to see whether they are the same in all cases. For if they are not the same, what is said is clearly homonymous. Thus, for example, the good in food is the productive in pleasure but in medicine it is the productive of health. . . . It follows that the good is homonymous. (107a3–12, Ross transl.)

This criterion of homonymy clearly connects with Aristotle's theory of definition *per genus et differentium* and with the definition of homonymy in the *Categories*. A difference in genus would show a difference in definition, the two definitions would not overlap, and so we would have homonymy. The definition of homonymy provides us with a better test than simply differences in senses or meanings, a test of "deep signification" or "deep meaning," as Shields calls it; because its application can show differences in essence signification, a difference in basic explanatory properties.[15] If the definiens of good are different in different kinds of applications, the properties signified by these different definiens are different.

To apply all this to good (or rather to *to agathon*), we would need at least one undisputed example where two things are good but there is a definition of good which is true of one but not of the other, or at least a genus of good which is true of one but not of the other. But here Aristotle faces another great difficulty: there is no uncontroversial definition of good he can appeal to. Indeed, as is well known, at least one notable philosopher, G. E. Moore, has argued that good cannot be defined at all. And in Aristotle's own time, by placing good at the very top of the Divided Line in the *Republic*, Plato implied that good has no genus and so cannot be defined, at least by genus and difference.

But what of the example from the *Topics* about the good in food and the good in medicine? The argument seems to be as follows. Suppose someone were to say of some particular food, say, chicken, that it is good, and of some particular medicine, say, penicillin, that it is good. The term good may be true of both but the genus of good is different in the two cases: in the case of food the genus is productive of pleasure, for penicillin it is productive of health. Hence the definition of good is different in the two cases and the two things are good homonymously; if so, what good signifies in one case is different from what it signifies in the other, and there is not a single property, common to the two cases, but two different properties by which these two things are good.

But how can we be sure that the genus of good is different in the two cases? Aristotle's example is controversial, to say the least. Surely some of the good of food is also that it is productive of health: if the chicken were delicious but poisonous we would not say that it was good, though pleasant. Does the good of food then have two genera, productive of pleasure and productive of health? How can that be if neither genus is subordinate to the other? Perhaps being productive of pleasure and being productive of health are species of a higher order property, for example being productive of good, which they have in common.

Shields examines two interpretations of the argument in *NE*, Bk. I, ch. 6, which "appeal neither to word sense nor to the doctrine of categories as such." One is Ackrill's proposal that the "criteria for commending different things as good are diverse and fall into different categories; and this is enough to show that 'good' does not stand for some single common quality" (Shields, 1999, pp. 201–4). Shields considers two interpretations of criteria, evidential and constitutive, and shows that the argument is unsuccessful in both cases.

In fact, on Ackrill's interpretation Aristotle's argument is both too weak and too strong. It is too weak because it is false to suppose that the different "criteria" (evidential or constitutive) we can use for calling different things good entitle us to infer that good is homonymous and nonunivocal. There are theories of goodness which suppose that the criteria or reasons for calling things good can differ while the definition of good remains the same; for example the theory of goodness of John Rawls. His definition in simpler cases is: "A is a good X if and only if A has the properties (to a higher degree than the average or standard X) which it is rational to want in an X, given what X's are used for, or expected to do, and the like. . . ." The properties it is rational to want in a house are different from the properties it is rational to want in a watch, but that does not show that good in "good watch" and "good house" does not signify the same property; the definition of good is the same in both cases, and the property can be the same, namely, having the properties it is rational to want in that kind of thing; even though the "criteria" we would give for the goodness of a watch and the goodness of a house are indeed different; Rawls even claims that the same definition explains why the reasons or criteria differ (1971, ch. 7, pp. 399ff., 405ff.).

On the other hand, if we forgo this criticism and accept the disputed premise, Aristotle's argument would be too strong. The number of reasons (criteria in either sense) why things are good is indefinite, if not infinite: every time we change from one kind of thing to another, it would seem, the reasons for calling things of the new kind good are different; the reasons for calling foods, medicines, cows, music, pleasures, virtues, and health good are all different. But if so, we now have a tremendous proliferation of definitions of good, as Ackrill himself noted; and this seems to be a *reductio ad absurdum* of Aristotle's argument.

The other version of the argument Shields discusses is the functional interpretation of McDonald,[16] which is set in the wider context of *NE*, Bk. I, ch. 7, which contains the famous function argument. Shields argues that this argument is unsuccessful in so far as it relies on the proposition that the categories themselves are functional kinds. But a functional argument can also be constructed without reliance on the categories, and Shields constructs it as follows:

1. For a functional kind F, the good for F consists in "that for the sake of which" Fs act.
2. That for the sake of which the members of any functional kind F act will be the end for those Fs.
3. Hence, for the functional kind F, the good for Fs consists in their end.
4. The ends for different functional kinds necessarily differ.
5. Hence, what goodness consists in for different functional kinds necessarily differs.
6. If (5) is true, then goodness is non-univocal.
7. Hence, goodness is non-univocal. (Shields, 1999, p. 205)

This seems a fair interpretation of part of McDonald's argument, the part which does not rely on the idea that the categories themselves are functional kinds. It relies on Aristotle's own functional theory of good, which seems similar to Plato's.[17] Shields (1999) says that "(7) is not established by (1)–(6)."[18]

I think a Platonist could reasonably say that there is a conflation here between the good of something and the property of being good (or goodness), parallel to a conflation between the end of something and the property of being an end. The fact that different kinds of things, actions and activities have different ends, as Aristotle and Plato both fully recognize, does not show that there is no property common to all ends, namely the property of "that for the sake of which something occurs (or is done)," or the property of being an end. Health and victory are different ends of different enterprises (medicine and strategy), but they are both ends, that for the sake of which physicians and generals act. Similarly, the good of various actions and activities is indeed different for different actions and activities – health for medicine, victory for strategy; but this does not show that the property of being good is different in the two cases. The shift can be seen in Shields's reconstruction of the argument: from "*the* good for" in (3) to "goodness" in (5).[19]

3 Aristotle's Argument from Final and Instrumental Goods

There is *one* noncontroversial distinction among good things, the distinction between instrumental and noninstrumental goods, which is common ground between Plato and Aristotle, as well as their modern counterparts in this dispute, G. E. Moore and G. H. von Wright. This can be appealed to in the present case to try to show that good is homonymous after all. The argument might go as follows: whatever the true definition of noninstrumental good, the definition of instrumental good will not be the same but rather something like "productive of noninstrumental good."[20] When we call exercise good and the experience of smelling a rose good, for example, the definition of good will not be the same in both cases: exercise can be good in that it is a means to the good of health, but smelling a rose can be good without it being a means to anything. So good is used homonymously at least in such cases, and there cannot be a either a single universal or a form good by the presence of, or participation in, which both exercise and smelling a rose are good.

Now in our text Aristotle has the Platonists concede this point but argue that there is a universal good common to all noninstrumental goods: the theory of the form of the good, he has the Platonists say, was meant to apply to these goods, things that are good in themselves (*NE*, Bk. I, ch. 6, 1096b8–25). And Aristotle goes on to attack the remaining view that all things good in themselves are good by the presence of the same form or universal good. So we have a two-stage argument (or possibly, two arguments), and as Shields remarks, the dialectic of the passage is not all that clear. Does Aristotle mean that the first stage of the argument does not count against the Platonists, because they meant to apply the theory of the form of the good *only* to things good in themselves to begin with? Or does he mean that the first stage of the argument refutes the Platonists' original theory (that *all goods* are good by the presence of a universal or a form good), and then he goes on to refute even the restricted remnant (that all things good in themselves are so by the presence of a universal or form good)?

Shields favors the second interpretation; indeed he thinks the first stage of the argument is the *only* one of Aristotle's arguments which is successful in refuting the Platonic good or a universal immanent good. I favor the first interpretation. I think Aristotle is correct in supposing that Plato did not regard the distinction as a basis for argument against his postulation of the form of the good; and I think Aristotle correctly agrees with Plato in this. For one thing, Plato does not hold the naive theory of universal good, according to which the form of the good is that by participation of which all good things are good. So far as I know, Plato never applies the one over many principle directly and simply to the set of all good things. For another, Plato distinguishes between the good and the beneficial, he defines the beneficial as "the productive of good," and he makes it clear that the relation "productive of" is not participation (*Hippias Major*, 296–7; see Woodruff's fine discussion [1982, pp. 70–7]). If exercise is good (only) as a means to health and health is good in itself, then exercise is good only in the sense of being productive of good; given the definition of the beneficial, exercise is good not by participating in the form of the good but in the form of the beneficial. Plato's definition of the beneficial amounts to an analysis of "exercise is good" into "excercise is productive of good"; in the latter statement the predicate is not good but productive of good; and good in that statement is in turn predicated not of exercise but of something good in itself – health. The full analysis of "exercise is good" would be "exercise is productive of health and health is good." Plato already has two properties or forms here, not one, the good and the beneficial; since his definition of the beneficial makes it clear that it cannot be the same property as the good by reference to which the beneficial is defined.[21]

Going now to the second stage of the argument, Aristotle asks: What belongs to this class of things that are good in themselves? Only the form of the good, or also such things as wisdom, sight, and certain pleasures and honors which would be pursued even alone by themselves? If the former, he says, "the form will be empty" (*NE*, Bk. I, ch. 6); that is, presumably, it will have no participants at all and so there will be nothing which is good by virtue of participating in that form. If the latter, then the account (definition) of the good will have to be the same in them all. But, he continues, "of honor, wisdom, and pleasure, just in respect of their goodness, the accounts are distinct and diverse. The good therefore, is not some common element answering to one Idea" (*NE*, Bk. I, ch. 6).

Once more, Aristotle's argument is cryptic, because he does not complete it by giving the different accounts or definitions of the good of honor, the good of wisdom, the good of pleasure, and so on. We have to go to other texts (and later to Aristotle's own theory of the logic of good) to fill in the argument. In a previous section (*NE*, Bk. I, ch. 4), he had argued that honor is not the good since men pursue it because it is a sign of their virtue; honor is good because and in so far as it a sign or evidence of something else which is good. Again virtue as a disposition is not identical with the good (because it is compatible with being asleep) but is good because its actualization, virtuous activity, is part of the good (happiness, *NE*, Bk. I, chs. 4, 7). And according to his theory of pleasure (*NE*, Bk. X, chs. 3, 4), pleasures are good in so far as, or because, they encourage and re-enforce the virtuous exercise of our practical and theoretical reason, which is good in itself. So, to complete the argument, the definitions of the goodness of honor, virtue, and pleasure, are all different: in the case of honor it is something like "evidence of virtue whose actualization is part of the good"; in the case of virtue it is something like "its actualization is part of the good"; and in the case of pleasure something like "encourages the disposition to rational activity which is good." Therefore, good is said homonymously even in the case of things good in themselves; and so there is no single Platonic form of good nor a universal good common to all these things. Nor is it by any single relation, such as participation, that these various things are related to the good, since the relation differs from case to case.

But one might now question whether on this understanding of the goodness of honor, pleasure, virtue, and the rest of them, these things are good in themselves. To use Aristotle's own test,[22] would honor be desired or pursued for itself, even if it were not a sign of virtue? Or virtue for itself, even if its actualization were not constitutive of happiness? Or pleasures if they were not re-enforcements of rational activities? If one says no, as one might be inclined in the case of honors, it would seem to follow that honors are not good in themselves; and in that case they drop out of the anti-Platonic argument as a nonrelevant case. And if one says yes, as one might be inclined to in the case of pleasures, it would seem to follow that the good of pleasure is not *simply* that it encourages rational activities; in *that* respect pleasure is not good in itself. Aristotle seems to be giving accounts of the goodness of honor, virtue, wisdom, and pleasure, which make their goodness depend in some way or other on the goodness of happiness; but in that respect they are not good in themselves, that is, in isolation from any relation to some other good. So far as this argument is concerned, there remains the possibility that the respect in which pleasure is good in itself, if it is at all, may well have something in common with the respect in which virtue or reason are good in themselves, if they are. If there is a genuine class of things good in themselves, Aristotle's argument has failed to destroy the possibility that they are good in themselves by some relation to a universal or transcendent good.

4   The Attack on the Ideality of the Form of the Platonic Good

Aristotle's next important argument attacks the separateness and ideality of the forms and of the form of the good:

> And one might ask the question, what in the world they mean by "a thing itself", if (as is the case) in "man himself" and in a particular man the account [definition] is one and the same? For in so far as they are man, they will in no respect differ; and if this is so, neither will "good itself" and particular goods, in so far as are good. But again it [the form of the good] will not be good any the more for being eternal, since that which lasts long is no whiter than that which perishes in a day. (1096a34–b5, Ross transl.)

In the first part of this passage, another cryptic argument, Aristotle asks what the Platonists can mean by "itself" in such phrases as "the Good itself," "Man itself," "Beauty itself" – phrases typically used by Plato in the dialogues to signify the forms good, man, beauty, as existing separately from their sensible participants.[23] He claims that the definition of the form man and of a particular man will be the same since they do not differ at all with respect to being man. What then can be the difference between a particular man as man and the form man, the difference signified by the phrase "itself"? And similarly, between the form good and particular goods? Here, we actually seem to have implicit Aristotle's distinction between the form man *qua* man and the form man *qua* form.

In the second half of the passage, Aristotle gives what he takes to be the Platonic answer to his question, an answer in terms of the *ideal* or *formal* attributes of the forms, the attributes the forms have *qua* forms: the difference is that the form man and the form good have the *ideal* attribute of being eternal, whereas their participants do not. And now Aristotle criticizes *this* difference. The criticism is that the ideal attribute of being eternal does not make a form *what it is to a higher degree* than its sensible participants which last only a little while; so there will be no difference with respect to being good between the good itself and the goods that participate in it, and the good itself will not be a greater good for being eternal, just as a white that lasts longer is no more white than a white that perishes in a day.[24]

Now in the first part of the argument, Aristotle appears to be assuming the Vlastos–Code interpretation of formal causality (see chapter 5 above): if the form man is the formal cause of Socrates being a man, then Socrates has all the defining features (proper attributes) of the form. So the form man and Socrates will not differ *qua* man. Presumably, if the definitions are not the same, then by Aristotle's definition of homonymy, man will be said in different ways in the two cases; and if so, the Platonic explication of, say, Socrates being a man, namely, that he participates in the form man, will be fallacious – an equivocation.[25] But if the form man and a particular man do not differ at all with respect to being man, how can the form man be a better man (indeed the best man) than a particular man? For similar reasons, the form good and Socrates, if Socrates is good, will not differ *qua* good and so the good will not be anything better than Socrates *qua* good.

But this seems to overlook the approximation interpretation of the relation of forms to sensibles: which concedes that sensible participants have the defining features (proper attributes) of the forms they participate in, but maintains that they have them to a lesser degree. A "better human being" *can* mean a person who has reached the age of reason or physical maturity and so is more completely a human being than an adolescent or a child, even though both have all the defining features of human being. And, Plato would add, no human being ever reaches completely and so exemplifies perfectly the human form. Except for the last statement, Aristotle may have to agree. Aristotle's theory of the good for man, as we shall see in the next chapter, is perfectionist, and it seems to allow for just that interpretation of better man we gave earlier. His definition of man is rational animal. And his theory of the good man and the good for man is that it consists in the exercise of practical and theoretical reason in accordance with the excellences (or virtues). Now a person can certainly be more or less rational (she can reason more or less well theoretically and practically), and so more or less rational animal; and the more so she is, the better a human being she is. Aristotle's theory of man and of a good man allows for all this, and in these respects it is not all that different from Plato. So if we lay aside the Platonic separation of the essence of man from individual men, Aristotle's present criticisms may be inconsistent with his own perfectionist theory of a good man and the good for man. In any case, the forms and their sensible participants having the same proper (definitional) features does not exclude the forms being ideal exemplars and so being the best objects of their kind, and thus the form of the good could still be what Plato said it was – the form common to all the ideal exemplar forms.

Perhaps, however, the point of the passage is different: if all the forms and their participants have in common the defining (proper) attributes of the forms, then this is also true of the form of the good. And if this is so, then the form of the good and its participants will have all the defining features of *that* form, and if this is so the form cannot be *better* than its participants. But this treats the form of the good as if it were on a par with any other Platonic form, as is shown by Aristotle's treatment of man and good, as if they were parallel. But they are not analogous in the relevant respect in Plato's theory, and they may not be in any theory of good. The form of the good is the most abstract form in Plato's theory; the proper features of the form of the good are the ideal attributes of all the other forms, abstracted from *their* proper attributes: in our shorthand, being perfectly what they are and nothing but that. The form of the good is a greater good than the form man only in the sense that it is goodness itself and not the partial goodness of some particular kind. When we come to sensible participants, the story of their goodness is different: if they are good, they do not have the defining feature of the form of the good: for none are perfectly what they are and nothing but that. If Socrates is a good human being, that means that he has all the defining features of human beings, perhaps to a higher degree than the average human being, though never as perfectly as the form human. If rationality, say, is a defining attribute of human beings, Socrates can be good in having that attribute to a higher degree than the average human being; he does not have perfect human rationality, he can be superstitious as well as rational. What makes him good is that he approximates to a higher degree the ideal attribute of perfect rationality, and by virtue of that the form of the good. But he is certainly not as good as the form man, not to speak of the good itself.

Now in the second half of our passage, as we saw, Aristotle brings in an ideal attribute of forms, their eternity, and he claims that it is not a good-making characteristic. The problem with this criticism is that it proceeds as if for Plato being eternal is a good-making characteristic *all by itself*. But being eternal is not the only ideal attribute of Platonic forms, and it may be a good-making characteristic only given other properties. We saw that, according to the *Symposium* and the *Republic*, besides being eternal, each form exists separately; further, each form is what it is (its proper attributes) in every "aspect" or "part" of itself, no matter compared to what, and to all who apprehend it; whereas its sensible objects participate in or resemble the form but fail to have its ideal attributes. I summed this up by saying that each form is completely what it is, and nothing but that, whereas its sensible participants are never completely such, and they are many other things besides. This is what being a form is, and what makes a form an ideal exemplar, the best thing of its kind and the best thing of its kind to know. To take an example favorable to Plato, the form line satisfies completely the Euclidean definition of line, "Length without breadth,"[26] whereas sensible lines always fall short of it: for example they always have some breadth however little, they change, from some points of view they may appear as surfaces, and they may have all sorts of accidental characteristics such color and a particular length. When we separate the essence of line, captured by the definition, from sensible lines we free it from the defects of materiality, space, and accidental features, so it can be completely line and nothing but line; and when we make it eternal we freeze it, as it were, in that perfect state, and that is what the form line is, conceived as an ideal exemplar. So it is not true, as Aristotle charges, that Plato thought that by simply being an eternal F the form F is a better F than an F that lasts a little while, except pos-sibly epistemologically. Being immune to change and being eternal are good-making characteristics of the forms, *given* their other ideal features – being perfectly what they are and nothing but that. Immunity to change, immutability, or eternity, are epistemological requirements for Plato: as we saw in the last chapter, these are properties objects must have if they are to be knowable. Thus the forms must have these properties if they are to be knowable. What makes the forms "the best objects to know," however, is not only this, but also that they are what they are perfectly and nothing but that; in short, they are "the best objects of their kind." Aside from the epistemological requirement, we could compare here eternity for forms to stability or efficiency for just institutions. Just institutions that are also stable (or, also efficient) are better than equally just institutions that are unstable. But stability is not by itself a virtue of institutions: it is a dubious virtue of unjust institutions (since it is likely that the stability will prolong the injustice), and efficiency would make unjust institutions worse than equally unjust but inefficient ones. The fact that a white that lasts longer is not more white than an ephemeral one does *not* show that if we had a sample of the purest possible white we would not want it to be as immune to change as possible. We would want just that; for then it would be the best possible measure of pure white and the best white. It is no accident that we want constant temperatures for our standard measures.

5   *The Attack on the Practicability and Usefulness of the Platonic Good*

In the last paragraph of our chapter, *NE*, Bk. I, ch. 6, Aristotle dismisses the theory of the form of the good as belonging to another branch of philosophy, not ethics but metaphysics. For "even if there is some one good which is universally predicable of goods or is capable of separate existence, itself by itself, it is clear that it would not be what human beings could do or possess; but we are now seeking some such thing" (Ross transl.).

A Platonic form is not the sort of thing one *could do* nor the sort of thing one *could possess*, but the good for a person must be just such a thing; so the form of the good is irrelevant to ethics and can be dismissed as a subject fit for metaphysics.[27] No clearer statement is needed to record Aristotle's attempt to free ethics from Platonic metaphysics.

Plato was aware of this objection, though, and answered it in the *Republic*, 480cd and 499–505; and so was Aristotle, who records the answer and objects to *it*. "Perhaps, however, some might think it worth while to know this [the form good] with a view to the goods that can be done or can be possessed; for having this as a sort of paradigm we shall know better the goods that are good for us, and if we know them shall attain them."

But, Aristotle claims, though this answer has some plausibility, it "clashes with the procedure of the sciences" (*NE*, Bk. I, ch. 6). For all the sciences aim to some good but none seeks knowledge of *the* (form of the) good; an improbable situation if this good were such a great aid. Besides, he adds, it is hard to see how a carpenter or a weaver would be benefited in his craft by knowing this "good itself"; or how "the man who viewed the idea itself will be a better doctor or general thereby."[28]

This last criticism, that Plato's good is useless, is similar to Sir Karl Popper's famous criticism:

Since it [the form of the good] is the sun and source of light in the world of Forms, it enables the philosopher-painter to discern its objects. Its function is therefore of the greatest importance for the founder of the city. But this purely formal information is all we get. Plato's Idea of the Good nowhere plays a more direct ethical or political role; never do we hear which deeds are good or produce good . . . [by] recourse to the idea of Good. . . . This empty formalism is still more marked in the *Philebus* . . . (1966, pp. 145–6)

Aristotle had attacked the practicability and the usefulness of the form of the good, and Popper has joined him in attacking its usefulness.

Plato would certainly be most sensitive to both objections. We saw that he says the form of the good is "that which every soul pursues and for its sake does all that it does . . ." But if the form of the good is neither *do*able nor *have*able, what sense is there in pursuing it? And if it gives us no information we can use in making choices, what sense is there in doing everything for its sake?

We saw that Aristotle is aware of Plato's answer to the practicability objection. Though the forms are not doable nor haveable, knowledge of them could still be valuable because they can be stable paradigms, ideal exemplars always there to be approximated in this world: no one can be a perfectly just man nor a perfect man, but if we know what these things are we can try to come close to these ideals – indeed this is the distinction between perfection and excellence. Plato likens the philosopher-king to a painter (*Republic*, 484 and 499–505) who tries to embody on canvas his ideal of the most beautiful man. It is no objection to his painting, that there is no such man. The philosopher-king, once he learns the perfect exemplars, will fashion his own soul after the ideal forms, and he will take the human soul and the human city as his canvas and fashion them also after the forms. Aristotle's objection to this is unsound: the special sciences are not concerned with the form of the good, even though all aim at some good, because goodness is not their subject matter, and because they take the goodness of their aim for granted. Thus medicine aims at producing and preserving health, the goodness of which it takes for granted. And in any case, Aristotle's objection is too strong, since it applies equally well to his own theory: medicine does not study Aristotle's good either, namely, the nature of happiness and virtue.

The last point applies equally well to Aristotle's last criticism, concerning the usefulness of knowledge of the form of the good. It is too strong a demand of *any* theory of good that knowledge of goodness helps one become a better doctor or general. Knowledge of Aristotle's good or happiness, as he characterizes it in *NE*, Bks. I and X, would certainly be of no use to anyone for becoming a better doctor or general, though it might help one become a better person and lead a better life.

But knowledge of the good or of goodness must be useful in some important way: it must be possible to put together knowledge of the good and relevant factual information and thus determine what things are good and how to live. This is a reasonable demand to make of a theory of good, quite distinct from the *un*reasonable demand that one be able to infer *directly* (without recourse to facts) from a theory of good what things are good. Popper is indeed correct to complain that *in fact* Plato does not show that his theory of the form of the good meets even the reasonable demand. One of the most puzzling features of the *Republic* is that Plato does not apply the theory of the form of the good to determine what is a good man and a good city. So the theory of the form of the good sits there, in the middle of the *Republic*, idle. Removed from any evident application it seems not only formal – which is no objection to it – but also useless, empty and barren. It is formal but not useless, however. The fact that Plato does not apply it does not show that it cannot be applied. Popper does not try to understand the theory: he simply puts together its formalism and Plato's not using it and concludes that it is useless. Popper and Aristotle are mistaken in this criticism. Plato's theory is not useless, either by itself or when put together with his functional theory. All theories of good*ness* are formal;[29] perhaps partly because in most of its uses good is an incomplete predicate and partly because good has such a wide range of application. Plato's theory may be the most abstract and formal of them all, because Plato thinks that everything there is partakes to some degree of goodness. But it is not useless. When we put together knowledge of what a human being is and what a human city is with Plato's theory of the form of the good, we obtain paradigms, perfect specimens, of a human being and a human city, and these can function as standards for ethical judgment and reform. The fact that Plato separated these perfect specimens into transcendental forms makes for a prolific ontology, but it does not affect the usefulness of his theory of good.

6   *Putting the Fragments of Goodness Back Together: Focal Meaning*

In his arguments against Plato's form of the good or a universal immanent good, Aristotle presumably does not mean to deny that there is any property "goodness" whatsoever. He holds that there is at least one thing which is synonymously good, namely, happiness. Now clearly there is not just a single happiness but many happinesses; the happiness of Socrates if he is happy, the happiness of Plato if he is happy, the happiness of Aristotle, and so on. And when we predicate good of all these happinesses we are saying that they are good synonymously. So there is at least one set of things whose members are said to be good in the same way, and at least one common good by relation to which all these happinesses are good. We can extend this conclusion to each set of things whose members are said to be good synonymously. Though health and pleasure might be said to be good homonymously because the good of pleasure and the good of health might have different accounts, all healths are presumably good in the same way, no matter whose health it is, and so the good of all healths can have the same account; and similarly with all pleasures, all virtues, all honors, and so on. Presumably, for each set of these different kinds of things there is a property "goodness" which they all have in common and by the presence of which they are good.

Now this opens up the radical possibility that there is an indefinite number of properties of goodness, which are not connected except by the linguistic accident of calling all these things in all these sets good; much as it may be a linguistic accident that minds, products, points, pencils, and musical notes are all called sharp. This possibility would seem to make a shambles of the idea that there is a science or an art of ethics whose subject is goodness.

The doctrine of the categories opens up a less radical possibility, to be sure. If good is predicated across all categories, and anything so predicated is said in as many ways as there are categories, then good is said in as many ways as there are categories. But this is compatible with good being said in a univocal way *within each* category. So, if there are ten categories and good is said synonymously in each, there may be ten different kinds of good, and each can be defined Platonically. This less radical possibility, seems less incoherent and less at odds with our linguistic practices, our intuitions, and our arts and sciences. Perhaps there are ten unrelated kinds of good and ten sciences or arts of ethics?

Faced with either possibility, however, Aristotle recoils, at least in *NE*, Bk. I, ch. 6.[30] He seems to appeal to the theory which G. E. L. Owen called "focal meaning," and now Shields calls "core dependence," to repair the damage and make ethics as a unified science possible again: "But what then do we mean by the good? It is surely not like the things that only chance to have the same name. Are goods one, then, by being derived from one good or by all contributing to one good, or are they rather one by analogy?" (*NE*, Bk. I, ch. 6, 1096b25ff., Ross transl.). The example he goes on to give illustrates the analogy possibility,[31] but the statement also contains the suggestion of core dependence. Perhaps Aristotle thinks some cases of good are going to be analogical, others core dependent; and this may be sufficient for having an art or science of ethics.

There are cases of homonymy in which it is not by chance that several things are called by the same name. Rather they are called by the same name because they are all related in some way or other to *one* of these things which are so named; that one thing is the "focal point" or "the core."[32] The healthy and the medical are Aristotle's prime illustrations of the theory:

> Just as everything which is healthy is related to health, some by preserving health, some by producing health, others by being indicative of health, and others by being receptive of health; and as the medical is relative to the medical art . . . and we shall also discover other things said in ways similar to these . . . so too being is said in many ways, but always relative to some one source. (*Metaphysics*, 1003a34-b6, Ross transl.).

Aristotle goes on to propose a core-dependence account for being within the framework of the categories, to make possible a science of being *qua* being. But we saw earlier that he treats good as parallel to being, which suggests that he thinks core dependence as applicable to good. The application of core dependence to good is meant to elucidate and help us understand not only the anti-Platonic varieties of goodness, but also their non-Platonic unity; a non-Platonic order in an anti-Platonic multiplicity but stong enough to make an art or science of ethics possible.

Shields developed Aristotle's examples and remarks into a sophisticated theory of core dependence (1999, p. 126):

> Aristotle's examples of core-dependent homonymy are intended to illustrate a general form of unity in multiplicity, which some, but not all, non-univocal terms enjoy. By extrapolating from these examples, it is possible to develop a general account of core-dependent homonymy along the general lines of CDH4. According to CDH4, core-dependent homonyms (i) are non-univocal because their accounts [definitions] are discrete [do not completely overlap]; (ii) have core and non-core instances whose relations are constrained by Aristotle's four causal scheme; and (iii) have core instances whose accounts are necessarily cited in the accounts of all derived instances, because they are the

archai of the derived instances in the sense of being asymmetrically prior to them.[33F]

From this general account of core-dependent homonymy (and Shields's intricate construction of it), one can see how difficult it would be to show that Aristotle's account of good conforms to it. Aristotle himself never undertakes to show this, nor is it clear that it is his view. But Shields's fine discussion enables us to see in a sketchy way how such an account might go. First, we have to grant that things that are said to be good are good homonymously, contra Plato; then we need to identify core and noncore instances of good; after that we have to discover whether the noncore instances of good bear to the core instances one or another of Aristotle's four causal relations; and finally, we have to see whether the account of the core instances of good is necessarily cited in the accounts of the noncore instances.

This looks at least as complex and demanding a theory of good as Plato's! And when we consider the vast variety of things that can be good, the application of core-dependent homonymy to good looks formidable – as formitable as the Platonic enterprise of finding a single property or set of properties for all the things that are good. Still, small illustrations are possible, and some big picture alternatives can be discerned.

Physical exercise being good and health being good provide an illustration, since we are fairly confident that physical exercise is an efficient cause of health, producing or preserving it; while the good of health is a formal or final cause of the good of physical exercise. If we assume that health and exercise are homonymously good, and that health being good is the core homonym and exercise being good is the core-dependent homonym, it looks as if the example can satisfy Shields's conditions, given the two relations we are confident of.

But if we now make a big leap to the vast set of all the things that are good, and we assume the anti-Platonic view that good things are homonymously good, the application of the core dependence to this class is anything but easy or clear.

To begin with, which is the core homonym of good? For Aristotle there seem to be at least three candidates. Perhaps human happiness being good is the core homonym; then presumably all other things being good are core dependent on happiness being good. On this hypothesis, to show that the remaining conditions are satisfied for all other things being good would be difficult indeed. The roots of a plant can be good, for example, but this goodness seems in no relevant (core-dependent) way related to human happiness. Aristotle might reply that ethics is concerned only with human good; but then the theory would not apply to all good things; and Aristotle would have a theory of human good, but not of good. Even aside from this, it is not clear how all other human goods would satisfy the relevant conditions of being related to human happiness. Here one might plausibly suppose that Aristotle would rely on the complex means–ends relations and part-to-whole relations that he works out between all other human goods and happiness. We get a glimpse of some of these relations in Aristotle's statement, at the end of his criticism of Plato (in *EE*, Bk. I, ch. 8), of what kind of good he is looking for:

> The good we are looking for is: best as end, as health, e.g. is best as the end of medicine; the cause of the goodness of all goods under it, as health is the cause of the goodness of wholesome food or exercise, the latter being the efficient causes of health existing, not its goodness; first among goods, as health, e.g. is first among the goods of the body; the end of all the goods practicable for human beings; the end of the supreme of all the sciences, politics, household management, and practical wisdom.

We will see some of these relations again when we work out his theory of the human good and happiness in the next chapter.

A second hypothesis would be that human beings being good (*qua* human) is the core homonym. This presumably would be favored by those who think that Aristotle has a virtue ethics, an ethics in which the good of character would have explanatory primacy over all other human goods. Once more, the scope of this hypothesis is limited to human good, and does not cover all good things. And once more, to see whether this is Aristotle's view, we have to examine his normative theory – on this hypothesis, his virtue ethics.

Finally, there is the hypothesis that the Unmoved Mover being good is the core homonym. Unlike the first two hypotheses, this cosmic hypothesis presumably has the range to accommodate all the remaining cases of being good, all of which would now be cases of core-dependent homonyms. If the rest of the conditions can be satisfied, here we would have a core-dependence theory accommodating all things that are good. This hypothesis goes beyond ethics to Aristotle's metaphysics. Aristotle will have to give up his claim that goodness is the subject of ethics, not metaphysics. And to determine whether this is Aristotle's view one would have to study not only his normative ethics but also his biology and metaphysics.

Notes

1 For criticism without sufficent exposition, see Popper 1966, vol. 1, pp. 145–6). Not a single piece on Aristotle's criticism known to me expounds even fleetingly the theory Aristotle criticizes; see also Barnes et al. (1977, pp. 222–3).

2 In this argument we have both the expressions "the good itself" and "the idea [form] of the good" and the argument purports to show that they refer to one and the same thing.

3 For the anti-Platonism of the *Categories* see, e.g., Lewis (1991, part 1).

4 The Pythagoreans may have thought of number as multiplicity of units. Under this conception one is not a number, the series of numbers would begin with the number two or the double. See, e.g., Aristotle, *Metaphysics*, 1087b33–1088a13; and Euclid, *Elements*, Bk. VII, defs. 1, 2.

5 Cherniss, 1944, Appendix 6. Here I try to go beyond Cherniss in developing the criticism so as to avoid the equivocation.

6 Woods (1996, pp. 70–4) exhibits many puzzles in the present passage. I am not sure whether he appreciates the merit of D. J. Allan's suggestion. The argument based on this suggestion need not have a different form; it can continue to be a reductio, as I show below. Allan's suggestion also has the merit of incorporating the self-predication assumption in the Platonic view, which is essential to Plato's theory of the form of the good.

7 We find both these premises in Aristotle's exposition of the theory in *EE*, Bk. I, ch. 8, though the argument Aristotle gives does not rely on the good being the best good, only on it being the first good.

8 The latest and best discussion is in Christopher Shields (1999). Shields discusses in detail the present argument, which he calls "the categorial argument," and argues that it fails to show nonunivocity for good.

9 G. H. von Wright (1966) argued that "good" has many uses and there is no single genus under which all the varieties of goodness fall; G. E. Moore (1903) argued for or perhaps assumed a "Platonic" view, that there is a simple property good(ness) which supervenes on all things that are intrinsically good.

10 Shields (1999, p. 198) raises a very good question about this part of the passage: "why suppose that goodness is said in as many ways as being is? Why suppose, that is, that goodness and being march in step at all?" Shields does not try to answer this question. I believe one of the merits of our interpretation of the theory of the form of the good in the *Republic* is that it does illuminate this question. Plato himself supposed that being and goodness "march in step," since according to his theory it is by virtue of the same properties that the forms are the best *and* the most real objects of their kind; and so did St. Augustine who followed him in this matter. For this reason Aristotle attacks them in a parallel way. But it should not be assumed that Aristotle claims that good is

said in many ways *because* being is; he says "*as* being is." Separate arguments are required in the two cases and Shields does indeed treat them separately and independently of each other.

11   A particular time and a particular place may both be opportune; how does it follow from time and place being in different categories that opportune is said in many ways? And how does it follow from *that* that being opportune is not something single and present in both cases? Why could not being opportune be for example, something like "being favorable to one's interests," a property which can be common to both opportune times and opportune places? Shields shows how a Platonist can reasonably question both these inferences that Aristotle seems to take for granted.

12   Though Shields does not claim that relying on the categories begs the question at issue, he gives special attention to two interpretations, those of Ackrill and McDonald, because they base Aristotle's argument on "foundations which appeal neither to word sense nor to the doctrine of categories as such" (1999, p. 201).

13   Von Wright argues not that "good" is ambiguous but that there are varieties of goodness or a "multiplicity of uses of the word 'good' ", e.g. medical goodness, instrumental goodness, hedonic goodness; and these "forms of goodness" are not species of a generic good – a point he takes himself to have in common with Aristotle's criticism of Plato. But von Wright also says that he does not "know how to argue conclusively for my opinion"; and he declines to say what he means by "forms of goodness." Like Aristotle, he has examples of different uses of good and no conclusive arguments against a generic form of good; unlike Aristotle, who has his theory of "focal meaning," or "core-dependent homonymy" as Shields calls it, von Wright has no theory which would unify in *some* way the various uses of "good," or bring "order in multiplicity" (1966, pp. 8, 12, 13). Like Humpty Dumpty, goodness is broken into pieces, with no assurance that the pieces can be reassembled.

14   Shields gives a definition of what he calls comprehensive homonymy: "x and y are homonymously F iff (i) they have their name in common, (ii) their definitions do not completely overlap." A good time and a good place are homonymously good if the definitions of good in the two predications do not completely overlap (1999, p. 11).

15   Shields (1999, pp. 54–6) discusses *Topics*, Bk. I, ch. 15 and finds that it contains some twelve "homonymy indicators." He picks out the present passage as containing the most important test, "signification." He says that good does not pass all twelve tests, and it passes none convincingly. Most of them would show differences in only "shallow meaning" or "shallow signification": the kind of differences any competent speaker of the language could spot – e.g. the difference between the bird crane and the machine crane. The test which uses the definition of homonymy goes deeper, to the essential properties sig-

nified by the definiendum and the definiens; something which a competent speaker of a language would not necessarily be able to get to, as is witnessed by the common difficulty of competent speakers to define terms which they use correctly (1999, ch. 2). See also Irwin (1981, pp. 523–44).

16 McDonald, 1989, pp. 150–74. This fine article was not available to me in 1987–8.

17 But Plato might disagree with Aristotle's functional classification of things (i.e. classification into "functional kinds," Shields [1999, p. 33]); although Plato might agree that we do so classify physical objects, he might claim that this is not the most fundamental classification, if function is a process or activity spread out in time; the most fundamental classification would be on the basis of participation in forms.

18 See pp. 66 and 207–8. "A Platonist should simply respond that goodness may, like belief, be second order, though univocal. Although it is true that it may be realized differently by different functional kinds, goodness may yet admit of a perfectly univocal account" (p. 66). Shields does not give an example of what such an account might be. Rawls's definition of good might be an example. I make a somewhat different criticism.

19 There is a similar shift in McDonald's language. On the one hand we have: "the notion of *good* is equivalent to the notion of an end." Presumably this means that at least for functional kinds being good and being an end are at least coextensive notions, possibly identical properties. He then speaks of "the thing, state or activity which constitutes something's end"; presumably, here he is speaking of the ends themselves – victory, health, rational activity, and so on – not the property of being an end or the concept of an end; and later he speaks of "the real nature or property which constitutes *the good for* some particular kind of activity or thing . . ." (1989, p. 167; my emphasis). Here it looks as if the ends themselves are spoken of as properties. Once more, a Platonist could reasonably protest that a property and the thing that has the property are being conflated; the notion of *good* is being conflated with the notion of *the good for x*. The fact that the good for human beings and the good for plants is different does not show that the property of being good is different in the two cases; any more than the end of human beings and the end of plants being different shows that the property of being an end is different in the two cases.

20 A definition of instrumental good might not use the notion of good at all, as Rawls's definition of primary goods (1971, pp. 62, 92). But Rawls is defining what Plato calls the useful, something which is necessary or effective for one's ends no matter what these ends are. Plato distinguishes the useful from the beneficial: the beneficial is "the productive of good," where good refers (ultimately) to noninstrumental goods (*Hippias Major*, 296–7). This accords with the way Shields takes the distinction.

21   I think the same point applies to the first premise of the two versions of the arguments against Plato on the basis of the distinction between final and instrumental goods, which Shields reconstructs (1999, pp. 213–15).

22   Aristotle's test is whether we would desire something even if it had no results or none of the good results it usually has; similar but not as radical as G. E. Moore's isolation tests; see, e.g., *NE*, Bk. I, chs. 4, 7, and *NE*, Bk. X, ch. 4, where the test is applied to such things as sight.

23   For discussions of separation, see Vlastos (1987); Fine (1995, pp. 51–2, 268–70). By "itself" and by the more elaborate "itself by itself" Plato, and Aristotle following him, signified that these entities existed separately from their sensible participants; for our purposes, let us say, separate in that they can exist whether or not any sensible participants exist.

24   See also Aristotle, *EE*, Bk. I, ch. 8: "What does it [in itself] express except that this formula [what is common to the sensible participants] has been rendered eternal and endowed with independent reality? But that which remains white for many days is not thereby whiter than that which has only been white for one day."

25   Some authors have maintained that on Plato's view the name of a form applies to the things that participate in it only derivatively, so that we have a case of *systematic* ambiguity (see Allen [1960, pp. 147–64]).

26   A Platonic definition (see Heath [1956, pp. 158ff]).

27   In *EE*, Bk. I, ch. 8, the argument is: the form of the good is unchangeable; what is unchangeable cannot be an end or a means; the practicable is an end or a means; therefore, the form of the good is not practicable.

28   In *EE*, Bk. I, ch. 8, the argument from the sciences is: the form of the good is not useful, because it is useful either to no science or to all alike, since the form of the good is that by the presence of which or similarity to which all other things are good. But it is not useful to all sciences alike; e.g. it is not useful to political science, whose good is the good of the city as a whole; nor is it useful to gymnastics, whose good is the good condition of the body.

29   See, e.g., Rawls (1971, ch. 7, p. 399). From his definition of "a good X" one could not infer directly what things are good; the definition tells us how to discover what things are good by telling us what sort of information we need to determine that; e.g. it tells us that to determine the goodness of a watch we need to know what a watch is normally used for and what properties make a watch efficient for that end.

30   In *EE*, Bk. I, ch. 8, 1217b, as Owen pointed out, Aristotle goes to the brink of ethical chaos and simply stays there: "nor is there one science either of being or of the good . . . so there can hardly be the province of one science to study the good per se" (1968).

31   "Certainly as sight is in the body, so is reason in the soul, and so on in other cases." Though Aristotle believes that some uses of good are analogical, it is difficult to see how the analogical uses by themselves could compensate for his pervasive fragmentation of goodness.

32   For a revision of Owen's classic treatment of focal meaning see Ferejohn
     (1980, p. 120): "A term T has *focal meaning* iff (i) T is 'said in many ways',
     and (ii) one of T's many *logoi* [definitions] is non-reciprocally contained in
     T's remaining *logoi* (i.e. its significata are logically prior to theirs)." Ferejohn
     and Shields agree that the theory goes beyond linguistic meaning, and
     depends on features of the world beyond language. See Shields's sophisticated
     account of "core dependence" (1999, ch. 4).

33   CDH4 reads: "a and b are homonymously F in a core-dependent way iff: (i)
     they have their name in common, (ii) their definitions do not completely
     overlap, (iii) necessarily, if a is a core instance of F-ness, then b's being F
     stands in one of the four causal relations to a's being F, and (iv) a's being F
     is asymmetrically responsible for the existence of b's being F" (Shields, 1999,
     pp. 124–5). As can be seen from this definition, core dependence is not purely
     a linguistic notion (as Owen may have thought), and it is quite complex and
     demanding. See Shields's application of it to life in chapter 7.

7

The Good of Desire, of Function, and of Pleasure

Aristotle's rejection of Plato's theory of forms and the form of the good frees his own theory of the good from Platonic metaphysics. For Aristotle, good is not transcendent nor eternal, existing separately on its own, but immanent, existing in the physical world, spread out in time. The good existing in the sensible world is not imposed on it from outside, as in Plato's *Timaeus*, where the divine craftsman stamps the goodness of the forms imperfectly on matter. Nor does the good of the world derive from a divine mind nor the goodness of a divine mind, as in the later Christian Philosophers. The good in the physical world is all the good there is.[1]

Aristotle's own theory of good is influenced by his biology, psychology, and the medicine of the day. His concepts of function and functioning well appear to rely heavily on his study of organisms and their organs, especially those of animal and humans. His theory of good is more comparable to Plato's *functional* theory of good.

But Aristotle was more sensitive than Plato to desire and pleasure playing a central role in the good life; more sensitive to the relevance of what people in fact pursue as good, to what they say about the good, and to what their practices in the arts and sciences can teach them about it. Here his procedures are perhaps more comparable to those of the Socrates of the early dialogues than to the speculative Plato of the *Republic*.

Accordingly, in *Nicomachean Ethics* (*NE*), Bk. I, Aristotle begins to work out his theory of the good for humans using two distinct lines of argument and two distinct concepts, the concept of *orectic* good, good as an object of desire, the popular good of most people; *and* the concept of functional or *perfectionist* good, the good most evident in biology and medicine. For seven and a half chapters in Bk. I Aristotle investigates the concept of *orectic* good and seems to build up a reasonable theory of the good for man on the basis of it. Then suddenly he begins an entirely new line of thought with the famous function argument, which relies on his biology and psychology; and this dominates the rest of *NE*. But in Bks. VII and X Aristotle also examines the good of pleasure and tries to bring it into line with his perfectionist theory.

Early in the twentieth century Aristotle's concept of *orectic* good received plenty of attention and was thought by some to be his own theory; his perfectionism and its implications were neglected. Because of his sensitivity to the claims of desire and pleasure to play a central role in the good life, at times he wrote as if he had a desire-based or even hedonistic theory of the good; and he has been so interpreted. He keeps citing what people say is good, what people pursue as good, and what people enjoy, as evidence for what is good. So, in Bk. I we find Aristotle paying a lot of attention to the notion of *orectic*[2] good and seemingly much less to perfectionist good. As a result his theory of the good has been difficult to interpret cleanly; and though his perfectionism is now more appreciated, the problems and implications of it need to be better understood, especially now that perfectionism on its own is getting some attention again (Hurka, 1993; Sen, 1985; and Nussbaum and Sen, 1992).

In this chapter I explore Aristotle's perfectionism and its implications, and compare it to his treatment of *orectic* and *hedonic* good. I argue that his view of the good is perfectionist. But his perfectionism, being more moderate and less metaphysically prolific, seems more plausible than Plato's, especially since he tries more successfully to reconcile his perfectionism with *orectic* and *hedonic* good; much as Rawls, working from the opposite direction, tries to reconcile his conception of the good, as the satisfaction of rational desire, with the perfectionism of Aristotle through his "Aristotelian Principle" (see below).

Aristotle discusses the *concept* of the good, its various *formal* features as a choice guiding concept; and also various *conceptions* of it, views as to the *content* of the good, for example, that the good is pleasure or honor or virtue. His discussion of the *concept* of the good appears to be neutral between orectic and perfectionist good. But his discussion of *conceptions* starts with orectic good, in which he relies on what people say, desire and choose, and ends up with perfectionist good, in which he relies on our evaluative practices in medicine and the arts and on his biology and psychology. I shall take these up in turn.

My main aim in the first two sections is to use the distinction between concept and conception of the good to clarify and systematize Aristotle's treatment of orectic good. My aim after that is to state clearly his theory of perfectionist good, expounding the famous function argument and discussing misunderstandings and objections to it; and then to see how he reconciles it with orectic and hedonic good.

1   The Concept of the Good

Unlike Plato, who usually begins ethical discussions with the virtues and eventually reveals the fundamental importance of the good for the virtues, Aristotle begins *NE* with the human good and he explicitly bases the discussion of the virtues on his earlier discussion of the good. And unlike *EE*, which begins in an easier way with common opinions about human happiness, *NE* starts abruptly with the most complex of the three central value concepts – not goods nor goodness, but *the* good (Kraut, 1989, ch. 1). This makes for difficult reading, but he begins with what he believes is the aim of the *study* of ethics, to discover the human good, knowledge of which is essential to the aim of ethics itself, to achieve that good. Accordingly he opens *NE* with the famous lines "Every art and every inquiry, and similarly every action and pursuit, is thought to aim at some good: and for this reason the Good has rightly been declared to be that at which all things aim" (Ross transl.).

Some commentators have found this and similar passages fallacious[3]: from the fact that several things aim at some good it does not follow that there is some unique good at which all these things aim: it is possible that each aims at some different good. But Aristotle shows himself aware of this possibility, here and in Bk. I, ch. 7: "But as there are numerous pursuits of arts and science, it follows that their ends are correspondingly numerous: for instance the end of the science of medicine is health, that of the art of shipbuilding a vessel, that of strategy victory, that of domestic economy wealth." And, "Now there do appear to be several ends at which our actions aim" (Ross transl.).

Aristotle's response in both passages is that not all ends are equally final, but can be ranked by degrees of finality. His distinctions among ends, best expressed in Bk. I, 7, are worth setting out here:

Some things we choose for the sake of other things and never for themselves, for example, wealth and flutes and other instruments. Some things we pursue for their own sake and also choose for the sake of other things, for example, honor, pleasure, intelligence, and virtue. And some things we pursue for their own sake and never for the sake of anything else, for example, happiness.

Following Keyt (1983), I will call the first kind of end *subservient*, the second *subordinate*, and the third *ultimate*. And Aristotle tells us in the same passage that the good we are seeking is an ultimate end. Let us refer to this as the first formal property of the good.

But this is still clearly compatible with the possibility that a person may have several (independent) ultimate ends, as well as that different persons have different ultimate ends. Yet, as we have seen, in the first sentence of *NE* Aristotle attributes a second and stronger formal property to the good: The good is *the* ultimate end of *all* human actions. Since he is aware that this is not entailed by the fact that all human actions aim at some end, why does Aristotle think that the good must have this second formal property, which is strong enough to entail the first?

The opening sentence of *NE*, Bk. I, ch. 2, contains a famous argument which seems intended as at least a partial answer to this question:

> If then there is an end of the things we do, which we desire for its own sake, the others being desired for the sake of it, and if we do not choose everything for the sake of something else (for at that rate the process would go on to infinity, so that out desires would be empty and vain), clearly this must be the good and the chief good. (Ross transl.)

It seems correct to take the statement inside the parenthesis as an indirect argument against the hypothesis immediately preceding it, i.e. that we choose everything for the sake of something else. If so, we can reconstruct the argument thus: Suppose we choose everything for the sake of something else. If this is true, then the process of choosing would go on to infinity, i.e. it would have no stopping place. If the process of choosing had no stopping place, our desires would be empty and vain. It false that our desires are empty and vain. Hence, it is false that we choose everything for the sake of something else.

The argument is very abstract and requires interpretation. What does Aristotle mean by the process of choosing? On the basis of his analysis of choice (in *NE*, Bk. III, chs. 2, 3), we can say he means discovering reasons for the action chosen, in the form of connecting up some end the agent has in view with an action which is a necessary or the best means to it. If so, the second premise presumably means that the reason given for the choice would not stop or completely satisfy the question For the sake of what did you choose the action? And this would be true under the initial hypothesis, in the sense that no end could be provided, which, pursued for its own sake, could stop a similar question from arising again and again ad infinitum. And what does Aristotle mean by saying that in that case our desires would be empty and vain? Perhaps, as Cooper suggests (1975, pp. 93ff.; see also Ackrill [1973]; Kenny [1977]; and Wedin [1981]), he means "altogether ungrounded," or perhaps, less strongly, ultimately ungrounded.

So interpreted, the argument is about the possibility of rational choice, or more globally, about the rationality of a whole life. It is not an argument that produces empirical evidence to the effect that each person or even one person in fact has at least one end which he or she desires for its own sake. Rather, it purports to show that if rational choice is to be possible there must be at least one such end; or, in the words of *EE*, Bk. I, ch. 2: "not to have one's life organized [where one has a choice] in view of some end [with reference to which he or she will do all acts] is a mark of much folly" (Ross transl.) A person who had such an end would have a beginning for her practical reasoning or her deliberations about what to do with her life, a beginning at which all her explanations of her rational voluntary actions would end.

The argument does not show that anyone must have exactly one ultimate end of all her actions, if she is to make rational choices. A plurality of ultimate ends for a single person, or for several persons, is compatible with the argument. Perhaps it does not even show that anyone must have at least one ultimate end: would we not be able to make rational choices if we simply had one or more *subordinate* ends? Apparently so: the doctor or the general, for example, can make rational choices assuming no other end than health or victory (see Charles [1984, pp. 148–55]). It seems that the most the argument shows is that not all our ends can be subservient, if we are to make rational choices. But Aristotle soon introduces nonformal considerations pertaining to the content of the good, for excluding all these possibilities.

Even this modest conclusion might be reasonably disputed by some philosophers, because the notion of rational choice implicit is too strong. If a man wants to make money in the stock market and he finds that the probability of a stock going up in price is far greater than its going down or remaining the same, is he not acting rationally in buying the stock? Do we need to know what kind of end making money is for him, or whether he has at least one ultimate or subordinate end in his life, to decide whether his choice is rational? It would seem not, either in common everyday situations where we judge the rationality of a particular choice, or in theoretical discussions of rational choice where some principle of expected utility maximization is used. Aristotle might concede the point for isolated particular choice situations but argue that a man's life as a whole (his plan of life) would not be rational if he had only subservient ends. Such a life would seem to be aimless and adrift: it would be difficult to know how to judge it happy or successful, or how such a person would make large decisions such as the choice of career or lifestyle.

For the moment, we can say that Aristotle attributes to the good the formal property of being the unique ultimate end of all actions and pursuits; however, he does not to prove that there is such a thing, but only that not all our ends can be subservient.

In *NE*, Bk. I, ch. 7, Aristotle attributes a third formal property to the good, that it must be self-sufficient, and defines it: "The self-sufficient we now define as that which when isolated makes life desirable and lacking in nothing" (Ross transl.) Aristotle does not tell us explicitly why he thinks the good must be self-sufficient, something that Plato also claimed in the *Philebus* (20c). But it does not seem to follow from an end being ultimate, that it is self-sufficient, since a person might have several ultimate ends. Whatever value an ultimate end has, it has all of it on its own, in contrast to a subservient end which derives all of its value from the ends it serves, and distinct from a subordinate end which has some value on its own and some value from the ends it serves. If a man had several ultimate ends and pursued some to the exclusion of others, his life would not be self-sufficient, since he would lack some goods with value of their own, which when added to his life would make it more desirable or choice-worthy. But if we assume the uniqueness condition built into the second formal property, that there is exactly one ultimate end at which all human actions aim, it would indeed follow that it is self-sufficient, provided that we think of it as composed of all the subordinate goods there are: for if it lacked even one of these it would not be self-sufficient, while if it had all of them it would lack nothing that had value on its own. In this passage Aristotle may be assuming the uniqueness condition, for reasons we shall see below.[4]

In sum, Aristotle attributes three formal properties to the good for a person: it must be an ultimate end, it must be the single ultimate end of all actions and pursuits, and it must be self-sufficient. The second property is plainly very strong, since it implies the first, and also the third given the proviso about subordinate goods. These properties are formal in the sense that the good has them irrespective of content or composition. Aristotle is perfectly aware that different people take the good or happiness to be different things, for example, pleasure or honor. But, he would presumably argue, though a person who thinks that honor is the good may be mistaken, in so far as that person takes honor to be the good she or he treats honor as if it had all these three properties.

2   *Different Orectic Conceptions of the Good*

In attributing formal properties to the good Aristotle apparently was relying on what he took to be the requirements of rational choice. But Aristotle is also interested in discovering the content or composition of the good for a person, and his discussions of formal properties is intertwined with questions about different particular compositions of the good. And in the latter he relies on what people say the good is or what they take to be the good as shown by their choices and behavior. In *NE*, Bk. I, ch. 4 Aristotle begins his discussion of conceptions of the good as follows:

> Verbally there is very general agreement; for both the general run of men and people of superior refinement say that it is happiness, and identify living well and doing well with being happy; but with regard to what happiness is they differ, and the many do not give the same account as the wise. For the former think it is some plain and obvious thing, like pleasure, wealth, or honor, they differ, however, from one another – and often even the same man identifies it with different things, with health when he is sick, with wealth when he is poor . . . (Ross transl.)

In ch. 5 he distinguishes three kinds of life by what the good is identified with: the apolaustic life, *pleasure*; the political life, *honor*; the contemplative life, *reason*. And he gives some preliminary reasons against the first two. He dismisses the first here as being "suitable to beasts," presumably taking it to refer only to the bodily pleasures we share with animals. And he says that those who pursue honor do so in order to be assured of their virtue, so the latter might better be thought to be the end of the political life; but even this appears to be incomplete because virtue is compatible with being asleep or inactive and also compatible with the greatest sufferings and misfortunes. As for wealth, it cannot be the good, for it is merely pursued for the sake of something else.

In the last remark we see Aristotle using one of the formal properties of the good to show that wealth is not identical with it: wealth is not an ultimate, nor even a subordinate good.

In ch. 7 Aristotle uses all three formal properties to show that the good or happiness is not identical with honor, pleasure, reason, or virtue:

> Now such a thing happiness, above all else, is held to be [an ultimate end]; for
> this we choose always for itself and never for the sake of anything else, but
> honor, pleasure, reason, and every virtue we choose indeed for themselves (for
> if nothing resulted from them we should still choose each of them), but we
> choose them also for the sake of happiness, judging that through them we shall
> be happy. (Ross transl.)

Happiness is an ultimate end, whereas pleasure, honor, virtue, reason, are
all subordinate ends, so no one of them is identical with happiness. Moreover, happiness is the ultimate end for the sake of which we choose these
subordinate ends.

Finally, self-sufficiency is applied to happiness, and used to show that
no one of the subordinate goods is identical with happiness:

> From the point of view of self-sufficiency the same result seems to follow:
> for the final good is thought to be self-sufficient . . . and such we think
> happiness to be; and further we think it the most desirable of all things, without
> being counted as one good among others – if it were so counted it would
> clearly be made more desirable by the addition of even the least of goods; for
> that which is added becomes an excess of goods, and of goods the greater is
> always more desirable. (Ross transl.)

From the definition of self-sufficiency and of subordinate goods it follows
that no one of them is self-sufficient or the most desirable of all things:
since each of the subordinate goods has value on its own, the addition of
any of them to any other would make the totality of the two more desirable, and a life which excluded any one of them would lack it and not
be self-sufficient. Moreover, from the self-sufficiency of happiness and the
existence of subordinate goods, it follows that happiness must include all
the subordinate goods; for if it excluded even one of them it would not
make life most desirable and lacking in nothing.

It is noteworthy that this argument favors the so-called "inclusive end,"
rather than the "dominant end" interpretation of the good for a person.
Ever since Hardie introduced this distinction, controversy has raged
whether Aristotle meant to include moral virtue in happiness (the so-called
"moderate intellectualism" view), or meant to identify happiness with the
intellectual virtue of theoretical wisdom ("strict intellectualism") as the
dominant end to which all other ends are subservient (Hardie, 1967;
Cooper, 1975; Keyt, 1983; Kraut, 1989; Broadie, 1991). The argument I
have just reviewed favors the inclusive end interpretation of the good and
moderate intellectualism. If moral virtue is a subordinate good, choice-

worthy for itself, having value on its own, and happiness is self-sufficient, it follows that moral virtue must be included in the life of happiness as a component, since its addition to intellectual virtue would make life more choiceworthy, while its subtraction would make life less than self-sufficient. However, it does not follow from the requirement of self-sufficiency alone that moral virtue must be part or component of happiness, as distinct from instrument; for it may be that moral virtue is instrumentally necessary for theoretical wisdom, and in such a case it would be included in the life of happiness, though not as a component, even if happiness were simply identified with theoretical wisdom.

Before Aristotle begins the function argument, he sums up the grand conclusion of his discussion so far of the concept of the good and the various conceptions of it: "Happiness, then, is something final and self-sufficient, and is the end of action" (Ross transl.).

Several large questions arise about Aristotle's discussion so far. To begin with, has he shown that there is such a thing as the good, i.e. something that has all three formal properties? We have seen that in his discussion of the concept of the good Aristotle has no general formal argument that shows that even a single person must have such a good, much less that there is such a thing which is the same for all people. A man with several ultimate ends, presumably independent of each other, could also make rational choices. Nor does Aristotle have a formal argument that the good must be self-sufficient. It may be, however, that Aristotle would argue plausibly that a man who had so organized his life that some one thing was the good for him would be able to make rational choices more extensively (in more or possibly all cases) than a man who had several ultimate ends. The latter for example, may have a problem in choosing rationally if several of his ultimate ends were in conflict in particular cases. Suppose a man takes virtue and pleasure to be his two ultimate ends; clearly he might be faced with choices which promote one and frustrate the other, for example, temperate or courageous or just acts. How is he then to choose rationally?

But in his discussion of *conceptions* of the good, does not Aristotle show that every man has a single ultimate end for the sake of which he does all that he chooses to do, namely happiness? In this discussion Aristotle relies on Vlastos's Eudaimonistic Axiom, that "[their] own happiness is desired by all human beings as the ultimate end of all their rational acts . . . [which] once staked out by Socrates, becomes axiomatic for all subsequent moralists of ancient antiquity" (Vlastos, 1991, ch. 8). If this principle is true, it follows that for every person there is some end which has

at least the first two formal properties of the good, i.e. it is the single ultimate end for the sake of which that person does all his or her rational
acts (acts chosen because they are efficient means to his or her ends). And
happiness is also thought to be self-sufficient, Aristotle claims, though it is
difficult to believe that some of the things Aristotle says people take happiness to be, such as health when they are sick or wealth when poor, are
thought by these people to be self-sufficient.

In any case, if it is true that every person desires happiness as the
single ultimate and self-sufficient end of all rational acts, it follows that
for every person there is an end which has all the three formal properties of the good. And if we assume the good to be the only thing
that has all three properties, it follows that for every person there is
something which is the good, as Aristotle understands the concept of the
good. So, if we add the Eudaimonistic Axiom and self-sufficiency to
Aristotle's analysis of the concept of the good, we see that Aristotle has a
plausible argument that there is such a thing as the good. And even if this
principle is not true of all people, it certainly seems to be true of some;
so it seems true that there is such a thing as Aristotle's good, at least for
some people.

A second large question is whether Aristotle has shown that the good
is the same for all people, at least for all those who have so organized their
lives that some single end is the good for them, an end they all identify
with happiness. Now we saw that Aristotle recognizes that even if all
people take happiness to be their single ultimate and self-sufficient end,
they differ about what happiness is, different persons taking it to be one
or another of (what Aristotle takes to be) subordinate ends, even subservient ends. And Aristotle has arguments to show that if any person takes
one of these ends to be identical with the good or happiness she or he
is mistaken, because people desire and choose each one of these for the
sake of happiness, so that none of them is an ultimate end; and if any
person takes any combination of these subordinate ends which does not
include all of them to be the good, she or he is mistaken, because such a
combination would not be self-sufficient. In such a case Aristotle would
say that the person is pursuing not the good but the apparent good. Our
question is whether these arguments are decisive. They are not, and
Aristotle seems to have recognized this. How so?

Suppose a man has so organized his life that he makes all his choices
with a view to obtaining pleasure and that he does not pursue pleasure
for the sake of anything else. If Aristotle says to him, "But we pursue pleasure for the sake of happiness," it is open to him to say, "I do not," or

more plausibly, "For me pleasure is the same thing as happiness." And if Aristotle says to him, "But would not your life be more desirable if you added honor or virtue or reason to it?" it is open to him to reply, "I pursue these things indeed, but only because and in so far as they are sources or means to pleasure and enjoyment – if I can get these pleasures without them I would be perfectly content." The point here is that within the line of argument Aristotle has pursued so far he has no good reply to these rejoinders, especially if such a man has had considerable experience with life, has made all his choices with a view to maximizing his pleasures, and he is perfectly content with the results.

The reason why this is so is that the notion of good Aristotle has used so far is the same as an end of action, an end of action being the same as the object of desire for the sake of which the action is done (desire in the broad sense of *orexis* in *De Anima*, Bk. III, ch. 9). We can see this in the opening statement of *NE* where Aristotle makes a transition from what all human enterprises aim at to the good. We can see it again in the opening paragraph of *NE*, Bk. I, ch. 7: "Let us again return to the good we are seeking, and ask what it can be. It seems different in different actions and arts; it is different in medicine, in strategy, and in the other arts likewise. What then is the good of each? Surely that for the sake of which everything else is done . . . and in every action and pursuit the end" (Ross transl.).

We can see the connection reaffirmed in *NE*, Bk. X, ch. 2, where Aristotle refutes a certain objection, probably Platonic, to Eudoxus' thought that "pleasure is the good because all things, both rational and irrational, aim at it": He says, "Those who object that that at which all things aim is not necessarily good are, we may surmise, talking nonsense. . . . If it were irrational creatures that desired the things in question, there might be something in what they say; but if intelligent creatures do so as well, can there be anything in it at all?" (Ross transl.).

We can see the connection also outside *NE*, where Aristotle explains the notion of final cause, the cause that explains an action teleologically: "The fourth cause is the goal, i.e. the good" (*Metaphysics*, 983a31–2, Ross transl.).

So, if the concept of good is the same as that of orectic end, something desired and for the sake of which actions are done, and the concept of *the* good is the same as that of the ultimate and self-sufficient end of all our actions, then the good will be the same for all people if they all have the same ultimate and self-sufficient end. But if different people have different ultimate and self-sufficient ends, as Aristotle recognizes, if follows just as much that the good is not the same for all.

To be sure, mistakes about goods and the good can be accommodated within this theory of orectic good. A woman might pursue wealth as the chief means to pleasure but find out that accumulating wealth causes her more pain than the pleasures it brings; or she might think that playing the piano better than any other person would be the good for her, but, having reached this goal, she might be lonely and discontent and decide this was not sufficient and that the good for her must include friendship and affection. But if we suppose such mistakes eliminated through experience, no reasonable inference can be made that such error-free persons would all agree and pursue the same thing as the ultimate and self-sufficient end of their lives. The concept of the good Aristotle has used so far is not, we might say, entirely relative and subjective, but it has built into it a good deal of relativity and subjectivity: it depends a lot on what people happen to want, and also on at least experienced individuals being the ultimate judges of what it is they want.

This is perhaps one of Aristotle's dissatisfactions with his discussion of the good so far. For after he sums up this discussion with "Happiness, then, is something final and self-sufficient, and is the end of action," he opens the famous function argument with "Presumably, however, to say that happiness is the chief good seems a platitude, and clearer account of what it is still desired" (*NE*, Ross transl.).

I take this to refer to the same problem made explicit earlier, that though men agree that happiness is the good, they disagree about what happiness is. The discussion of good as orectic end was useful in bringing out certain formal features of the good, which are important for understanding rational choice; perhaps because good as orectic end suits rather well means–ends deliberative reasoning, the kind of reasoning Aristotle employs in his analysis of rational choice, a point John Cooper has emphasized. At the same time, good as orectic end leaves the *content* of the good wide open: the good for anyone can be anything that she desires as the ultimate and self-sufficient end of all her actions. Some ethical theorists, such as nonteleologists, might be content with this state of affairs, since for them the right is prior to the good and so it can limit the excesses of orectic good (see, e.g., Rawls [1971 pp. 31, 425; 1982]). But Aristotle is not. And I take the function argument to be his attempt to provide a different basis from desire, a perfectionist basis, for determining the content of the good for people, a content importantly the same for all.

3   Aristotle's Functional-Perfectionist Theory of Good

Unlike Aristotle's discussion of orectic good, his function argument has been the subject of broad disagreements among commentators. Opinions range all the way from "a piece of unnecessary Aristotelian metaphysics" (Austin, 1967), to "too abstract to be informative" (Cooper, 1975), to "one of the two lines of argument in Bk. I" (Anagnostopoulos, 1980), to "his own account of the good" (Irwin, 1985), to "his own view" (Hardie, 1980), to "the center-piece of Bk. I" (Keyt, 1983).[5] My discussion will show that Austin was off the mark, and that the argument is more informative than Cooper allows, at least if it is reasonably filled in; and that while Hardie, Irwin, and Keyt are essentially correct, Anagnostopoulos also has an important point. The functional-perfectionist account of the good is indeed Aristotle's own. But Aristotle does have another line of argument, as we have seen already; and he wants to take into account good as orectic end, which is the more popular notion of the good, and to reconcile the two as much as possible. We shall see this reconciliation in Bk. X, in Aristotle's considered and final view on the value of pleasure.

Our first task is to reconstruct and interpret the function argument; our second to consider misunderstandings and objections to it. After that we shall compare *orectic and hedonic* good with *functional-perfectionist* good and see how Aristotle tries to reconcile them.

Aristotle's function argument, given in *NE*, Bk. I, ch. 7, 1097b22–a18, is notoriously compressed and obscure. The clearest and most detailed interpretation known to me is by David Keyt, who reconstructs it as a valid deductive argument, drawing from other writings of Aristotle to fill in and clarify various premises (1983, pp. 366–8; see also Irwin [1985, pp. 15–17, 304–5]).

1.   In the animate world there are four general functions: to use food and reproduce, to perceive, to move from one place to another, and to think. Accordingly, there are three general forms of life[6]: the nutritive and reproductive, shared by all animate things, the perceptive, shared by all animals, and the life of reason, practical and theoretical, which is special to man (*De Anima*, Bk. I, ch. l; Bk. II, ch. 4; Bk. III, ch. 9; *Politics*, Bk. VII, ch. 13).

2.   One form of life is lower than another if and only if normal members of the first lack a function that normal members of the second possess. Thus plants are lower than animals, animals with fewer sense

modalities lower than those with more, and nonhuman animals lower than man (*De Anima*, Bk. II, ch. 2, Bk. III, ch. 12).

3. A form of life or an activity of the soul is the distinctive function of a kind of living thing if and only if every normal member of this kind and no member of a lower kind can perform it (*NE*, Bk. I, ch. 7).

4. The distinctive function of man is a theoretical and practical activity of reason (*NE*, Bk. I, ch. 7).

5. A good member of a kind is one that performs the distinctive function of that kind well (as compared to other members of the kind) (*NE*, Bk. I, ch. 7).

6. Hence, a good man is one who performs well the activities of practical and theoretical reason, i.e. one who deliberates well about what to do and reasons well about what is true (from 4 and 5; and *NE*, Bk. VI).

7. A member of a kind performs its distinctive function well if and only if it performs it according to (or "performs it by") the virtue or excellence appropriate to that kind (*NE*, I, 7, II, 6).

8. The good of a member of a kind is to be a good member of that kind (supplied premise, possibly in the text of *NE*, I 7).

9. Hence, "human good [the good for man] is [rational] activity of soul according to virtue, and if there is more than one virtue, in accordance with the best and most complete [perfect]" (Aristotle's actual conclusion).

As in Aristotle's discussion of the good as orectic end, his function argument contains a formal and a material part, a concept and a conception. The formal part contains a definition of distinctive function, of being good of a kind, implicitly of the good of a kind; implicitly also a definition of virtue,[7] in the broadest sense, applicable to all things with functions. The material part, which seems to be based on Aristotle's psychology and biology, fills in a person's distinctive function and gives consequent general descriptions of a good person and the good for a person.

The definition of distinctive function and the whole formal part has obvious affinities to Plato's definition of function at the end of the *Republic*, Bk. I: "Would you agree to define the function of a thing [of a given kind] as what only [that kind] of thing can do or can do best [most efficiently]?" (author's transl.). Here we have only a partial correspondence: Plato's *exclusive* function corresponds to Aristotle's *distinctive* function. But though Aristotle does not use Plato's notion of *optimal* function here, he does use it in the *Politics* to determine who should rule.

Both Plato and Aristotle illustrate their definitions of function with artifacts, roles and occupations, organs of animals, and animals. The definitions and the examples show that the concept of function Plato and Aristotle are using makes essential reference to characteristic (or optimal) capacities or potentialities of an object and the activities to which these issue, and not necessarily to human (or divine) desires or purposes. This is crucial for understanding their theories, because good is defined by reference to *this* concept of function; as a result, we clearly have here a theory of good which is neither a desire-satisfaction theory nor a hedonistic one.

In the function argument Aristotle does define good in terms of function, in premises 5 and 8. This is worth noting because of the ongoing controversy about the nature of Aristotle's teleology and his teleological explanations especially in biology. Do such explanations rely on some notion of good, imported into biology and independent of it, to determine ends or functions? Some have argued that Aristotle needs to build into "the analysis of actualization the required normative component"; he needs some notion of good to pick out what the function or the end of a thing is; observing what a thing comes to be is not enough, since, among other things, living things come to be weak, senile, and dead. John Cooper appears to attribute a similar view to Aristotle, though perhaps not as explicitly, when he tells us that by "a goal" Aristotle understands "something good". Alan Gotthelf, on the other hand, has argued in some detail that Aristotle does not use, or need to, the notion of good to determine function; maximum efficiency and capacity for maintenance, for example, might well be sufficient for determining what is to be actualized (Kahn, 1985; Gotthelf, 1987a). This controversy is complex and deep, and some of it at least is beyond the scope of this book – certainly the parts of it concerned with explanations in Aristotle's biology. But for our purposes, it may help to remind ourselves of two crucial points, one historical, the other philosophical.

We have a relevant historical model of normative teleological explanations in Plato, if we put together passages in *Phaedo*, *Republic*, and *Timaeus*.[8] The first of these tells us that one kind of cause explains by reference to what is good or best: we would understand why the earth is round if we could see why it is better that it be round than have any other shape. In the theory of the form of the good in the *Republic* Plato provides an account of the good independent of function. And in the *Timaeus* he provides an agent, the divine craftsman, who knows this good and fashions the sensible world accordingly using the perfect forms as models. The the-

ories of the *Republic* and the *Timaeus* make sense of the teleological explanations of the *Phaedo*: teleological explanations of phenomena in the sensible world do use an imported and independent notion of goodness: the
forms as ideal exemplars with the form of the good as their essence: the
forms are formal causes, the divine craftsman the efficient cause who
brings order into the physical world for the sake of approximating the
forms, which are thus also final causes of the divine craftsman's activity.
Our question is whether Aristotle has something similar or analogous. Well,
in Aristotle forms are not imposed on matter from the outside, there is
no divine creator of species (the Unmoved Mover is not such a creator
and species are never created), and good is spread out in time. One might
reply that in teleological explanations of human conduct Aristotle does
use the notion of good to determine goals or functions. For example in
De Anima, Bk. III, chs. 9, 10, 11 teleological explanations of human action
appear to be normative: human action is explained by reference to practical reason and desire; and, as Aristotle tells us, "it is always the object of
desire which produces movement, but that is either the good or the apparent good . . ." (Ross transl.). (433a27–8). Apparently for human beings the
form of explanation is: P does x because P desires something y which P
thinks is good, and P thinks that x is necessary for y or the most efficient
means to y. Now in the last clause only the notion of good as necessary
or efficient means to something else is used, and this can be given a non-
normative, purely quantitative interpretation. The other occurrence of
good is not necessarily to good as means. But we might note, first, that
the explanation could work just as well without reference to good as end,
though without it we might not know why the person ultimately desires
y. Second, it is not clear at all that in the *De Anima* type of explanation
good is used to determine goal or function. The explanation is perfectly
compatible with the theory of orectic good I expounded earlier, in which
desire determines what is good, within the formal restrictions on desire
imposed by practical rationality. Within the orectic theory it is desire that
determines what is good, not conversely: good is explicated by reference
to the object of desire, not conversely; though this is compatible with the
object of desire being the good or the apparent good.

The philosophical point is that Aristotle cannot have it both ways:
define good in terms of function and function in terms of good; at least
not within the same discipline. Maybe in his biology he sometimes uses
the notion of good to determine function or end,[9] but in his ethics he
cannot, at least not in his functional theory of good. Aristotle tells us
clearly that the good and the well are thought to reside in the function,

not the other way around; and that is why we look at the function of things to determine their good – this is the central idea of the function argument! So, since he defines good in terms of function, he cannot also define function in terms of good without going around in a vicious circle. And he does not. The function argument picks out the distinctive function of a human (common functions as well) without any reliance on normative concepts, much as the notion of exclusive function in Plato does not rely on any normative concepts. Premises 2 and 3 of Aristotle's function argument, which together determine distinctive function, make no use of normative concepts. One might think that the notions of "higher" and "lower" forms of life do implicitly appeal to normative notions, but I think they need refer only to more and fewer powers within an ordered series.[10]

Aristotle takes the definition of functional good on which he relies as something widely accepted: "for all things that have a function or activity, the good and the well is thought to reside in the function . . ." "The good" of a thing residing in the function is reflected in premise 8, the "well" in premise 5: the idea is that for anything with a function, to do well just is to perform its function well; and the good for it (or some of the good for it) resides in the performing well of its function. Like Plato, Aristotle thus puts forward his explication of good in terms of function as if it were uncontroversial.[11] Both theories do have a lot of initial plausibility, perhaps derived from the examples of artifacts, roles, and occupations – these examples appear to be the logical home of the theories. But in these cases the notion of function is not necessarily the psychobiological concept Aristotle appears to be using, but that of purpose or standard use. Like ourselves, the ancients evaluated artifacts and people in roles and occupations by how well they do what they are supposed to do. But what they are "supposed to do" may be a different and easier concept in these cases than it is for natural living things in medicine and biology. A good flautist is one who plays the flute well, and a good eye is one that sees well. And the same holds for the good of these things: the good of a flautist, as a flautist, is whatever enables her to play the flute well or better, a better flute or an enhancement of her skills; and whatever enables an eye to see well or better is good for the eye; for example, a certain flexibility in the shape of the lens which helps focus light rays on the retina. Thus it looks as if the theory of good is the same for both kinds of cases. But if the notion of function is significantly different for flautists and eyes – one making essential reference to human purposes the other not – the resulting theories of good may be fundamentally different, and the initial plausibility Aristotle's theory has may rest on this "ambiguity" in the notion of function.

Perhaps this is one reason why Aristotle's application of his functional theory to human beings, in the function argument, has been extremely controversial.

4 Objections to Aristotle's Functional Theory of Good

The most common objection is that humans were not made or designed for a purpose, or at least we have no acceptable evidence that they were.[12] I believe that this is a major misunderstanding of Aristotle's view: it uses a narrower concept of function, "what a thing is made for or designed to do." Both Aristotle's definition of function, which makes no reference to a thing being made for a purpose, and his application of the concept to organs of animals in his biology, as well as current applications of it in medicine, show clearly that this objection is mistaken. In his biological works Aristotle identifies functions of parts of animals without ever making any appeals to a designer of animals or their parts (Gotthelf, and Lennox, both in Gotthelf and Lennox, 1987). The way in which Aristotle arrives at the function of a person in the function argument, without any appeal whatsoever to design or designer, shows the same thing. The question whether a person has a distinctive (and essential) function in Aristotle's sense is the same as the question whether a person has certain capacities or powers that no other living thing has; specifically the capacities to deliberate about means and ends and to do theoretical research; or, to deliberate about *what to do* and to find out *what is true* (De Anima, Bk. III, ch. 10; and NE, Bk. VI, chs. 1 and 2). We know that a person does have these capacities and powers, and as far as we know even now, only a person does.[13]

Moreover, Aristotle's concept of distinctive function was neither arbitrary nor stipulative. It accorded with practices in medicine and biology, where functions were assigned on the basis of distinctive activities and the contributions parts and organs make to the life of the animal. In *Parts of Animals* Aristotle uses this concept of function constantly and routinely in trying to understand the causes of animal life, and he also supposes without argument that the functioning well of the various parts of animals, tissues, fluids, and organs, is good for the animals, that is, necessary or efficient means to their continued existence or their well-being.[14]

Though Aristotle's concept of function appears to be psychobiological, it can accommodate the notion of function we find in the arts and crafts, in roles and occupations, the notion we usually apply to artifacts. This is so because Aristotle's concept of function is broad enough to *include* the narrower notion of function as what a thing was made for, in normal cases most of the time: when we make a thing for a purpose, for example, a pump for moving liquids against gravity, we usually endow it with some structures and capabilities which other kinds of things do not have, and so the purpose for which it was made turns out to be its Aristotelian function. Theoretically, using Aristotle's concept of distinctive function, we could discover experimentally the function of a pump without knowing what it was made for, though this could turn out to be a large and costly enterprise.

A whole series of objections has been made to Aristotle's use of *distinctive* function. To begin with, why should we confine a person's function to things only humans can perform, as the function argument seems to do? Well, Aristotle does *not* deny that human beings have other essential functions besides thinking practically and theoretically; they have functions in common with animals and even with plants, such as nutrition and reproduction, locomotion, sense perception and even (some) affective responses such as pleasure and pain, desire and fear. The function argument actually *includes* all these as *common* human functions. On Aristotle's view human beings are essentially animals as well as rational beings: their animality distinguishes them from plants, but within animals it is their rationality that distinguishes them from other kinds of animals, what makes them *human* animals. His theory of distinctive function, based on his theory of the *differentia* of a species, does not deny common functions – functions of the genus within which the differentiation of species is made.

But Aristotle gives a unique or central role to the differentiating functions among all the essential functions. What is this role? Perhaps David Balme is correct in suggesting that in his biological works Aristotle was not concerned so much with typology or classification but rather with discovering the causes of, and thus understanding, animal and human behavior.[15] The centrality of distinctive function is to be found in the explanations we seek of structures, parts, lifestyles, and behaviors. Taking into account final as well as other causes, we can perhaps say that the notion of distinctive function combines two ideas: a function without which we cannot explain at least some aspects of an animal's life; *and* at the same time a function for the sake of which other functionings exist, or at least a function that other functionings serve (*De Anima*, Bk. II, chs. 2, 3, 4). The distinctive human functions would thus be ones without which we could not understand at least some aspects of human life *and* which all other human activities (at least) serve. Perhaps this can be seen in Aristotle's explanation of human action, in *De Anima*, Bk. III, chs. 12, 13, where reason must be brought in to explain typical human actions; in his account of deliberation in *NE*, Bk. III, which makes deliberation essential to understanding choice; and in his account of theoretical reason in *NE*, Bks. VI and X, which makes the search for truth essential to understanding systems of human thought.

The same kind of theory of the relations among all the living functions emerges from Aristotle's discussion of the functions of all living things in *De Anima*, Bk. II, ch. 3, and Bk. III, ch. 12. He begins with an enumeration of the general living functions: "nutrition, sense-perception, desire, movement in respect of place, and thought" (414a30). He then argues, on the basis of what is found in nature, that some of these functions (can) exist without the others but not conversely: nutrition *can* exist without sense perception, as it *does* in plants, but sense perception does not exist without nutrition. And the same for the pairs: touch and other senses, sense perception and desire, desire and movement, movement and thought. Since the relation is transitive, it follows that thought does not exists without *all* the others (in mortal);[16] movement does not exist without the remaining three, desire without the remaining two, and sense perception without nutrition. In *De Anima*, Bk. III, ch. 12, he takes these propositions for granted, and infers from them *and* from the most general assumption of his teleology – that "everything in nature exists for the sake of something"[17] – that, e.g., in animals sense perception exists for the sake of movement, and similarly with the other pairs. Aristotle apparently does not distinguish between, say, nutrition *serving* sense perception and nutrition *existing for the sake of* sense perception; the former may be compatible with the theory of evolution, the latter may not be.[18] It is in fact doubtful that even the first inference holds: from nutrition existing without sense perception (in plants) but not conversely (in animals) to nutrition serving sense perception; at any rate, the converse is also true since animals certainly use their senses to obtain food. And the second inference certainly does not hold: from nutrition serving sense perception to nutrition existing (in animals) for the sake of sense perception. Do these inferences hold if we add the premise that everything in nature exists for the sake of something? Not necessarily, if each function can serve the others.

Whatever the truth of *this* matter is, it remains true that Aristotle thought that all the other essential human functions serve and exist for the sake of the functions of practical and theoretical reason – indeed for the *exercise* of these functions and not merely their existence as capacities. And of course he also held that the full development and exercise of distinctive functions is the goal, the final cause of the organism: the final cause of the individual organism is to become fully what its kind essentially is.

However, even if we accept a central role for distinctive function, we might dispute Aristotle's identification of rationality as the distinctive human function. How about the ability to make fires, have sexual intercourse year around, kill for fun, or tell jokes? Aren't all these activities distinctively human? Here we must remember that for Aristotle rationality is a set of broadly based properties, some of which may after all turn out to be centrally involved in the above activities. These apparent counterexamples may not turn out to be as forceful as they appear at first glance. Why don't other animals make fire? Till we understand this, the fact that only humans make fire is not a very deep objection to Aristotle assigning rationality as the distinctive human function; it may be, for example, that when we have an answer we would be willing to count making fires as a prime example of practical rationality. In addition, we must remember that it is not only distinctiveness that is involved in Aristotle's notion of differentia – the attribute must also be essential: the individual animal perishes if it loses it, and without it the species cannot be picked out (at all or as well) from the rest of the genus. Perhaps practical and theoretical rationalities fit these requirements a lot better than telling jokes, distinctive of humans and important as this may be. Finally, it may be the breadth and centrality of rationality in the understanding of human life that gives Aristotle's choice of rationality such great force. It is difficult to understand any important human activity, it seems, without practical and theoretical rationality, understood in the broad sense of the cognitive capacities for practical and theoretical thought. Inventing and using language, cultivating land, building cities, making and using artifacts, the creation of the arts, the discoveries of the sciences – all these are clearly distinctive and enormously central human activities which could not exist without the distinctive human cognitive capacities; at least they do not in fact exist in animals without these capacities.

But even if we accept rationality as the essential and distinctive human function, why should *the good* for a person lie in his or her distinctive function, a question which Thomas Nagel has pressed (in Rorty, 1980, pp.

7–14)? Here we must first remind ourselves that, just as Aristotle does not deny that humans have other essential functions besides rationality, so he does not deny that a human being's *total good* will include *in some way or other* well functioning in nutrition, reproduction, perception, affective response, and even locomotion. He does not deny, for example, that health is a good, indeed an important one, even though the good of health lies in the well doing of many activities we have in common with animals. Nagel himself does not deny that some human good lies in the well doing of such rational activities as deliberating, proving theorems, or constructing experiments. Once more, the issue concerns the primacy or centrality Aristotle attributes to the good of rationality among all human goods, and the subordination or subservience of other goods to it. And here we can say that in general the primacy and centrality of the good of rationality among all human goods will depend on the primacy and centrality of the function of rationality among all human functions, in all of human life. And when we look at the scope and depth of rationality, we can see that the good of rationality is indeed enormous. Rationality, practical and theoretical, enables us to understand ourselves, to create and understand the typical human activities. But it also enables us to understand the rest of the universe. Practical rationality enables us to understand and serve not only our own survival and growth but that of communities and nations and indeed the whole species, and even the survival of other species. More fundamentally, theoretical rationality enables us to use language and abstractions to understand and build up theories about ourselves, our development as individuals, our species, the differences between us and other animals, animals and plants, organic and inorganic matter, the earth and the heavens, the whole universe. Aristotle knew this much, even without the benefits of knowing the theory of evolution, the genetic code, modern physics and chemistry, decision and game theory. Even with his modest knowledge, he could see that rationality far outstrips other animal functions in scope and depth, theoretical rationality even reaching the powers of the gods (*NE*, Bk. X, ch. 7).

Sense perception comes in second; though it is fundamental and enormously useful to animals with theoretical rationality; indeed for Aristotle it is a necessary beginning of knowledge in such animals. Its powers are severely limited in scope – to relatively near sensible objects; and it has no depth: it can tell us that something is the case but not why. We can presumably see this in the lives of the rest of the animal kingdom: dolphins, lions, and whales are indeed marvelous animals, with some animal powers far surpassing the same powers in human beings; but they hardly create anything other than replicas of themselves, and they do not even study themselves. Moreover, sense perception does not know how to use rationality, but rationality knows how to use sense perception. Seeing clearly or seeing far can serve both eagles and humans; but in humans it may be put not only to the uses eagles put it, but also to discovering the structure of the heavens or appreciating the Sistine Chapel. In eagles seeing well derives its value from, and is put in the service of, the eagle's need to survive, grow, and reproduce; in humans it also derives value from the role of observation in science, and the appreciation of visual beauty in nature and art. Rationality, especially theoretical rationality, enables us to go beyond "thoughts of mortality"; and "though it be small in balk, in power and value it far surpasses all the rest" (*NE*, Bk. X, ch. 7, 1178a).

If we *are*, above all, our rationality, would not the good of rationality be above all *our* good? Even if sometimes we envied the simpler life of an eagle, would we, even if we could, want to lead a life of such severe limits? "Moreover, each person would seem to be his understanding, if he is his controlling and better element; it would be absurd, then, if he were to choose not his own life, but something else's" (*NE*, Bk. X, ch. 7, 1178a).

Even if we lay all this aside, we face another objection to the function argument, to the premise that a good person is a person who performs her function well: a person is not an instrument, something to be used, and so it is a mistake to evaluate a person by how good such an instrument she is. But, so the objection continues, this is just what the function argument does, it evaluates a person instrumentally, by how good she or he is in performing a function. This too is a misunderstanding, though probably a more complex one. For one thing, for Aristotle functioning well may be instrumental in producing things, but not necessarily in acting virtuously or thinking well – indeed we see this in his distinction between doing and producing. Functioning well for a carpenter is purely instrumental, a means to a good product; acting temperately is not entirely instrumental; nor is thinking well purely instrumental. For another, it is misleading to think of instrumentality as the correct relation between a good person and acting virtuously: a good person is one who acts virtuously; as a disposition, a virtue may indeed cause or enable one to act virtuously, but the disposition is not a means to acting virtuously. Further, the objection may be based on the Kantian view that it is morally wrong to use a person as a means or only as a means, which might be thought to imply that it is wrong to evaluate a person as a means. This objection is clearly without foundation in the case of the flautist, whom we

evaluate by how well she or he plays the flute. But it also has no application to the Aristotelian view that a good human is one who performs
well the human function. The Kantian objection is that it is morally wrong
to use *another* person as only a means to *one's own* purposes. But
Aristotle's view is that a person is a good person if she or he performs
well the function of human beings; she or he is not evaluated by how
well she or he serves the purposes of *another*.

Finally, objection has been made to the implicit premise of the function argument, that the good for human beings consists in or includes
being a good human being. Aristotle, it is said, is confusing two notions
of goodness: being good of a kind with what is good for a kind; and
within that confusion, he is confusing being a morally good person with
the good for a person. I think we have to say that it is extraordinary that
in the function argument Aristotle seems to take it for granted that being
a good person is the good or the principal good of that person. It is as if
the greatest controversy in Plato's *Republic*, whether justice brings happiness to the just, has already been decided and we can assume the Platonic
position without argument. It is equally extraordinary that the controversy
is not acknowledged and the assumption is not explicitly argued in the
whole of *NE* (see Young, from 1988 on). But I do not think we can say
that Aristotle confuses the two notions of goodness. For example, in *Politics*, Bk. III, ch. 6, he distinguishes between deviant and correct constitutions on the basis of whose good their kind of justice promotes, the good
of the rulers or the good of all. And he acknowledges and argues against
a position such as that of Thrasymachus, that justice is what is to the
interest of the ruling party; the implication of such a position is that it is
not necessarily to the interest of the subjects to act justly (*Politics*, Bk. III).
So Aristotle is not confusing the notions of being just (being a good
person) and being benefited (the good of a person).

But the function argument does assume, first, that the functioning well
of a being of a certain kind is the good (or the chief good) of beings of
that kind, and this for all the essential functions, common and distinctive;
second, it assumes that the well functioning of the distinctive function is
the central or primary good among all the goods of well functioning. As
applied to human beings, the first assumption has as much initial plausibility as the claim that the satisfaction of desire is the good for a human.[19]
In medicine, for example, this first assumption is taken for granted: the
well functioning of parts and of the whole human organism is assumed
to be an important part of the human good. Desire has nothing to say
about it: if a man did not happen to desire to function well physically, to

see well for example, this would not make his seeing well any less good
for him. And I submit we assume something similar in all our theories of
education, physical and mental: the development and well functioning of
human physical and intellectual powers is assumed to be an important part
of the human good. And here too desire has nothing to say about it, except
to serve as a motivator. The second proposition, that the development and
well functioning of a person's mental powers is the primary or central
human good, is assumed in the function argument; but as we have seen,
it is at least partly argued for in *De Anima*, Bk. II, ch. 3, and Bk. III, ch.
12, where it is argued that the other human functions *serve* the mental
powers, and arguably exist for their sake.

One might reply that there are other human goods besides the well
functioning of all the essential human functions, common and distinctive:
for example, good birth, good looks, wealth, powers and offices, reputation and honors, friends, and all the rest of their kind. These are the goods
of the body and social goods whose value, Socrates had argued, depends
on wisdom and virtue. We have seen that Aristotle acknowledges these
goods and attributes to them instrumental value within the orectic conception of the good. But after the function argument, he returns to them
(in *NE*, Bk. I, chs. 8–12). Here, and again in Bk. X, ch. 8, he acknowledges that they have value, and he tries to account for that value on the
basis of his functional theory. He certainly does not deny that these are
goods and that they have a place in the happy life. The only question is
what kinds of goods they are, and what is their place in the good life. His
attitude toward them and his strategy about them is similar as in his treatment of pleasures – external goods have no value of their own and independently of the exercise of wisdom and the virtues – though the roles
of external goods and pleasures are different.

John Cooper (1985) has argued that external goods play a more important role in Aristotle's ethics than in Socrates or Plato. Cooper finds that
Aristotle places their value, first, in their instrumentality for virtuous
action: they are either necessary for virtuous activity, as money is for generous actions, or especially effective for virtuous actions, as political position is for promoting the public good. Second, external goods help in not
impeding or in enhancing virtuous actions by supplying "preferred circumstances" for the fullest exercise of the virtues. A good violinist can play
well with almost any violin but plays at his best when in good form and
with the best violin (see *NE*, Bk. X, chs. 3, 4, on the best exercise of a
faculty); similarly, a virtuous person can exercise her virtue even in meager
circumstances, but best if she is wealthy, good-looking, has friends and con-

nections, honors and reputation. In such cases her happiness will not be "disfigured," but be more complete and blessed.[20]

Cooper notes that Aristotle's view of external goods was influenced by Socrates' treatment of them in the "crucial texts for the whole later development of Greek moral philosophy" of *Euthydemus*, 278ff. and *Meno*, 87ff. – the passages we examined in chapter 2. He implies that Socrates may not have realized as clearly as Aristotle did that external goods play the first two roles in virtuous action, "either as part of the context of action or as instruments to be used in it." But in any case, Cooper says that even if we concede to Socrates that "their value is not independent of the value of virtuous action, that does not mean that the good that virtue does [which lies in the exercise of virtue] is available without them. Socrates, then, was wrong to say or imply that happiness is possible without these goods" (1985, p. 190). Perhaps, though this difference between Socrates and Aristotle does not require that external goods are constituents of happiness; their being necessary conditions suffices. But how much of external goods is necessary for happiness? As we interpreted Socrates' position, a minimal amount of external goods – a baseline – is necessary for wisdom and virtue, for a wise and virtuous use of such goods; certainly enough, for example, for maintaining one's body in health and strength and one's mind sound, so that one can perform virtuous actions.[21] Socrates might also agree that one's happiness would be more complete and blessed with more than a minimal amount of external goods.[22]

Aristotle's view of external goods and his perfectionist is clear, if we assume the first two roles for external goods, instrumentality and preferred circumstances. The virtuous person desires external goods because and in so far as they are necessary or effective instruments for virtuous activity, or because and in so far as they provide preferred circumstances for the best and most complete exercise of virtue. This Cooper has illuminated and established, and it is sufficient to account for what Aristotle says about external goods, and to mark important continuities with, as well as subtle differences from, the Socratic view. Whether external goods are constituents of happiness remains problematic; and though they can be aimed at in virtuous activity, such aims need not be subordinate goods, and certainly not ultimate; their previous two roles are sufficient to explain their being aimed at in many cases.[23]

To sum up: Aristotle's conception of the human good *includes* all the human well functionings, common and distinctive, physical and mental, social and political, *and* the external goods, social and physical. But it assigns to them different places and roles in the good and happy life: the greatest single good, desired for itself and not as a means to anything, is the well functioning of theoretical reason; but this by itself is not a complete good, at least not for human beings. The next greatest single goods are the well functionings of practical reason or the exercise of the virtues of character, desired for themselves *and* for enabling theoretical reason to function well; these are subordinate goods. The well functioning of the essential functions we have in common with animals, are subservient goods, desired for the sake of the subordinate and ultimate goods; they enable and enhance the performance of practical and theoretical functions of reason. Social goods provide the instruments and circumstances for the well functioning of practical reason. Not being aware of the fantastic modern material demands of research in the sciences, Aristotle thought that far fewer external goods were necessary for the functioning of theoretical reason and that the life of theoretical wisdom was the most self-sufficient.

There may still be objection that it has not been establishd that functioning well, in the sense of acting in accord with virtue, is the good or part of the good for man. It may be granted that the well functioning of theoretical and practical reason, conceived on the analogy of physical well functioning, is part of the human good. But why should we assume that such well functioning, at least practical well functioning, is acting virtuously and so constitutes being a good human being? Here we need to see the relation between the functional account of the good and virtue. Aristotle of course *says* that the human good is activity of practical and theoretical reason in accordance with virtue. But why is the well functioning of practical and theoretical reason the same as activity of reason in accordance with virtue? Can't a person's practical reason function well in calculating how to act badly – to steal, for example? This large objection to the functional theory has to do with the interpretation of the relation between function and virtue, and well functioning and acting virtuously. We need to see how the function argument works itself out relative to the virtues. We shall do some of this in the next chapter, when we take up the structure of Aristotle's ethical theory, the threat of circularities, and paucity of practical content.

5   Orectic, Hedonic, and Perfectionist Good

For the rest of this chapter, we turn to the most obvious omission of the function argument, the good of pleasure. What is the role of pleasure in the happy life, and how does pleasure fit into the function argument?

In this discussion we need to remember constantly that Aristotle had a perfectionist theory of good; or at least we need to make this hypothesis consistently and see if we can understand his account of pleasure better. Aristotle's perfectionism deserves to be taken seriously, both because it is his real theory of good, and because perfectionist theories are *the* great alternative to desire-based and hedonistic theories, as Sidgwick, himself no perfectionist, reminds us (1981, pp. 9–11).

In comparing Aristotle's discussions of good as orectic end and good as well functioning, we are struck first of all by the apparent lack or relation between the two: in the whole discussion of the good (to the middle of Bk. I, ch. 7) there is no reference to function, and in the function argument there is no reference to desire. We could of course say that for Aristotle the end of a thing and its distinctive function are one and the same, the final cause of that thing. And we could produce some evidence for this (*De Anima*, Bk. I, ch. 1; Irwin, 1985, pp. 396, 404; Keyt, 1991). But I do not believe that Aristotle assumes this in his ethics, and it might well be that to do so would be begging the question in disputes with hedonistic or desire-based theories. After all, a person might simply not *want* to do what Aristotle theorizes is a human function. And in fact Aristotle does not proceed by relying on this assumption. His evidence for good as orectic end consists of what people in fact desire and what they say they want; and we saw that in Bk. X, ch. 2, in his discussion of Eudoxus' psychological hedonism, he defends this evidence. His argument for functional or perfectionist good, on the other hand, is drawn from our evaluative practices in the arts and medicine, where we do evaluate functionally, and from his psychology and biology. But Aristotle, characteristically, wants to reconcile these two lines of thought as much as possible; and so we need to look at the role of the function argument within this larger framework and see how functional good can be related to orectic good.

Our main clue is Aristotle's acknowledgment of the disagreement among men about what happiness or the good is: the function argument is supposed to determine the content of the good or settle disagreements about ultimate ends, the main thing which any theory of good as orectic end fails to do. But the function argument need not, and in any case does not, retract the formal features of the good as orectic end, namely, that it is the ultimate and self-sufficient end of all action. It is the good as having these formal features whose content the function argument seeks to deter-

mine, as Keyt and Irwin tell us. Aristotle nowhere retracts these formal
features, perhaps because the good as orectic end best exhibits the formal
features that make rational choice easiest and simplest, and because it
assures us that there is such a thing since humans do desire their own happiness as the ultimate and self-sufficient end of all their actions. But
humans, alas, disagree about what happiness is, and in fact desire different
things as the ultimate and self-sufficient end of their actions; and if we
stay with desire we cannot rationally resolve such disagreement. So we
change over to good as well functioning and try to determine the content
of the good on the basis of that. If there is disagreement *here* we can try
to resolve it rationally by appealing to facts in biology, anthropology, psychology, and so on. But this is no reason to retract the formal features of
the good as orectic end, because the content the function argument determines can also have these features. The distinctive human functions can
be the ends of conduct; though whether they are in fact the ultimate ends
of human desires is another question, one which Aristotle faces and tries
to handle in his account of pleasure, as we shall soon see.

So, at the formal level, we might say, there is no conflict between good
as orectic end and good as well functioning, nor between the good as the
ultimate and self-sufficient end of all our actions and the good as the
excellence of functionings essential and characteristic of humans; the latter
could be the ultimate orectic end and the former excellent human
functionings.

But at the material level there are some spectacular differences, even
possible conflicts, between the two accounts. And if we take seriously the
interpretation which makes the functional account, material and formal,
Aristotle's true view of the good, we have to look at the implications of
this, and also consider how these differences and conflicts might be
somehow reconciled.

One difference is that the functional theory tells us that the good or
happiness is *activity*. This is a departure from the model of happiness as
consisting in the possession of good things; a model we find in Plato
as late as the *Symposium*, and one that goes well with the notion of good
as orectic end, since desire was thought of as possessive and acquisitive
(Santas, 1988, ch. 2). If the good is activity, then anything which is good
either *is* activity, or is good by virtue of some suitable relation to activity.
Moral virtue, for example, is not activity but a state of character or disposition; but the exercise or actualization of that disposition is activity
which is good, and the good of virtue as disposition lies in that relation.[24]

Honor is further removed from activity but still connected with it: the good of honor consists in its being evidence of virtue.

That the good is activity is no accidental feature of Aristotle's philosophy. It has deep connections with his biology and metaphysics, in which basic classification is made by characteristic and essential functions, functionings constitute the actuality of a thing, and this (second) actuality is prior in time, in nature, and in definition to potentiality.[25] And the basic intuition of any perfectionist view of the good is that the good of each kind lies in the development and exercise of its characteristic and essential powers or potentialities. And such developing and exercise are activities of one kind or another.

But perhaps the most spectacular difference in content between Aristotle's accounts of good as orectic end and as well functioning is the difference in subordinate goods. In his account of the good as orectic end, as we saw, Aristotle argues that reason, virtue, pleasure, and honor are subordinate, not ultimate, goods, since we desire them for themselves and also because we think that through them we become happy. So, given the uniqueness, ultimacy, and self-sufficiency of the good and the above subordinate goods, it was reasonable to think that Aristotle's view, within the account of the good as orectic end, was that the good was composed of all subordinate goods. But when we look at the content of the good determined by the function argument, we find reason and virtue conspicuously present, and honor and pleasure spectacularly absent.

With honor we can perhaps dodge the problem, appealing to Aristotle's earlier remark, within the account of orectic good, that honor is after all pursued because it is deemed to be evidence of virtue, rather than for itself. So honor seems to be removed from the class of subordinate goods.

But what of pleasure? On the theory of good as orectic end, pleasure would seem to have a nearly undisputed claim to be a subordinate good or an ultimate good, and we saw Aristotle acknowledge this in Bk. I. But on the functional-perfectionist theory of the good, pleasure would seem to have no claim to intrinsic value.

Aristotle's story on pleasure is too long, too difficult, and too disputed (see Gosling and Taylor [1982]). But our discussion of Aristotle's theory of perfectionist good has some definite implications for interpreting Aristotle's theory of pleasure; and I want to bring these out, because they are a useful context in which to try to understand his struggles with pleasure, a context almost universally neglected.

To begin with, if Aristotle has a perfectionist theory of good then his account of pleasure has to fit into that theory, or at least should be seen as an attempt to make it fit. Second, Aristotle's functional argument makes no reference to pleasure, any more than it does to desire. So, if pleasure is some sort of good, or pleasures are in some way good, they have to be so in virtue of some relation to the things the theory explicitly says are "part" of the good, namely, reason and virtue. And of course it is no accident that Aristotle in fact has a whole host of pleasures he finds good, indeed the best pleasures, whose good he relates to the exercise of reason and the virtues, by a version of what Rawls calls the "Aristotelian Principle": the person who excels in the exercise of practical and theoretical reason enjoys these activities because and in so far as he or she excels in them. The enjoyments of reason and virtue attend the excellent exercise of these things and, for Aristotle, they are good because reason and virtue are good.

Third, if the good is activity, then if pleasure is good, it follows either that pleasure *is* activity, or that it is so related to activity that the good of pleasure can be accounted for by the good of activity. So of course it is no accident but a direct consequence of this that Aristotle in *NE*, Bk. VII, chs. 11–13, gives a run to the hypothesis that pleasure *is* activity. And in *NE*, Bk. X, chs. 1–5, where in my opinion he gives up that hypothesis, he tries the other alternative, that pleasure is not identical with activity but bears some relation to it that accounts for the value we attach to pleasure.

What the relation is has been hotly disputed: some say the enjoyment of an activity is a final cause of the activity, some that it is a formal cause (Irwin, 1985; pp. 276–7; Gosling and Taylor, 1982, ch. 13); some stress the "bloom of youth simile" but don't know what to make of it. A perfectionist reading of Aristotle's theory of the good supports the main things he says about the relations in *NE*, Bk. X, chs. 4, 5, and the main things Urmson attributes to him in his classic article (1967). First, the enjoyment of an activity is posterior in nature to it, or existentially dependent on it; and this makes good sense, since I can, say, play golf without enjoying it but I cannot enjoy playing golf without playing it. Second, it is posterior in definition, since in identifying or sorting out enjoyments we have to make reference to the activities enjoyed and not conversely. And third, and perhaps consequently, the value or the good of an enjoyment depends on the value of the activity enjoyed, and pleasures can be ranked by the value of their activities. So, the being, the nature, and the value of pleasure all "depend on" activity.

The third relation, the dependence of the value of enjoyment on the value of the activity enjoyed, is clearly what we would expect from Aristotle's perfectionist account of the good, since on that account pleasure, like anything else, has no value unless it is or is related in some way to excellent functionings essential and characteristic of humans. It is important to note that Aristotle agrees with the hedonist that these pleasures have value, though he disagrees on what makes them valuable.

The first two relations are probably incompatible with hedonism, since they undermine the notion that activity is chosen for the sake of pleasure: if the activity is prior in nature and definition to the enjoyment, then the activity cannot simply be *a* means to that pleasure. These relations, if correct, provide Aristotle's answer to the hedonist who earlier conceded that virtue and reason would add value to a life, but argued that their value would consist in the pleasures to which they are means; if the hedonist could get the pleasures of reason and virtue without reason and virtue, he would be perfectly content without reason and virtue. Aristotle's answer is that this is not possible: if the enjoyments of reason and virtue are naturally and definitionally posterior to the activities of reason and virtue, they cannot be had without the exercise of reason and virtue. To paraphrase Urmson's charming phrase, one could not chance to get the enjoyment of playing the violin from eating Athenian pastries.

Finally, if Aristotle is a perfectionist about the good he cannot also be a hedonist, and indeed he is not.[26] At the end of *NE*, Bk. X, ch. 3, after the dialectical discussion of hedonism and antihedonism, he tells us clearly that pleasure is not the good, and that some pleasures are not desirable. But he also says that some pleasures are desirable or choiceworthy in themselves. This last is what is left, I think, of his view in *NE*, Bk. I, ch. 7, where in his discussion of the good as orectic end he showed himself sensitive to the claims of desire and pleasure to be the good, and where he allowed that pleasure is a subordinate end. This may present some difficulty if he means that some pleasures have value of their own, since he cannot hold this and also the perfectionist position he takes up in *NE*, Bk. X, chs. 4, 5, that all the value of enjoyment is derivative from the value of the activity enjoyed. And in addition, there is the difficulty in understanding his statement, that pleasure "completes" or "perfects" the activity; though he makes it clear that the pleasure is not what makes the activity the best of its kind – it is the condition of the faculty or organ and the suitability of its object that does that; and this is certainly consistent with perfectionism.

Despite these difficulties of detail, it is clear that Aristotle accounts for the value of pleasure as a perfectionist would, just as John Rawls accounts for the value of perfection as a desire theorist would. The comparison is instructive because they both happen to have in common what Rawls appropriately calls the "Aristotelian Principle," but make different use of it: "Other things equal, human beings enjoy the exercise of their realized capacities (their innate or trained abilities), and this enjoyment increases the more the capacity is realized, or the greater its complexity" (1971, pp. 426ff.). To account for the value of developing and exercising our faculties Rawls, who has a desire-based though not hedonistic theory of the good, must bring them within the scope of desire. After all, to use one of Rawl's, own examples, if a talented mathematician enjoys counting blades of grass more than anything else, Rawls has to say, and does say, that this is the good for him (or, a plan of life organized around that activity), even though evidently the man is wasting his talents and his life. But if the Aristotelian Principle is true, we in fact tend to enjoy the development and exercise of our faculties, and so we want to do that after all, and blades of grass cases will be rather rare. The thrust of Aristotle's account of pleasure is to use the same principle, but from the reverse direction: not to account for the value of the development of our faculties, which on his perfectionist view is intrinsically valuable, but to account for the evident value of the enjoyment of such development and exercise. Enjoying the development and exercise of our essential faculties encourages us to develop them further and exercise them more excellently, and this is precisely the reason why we value such enjoyment.

Notes

1 For such contrasts, see Cooper (1987, pp. 249–50); for disagreements, Kahn (1985).

2 *Orexis* is Aristotle's general term for desire, under which he puts appetite, rational desire ("wish"), and anger-like feelings (*De Anima*, Bk. III, chs. 9, 10).

3 Ackrill, 1973, p. 241; Kenny, 1977, p. 26; Broadie, 1991, who acquits Aristotle of fallacy.

4 For more discussion of this complex property, see Irwin (1985); Kraut (1989, pp. 13–14); Crisp (1994).

5 Austin, 1967; Cooper, 1975, p. 145; Anagnostopoulos, 1980; Hardie, 1980, p. 22; Irwin, 1985, p. 204; Keyt, 1983. See also Kraut (1989); Broadie (1991); Whiting (1988); Lawrence (2000).

6 There are many more functions which the argument bypasses: sense perception includes several modalities not always found together; sense perception
brings with it pleasure and pain *and* so desire (*De Anima*, Bk. II, chs. 2, 3;
Bk. III, chs. 8–12). A more complete enumeration would give us the capacities and functions of nutrition, growth and decay, reproduction, sense perception, desire, locomotion, and reason. Plants have the first three, animals
other than man the first three and the second set of three, and man has all
six and reason.

7 This apparent definition or characterization of virtue may be ambiguous: is
Aristotle defining functioning well in terms of virtue, or virtue in terms of
functioning well? See chapter 8 below.

8 See Strange (1999); and Fine's introduction in Strange (1999). Though
Strange does not integrate his discussion with my own interpretation of the
form of the Good, I believe the two discussions go well together.

9 Cooper, 1987, pp. 245, n. 4: "That the concept of a goal is the concept of
something good is a view Aristotle inherited from Plato's *Phaedo*." Gotthelf
(1987a, pp. 237–42) tries to show that good in Aristotle's biology can be
understood naturalistically, including the assumption that nature never does
anything in vain but always acts for the best.

10 Part of the ordered series: nutrition, sense perception, desire, locomotion,
thought. Each successive function presupposes the previous one, since it does
not exist in a living thing without it. So we can add them successively to
get higher forms, but not randomly. Aristotle also thought that each function
serves the one after it and exists for its sake.

11 For a defense, see Cooper (1996).

12 In Sartre (1957); even in Hardie (1968, pp. 23–5).

13 Even Darwin grants that man has such superior posers over other known
living things, though for him the differences are a matter of degree rather
than kind and his explanation, relying on accidents of mutation and on
natural selection, would be different from Aristotle. See Porter and Graham
(1993, pp. 350ff.).

14 See the illuminating discussions, by M. Furth, D. Balme, and A. Gotthelf, of
Aristotle's treatment of structures and functions in his biology, in Gotthelf and
Lennox (1987, especially pp. 36–8, 52, 88, 192).

15 "Aristotle's Use of Division and Differentia," in Gotthelf and Lennox, 1987.

16 With the exceptional exception of the Unmoved Mover?

17 For discussion of this assumption see, e.g., A. Gotthelf, in Gotthelf and Lennox
(1987, pp. 185ff.).

18 Whether teleological explanations are compatible with evolution is,
surprisingly, a disputed question. See, e.g., Wright (1976); and Ayala
(1998).

19 Sen (1985) argues that well functionings are part of the human good, and
Cooper (1996) connects well functioning with the development and exer-

cise of one's innate powers and faculties. See also John Rawls's (1971) use of the "Aristotelian Principle."

20   Cooper argues, further, that external goods are for Aristotle *constituents* of happiness (1985, pp. 176, 192). It is not clear to me how external goods, most of which are not activities (friends, property, reputation), can be parts of happiness, which is activity.

21   As Cooper notes, external goods can include social *and* bodily goods. This is my use in this discussion, since this is the Socratic use in *Gorgias* and elsewhere.

22   Cooper notes a third role yet for external goods, and tries to show that it is integral to Aristotle's theory. This role is "as objects of pursuit or goals of action in virtuous activity. . . ." (1985, pp. 192–4). This is a different role from the two noted earlier; it is not clear to me whether this is compatible with Aristotle's perfectionism or the conclusion of the function argument, or his virtue ethics. Perhaps this third role fits with Aristotle's view that virtuous action is desirable for itself and for its results: e.g. health for temperate actions, victory for courageous actions. But this is an incomplete picture for Aristotle: why are health and victory desired? Presumably, health is prized because it is a necessary condition for the full exercise of the virtues; and victory because it enables the city to remain free and the citizens to develop and exercise their virtues, personal and political. Health and victory are certainly not ultimate goods for Aristotle, not even subordinate goods. When Aristotle discusses virtue as a subordinate good, he says that it is desired for itself *and* for the sake of *happiness* (*NE*, Bk. I, ch. 7). What then is *this* happiness – the possession and maintenance of external goods?

23   Many, perhaps most, choices in life are made in view of subservient ends and goods. Witness agriculture, commerce, and many crafts, trades and businesses: almost everything done in these is for the sake of such goods as food, shelter, clothing, and property, and wealth. We need not suppose that any of them are subordinate goods to account for their being ends of innumerable actions and activities. And in Aristotle's discussion of orectic good we saw him classifying wealth as a subservient end in the blink of an eyelid.

24   Young, 1988. The good of temperance, subtly delineated by Young, is, I believe, perfectionist; in an area of life in which we deal with our animality, choices involving some of our desires and pleasures for food, drink, and sex, this virtue enables us to have correct attitudes and make correct choices. Temperance enables us to become *rational* animals to a higher degree, and this is a perfectionist good.

25   See Irwin (1980, especially pp. 39–41; and 1988). For priority in nature and in definition, see Keyt (1991, pp. 126ff.).

26   Gosling and Taylor (1982) seem to think that Aristotle is an ethical hedonist (see ch. 14, section 6, part 1). For criticism of this see Urmson (1984, pp. 215–17).

8

The Good of Character and of Justice

Aristotle's ethics is usually thought to be the paradigm of virtue ethics: an ethical theory in which the good of character has explanatory primacy over all other values. Some philosophers have seen this structure as an advantage of Aristotle's theory: it highlights the virtues of character, which the moderns seem to neglect; and it avoids the vicious circularity it would fall into if it had the structure of a teleological ethical theory. Other philosophers have claimed that a virtue ethics cannot account for the virtue of justice, which needs a different framework that gives explanatory primacy to the rightness of principles, as modern Kantian or deontological theories do. To complicate matters further, several structures have been proposed for a virtue ethics, and it is not clear which of these structures, if any, Aristotle's ethics has.

1 Is Aristotle's Ethical Theory Circular?

It is convenient to begin with the charge that Aristotle's theory contains vicious circularities which deprive it of suffecent practical content, since this raises the issue of structure of the theory and the role of the good in it.

Sidgwick made the charge of circularity a century ago, but he is not alone. Sandra Peterson says that "the appearance of explanatory circularity in the *Nicomachean Ethics* is positively dizzying." She cites no fewer than "fourteen apparitions" which writers have "seen" and tried to make disappear, from Aquinas to Grote and Greenwood, to Ackrill and Cooper (Peterson, 1992). But not all of them have the same circularity in mind.

I believe there are two main apparent circularities. The most fundamental is brought up by Sidgwick, on the assumptions that Aristotle had a teleological ethical theory *and* a perfectionist theory of the good.

Sidgwick has essentially the same conceptual framework for ethical theories as John Rawls and other recent writers: there are two ways in which an ethical theory can relate the right and the good: ultimate good may be conceived independently of the right and the right is conceived as what promotes ultimate good; or, "conduct is held to be right when conformed to certain precepts or principles of Duty, intuitively known to be unconditionally binding," and "without consideration of ulterior consequences" (Sidgwick, 1981, pp. 3, 96, 391; for Rawls's definition see 1971, pp. 24, 30). Sidgwick called the second type of ethical theory "intuitional," the usual name being "deontological"; while the first type, of which utilitarianism is an example, is called teleological (or consequentialist when it insists on an instrumental relation of right conduct to the good).

Now when it comes to Ultimate Good, Sidgwick says that there are two ends which have

> a strongly and widely supported claim to be regarded as ultimate rational ends ... Happiness and Perfection or Excellence of human nature – meaning here by "Excellence" not primarily superiority to others, but a partial realization or, approximation to, an ideal type of human Perfection. (1981, p. 9)

Sidgwick sees no problem of circularity in a teleological ethical theory with happiness as the ultimate good, if happiness is pleasure (as in Bentham and Sidgwick), or (we might add) the satisfaction of rational desire, since these can be specified independently of the right.

But Sidgwick sees a logical difficulty in a teleological ethical theory with perfection or excellence of human nature as the ultimate good, when "[moral] virtue is commonly conceived as the most valuable element of human Excellence . . ." (1981, p. 11). If we use *moral* virtue (virtue character) to define excellence or perfection, then we cannot also define such virtue as what promotes excellence or perfection, without going around in a logical circle; a circle which would be evident in such explications as "virtue is what promotes virtue," or "virtue is what promotes virtue and . . ." (1981, p. 392) To make reference to *moral* virtue in defining ultimate good violates the first condition of a teleological theory, the independence of the good from the right; and once such a condition is violated, either a teleological structure has to be given up or we fall into circularity.

To avoid such circularity, Sidgwick classified *modern* ethical theories which take the ultimate good to be excellence or perfection, as intuitional, i.e. deontological, on the assumption that the chief part, or all of, excellence or perfection is moral virtue (1981, p. 3).[1] But, he argued, the ancients, even allowing for their greatness, were guilty of falling into the circle. Sidgwick correctly perceived, in my opinion, that most ancient Greek ethical theorists were perfectionists, that is, they thought the ultimate good was, partly or wholly, perfection or excellence. But, he argued, they were also teleologists: they explicated virtue in terms of promoting the good. Having done that, however, they failed to see that they could not also explicate the good in terms of virtue; not only the Stoics who seemed to have thought that virtue is all of the good (and so their circle is "Virtue is what 'promotes' virtue"), but also Plato and Aristotle who counted moral virtue as *one* element or part of the good; so for them the circle is "moral virtue is what promotes moral virtue and, e.g. wisdom" (1981, pp. 375–6). They explicated the good by reference to virtue and virtue by reference to the good.

The second major circularity is usually located in Aristotle's analysis of the relation between moral virtue and practical wisdom. In his definition of virtue of character (*NE*, Bk. II, ch. 6), as a disposition to choose the mean relative to us as the person of practical wisdom would choose it, he has reference to practical wisdom, the intellectual virtue (virtue of thought) which is supposed to guide our choices. But in his analysis of practical wisdom (in *NE*, Bk.VI), practical wisdom starts deliberation from right or correct ends, and these are provided by moral virtue; so we seem to have a reference back to moral virtue in the analysis of practical wisdom. This looks like another circle (Peterson, 1992; Broadie, 1991), a circle within Sidgwick's larger circle!

Now these two apparent circles are plainly not the same. But we may well wonder how they are related – an issue we have never seen discussed. If Aristotle's ethical theory is teleological and his theory of the good perfectionist, we can see that Sidgwick's circle, assuming it obtains at all, would be the more fundamental of the two; but the second circle is to be expected if Sidgwick's circle is assumed. How so? If the theory is teleological, moral virtue is what (dispositions, actions, etc.) promotes the good; and if the theory of the good is perfectionist *and* moral virtue is part of perfection, then moral virtue is part of the good, and we have Sidgwick's circle – "moral virtue is what promotes moral virtue *and* . . ." But if this is so, we seem to get also the second circle: if moral virtue is part of *the* good, then practical wisdom, whose function is to discover the necessary or most effective means to this good, must always take as *an* end of such means the states of character which constitute moral virtue: in the sense that no matter what other ends are aimed at, the means chosen must promote or at least not destroy the disposition which is moral virtue. Otherwise the means chosen are not correct, and the wisdom in question might be Aristotle's "cleverness" – an ability to choose necessary or efficient means no matter what the ends. So this second circle, or at least its appearance, is really the result of a constraint on the ends of conduct imposed by a moral perfectionism of the good on a teleological ethical theory.

An unfortunate but predictable result of these circularities, Sidgwick thought, is that ancient Greek ethical theories lack sufficient practical content; as guides to choice and conduct they are not specific enough for deciding what humans ought to do. Now some loss of practical content may well be expected from major circularities in an ethical theory; circularity between definitions or explications can be vicious because it can result in lack of the information we need from the definitions. This is a modern stock objection to Aristotelian ethics, as old as Grotius. Except for justice, a crucial and neglected exception we take up later, one can read Aristotle's analysis of courage, temperance, or generosity, and still have no specific guidance about what to do. As Sidgwick puts it for the doctrine of the mean, "Nor, again, does Aristotle bring us much nearer such knowledge by telling us that the Good in conduct is to be found somewhere between different kinds of Bad. This at best indicates the *whereabouts* of virtue: it does not give us a method for finding it" (1981, pp. 375–6, 343–4).

The issues of circularity and practical content are related. If Aristotle's theory does not lack practical content, any more than could be reasonably expected for the subject matter, then even if there are circularities, perhaps they are not vicious – the theory can still be a reasonable guide to choices. We shall pursue later the issue of practical content as a separate line of investigation independently of the issues of circularity.

Now Sidgwick's charge of circularity has certainly been influential. In the last century the tendency has been to try to get Aristotle out of Sidgwick's circle by arguing either that he had a purely instrumental view of the relation of virtue to happiness, and thus could specify happiness independently of virtue; *or*, that he did not have a teleological ethical theory, and thus happiness or the good need not be determined independently of virtue.

W. D. Ross made the first of these major moves: "Aristotle's ethics is definitely teleological; morality for him consists in doing certain actions not because we see them to be right in themselves but because we see them to be such as will bring us nearer to the 'good for man'." Ross was aware of one difficulty in his interpretation, namely, Aristotle's view that virtuous action is "desirable or valuable in itself," but he says that this is not consistent with Aristotle's teleological ethics, and implies that the inconsistency is in Aristotle (1959, pp. 184, 190; Vlastos, 1991, ch. 8).

There are, however, other options within a teleological structure with a perfectionist theory of good. One is that Aristotle had a "strict intellectualist" view in which perfection is *constituted* by the intellectual virtues, not the *moral* virtues or the virtues of character. In such a case Sidgwick's circle would not obtain. Another possibility is that there is an apparent circle between moral virtue and happiness, but it can be eliminated on further analysis. Or, there is a circle that cannot be eliminated but is wide enough so as neither to be vicious, nor to deprive the theory of sufficient practical content. We explore all these possibilities later on.

John Cooper has made the second major move. He clearly says that Aristotle's theory is not teleological, using Rawls's definition, on the ground that Aristotle's theory violates the first condition, the independence of the good from virtue: "eudaimonia is itself not specified independently of virtuous action . . ." (Cooper, 1975, pp. 87–8, and nn. 113, 114). And he is correct, in that we have strong textual support for it in the function argument and elsewhere; though, as I shall argue, this is not the end of the matter. A problem with this second defense to Sidwick's objection is that it takes the form of arguing that the distinction between teleological and deontological theories does not apply at all to ancient ethical theories; Aristotle did not have a deontological theory either, as indeed Cooper makes explicit (1975, p. 88). But if Aristotle's ethical theory is neither teleological nor deontological, what is its structure?

Perhaps Aristotle had a virtue ethics, whose structure falls outside the modern dichotomy of teleological and deontological theories. But what is the structure of such a theory? The advantage of Sidgwick's and Rawls's classification of ethical theories is that it is clear-headed. The modern elaborations of teleological ethical theories by utilitarians and of deontological theories by Kant and Rawls have done much to clarify the structures of these theories. But the same cannot be said about the structure of virtue ethics, though there has been some progress recently. So here we face the difficulty of becoming clear about the structure(s) of virtue ethics, before we can even take up the question whether Aristotle had a virtue ethics.

2   Did Aristotle Have a Virtue Ethics?

Surprisingly, some writers have suggested that Aristotle did not have a virtue ethics, but Plato did; though most writers seem to have Aristotle in mind when criticizing or defending a virtue ethics (Slote, 1989; Trianoski, 1990; Watson, 1990; Schneewind, 1990). This division of opinion reflects controversy on two fundamental questions: What is a virtue ethics? And, what is the structure of Aristotle's ethical theory? Some philosophers have recently tackled the first question (see Schneewind [1990]; Trianoski [1990]; and Watson [1990]), while a number of philosophers and classicists have wrestled with the second (Sidgwick, 1981, intro., chs. 9, 13; Ross, 1949; Cooper, 1975, pp. 87–8, 125–35).

There is agreement among friends and foes of virtue ethics that there are significant contrasts between an ethics of virtue and an ethics of principles and rules (Schneewind, 1990). What are they?

Some strong contrasts have been isolated recently. A "*pure* ethics of virtue," writes Trianoski, makes two claims: (1) "at least some judgments about virtue can be validated independently of any appeal to judgments about the rightness of actions"; and (2) "it is this antecedent goodness of traits which ultimately makes any right act right."[2] He claims that Plato, in his definition of soul justice in *Republic*, Bk. IV, satisfies both these conditions and so has a pure virtue ethics; and Aristotle "might be read" so as to satisfy them.

We find the Platonic view in *Republic*, 443e–444a: the man who has attained order (justice) and harmony (temperance) in his soul will

> then and only then turn to practice . . . in the getting of wealth or the tendance of the body or in political action or private business, in all such doing believing and naming the just and honorable action to be that which preserves and helps to produce this condition of soul, and wisdom the science that presides over such conduct . . . and the unjust action to be that which tends to overthrow this spiritual constitution . . ." (Shorey transl.)

Earlier Plato had defined justice in the soul (a virtue of persons) without reference to conduct at all, as a psychic state in which each of the three parts of the soul is performing its own optimal function: reason rules, spirit defends, and appetite obeys reason on the satisfaction of bodily needs. So here we do indeed seem to have the two conditions of a pure virtue ethics satisfied. Though this is not an adequate interpretation of Plato's theory of justice,[3] it can serve here as an example of a "pure virtue ethics."

Gary Watson (1990) tries to isolate a virtue ethics which falls outside the modern conceptual framework of teleological and deontological ethical theories, in which moral worth or moral virtue is derived from, or defined in terms of, the right or the good. His view is of historical and theoretical interest. Perhaps Watson has succeeded in identifying a structure which fits and illuminates Aristotle's theory.

The conceptual schema defining this Watsonian (1990) ethics of virtue is as follows:

> 1. Living a characteristically human life (functioning well as a human being) requires possessing and exemplifying certain traits, T. 2. T are therefore human excellences and render their possessors to that extent good human beings. 3. Acting in a way W is in accordance with T (exemplifies or is not contrary to T). 4. Therefore, W is right (good, or wrong).

It appears from 3 and 4 that in a virtue ethics right conduct is defined in terms of, derived from, validated, or explained, by reference to the virtues as states of character. And this appears contrary to the way modern nonvirtue ethics theorists have proceeded, from Grotius to Rawls. Rawls's characterization of "the fundamental moral virtues" as "the strong and normally effective desires to act on the basic principles of right" (1971, p. 436), is essentially the same in the relevant respect as that of Grotius (Schneewind, 1990, pp. 46–8); not to speak of John Locke who makes the matter explicit: "By whatever standard soever we frame in our minds the ideas of virtues or vices . . . their rectitude . . . consists in the agreement with those patterns prescribed by some Law" (1959, p. 358).

The writers reviewed above do not say explicitly enough in what sense the virtues of character are more fundamental. Trianoski speaks of judgments about virtue being "validated" independently of judgments about the rightness of actions, and about the goodness of traits "making" right acts right; Watson speaks of "explanatory primacy"; Locke and possibly Rawls could be interpreted as offering definitional remarks.

In Aristotle, *one* way the issue could be posed is by using his notion of *priority in definition*: one thing is prior in formula [definition] to another if and only if the one is mentioned in the definition of the other but not the other in the definition of the one.[4] If, for example, Rawls defines a just person as one who has strong and normally effective desires to act according to principles of justice, and in his statement of principles of justice he makes no reference to just persons, then in his theory just principles would be prior in definition to just persons.

So *one* contrast between a virtue ethics and an ethics of principles may be whether the virtues as traits of character are to be defined in terms of principles of right conduct, as Grotius, Locke, and Rawls might be read to be saying, or whether principles of right or right conduct are to be defined in terms of the virtues, as the virtue theorists would have it.

There may also be other relations between the virtue of persons and the rightness of their acts, relevant to our issue: logical derivability, causal relations, ontological relations, relations of "finality" — what is desired and pursued for the sake of what. The Aristotelian texts are full of remarks about such relations, and we must be sensitive to them.

There is a second question to be answered, besides the relation between the goodness of character and the rightness of acts, perhaps more difficult and controversial: What is the relation between virtue and good?

Watson admits that his schema for a virtue ethics appeals "to several notions of good: to functioning well as a human being, to being a good human being, to being a human excellence (perhaps also to being good for one as a human being)." But, he claims, there is no "essential appeal to the idea of a valuable state of affairs or outcome from which the moral significance of everything (or anything) else derives" (1990, p. 459.) It is not entirely clear what is this notion of a good state of affairs or a good outcome, other than the notions of good Watson has listed as being appealed to. Why, for example, is not functioning well an example — even a paradigmatic one — of a good outcome? We shall indeed find that in Aristotle functioning well may be the most fundamental normative concept.

Watson distinguishes his virtue ethics from "character utilitarianism," which he believes is not a virtue ethics. According to this theory, (1) the virtues are human traits that promote human happiness [the good] more than alternative traits; and in turn, (2) right conduct is defined as conduct which is contrary to no virtue and wrong conduct as conduct contrary to some virtue. Because of (1) Watson calls this character utilitarianism an "ethics of outcome" rather than a virtue ethics, though by (2) it satisfies the first condition by which writers distinguish a virtue ethics, the priority of virtue over right conduct.

Character utilitarianism gives a more prominent role to the virtues than do rule or act utilitarian theories or deontological theories; and perhaps some writers have read Aristotle as a character utilitarian. But we shall find that for Aristotle functioning well is prior in definition to, and more final than, the state of character that enables one to do so. It is very doubtful that he is a character utilitarian.

There is a third view which, Watson says, is "naturally called an ethics of virtue." According to it, (1) right conduct is defined in terms of the virtues; but (2) the virtues are either the sole or the primary *constituents* of the good (or happiness), this being its essential difference from character utilitarianism which seems to take the virtues as instrumental to happiness (Watson, 1990, p. 457). Here it would appear that both right conduct and the good are defined in terms of the virtues; so it would be difficult indeed to see how this fails to be an ethics of virtue.

In *sum*, we have three different theories which might be counted as a virtue ethics: Watson's theory, the constitutive theory, and character utilitarianism. What all three share in common is the definitional priority of virtue as a state of character over right conduct. Where they differ is in the relation of virtue to good or to the good. This relation may not completely clear till a theory of virtue is in place. Aristotle, whatever the structure of his theory, has arguably the most developed theory of virtue we have up to now, some twenty-three centuries later. Because of this and because the structures we have identified are not completely clear since they lack a theory of virtue, we have a chance, in examining Aristotle's ethical theory, to clarify both the question of the structures of ethics of virtue and the question of the structure of Aristotle's ethical theory. The structures we have identified can serve as guiding hypotheses, for identifying the structure of Aristotle's theory and for clarifying an ethics of virtue.

Does Aristotle's theory have any of these structures?

Before we can answer this question, though, we must consider a significant and much neglected possibility. Our investigation so far presupposes that whatever analysis of virtue Aristotle has, it is the same for all the virtues of character. But this overlooks the possibility that *some* virtues, such as generosity and benevolence, are susceptible to a virtue ethics analysis, while others, such as justice, are not. This is a possibility for any ethical theory. I believe it is also a live possibility for Aristotle's theory and one which, so far as I know, has not been examined.

In an illuminating modern historical sketch, J. B. Schneewind (1990) discusses the contemporary complaint, made by such writers as P. Foot and G. H. von Wright, that modern moral philosophers have neglected the virtues. Schneewind reviews such founders of modern moral philosophy as Grotius, Locke, Hume, Kant, and Adam Smith. He makes out a plausible (to me, pretty convincing) case that these writers did not neglect the virtues; indeed Hume might well be thought of as a virtue ethics theorist; and Kant (1981) certainly devoted much analysis to the virtues, though not in the most widely read of his moral writings, the *Foundations*. Rather, Schneewind finds, these writers were pretty much in agreement that an Aristotelian virtue ethics is not adequate for such virtues as justice; to analyze justice, even in Hume, we need a principles- or laws-centered framework. Schneewind further argues that these writers used the distinction between perfect and imperfect duties – in Hume the analogous distinction between natural and artificial virtues – to give a limited role to a virtue ethics analysis. Such virtues as generosity and benevolence receive virtue ethics analysis; their duties are "imperfect," indefinite; it is up to the agent to decide when, to what extent, and toward whom to be generous. But justice, whose dutes are "perfect," definite or specific in all these respects, and enforceable, requires reference to principles and/or laws in its analysis. A virtue ethics analysis, all these writers agree, is inadequate for the "artificial" virtue of justice and its "perfect" duties. The misfortune of virtue was not its neglect, Schneewind argues, but the finding in modern times that a virtue ethics analysis is inadequate for a central part of morality, such as justice.

It is not within the scope of this book to discuss the accuracy of Schneewind's thesis; so far as I know it seems correct. However, both Schneewind and the writers he examines appear to presuppose that Aristotle had a virtue ethics for *all* the virtues. This is the common understanding of Aristotle, the received opinion. I believe that this is incorrect. It is a thesis of this chapter that Aristotle may have had a virtue ethics analysis for *some* of the virtues, such as generosity and magnificence; but definitely *not* for the virtue of justice. For such virtues as temperance and courage, the picture is ambiguous and thus unclear.

In our review of the evidence, we shall find that Aristotle's *general* analysis of virtue and happiness in the function argument, appears to have a circular teleological structure, but the circle may be eliminated on further analysis; alternatively, it may be viewed as a constituent of virtue ethics, thus accounting for having both of these major interpretations in the literature. When we next look at Aristotle's specific analyses of particular virtues of character, the story is different: his analysis of justice seems to have the structure of a teleological theory, something perhaps not appreciated because he separated ethics and politics and the two are not usually studied together. Further, a separate investigation into the issue of paucity of practical content, independent of issues of structure, shows that his theory of justice has plenty of practical content; and so if there is a circle it appears to be harmless. Finally, his analyses of the other virtues such as temperance, courage, and generosity, is somewhat ambiguous and come closer to displaying one of the structures of virtue ethics, though probably a non-Watsonian one; and these analyses do display the paucity of practical content characteristic of virtue ethics.

3 Aristotle's General Analysis of Virtue and Functional Good

For the structure of Aristotle's ethics let us look again at the crucial function argument discussed in the last chapter. Its conclusion is that "human
good [the good for a person] is [rational] activity of soul according to
virtue, and if there is more than one virtue, in accordance with the best
and most complete [perfect]." This seems a clear example of Aristotle
defining human good by reference to virtue; and this seems to be his
settled and considered view, since in his final thoughts about human good
and happiness in Bk. X, ch. 6, he starts by repeating this very conclusion
and making the very same reference to virtue in his account of happiness.
But is there a vicious circularity here? What exactly is it a reference to?
And is it essential or can it be eliminated?

Now there is *no* circularity *if* the reference is exclusively to the *intellectual* virtue of theoretical wisdom, while *moral* virtue is brought in at a
later stage by some instrumental or other nonconstituent, nondefinitional
relation. Since W. F. R. Hardie introduced the distinction between dominant and inclusive ends, there has been renewed and raging controversy
among Aristotle's commentators, whether the conclusion of the function
argument is to be given an exclusionary or inclusive interpretation
(Hardie, 1967; Keyt, 1991; Kraut, 1989; Cooper, 1975, 1999; Crisp, 1994).
On an inclusive interpretation, the good or happiness is an inclusive end
and the reference to "complete virtue" is a reference to all the virtues,
intellectual and moral. On the exclusionary interpretation the good or
happiness is a dominant end and the reference is *only* to the intellectual
virtue of theoretical wisdom. But Sidgwick's objection is to the circularity between the good and the right, and the right can only be represented
in Aristotle by *moral* virtue (or the virtues of character), not by the intellectual virtue of theoretical wisdom. So if happiness consists entirely in
the exercise of theoretical wisdom, as the exclusionary interpretation has
it, then there is no circle between the right and the good.[5] The theory
can be teleological, with the value of moral virtue being instrumental, or
in some other nonconstituent, nondefinitional relation to theoretical
wisdom; and it does not violate the first condition of a teleological theory,
the independence of the good from the right.

Unfortunately, there is no agreement on the exclusionary interpretation, so we cannot ignore the question whether on the inclusive interpretation – the interpretation Sidgwick took for granted – there is
circularity between the right and the good. On the assumption of the

inclusive interpretation, then, we must now examine the conclusion of the function argument, to determine what exactly the reference to moral virtue is, and whether it can be eliminated.

Since we are dealing with a question of structure, we might try to understand Aristotle's procedure in the function argument by extracting from it a general formal theory of good and virtue. We can then look to this theory for clues of the structure and procedure in Aristotle's application of it to a person. The central question here is what concepts are the most fundamental, or what is prior in definition.

The formal theory, which appears to be the logical backbone of Aristotle's function argument, seems to contain at least the following propositions (applicable to things with functions):

1. An F does well as an F if it performs well the function of Fs.
2. A good F is an F which performs well the function of Fs.
3. The good of an F "depends" on its performing well the function of Fs.
4. The virtue of an F is that by [the presence of] which it (a) is a good F and (b) performs well the function of Fs.
5. A good F (is an F which) has the virtue of an F. (From 2 and 4(a).)
6. The virtue of an F is [the?] good for an F. (From 3 and 4(b).)

The last two are derived propositions. Propositions 1 and 3 capture Aristotle's remark that the well and the good of a thing reside and/or depend on its function. The analogies in the passage might be thought of as inductive evidence for the main propositions of the theory.[6] These analogies may be the logical home of the theory, but when applied to a person all these propositions become controversial, with 3 and 6 the center of controversy.

The most fundamental concept in this formal theory seems to be that of function, since reference to it seems to be made directly (1, 2, 3, 4) or indirectly (5, 6) in all the propositions of the theory. And the most fundamental *normative* concept seems to be that of functioning well, since reference to it is made in the explications of other main normative concepts of the theory, the good of an F, a good F, and the virtue of an F, but not conversely. In Aristotle's terms, functioning well is prior in definition to the remaining normative concepts.

We obtain the same result from Aristotle's metaphysical view that actuality is both more final and prior in definition to potentiality. The virtues are "first" (learned, habituated) actualities of inborn human potentialities, while the exercise of the virtues are "second" actualities. And second actualities are both prior in definition and more final than first actualities (*De Anima*, Bk. II, ch. 4; Ross, 1961, pp. 224–51; Irwin, 1985, pp. 385–6). Courageous actions, for example, are second actualities and so more final and prior in definition to the state of character which is the virtue of courage, a first actuality of the potential for courage human beings are born with. Similarly, temperate actions are prior in definition to the virtue of temperance, and just actions prior in definition to the personal virtue of justice (*NE*, Bk. V, ch. 1).

If this analysis of the formal structure of the functional theory is correct, and if this concept of functioning well, at least when applied to human beings, can be understood without reference back to virtue of character, then we can have a noncircular teleological ethical theory. And this can be true of the function argument. For though reference to virtue is made in specifying the good of an F in proposition 6, this reference can be eliminated, if virtue itself can be defined in terms of functioning well.

4 Can Moral Virtue be Explicated by Functioning Well?

Virtue in the conclusion of the function argument is ambiguous: it may refer to a standard of excellence by which performance is judged, or to the disposition which causes and promotes well functioning. Aristotle's phrase "*according* to virtue," supports the standard of performance interpretation; "that *by which* a thing performs its function well" refers to the disposition and supports the causal interpretation.

The causal interpretation fits the case of the arts and organs, where the virtue is a skill, a trained ability, or educated talent, or for organs, a structure/composition which causes well functioning; and it can be used to give a noncircular teleological interpretation of Aristotle's ethical theory. The builder's skill can be defined in terms of producing good buildings, and reference to such skill need not enter into the definition of a good building; further, "right" action for a builder is whatever contributes to the production of a good building, and reference to such action need not enter the explication of good building. A good building in turn will be explicated in terms of the function of buildings. But these are cases of *production*, in which Aristotle explicitly recognizes the independence of the product from the process. Further, Aristotle's discussion of the differences between the virtues and skills (in *NE*, Bk. II, ch. 4), stands in the way of this simple interpretation: for actions to be virtuous, he says, it is not enough that they are "right" [i.e. temperate or courageous]; the agent must know they are right, she or he must have chosen them and chosen them for their own sake, and she or he must have done so from a firm disposition. So, unlike the skills, virtuous action, which is functioning well in the case of living in general, seems to refer us back to the disposition and knowledge of the agent. Whether this reference back is viciously circular remains to be seen.

On the other hand, the standard of performance interpretation seems to introduce into the concept of the human good a moral standard by which functioning is to be evaluated. Courage is to be thought of as a standard by which the performance of a soldier is evaluated: to perform the function of a soldier well is to act courageously, as a courageous man would. Here functioning well seems to be referred back to a moral virtue. And when Aristotle seems to make the virtuous person a standard of what is good and pleasant, as in the case of temperance, he seems to be using virtue as the fundamental notion, not functioning well.

Another obstacle yet to a simple teleological interpretation is Aristotle's view that virtue is a subordinate end. If virtue were a subservient end, the theory could be teleological without circlularity, since purely instrumental means need not enter into the definition of the ends they serve. But Aristotle tells us that virtue is desired for its own sake and for the sake of happiness, and thus would seem to be part of the good; so, through another route, we seem to have a reference to virtue in the definition of the good.

But what exactly is part of the good or happiness? There is a parallel ambiguity here to the ambiguity between cause and standard of performance: though the genus of virtue is disposition, references to virtue may nevertheless be references to the *disposition* or state of character, which is a first actuality; *or* to *activity* or action which is the exercise of the disposition and is a second actuality. It would be natural to interpret references to virtue as a standard of performance to be references to activity and to conduct, rather than to the disposition: it is courageous acts or temperate *acts* that can be standards of performance, not in any direct way the disposition; it is a record performance in track and field that can be a standard for runners, not in any direct way the skill and talent involved. When Aristotle makes the virtuous person a standard of what is truly pleasant or what is good, he presumably means that it is that person's conduct, not just the disposition, which is the standard. And when he says, in the conclusion of the function argument, that happiness is activity of the soul "according to virtue," he must be referring to the excercise of the disposition, the second actuality, if he is referring to a standard of performance.

The same ambiguity infects the notion of virtue being desired for itself and being part of happiness: is it the disposition or the activity that is desired for itself? What must be meant is that virtuous activity is desired for itself and is part of happiness. It is not virtue as a disposition that is part of happiness, but the exercise of the disposition, which is activity. Happiness is activity. How could a disposition be part of activity? The relation of first to second actuality is not that of part to whole in any plausible sense.[7] Virtuous activities can be part of happiness in a straight-forward sense: the activity which is happiness can be literally made up of activities. Moreover, it is virtuous activity that is to be pursued for its own sake, the cultivation of the disposition being pursued because of what it enables us to *do*; for the first actuality is for the sake of the second actuality (*De Anima*, BK. II, ch. 4, and Bk. II, ch. 13).

So the reference to virtue in the conclusion of this argument, must be a reference to activity, *if* it is virtuous *activity* which is desired for itself and is part of happiness, and *if* the reference is to a standard of perfor-mance. Virtue the disposition can be defined by a causal or enabling rela-tion to that activity. That is how Aristotle thinks of virtue in general in *NE*, Bk. II, ch. 6, where once more we get the analogies to organs and animals.

If I am correct so far, the definition of happiness at the conclusion of the function argument can be rephrased as follows: Happiness is activity of soul which manifests reason and which is virtuous (and if there is more than one kind of virtuous activity the best and most complete [perfect]). Here the reference is explicitly to activity, not to disposition; but still to virtuous activity, so the threat of Sidgwick's circle very much remains. However, we are out of the circle if we can show that *this* reference can be eliminated: that is, it is explicable in terms of well functioning without vicious reference back to virtue. I believe it is, and the formal theory shows us the way: to say that an activity is virtuous is to say that the function-ing which constitutes the activity is performed well. The analogy by which virtue is introduced in the function argument indeed says just this: "virtue being added with respect to superiority in the performance of function." And so does the immediate hypothetical before the conclusion: "and if the function of a good man is to do these things well and nobly,[8] and if this is done well by its appropriate virtue . . ."

To be sure, reference to the disposition cannot be totally eliminated; because, on Aristotle's view, to act virtuously a person must act knowingly, he or she must choose the act for its own sake, and act from a firm state of character. But none of this reintroduces vicious circularity. The firm state of character is a reference to the state of the relevant feelings which enable the person to do the act reason selects; "for its own sake" means something like, "because it is a courageous thing to do," rather than, say, because it will bring me a fortune if I win; and knowledge (practical wisdom) refers to knowledge the circumstances and objects of the act, what is at stake, what is to be feared, what might be won. If a courageous act can be explicated by functioning well, there is no circle in the relevant sense. Aristotle is not appealing to the dispositional elements to discover what act, among the various options, would be the right thing to do; *that* is the function of reason, as Aristotle tells us in the very definition of virtue.

Aristotle's analysis of virtuous action, as making reference to the cognitive and motivational state of the agent that cannot be eliminated, is shared by theorists who do not have a virtue ethics, writers who take laws or rules as primary over a virtuous disposition. For example Rawls's general characterization of the moral virtues as "the strong and normally effective desires to act on the basic principles of right" (1971, p. 436), shows clearly enough that on his own view "virtuous action" will indeed make reference to (the relevant) cognitive and motivational state of the agent: it makes reference to desire and knowledge of principles of right (and their relevant application). But this clearly does not imply that any appeal is made to these elements to determine what the right act is; we do *that* by applying the basic principles of right. Ross's distinction between *action* and *act* could also be used here: virtuous act refers to the rightness of the act, virtuous action to a right act done from a virtuous motive.

The solution to our problem now depends on whether a person's virtuous activity can be explicated in terms of functioning well *and* functioning well can be explicated without further reference back to virtue. I propose to show that this is so in two test cases: the definition of moral virtue, and the definition of justice.

5   States of Character and Practical Wisdom

Having decided that virtue is a disposition, and taking it for granted from his formal theory that the virtue of a man is something by which he is a good man and which enables him to perform his function well, Aristotle asks what sort of disposition it can be, and in response brings in choice and the theory of the mean. It is clear in this discussion that the mean is supposed to provide a standard of well functioning. Indeed in the middle of the discussion of the mean, after giving examples of the mean relative to us in eating and exercise, he tells us, "If therefore the way in which every art or science performs its work well is by looking to the mean and applying it as a standard to its works (functions) . . . it will follow that virtue aims at hitting the mean" (1106a8–16, Ross transl.). So, the definition of moral virtue which comes at the end of this discussion is supposed to explicate virtue, the disposition, in terms of choice and well functioning and well functioning in terms of the mean: "Virtue then is a state of character concerned with choice, lying in the mean, i.e. the mean relative to us, this being determined by a rational principle, and by that principle which the man of practical wisdom would determine it" (1107a, Ross transl.).

In the context supplied, this definition explicates moral virtue in terms of disposition to choose those actions and activities which constitute well functioning for a human as an animal the feelings and actions of which are capable of being informed and directed by reason; and it does so by reference to the theory of the mean. For temperance, for example, which is concerned with well functioning in the activities of eating, drinking, and sex, the definition explicates the virtue in terms of the disposition to choose the mean in such activities and their enjoyments.[9]

But this explication of well functioning in terms of choice of the mean still has two problems. First, the theory of the mean does not seem specific enough to guide choice, as Sidgwick and Grotius claim. The complaint is familiar and notorious: when we ask what the rational principle is by which we are to choose the mean, we get no answer in Bk. VI. I shall return to this when I discuss paucity of practical content for justice, courage, and temperance.

Second, in the definition of moral virtue we have reference to practical wisdom; but in Bk. VI, when practical wisdom is distinguished from cleverness, we have reference back to moral virtue: apparently, practical wisdom is knowledge of efficient means to *virtuous* ends, whereas cleverness is knowledge of efficient means to *any* ends a person has. So it looks as if functioning well, i.e. choosing the mean, is not explicated independently of moral virtue.

Why does Aristotle refer back to moral virtue in his distinction between practical wisdom and cleverness, and what sort of reference is it?

What Aristotle does in *NE*, Bk. VI, is to distinguish practical wisdom from other intellectual virtues, to delineate what it is wisdom about, and to determine the contribution practical wisdom makes to the life of virtue and happiness. Some of this is reflected in his definition of practical wisdom in Bk. VI, ch. 5: "Practical wisdom is a state grasping the truth, involving reason, concerned with action about what is good or bad for a human being" (Ross transl.).

Here there is no reference to moral virtue; the normative concepts the explication uses are truth and what is good *for* a person. This is perfectly compatible with a teleological conception of virtue, and there is no Sidgwickian circle. The context of this cryptic definition explains its main elements, and confirms that the virtue is teleologically conceived. All wisdoms are virtues by which we grasp the truth of something; practical wisdom, unlike theoretical, is that by which we can grasp the variable truths about effective means, and by which we can reason truly from ends to effective means.[10] The contribution which the virtue of practical wisdom makes is in the deliberation through which we discover the best means; it enables us to perform well the function of deliberating. Since deliberating well is necessary for attaining any ends, it is necessary for attaining the subordinate and ultimate ends which consititute the human good. And since deliberating about means is an exclusive and essential human function, deliberating well, besides enabling us to discover correct means to ends, is also a subordinate end and part of the human good: for it exhibits one sort of essential well functioning, and according to the function argument well functioning of an exclusive and essential function is part of the human good. As Aristotle says (in *NE*, Bk. VI, ch. 12), practical wisdom is desirable for itself and also for the effects it produces. So far so good.

But Aristotle also wishes to distinguish practical wisdom from cleverness. The latter seems to be what the moderns, Hume and Rawls for example, call practical rationality – taking effective means to one's ends, *no matter what one's ends are*. Aristotle wishes to distinguish cleverness from practical wisdom because cleverness or Humean rationality is not a virtue: a virtue enables us to function well, choosing cleverly does not necessarily do so. Whether in behavior toward oneself or others, one can choose effective means to bad ends, and in neither case is one functioning well. One can choose efficient means to the pleasures of recreational drugs and harm oneself, even more than if one had chosen less effectively; and one can choose the most efficient means to embezzling funds and in this one harms others, even more than if one had chosen less effectively. So Aristotle has practical wisdom beginning with good ends, i.e. ends supplied by moral virtue. And so we seem to have a Sidgwickean circle once more.

But this is misleading. What Aristotle is worrying about here (*NE*, Bk. VI, ch. 12) is not distinguishing the virtuous man from the wrongdoer, but the virtuous man from the man who does the right thing wrongly, i.e. "unwillingly" or "in ignorance," or "for the sake of something else and not for itself" (see 1144a15–25). Here the man is hitting the mean, but not from choice, or accidentally, or for some end beyond the act and not for the act itself. Because of these three factors the man's "wisdom" is only cleverness, though in hitting the mean it resembles the virtue of practical wisdom. But the good man hits the mean "from choice" and "for the sake of the acts themselves" (1144a20–5). And it is precisely these two elements that moral virtue, the disposition, supplies; practical wisdom, the intellectual state, becomes a virtue by hitting the mean, but only when these two elements supplied by moral virtue are present. So, what moral virtue supplies are not some ends other than what practical wisdom supplies, but a firm inclination to choose the mean for its own sake. In the virtue of temperance, for example, which is concerned with functioning well physically and with the rational regulation of (some of our) animality, functioning well consists in choosing the mean with respect to the pleasures of food, drink, and sex, the animal pleasures: practical wisdom determines this mean, while the emotional element of the moral virtue of termperance inclines us to choose that mean and choose it for its own sake.

Does this explain adequately Aristotle's remark that moral virtue sets the ends and practical wisdom finds the means? Perhaps we can be clearer here by imagining moral virtue (virtue of character) *apart* from practical wisdom: if we take away practical wisdom, all that we have left is a certain habituated tendency to fare well with respect to the feelings appropriate to the various moral virtues. This tendency neither *discovers* nor in any way *cognitively* determines the subordinate or ultimate human ends, any more than it discovers or determines any major means to such ends; only reason and wisdom can do either of these. The tendency to fare well means that the feelings have been habituated so that the person wants to and even enjoys acting according to what reason says is the mean. Thus in the case of temperance, the noncognitive part of the contribution of that virtue is that the temperate person has been habituated so as not to have excessive or deficient appetites for food, drink, or sex; and so as to enjoy the corresponding activities when they fall on the mean. That is all that can be meant by moral virtue setting the end while practical wisdom finds the means; it is all that can be meant because when we take away practical wisdom from moral virtue there is no cognitive element left. From the point of view of discovering or validating means *or ends*, moral virtue, apart from wisdom, is simply blind.

Further, when we look to see how Aristotle in his *practice* tries to settle disputes about ends, subordinate or ultimate (e.g. in *NE*, Bk. I, chs. 4, 5, 7, and Bk. X), it is by such things as appeal to what men in fact pursue as subordinate or ultimate ends, what they say are the ends of their lives; or by the function argument. And if we ask ourselves what Aristotelian psychic faculty is at work in these arguments, we have to say that it is reason, theoretical or practical: for his arguments about ends are either dialectical from the opinions of the many or the wise, or demonstrative from the nature of human beings and their place in the kingdom of living things. So we have to say that in Aristotle's view it is reason, arguing dialectically or by demonstration, that settles questions about ultimate ends, and practical reason that discovers the means to them.

What the moral disposition, considered apart from reason, contributes is the regulation of the feelings relevant to the ends and means reason discovers. What it does not contribute is to discover or validate ends of, say, temperance, health and the rational regulation of animality; or ends of courage, freedom, and independence of one's country. And if the moral disposition, apart from practical and theoretical wisdom, cannot discover human ends or means to them, then there is no relevant circle, when in the analysis of practical wisdom Aristotle refers us back to the moral disposition; for it is not an appeal to determine what acts are right.

The disposition is also valuable because it brings stability into the notion of a virtuous person: she is not one who does the right thing only occasionally or unpredictably or only in fair weather. The virtuous person, because she has a steady disposition to act according to the mean, can be counted upon to follow the guidance of practical wisdom.

6   Aristotle's Analysis of Justice: Not a Virtue Ethics

For Sidgwick's problem *and* for the controversies over virtue ethics, there is no more instructive case than Aristotle's analysis of justice, the very virtue ironically neglected in discussions of virtue ethics. The case of justice is crucial, for it is a big and central part of virtue and rightness, whether in Aristotle or in Rawls. What Aristotle calls *general* justice includes all the moral virtues in so far as they are concerned with our behavior toward others; and his *particular* justice includes distributive justice and the justice of punishment. So his general justice takes up all of rightness, and his particular justice a huge and central part of it. If Aristotle's account of justice is in terms of what promotes some good and the explication of that good does not make reference to justice, then do we have a refutation of Sidwick's criticism. Moreover, if he explicates justice as a personal virtue in terms of the justice of laws and constitutions, then he does not have an ethics of virtue for justice. And if his account of the justice of constitutions is sufficiently detailed then his theory of justice does not suffer from a paucity of practical content. We shall find that all this is so.

Finally, we may compare his theory of justice with his theories of such other virtues as temperance and courage, which seem more problematic in all three respects, and consider whether we can illuminate their problems.

Let us look briefly at Aristotle's procedure in his attempt to define justice. Here we sketch the bare essentials, for we are concerned mainly about the structure of his theory; detail will come in only to show there is no paucity of content.

He begins with a characterization of justice the disposition: "Now we observe that everyone means by justice the disposition which makes us doers of just actions, that makes us do what is just and wish what is just. In the same way we mean by injustice the state that makes us do injustice and wish what is unjust" (*NE*, Bk. V, ch. 1, 1129a, Irwin transl.). This is a partial explication of justice as a disposition in terms of just actions, the reverse of Plato's explication of just actions by reference to psychic justice, evidence pointing away from a virtue ethics, since it makes the justice of actions definitionally prior to justice as a state of character.

The rest of Aristotle's procedure is (1) to explicate just actions in terms of lawful actions for general justice; and in terms of proportional equality for particular distributive justice; (2) in turn just laws and just proportional equality are explicated in terms of just constitutions; and finally (3) just constitutions are explicated in terms of the contribution a constitution makes to the end or the good of the state.

Having noted that justice and injustice are said in many ways, Aristotle begins with the unjust person: one can be said to be unjust in the sense of being lawless (acting contrary to laws) and in the sense of "having more"; and similarly with the just person. "Hence what is just will be what is lawful and what is equal" (1129b). Accordingly, he distinguishes *general* justice, identified with what is lawful in all our behavior toward others and called "complete virtue" (1129b31); and *particular* justice, one kind of which is concerned with the distribution of "honor [offices], wealth, and the other divisible assets of the community, which may be allotted among its members in equal or unequal shares" (1131b);[11] the other kind of particular justice being corrective (not discussed here).

The explication of general justice in terms of law is very strong evidence for a negative answer to our question: Aristotle does not have a virtue ethics for all the virtues, since this explication makes just law primary over just dispositions. Three times in the first two chapters of Bk. V does Aristotle explicate just conduct in terms of lawful actions. Remarkably, even for courage and temperance, some of which can be parts of general justice, and in which the doctrine of the mean is pre-eminent, he gives rules of action specific enough to guide choice:

> But the law also prescribes certain conduct: the conduct of a brave man, for example, not to desert one's post, not to run away, not to throw down one's arms . . . that of the temperate man, for example not to commit adultery or outrage; that of a gentle man, for example, not to strike, not to speak evil . . . and so with the actions exemplifying the rest of the virtues and vices, commanding these and forbidding those – rightly if the law has been rightly enacted, not so well if it has been made at random. (1129b20–30)

As the last sentence indicates, Aristotle is aware that laws themselves may be just or unjust. And in the next stage of his analysis he gives a criterion for judging the justice of laws, a criterion which seems teleological:

> Now in every matter they deal with the laws aim either at the common benefit of all, or at the benefit of those in control, whose control rests on virtue or on some other such basis. And so in one way what we call just is whatever produces and maintains happiness and its parts for a political community. (*NE*, Bk. V, ch. 2, 1129b, Irwin transl.)

Here he seems to be saying clearly that the justice of laws depends on their promoting the good of the whole community, and this is clearly a version of a universalist or nonegoistic teleological ethical theory; *or*, the good of those who make the laws, a version of egoistic teleological ethical theory, earlier expounded by Plato's Thrasymachus; constitutions of this latter type Aristotle in the *Politics* calls "deviant."[12]

In the *Politics* the position concerning particular justice is in this respect similar, though here we get a two-step analysis: just laws are laws "constituted in accordance with right constitutions" (1282b); and the rightness of constitutions is then determined by how far they promote the *common* interest, the interest of all, rather than the interest of rulers (1279a).

Thus, both in *NE* and *Politics*, we have teleological accounts of justice: just conduct is *ultimately* explicated in terms of promoting the good. But we must remember that Aristotle's analysis has several stages: just dispositions, just actions, just laws, right constitutions, the good. And we still need to examine whether *this* good is explicated by reference back to justice and so circularly.

Returning to particular justice, Aristotle next asks, What distribution of the divisible goods of office, honors, and safety is just distribution? He reasons that since the unjust person is one who "has or takes more," that is, more of the divisible goods or less of the opposite evils, the just person must be the one who has and takes something between the more and the less, and that is in some sense the equal. And since the equal is somewhere between the extremes of the more and the less, he also brings in his theory of the mean and says that the equal is a mean. What happens next is instructive. For other virtues, Aristotle is content to argue that virtuous acts, courageous, temperate, or generous, fall on the mean; there is no further analysis of the mean, in terms of rules for determining the mean. But for particular justice the mean is said to be the equal, between the extremes of the more and the less, *and* we get a precise mathematical analysis of the equal.[13] Everyone agrees, Aristotle claims, that the equality in question is in proportion to worth (axian) of some sort, and that this is a geometrical, as distinct from an arithmetical, proportion. Accordingly, a distribution is just to the extent that the value of the things (the divisible goods) it assigns to one person stands to the value of the things it assigns to another as the worth of the one person stands to the worth of the other.[14]

In the next stage of his analysis, Aristotle notes that people agree on the evaluation of the things distributed, but they disagree on what this worth should be, which is the basis for the distribution. "All agree that the just in distribution must be according to worth of some sort, though all do not recognize the same sort of worth; but democrats say it is freedom, oligarchs wealth, and aristocrats virtue" (*NE*, Bk. V, ch. 3, 1131a25–9, Ross transl.). Accordingly, we have three different conceptions of distributive justice, under the same concept. In the *Politics* Aristotle gives us a detailed analysis of the different constitutions based on these different conceptions of distributive justice; and of the institutions which embody these different constitutions. Thus a democratic constitution, according to which all free-born citizens should have an equal share of

political authority, includes several institutions and rules which embody
this democratic political egalitarianism: universal membership of free men
in the Assembly, rotation in other offices, terms of office, selection by lot
and by election, and so on (*Politics*, Bk. VI, chs. 1–3).

In the final stage of his analysis of justice Aristotle attempts to resolve
the disagreement among these three conceptions (democratic, oligarchic,
and aristocratic) and to determine which constitution(s) are just, or at least
to rank them by how far they are just.

He begins by arguing that it cannot be superiority in any respect whatsoever (e.g. a person's height) that is a ground for distributing greater shares
in offices; and he gives a *reductio ad absurdum* to rule out this possibility. It
must rather be something which is related to the office, such as fitness for
the office or contribution to the end for which the office exists, that is a
ground for distribution (*Politics*, Bk. III, ch. 12). But this does not settle
the matter; for one thing, free birth, wealth, and virtue all make some contribution; for another, each of the three proponents, democrat, oligarch, or
aristocrat, can still claim that their attribute makes the greatest or only
contribution: who is correct, Aristotle says, depends on what the function
or the end of the state is. (*Politics*, Bk. III, ch. 13). For example:

> If property were the end for which men came together and formed an
> association, then men's share [in the offices and honors] of the state would be
> proportionate to their share of property; and in that case the argument of the
> oligarchical side . . . would appear to be a strong argument. (*Politics*, Bk. III, ch.
> 9, 1280a, Barker transl.)

To resolve the matter, we need to know what the function or the end of
the state is (*Politics*, Bk. III, ch. 13). Aristotle argues against several proposed ends taken individually, and proposes an inclusive end. The end of
the state is not only life or only a shared life; it is "a good life" or a "fine
or noble life" or "a perfect and self-sufficient life" (*Politics*, Bk. III, chs. 9
and 13). And for that end, Aristotle argues, superiority in free birth and
wealth are not enough for distributing shares of office but virtue must
above all be included.

Now it might be thought that the "contribution to the job" criterion
is some sort of deontological principle of desert, rather than a maximizing principle: just as punishment must fit the crime, so awards of offices
must fit the social contribution made. But the fitness for the job (*ergon*)
criterion and the flautist analogy ("nobody will play better for being better
born . . ." [1282b]) assure us, I think, that the criterion is proposed with

a view to assuring the performing well of the function. Whatever the correct end or the function of the city is, Aristotle is saying, shares of offices should be assigned with a view to performing that function or serving that end well. And this is a maximizing principle: for the good of the city and the performing well of the functions of the city are identical.

The teleological character of his argument comes out also in the crucial opening lines of *Politics*, Bk. III, ch. 12, in which he takes up where he left off in the discussion of justice in *NE*:

> In all arts and sciences the end in view is some good. In the most sovereign of all the arts and sciences – and this is the art and science of politics – the end in view is the greatest good and the good which is most pursued. The good in the sphere of politics is justice; and justice consists in what tends to promote the common interest. (Barker transl.)

But if the argument is teleological, is it not also circular? Aristotle appears to be using the notion of virtue in the specification of the end of the state. The end of the state is not simply life or shared life but also a good life; and the notion of good life or happiness he is using seems to be that of *NE*, which makes reference to virtue. But is this not circular once more? The concept of a just man is explicated by just actions; just actions by just laws; just laws by just constitutions; and just constitutions are explicated in terms of (a) promoting the common good of all the citizens rather than the good of the rulers, and (b) distributions of shares of offices in proportion to the worth which promotes most the common good. The good of the citizens is said to be not mere life or shared life but a good life and a life of happiness; that is, presumably, an active life of reason according to virtue; that is, presumably, a life in accordance with courage, temperance, justice, wisdom, and so on. In a chain of arguments attemping to discover what justice is we have ultimately used the notion of the good of the city, and in specifying that we have used justice. Is this not circular?

Perhaps. Aristotle does not actually specify justice in his explication of the end or good of the state. What he has in mind may be the virtue of political practical wisdom (see, e.g., *Politics*, Bk. VII, chs. 11, 12). The threat of a circle remains because of his view, as old as Socrates in Plato's *Gorgias*, that the end of the state, and so the end of a constitution and its laws, is not merely such goods as self-preservation, the protection of property and life, the wealth of the nation, and protection from external threats; but also the promotion of living virtuously, the cultivation of good character, including being a just person (*Politics*, Bk. III, ch. 9; Keyt, 1991). So, though so far as I have been able to determine there is no explicit circularity in our texts, that is, a definition or description of the end of the state which explicitly includes justice, the appearance of circularity remains.

It is instructive to compare here the lesser constitutions, such as the deviant constitutions of oligarchy or democracy or tyranny, and even some correct constitutions such as polity. In these constitutions there is no circle or even the appearance of one. In oligarchic justice, for example, offices are distributed in proportion to (the ability to create and maintain) wealth, and the creation, maintenence, and security of wealth is the end or the good of the oligarchic city. There is no circularity here between justice and the good of the city. But in Aristotle's own account of justice, the best constitution distributes offices on the basis of virtue, as well as freedom and wealth; and it promotes the good of virtue for all the citizens, as well as the goods of defense, property, and so on. In both occurrences of "virtue," the term presumably refers to all the virtues, and this would include justice. So if by the best constitution Aristotle means the most just constitution, we seem to have some circularity or the appearance of one.

7　Paucity of Practical Content: Justice and the Other Virtues

All three interpretations of the concept of distributive justice in *Politics* provide plenty of practical content. From the analysis of the justice of a democratic constitution, for example, it follows that it would be unjust to deprive someone both of whose parents were free and citizens of the right to participate and vote in the Assembly; unjust not to give someone his rotating share in office in the Council and the Jury Courts; unjust not to have limits to terms of office, and so on. Similarly with his analysis of oligarchic justice, which assigns offices in proportion to wealth. In general, as Keyt has shown,[15] Aristotle's four-step procedure (just person, just action; just action, lawful action; lawful action, just laws; just laws, just constitution),[16] will give us a lot of standards by which to judge individual conduct, though of course not perfectly so.[17] If Aristotle's account of justice is teleological and circular, the wealth of practical content in his account suggests that the circularity is pretty harmless.

But we have no such richness of practical content in Aristotle's analysis of courage or temperance. The theory of well functioning and the mean seems to give us very different results for justice and for the other moral virtues, that is, much more specific and fruitful in choice-guiding for justice. Part of the reason for this may be that for distributive justice Aristotle was able to give a mathematical formulation to the equal or the fair, geometrical proportion, and he was also able to specify several different bases for the proportionally equal distribution of goods of offices, wealth, and safety. In addition, justice is a virtue that applies to institutions as well as to individuals, as John Rawls has so forcibly reminded us by making justice a virtue primarily of the basic institutional structure of society. And institutions almost by definition have rules. So Aristotle was able to rely on institutional rules – such rules of election to office, terms of office, rotation in office, and so on – which can serve as guides to action. In sum, in the case of justice Aristotle was aided by the established relation of justice to equality – which is susceptible to mathematical analysis – and by the institutional character of justice.

But for temperance and courage Aristotle is unable to give any mathematical formulation of the mean which would allow us to derive rules of what constitutes temperate or courageous action. One reason Aristotle gives for this inability is that the mean is relative to the individual, taking this apparently to mean that it varies too much to receive quantitative formulation. And so he says it is a matter of "perception," meaning not necessarily sense perception but intuitive judgment of what individual action is correct, what the mean relative to us is in the particular circumstances we find ourselves in. Or, he cites the virtuous person as the model to follow. The reference to the virtuous person and the person of practical wisdom is an individual model device, in the absence of measurability and a mathematical formula.

Aristotle is perfectly aware of this lack of exactness in his theory of the mean (see Anagnostopoulos [1993, ch. 5]). Indeed he prefaces his first discussion of the mean with the remark that matters of conduct have nothing fixed or invariable about them, "but the agents themselves have to consider what is suited to the circumstances on each occasion, just as is the case with the art of medicine and navigation" (1104a5–10). The reference to medicine is crucial. As D.S. Hutchinson has shown (1988, pp. 18–24), this lack of exactness was standard theory in medicine. Thus the author of *Regimen* tells us:

> If . . . it were possible to discover for the constitution of each individual a due proportion of food to exercise, with no erring either of excess or insufficiency, one would have discovered exactly how to make men healthy. But . . . this dis-

covery cannot be made. . . . There are many things to prevent this [such a discovery]. First, the constitutions of men differ . . . then the various ages have different needs. Moreover there are situations of districts, the shifting of winds, the changes of the seasons, and the constitution of the year. Foods themselves exhibit many differences . . . all these factors prevents its being possible to lay down rigidly precise rules in writing. (Bk. I, ch. 2, and Bk. III, 67, transl. Jones)

The author appears to be saying that there are too many – perhaps an indefinite number – of variables involved in the choice of the mean in eating and exercise, and thus no hope of an exact mathematical formulation of such a mean. Significantly, he goes on to say that if a doctor were constantly present when the patient exercised, the doctor would be able to find the mean in exercise and food; perhaps because in the particular circumstances of a particular patient the doctor has to watch out for only a small number of actual variables at work, out of the indefinitely large set of possible variables. So the absence of a mathematical formulation, and even its alleged impossibility, did not keep doctors from successfuly finding the mean for particular patients in their particular circumstances. Aristotle was simply taking over both parts of this theory of the mean in medicine: its theoretical lack of precision and mathematical formulation, and its success in practice for the expert doctors. The parallel for ethics is a theoretical lack of precision and mathematical formulation, and the success in practice for people of practical wisdom.

For temperance the medical theory of the mean was of direct relevance, since temperance is concerned with the rational regulation of the activities and pleasures of eating, drinking, and sex, where health or physical well functioning is one of the standards of temperate behavior. Courage is further away from medical cases, and the difficulties of finding the mean here are even greater.

The difficulties of mathematical formulation and an exact account of the mean are still with us. Have we done any better at all in specifying rules for such virtues as temperance and courage? Sidgwick certainly had not done any better in his analysis of these virtues a century ago. And when Rawls characterizes the moral virtues as "strong and normally effective desires to act on the basic principles of right," what principles of right has he identified for courage or temperance or benevolence?

But here Schneewind's thesis may become relevant: the duties of courage, temperance, generosity, benevolence and love may all be imperfect duties: the problem here is not an epistemic one, lack of knowledge of principles or rules which is responsible for the indefiniteness of these duties; the problem is not that we have not yet discovered rules of how much, when, toward whom, and so on. It is the nature of these duties to be indefinite. Their nature allows for discretion, something Aristotle might recognize in his reference to the man of practical wisdom as a standard.

The case of temperance, though, is instructive. For healthy nutrition and exercise, two standards of temperance, a mathematical formula, relativized to individual body weight, height, age, and fat content, may now be possible. The relativity of the mean here is not necessarily to an individual, but rather to a body type: and this can be measured and specified. Apparently, there are indeed many variables, but their number is finite and their relations discoverable. For courage it is difficult to see how such a thing is possible. We saw that Aristotle gives some rules of courageous acts; but they may be rules which hold only for the most part, and individual judgment is still necessary.

8   Summary and Conclusion

Aristotle's theory of justice is teleological. If it contains a circle it is remarkably hard to detect, and in any case it is harmless since his analysis of justice contains plenty of practical content. And since his account of justice as a virtue of persons is clearly, unlike Plato's, in terms of just conduct, just laws, and just constitutions, Aristotle does not have a virtue ethics for justice. His analysis of the other virtues, such as courage, temperance, and generosity, does not display a clear teleological structure or a clear sufficiency of practical content. His particular analyses of these virtues look like virtue ethics and have been traditionally so taken. But even this diagnosis is troubled by Aristotle's metaphysical view that second actualities are prior in definition and more final than first actualities, and thus that human functioning well is prior to and more final than the psychic states that enable it to do so.

Aristotle's views about justice and goodness are in important ways anti-Platonic, and our study suggests some hypotheses about the deeper roots of their differences.

One root may be Plato's unusual view that the justice of persons and the justice of societies are isomorphic: within this formal framework he deduced the justice of persons from the justice of society, but he still defined the justice of persons independently of the justice of society. This may have been a working out of the Socratic primacy and emphasis on the state of our souls. Or it may have been a working out of the Platonic primacy of form over function. Aristotle broke decisively with this view of justice and began the tradition which has been dominant since, that a just person is one who subscribes to the principles of a just society, the principles and institutions by which a society is just. And on such a view, a theory of justice can be teleological or deontological but not a virtue ethics.

Aristotle's primacy of second over first actualities, of functionings over states or dispositions, is equally anti-Platonic. Here Aristotle may have been influenced by his biology, which appears to be primarily functional: for all living things their activities are prior in definition and more final than their psychic dispositions which may be conceived structurally.[18] Plato's thought was dominated by the theory of forms, in which form or structure takes primacy over functionings. And this makes a difference to his conception of goodness and what is the most basic value concept. Functionings are spread out in time; Platonic forms are not in time at all. In Plato the structures of physical entities are shadows of timeless forms, they are to be characterized by some relation to such forms, and their temporal functionings are to be explained and understood ultimately in terms of forms. The best objects of their kind are such timeless forms, and goodness the super abstract property by which they are the best. But as we saw Aristotle rejected this view. In Aristotle, goodness resides in activity, human goodness in human activities, and the goodness of activity is to explain all other value.

Notes

1   Rawls does not follow Sidgwick in this, but classifies perfectionism as a teleological theory, and criticizes it on other grounds, not on circularity (1971, pp. 25, 325–32). For a fine discussion of moralistic perfectionism, which takes moral virtue to be part of perfection, see Hurka (1993).

2   Trianoski, 1990, p. 336. Similar contrasts are made by W. Frankena, and R. Brandt (Brand, 1981, pp. 271–92).

3   Plato also has a concept of social justice, which is defined in terms of principles of conduct, so the matter is more complex (see chapters 3 and 4 above).

4   See Ferejohn (1980, pp. 117–28); and Keyt (1991, p. 126); e.g. right angle is prior in definition to acute angle, since an acute angle is an angle that is less than a right angle.

5   On some versions of the exclusionary interpretation, the highest happiness consists of theoretical wisdom, but a second-grade happiness, available to the common person, consists of moral virtue (Kraut, 1989). Here there would be a circle relative to the second-grade happiness.

6   "As in the case of the flute player and the sculptor and every artist, and in all cases where there is a function and action, the good and the well is thought to depend on [reside in] its function, so it may be thought in the case of man. . . ." (*NE*, 1096b, Ross transl.).

7   See Aristotle's discussion of part and whole in *Metaphysics*, Bk. V.

8   "Nobly" may be thought to reintroduce the circle, but as Irwin notes, "nobly" normally indicates or makes reference to promotion of the good of others. See *NE*, Bk. I, ch. 2, 1094b: it is "finer" or "nobler" to preserve the good of the city because the good of a whole city is greater than that of any individual in it.

9   Young, 1996. I enirely agree with Young's view that "location" depends on "intermediacy." See also Young (1989, pp. 521–42).

10 For a systematic collection of Aristotle's examples of practical reasoning, see Santas (1969).

11 For another such good, security, see 1130b and 1129b.

12 "Deviant" constitutions seem versions of egoism Rawls calls "first person dictatorship" (1971, p. 124).

13 For justice I take the mean to be derivative of proportional equality: the mean for distributive justice is whatever the theory of justice as proportional equality says it is. For more discussion, see Young (1989, pp. 233–49).

14 The language is taken from Keyt (1991, p. 24; see also 1991). I am relying considerably here on Keyt's clear-headed exposition of Aristotle's theory of justice. Since Keyt does not take up the issues I am discussing, his exposition may be regarded as neutral.

15 Keyt (1991, 1991) explicitly raises the question of content and gives a convincing positive answer.

16 Being a complex and abstract social concept, justice needs a multistage analysis; cf. Rawls (1971, ch. 4).

17 In Aristotle's favored theory of just constitutions, deriving practical content in particular cases might be more difficult, since his standard of worth includes virtue, freedom, and wealth, and it is not easy to compare, measure, or weigh these against each other. See Keyt (1991, p. 247).

18 This is a complex matter. See, e.g. M. Furth's fine analysis (1988), and much of the discussion in Gotthelf and Lennox (1987).

Bibliography

Ackrill, J.L., *Aristotle's Ethics*, London, 1973.

Ackrill, J.L., "Aristotle on 'Good' and the Categories," in Barnes, 1977.

Adkins, A.W.H., *Merit and Responsibility*, Oxford, 1960.

Allan, D.J., "Aristotle's Criticism of Platonic Doctrine Concerning Goodness and the Good," *Aristotelian Society Proceedings*, London, 1963–4.

Allen, R.E., "Predication and Participation in Plato's Middle Dialogues," *Philosophical Review*, 69, 1960.

Allen, R.E., *Plato's Parmenides*, Minneapolis, 1983.

Anagnostopoulos, Georgios, "Aristotle on Function and the Attributive Nature of Good," in Depew, 1980.

Anagnostopoulos, Georgios, *Aristotle on the Goals and Exactness in Ethics*, Los Angeles, 1993.

Annas, Julia, *An Introduction to Plato's Republic*, Oxford, 1981.

Annas, Julia, *The Morality of Happiness*, Oxford, 1993.

Annas, Julia, *Plato's Ethics Old and New*, Cornell, 1999.

Anton, J., and A. Preus, eds., *Essays in Ancient Philosophy*, vol. 2, 1983.

Augustine, St., *The Confessions*, transl. and ed. J.K. Ryan, New York, 1960.

Austin, J.L., "Agathon and Eudaimonia in the Ethics of Aristotle," in J.M. Moravcsik, ed., *Aristotle*, London, 1967.

Ayala, F.J., "Teleological Explanations," in Ruse, 1998.

Barker, E., *The Politics of Aristotle*, Oxford, 1946.

Barnes, J., et al., eds., *Articles on Aristotle: Ethics and Politics*, London, 1977.

Barnes, J., ed., *The Complete Works of Aristotle*, 2 vols., Princeton, 1984.

Barry, Brian, *Political Argument*, Berkeley, 1965.

Barry, Brian, *Theories of Justice*, vol. 1, Berkeley, 1989.

Barry, Brian, *Political Argument*, Berkeley, 1990.

Benson, H.H., ed., *Essays in the Philosophy of Socrates*, Oxford, 1992.

Berlin, Isaiah, *Four Essays on Liberty*, London, 1969.

Bobonich, C., "Plato's Theory of Goods in the *Laws* and the *Philebus*," in Cleary and Wians, 1997.

Brandt, R., "W.K. Frankena and the Ethics of Virtue," *Monist*, vol. 64, 1981.

Broadie, S., *Ethics with Aristotle*, Oxford, 1991.

Broome, John, *Weighing Goods: Equality, Uncertainty and Time*, Oxford, 1996.

Burnyeat, M.F., "Platonism and Mathematics: A Prelude to Discussion," in A. Graeser, ed., *Mathematik und Metaphysik bei Aristoteles*, 1988.

Charles, David, *Aristotle's Philosophy of Action*, London, 1984.

Cherniss, H., *Aristotle's Criticism of Plato and the Academy*, 1944.

Cleary, J., and W. Wians, eds., *Proceedings of the Boston Area Colloquium in Ancient Philosophy*, Boston, 1997.

Code, A., "Vlastos on a Metaphysical Paradox," in Irwin and Nussbaum, eds., 1993.

Cooper, J.M., *Reason and Human Good in Aristotle*, Cambridge, Mass., 1975.

Cooper, J.M., "Plato's Theory of Human Motivation," *History of Philosophy Quarterly*, vol. 1, 1984.

Cooper, J.M., "Aristotle on the Goods of Fortune," *Philosophical Review*, vol. 5, April, 1985.

Cooper, J.M., "Hypothetical Necessity and Natural Teleology," in Gotthelf and Lennox, 1987.

Cooper, J.M., "Reason, Moral Virtue, and Moral Value," in Frede and Striker, 1996.

Cooper, J.M., "The Psychology of Justice in Plato," in Cooper, 1999.

Cooper, J.M., *Reason and Emotion*, Princeton, 1999.

Crisp, Roger, "Aristotle's Inclusivism," *Oxford Studies in Ancient Philosophy*, vol. 12, 1994.

Crombie, I.M., *An Examination of Plato's Doctrines*, 2 vols., London, 1962.

Cross, R.C., and A.D. Woozley, *Plato's Republic*, London, 1964.

Daniels, N., *Reading Rawls*, New York, 1974.

Dawkins, R., *The Selfish Gene*, Oxford, 1976.

Dennis, M.J., "Scarce Medical Resourses," in Elster, 1995.

Depew, D., ed., *The Greeks and the Good Life*, Indianapolis, 1980.

Elster, Jon, *Sour Grapes*, Cambridge, UK, 1985.

Elster, Jon, ed., *Local Justice in America*, New York, 1995.

Ferejohn, M.T., "Aristotle on Focal Meaning and the Unity of Science," *Phronesis*, 25, no. 2, 1980.

Ferejohn, M.T., "Socratic Thought Experiments and the Unity of Virtue Paradox," *Phronesis*, vol. 29, 1984.

Fine, Gail, *On Ideas*, Oxford, 1995.

Fine, Gail, "Knowledge and Belief in *Republic* 5–7," in Fine, 1999.

Fine, Gail, ed., *Plato*, vols. 1, 2, Oxford, 1999.

Frede, M., "The Affections of the Soul", in Schofield and Striker, 1986.

Frede, M., and G. Striker, eds., *Rationality in Greek Thought*, Oxford, 1996.

Freud, S., *The Complete Psychological Works of Sigmund Freud*, vols. 1–26, ed. J. Strachey, London, 1953.

Furth, M., *Substance, Form, and Psyche*, Cambridge, UK, 1988.

Gosling, J.C.B., and C.C.W. Taylor, *The Greeks on Pleasure*, Oxford, 1982.

Gotthelf, Allan, "Aristotle's Conception of Final Causality" in Gotthelf and Lennox, 1987.

Gotthelf, Allan, "First Principles in Aristotle's *Parts of Animals*", in Gotthelf and Lennox, 1987.

Gotthelf, A., ed., *Aristotle and the Nature of Living Things*, Pittsburgh, 1985.

Gotthelf, A., and J. Lennox, eds., *Philosophical Issues in Aristotle's Biology*, Cambridge, UK, 1987.

Grote, G., *Plato and Other Companions of Socrates*, 4 vols., 4th ed., London, 1888.

Hardie, W.F.R., *Aristotle's Ethical Theory*, Oxford, 1968.

Hardie, W.F.R., "The Final Good in Aristotle's Ethics," in Moravcsik, 1967.

Harman, G., *The Nature of Morality*, New York, 1977.

Heath, T.L., ed., *Euclid's Elements*, vol. 1, New York, 1956.

Hintikka, Iaakko, "Time, Truth, and Knowledge in Ancient Greek Philosophy," *American Philosophical Quarterly*, vol. 4, January 1967.

Hintikka, Iaakko, "Knowledge and its Objects in Plato," in Moravcsik, 1974.

Hippocrates, *Regimen in Health*, vol. 1, W.H.S. Jones, transl., Cambridge, Mass., 1923.

Hume, D., *Treatise of Human Nature*, ed. L.A. Selby-Bigge, Oxford, 1955.

Hurka, Thomas, *Perfectionism*, Oxford, 1993.

Hutchinson, D.S. "Doctrines of the Mean and the Debate Concerning Skills in Fourth Century Medicine, Rhetoric and Ethics", in R.J. Hankinson, ed., *Method, Medicine, and Metaphysics*, Edmonton, 1988.

Irwin, T.H., "The Metaphysical and Psychological Basis of Aristotle's Ethics," in Rorty, 1980.

Irwin, T.H., "Homonymy in Aristotle," *Review of Metaphysics*, vol. 34, 1981.

Irwin, T.H., transl., *Aristotle: Nicomachean Ethics*, Indianapolis, 1985.

Irwin, T.H., *Aristotle's First Principles*, Oxford, 1988.

Irwin, T.H., "Aristotle's Defence of Private Property," in Keyt and Miller, 1991.

Irwin, T.H., "Socrates the Epicurean," in Benson, 1992.

Irwin, T.H., *Plato's Ethics*, Oxford, 1995.

Irwin, T.H., *Plato: Gorgias*, Oxford, 1979.

Irwin, T.H., and M. Nussbaum, eds., *Virtue, Forms, and Love*, Edmonton, 1993.

Kafka, Gregory, *Hobbesian Moral and Political Philosophy*, Princeton, 1986.

Kahn, Charles, "The Place of the Prime Mover in Aristotle's Teleology," in Gotthelf, 1985.

Kahn, Charles, "Plato's Theory of Desire," *Review of Metaphysics*, vol. 41, 1987.

Kahn, Charles, *Plato and the Socratic Dialogue*, Cambridge, UK, 1996.

Kant, I., *Foundations of the Metaphysics of Morals*, trans. L.W. Beck, Liberal Arts, New York, 1981.

Kenny, A., "Aristotle on Happiness," in Barnes et al., 1977.

Keyt, David, "The Mad Craftsman of the *Timaeus, Philosophical Review*, vol. 80, no. 2, 1971.

Keyt, David, "Intellectualism in Aristotle", in Anton and Prens, 1983.

Keyt, David, "Aristotle's Theory of Distributive Justice," in Keyt and Miller, 1991.

Keyt, David, "Three Basic Theorems in Aristotle's *Politics*," in Keyt and Miller, 1991.

Keyt, D., and F. Miller, eds., *A Companion to Aristotle's Politics*, Oxford, 1991.

Korsgaard, C., "Two Distinctions in Goodness," *Philosophical Review*, vol. 92, no. 2, April, 1983.

Korsgaard, C., "Aristotle and Kant on the Source of Value," in C. Korsgaard, *Creating the Kingdom of Ends*, Cambridge, UK, 1996.

Kraut, Richard, "Egoism, Love, and Political Office," *Philosophical Review*, vol. 82, 1973.

Kraut, Richard, "Reason and Justice in the *Republic*," in Lee, Mourelatos, and Rorty, 1973.

Kraut, Richard, *Aristotle on the Human Good*, Princeton, 1989.

Kraut, Richard, ed., *The Cambridge Companion to Plato*, Cambridge, UK, 1992.

Kraut, Richard, ed., *Plato's Republic*, New York, 1997.

Lawrence, Gavin, "The Function of the Function Argument", *Ancient Philosophy*, 2000.

Lear, Jonathan, "The Politics of Narcissism," in Irwin and Nussbaum, 1993.

Lear, Jonathan, "Inside and Outside the *Republic*," in Kraut, 1997.

Lee, E.N., A.P.D. Mourelatos, and R.M. Rorty, eds., *Exegesis and argument*, Assen, 1973.

Lennox, J., "Kinds, Forms of Kinds, and the More and the Less in Aristotle's Biology," in Gotthelf and Lennox, 1987.

Lewis, F.A., *Substance and Predication in Aristotle*, Cambridge, UK, 1991.

Locke, John, *An Essay On Human Understanding*, New York, 1959.

Malcolm, John, *Plato on Self-predication of Forms*, Oxford, 1991.

McCabe, David, "Knowing about the Good: A Problem with Antiperfectionism," *Ethics*, 110, no. 2, 2000.

McDonald, Scott, "Aristotle and the Homonymy of Good," in *Archiv für Geschichte der Philosophie*, vol. 71, 1989.

McDonald, Scott, *Goodness and Being*, New York, 1991.

Miller, F.D., *Nature, Justice and Rights in Aristotle's Politics*, Oxford, 1994.

Mirrlees, J.M., "The Economic Uses of Utilitarianism," in Sen and Williams, 1988.

Miller, F.D., "Plato on the Parts of the Soul," in J. Van Ophuijsen, ed., *Plato and Platonism*, Washington, D.C., 1999.

Moore, G.E., *Principia Ethica*, Cambridge, UK, 1903.

Moravcsik, J.M., *Patterns of Thought in Plato*, Berkeley, 1974.

Moravcsik, J.M., ed., *Aristotle*, New York, 1967.

Moravcsik, J.M., *Plato and Platonism*, Oxford, 1994.

Mourelatos, A.P.D., "Plato's 'Real Astronomy': *Republic* 527D–531D", in John Anton, ed., *Science and the Sciences in Plato*, New York, 1980.

Murphy, R.N., *The Interpretation of Plato's Republic*, Oxford, 1951.

Nagel, Thomas, "Aristotle on *Eudaimonia*," in Rorty, 1980.

Nahamas, A., "Plato on the Imperfections of the Sensible World," *American Philosophical Quarterly*, April 1975.

Nettleship, R.L., *Lectures on the Republic of Plato*, London, 1901.

Nussbaum, M., *The Fragility of Goodness*, Cambridge, UK, 1986.

Nussbaum, M., and A. Sen, eds., *The Quality of Life*, Oxford, 1992.

Owen, G.E.L., "Logic and Metaphysics in Some Earlier Works of Aristotle," in G.E.L. Owen and I. During, eds., *Aristotle and Plato in Mid-Fourth Century*, Gothenburg, 1960.

Owen, G.E.L., "Dialectic and Eristic in the Treatment of Forms," in G.E.L. Owen, ed., *Aristotle on Dialectic*, Oxford, 1968.

Patterson, Richard, *Image and Reality in Plato's Metaphysics*, Indianapolis, 1985.

Penner, Terry, "Desire and Thought in Plato," in Vlastos, 1971.

Penner, Terry, *The Ascent from Nominalism*, Dordrecht, 1987.

Penner, Terry, "Socrates on the Impossibility of Belief-Relative Sciences," in John C. Cleary, ed., *Boston Area Colloquium in Ancient Philosophy*, Lanham, Md., vol. 3, 1988.

Penner, Terry, "Desire and Power in Socrates," *Apeiron*, vol. 24, no. 3, 1991.

Penner, Terry, and C.J. Rowe, "Desire for the Good," *Phronesis*, 29, no. 1, 1994.

Perry, R.B., *A General Theory of Value*, New York, 1926.

Peterson, Sandra, "Apparent Circularity in Aristotle's Account of Right Action in the *Nicomachean Ethics*," *Apeiron*, vol. 25, June, 1992.

Popper, Karl, *The Open Society and its Enemies*, vol. 1, London, 1966.

Preston, Beth, "Why is a Wing like a Spoon? A Pluralist Theory of Function," *Journal of Philosophy*, vol. 95, no. 5, May, 1998.

Porter, D.M., and P.W. Graham, eds., New York, 1993.

Rawls, John, "Justice as Fairness: Political, not Metaphysical," *Philosophy and Public Affairs*, vol. 14, 1985.

Rawls, John, *A Theory of Justice*, Cambridge, Mass., 1971.

Rawls, John, "Social Unity and Primary Goods," in A. Sen and B. Williams, eds., *Utilitarianism and Beyond*, Cambridge, UK, 1982.

Rawls, John, *Political Liberalism*, New York, 1993.

Reeve, C.D.C., *The Philosopher-Kings*, Princeton, 1988.

Reeve, C.D.C., "The Naked Old Woman in the Palaestra," in Kraut, 1997.

Rodebusch, George, *Socrates, Pleasure, and Value*, Oxford, 1999.

Rorty, A., *Essays on Aristotle's Ethics*, Berkeley, 1980.

Ross, W.D., *The Right and the Good*, Oxford, 1930.

Ross, W.D., *Aristotle: De Anima*, Oxford, 1961.

Ross, W.D., *Aristotle*, New York, 1959.

Ruse, M., ed., *Philosophy of Biology*, New York, 1998.

Sachs, David, "A Fallacy in Plato's *Republic*," *Philosophical Review*, vol. 72, 1963.

Santas, G., "Aristotle on Practical Inference, the Explanation of Action, and Akrasia," *Phronesis*, vol. 14, no. 2, 1969.

Santas, G., "Hintikka on Knowledge and its Objects in Plato," in Moravscik, 1974.

Santas, G., *Socrates*, Routledge, London, 1979.

Santas, G., "Two Theories of Good in Plato's *Republic*," *Archiv für Geschitche der Philosophie*, 1984.

Santas, G., "Plato on Goodness and Rationality," *Revue Internationale de Philosophie*, 156–7, 1986.

Santas, G., "Justice and Democracy in Plato's *Republic*," in O. Gigon and M.W. Fischer, eds., *Antike Rechts und Sozialphilosophie*, Bern, 1988.

Santas, G., *Plato and Freud*, Oxford, 1988.

Santas, G., "Knowledge and Belief in Plato's *Republic*," *Boston Studies in the History and Philosophy of Science*, Boston, 1990.

Santas, G., "The Form of the Good in Plato's *Republic*," *Philosophical Inquiry*, Winter, 1980"; also in Anton and Preuss, 1983, and in Fine, *Plato* 1, 1999.

Sartre, J.-P., "Existententialism is a Humanist," in W. Kaufmann, ed., *Existentialism*, New York, 1957.

Schneewind, J.B., ed., *Moral Philosophy from Montaigne to Kant*, vols. 1, 2, Cambridge, UK, 1990.

Schneewind, J.B., "The Misfortunes of Virtue," *Ethics*, vol. 100, no. 5, October, 1990.

Schneewind, J.B., "Natural Law, Skepticism, and Methods of Ethics" in *Journal of the History of Ideas*, vol. 29, 1991.

Schneewind, J.B., "Modern Moral Philosophy: From Beginning to End?" in P. Cook, ed., *Philosophical Imagination and Cultural History*, Durham, N.C. 1993.

Schofield, M., and G. Striker, eds., *The Norms of Nature*, Cambridge, UK, 1986.

Scolnicov, Samuel, "Reason and Passion in the Platonic Soul," *Dionysius*, vol. 2, 1978.

Sen, A., "Well-Being, Agency and Freedom," *Journal of Philosophy*, 82, April 1985.

Sen, A., and B. Williams, eds., *Utilitarianism and Beyond*, Cambridge, UK, 1988.

Shields, Christopher, *Order in Multiplicity*, Oxford, 1999.

Shorey, P., "The Idea of the Good in Plato's *Republic*," *University of Chicago Studies in Classical Philology*, vol. 1, 1894.

Shorey, P., transl., *Plato: Republic*, 2 vols., Cambridge, Mass., 1935.

Sidgwick, Henry, *The Methods of Ethics*, 7th ed., Indianapolis, 1981.

Slote, M., *Goods and Virtues*, Oxford, 1989.

Smith, Adam, *The Wealth of Nations*, London, 1937.

Smith, N.D., and T. Brickhouse, "Socrates on Goods, Virtue, and Happiness," *Oxford Studies in Ancient Philosophy*, vol. 5, 1987.

Smith, N.D., and T. Brickhouse, *Plato's Socrates*, Oxford, 1994.

Smith, N.D., "Plato and Aristotle on the Nature of Women," *Journal of the History of Philosophy*, vol. 21, 1983.

Sorabji, Richard, "Rationality" in Frede and Striker, 1996.

Strange, S., "The Double Explanation of the *Timaeus*" in Fine, *Plato*, vol. 1, 1999.

Sullaway, S., *Freud: Biologist of the Mind*, Berkeley, 1970.

Taylor, C.C.W., "Plato's Totalitarianism," in Kraut, 1997.

Trianoski, M., "What is Virtue Ethics All About?" *American Philosophical Quarterly*, vol. 27, no. 4, 1990.

Urmson, O.J., "Aristotle on Pleasure," in Moravcsik, 1967.

Urmson, O.J., "Pleasure and Distress," *Oxford Studies in Ancient Philosophy*, vol. 2, 1984.

Vlastos, G., "The Third Man Argument in the *Parmenides*," *Philosophical Review*, vol. 63, 1954.

Vlastos, G., "Degrees of Reality in Plato," in R. Bambrough, *New Essays in Plato and Aristotle*, New York, 1967.

Vlastos, G., "Reasons and Causes in the *Phaedo*," *Philosophical Review*, vol. 78, 1969.

Vlastos, G., *Plato*, vol. 2, New York, 1971.

Vlastos, G., "The Theory of Social Justice in the Polis in Plato's *Republic*," in H. North, ed., *Interpretations of Plato*, Leiden, 1977.

Vlastos, G., *Platonic Studies*, 2nd ed., Princeton, 1981.

Vlastos, G., "Separation in Plato," *Oxford Studies in Ancient Philosophy*, vol. 5, 1987.

Vlastos, G., "Was Plato a Feminist?" *Times Literary Supplement*, March 17, 1989.

Vlastos, G., *Socrates*, Ithaca, 1991.

Vlastos, G., *Socratic Studies*, Cambridge, UK, 1994.

Watson, Gary, "Kant on Happiness in the Moral Life," *Philosophy and Phenomenological Research*, 1984.

Watson, Gary, "On the Primacy of Character," in O. Flanagan and A. Rorty, eds., *Identity, Character and Morality*, Cambridge, Mass., 1990.

Wedberg, A., *Plato's Philosophy of Mathematics*, Stockholm, 1955.

Williams, B., "The Analogy of City and Soul in Plato's *Republic*, in Kraut, 1997.

Wedin, M., "Aristotle on the Good for Man," *Mind*, vol. 90, no. 358, 1981.

White, N.P., *Plato on Knowledge and Reality*, Hackett, Indianapolis, 1976.

White, N.P., *A Companion to Plato's Republic*, Indianapolis, 1979.

White, N.P., "The Ruler's Choice," *Archiv für Geschichte der Philosophie*, vol. 68, 1986.

White, N.P., "Plato's Metaphysical Epistemology," in Kraut, 1992.

Whiting, J., "Aristotle's Function Argument: A Defence," *Ancient Philosophy*, vol. 8, 1988.

Woodruff, Paul, *Plato: Hippias Major*, Hackett, Indianapolis, 1982.

Woods, M., *Aristotle: Eudemian Ethics*, 2nd ed., Oxford, 1996.

Wright, L., "Functions", *Philosophical Review*, April, vol. 82, no. 2, 1973.

Wright, L., *Teleological Explanations*, Berkeley, 1976.

Wright, G.H. von, *The Varieties of Goodness*, New York, 1966.

Young, Charles, "Aristotle on Temperance," *Philosophical Review*, vol. 97, 1988.

Young, Charles, "Aristotle on Justice," *Southern Journal of Philosophy*, vol. 27, 1989.

Young, Charles, "The Doctrine of the Mean," *Topoi*, vol. 15, 1996.

Zeyl, Donald, "Socrates and Hedonism, Pr. 351b–358d," *Phronesis*, vol. 25, 1980.

Index

Ackrill, John, 204, 220n12, 228, 259
Adkins, A. W. H., 19, 21
Allan, D. J., 198, 219n6
Allen, R. E., 222n25
Anagnostopoulos, Georgios, x, 56n26,
  106n18, 194, 236, 256n5, 285
Annas, Julia, x, 99, 112, 121, 150,
  161n23, 168
Anscombe, E., 123–4
Augustine, St., 167, 187
Austin, John, 236, 256n5
Ayala, F., 257n18

Balme, D., 242, 257n14, 257n15
Barnes, Jonathan, 219n1
Barry, Brian, 5, 16n2, 49–50, 60, 152,
  158n7
Benson, H. H., 104n2
Berlin, I., 3
Brandt, R., 147, 288n2
Broadie, S., 231, 256n3, n5, 261
Broome, John, 147, 148
Burnyeat, M., 192n2

Charles, David, 228
Cherniss, H., 219n5
Code, Alan, 172, 173, 174–8, 192n2
conditional value, 33–8
Cooper, John, 16n10, 21, 33, 119,
  158nn4–9, 160n14, 161n23, 228,
  231, 236, 238, 248–9, 256n1, n5,
  257n9, n11, n19, 258nn20–22, 259,
  263, 269

Cooke, Dale, x
Crisp, Roger, 17n10, 256n4, 269
Crombie, I. M., 168
Cross, R. C., 112, 193n14

Daniels, N., 93
Darwin, Charles, 11, 257n13
Dawkins, Richard, 11
Dennis, M. J., 21

Elster, Jon, 7, 147, 148, 165n50
ends, 226–35
  dominant, 231
  and good, 226–35
  inclusive, 231–2
  subordinate, 230–5
  subservient, 226–7
  ultimate, 230–5
eudaemonistic axiom, 22, 25, 32, 120,
  232

Ferejohn, M. T., x, 36–7, 46, 223n32,
  288n4
Fine, Gail, 192n5, 222n23, 257n8
forms, 167–91
  and function, 187–91
  and good, 180–7
  and knowledge, 169–80
Frede, M., 162n29
Freud, S., 17n8, 131, 160n12, 161n21,
  153–4
function
  and desire, 69–71, 255–6

function (*cont.*)
  and good, 72–5, 187–91
  and happiness, 93–5, 236–50
  and health, 134–8
  and justice, 75–84, 117–25
  definition of, 67, 69–72
  and pleasure, 250–6
Furth, M., 257n14, 289n18

Good
  and desire satisfaction, 70–1, 141–9,
    233–5
  and form, 178–91
  the Form of, 180–7, 196–214
  and function, 66–77, 236–41, 187–91
  and functional definition of, 67, 72–3,
    236, 240–1
  and pleasure, 51–3, 233, 250–5
  and Platonic Forms, 178–214
  questions about, 12–16
Goods
  classification of, 21–2
  conditional and unconditional, 33–8
  isolation tests for intrinsic, 42–7
  invariant, 36–7
  and justice, 6–9, 75–84, 93–5, 125–9
  primary, 23
  rankings of, 20–4
  self-sufficient, 37–8, 230–2
Gosling, J. C. B., 16, 52, 55n17, 254,
  258n26
Gotthelf, Allan, 238, 241, 257n9, n14,
  n15, n17, 289n18

Happiness
  and desire satisfaction, 69–70, 141–9,
    232–5
  and function, 94–5, 236–50
  and good, 45–8
  and virtue, 29–33, 59–65
  and wisdom, 33–8, 45–6
Harman, G., 107n33
Hardie, W. F. R., 231, 236, 257n12,
  269
Heath, Sir Thomas, 179, 222n26

Hesiod, 19
Hintikka, J., 179, 192n5, n11
Hobbes, T., 5, 7, 13
Hume, David, 10, 14, 21, 28–9, 92,
  104n4, 119–21, 126, 129–33,
  160n12, 162n23, n28, 276
Hurka, Thomas, 48, 78, 108n39, 225,
  288n1
Hutchinson, D. S., 285

Irwin, T. H., 24, 52, 54n3, 55n12, n17,
  n20, 58, 108n36, 109n56, 119, 121,
  160n12, 161n23, 162n27, n31,
  164n44, 221n15, 236, 251, 254,
  256n4, 258n25, 271
isolation tests, 42–5
isomorphism, of soul and city justice,
  111–17, 150–3

Justice
  and good, 6–9, 75–84, 93–5, 125–9
  individual, 112–13, 125–9
  social, 75–87, 278–84

Kahn, Charles, 55n17, 161n23, 238,
  256n1
Kant, I., 13, 33, 38–41, 51n2, 53, 53n24,
  n25
Kenny, A., 228, 256n3
knowledge
  and forms, 169–80
  value of, 42–5
Keyt, David, x, 17n10, 21, 105n14,
  110n68, 163n37, 182–3, 227, 231,
  236, 251, 258n25, 269, 284, 288n4,
  289n14, n15, n17
Korsgaard, C., 38, 39, 42, 70, 73
Kraut, R., 17n10, 159n10, 162n27, 226,
  231, 256n4, n5, 269, 289n5

Lawrence, Gavin, 256n5
Lewis, Frank, 219n3
Lennox, J., 241, 289n18
Lear, Jonathan, 159n10, 160n11
Locke, John, 265

Malcolm, John, 172–3, 178, 182, 192n2
McCabe, David, 17n5
McDonald, Scott, 187, 204, 220n12, 221n16, n19
Mill, J. S., 7
Miller, Fred, x, 21, 110n66, 160n12
Mirrlees, J. M., 56n33
Moore, G. E., 7, 10, 13, 33, 42–5, 56n29, 70, 201, 202, 205, 219n9, 222n22
Mourelatos, A., 180

Nahamas, A., 173
Nagel, Thomas, 93, 244–5
Nussbaum, Martha, 92, 225

organic unities, 42–7
Owen, G. E. L., 182, 215, 222n30, 223n32

Parsons, Talcott, 5, 49–50
Patterson, Richard, 192n2
Penner, Terry, 53n2, 54n11, 104n6, 119, 123, 160n12, 192n5
Peterson, Sandra, 259, 261
pleasure, and good, 51–3, 250–6
Popper, Sir Karl, 110n67, 163n34, 168, 212–14, 219n1
Preston, Beth, 106n27

Rawls, John, 3, 6, 7–8, 15, 17n6, 23, 34, 49–50, 54n6, 55n19, 57n33, 60, 61, 73, 76, 84, 92, 104n4, 107n31, 109n54, 110n63, 126, 152, 162n30, 165n47, 170, 194, 203, 221n20, 222n29, 235, 256, 260, 265, 274, 288n1, 289n12, n16
reason
   and passion, 129–33
   practical, 274–5
   theoretical, 274–5
Ross, W. D., 70, 107n31, n32, 262, 271, 274, 275
Rudebusch, G., 52, 54n4

Sachs, David, 104n5, 165n51
Schneewind, J. B., 3, 6, 8, 264, 265, 267–8, 286
Scolnicov, Samuel, 160n12
Sen, A., 92, 225, 257n19
Shields, Christopher, 202–5, 215–16, 219nn8–11, 220nn12–15, 221nn17–18, n20, 222n21, 223nn32–3
Shorey, Paul, 167, 168
Sidgwick, Henry, 3–7, 9–10, 42–5, 48, 154–5, 251, 259–63, 278, 286
Smith, Adam, 49, 81–2, 84
Smith, N. D., 110n68
Sorabji, Richard, 110n68
soul (psyche), 117–25
Strange, S., 257n8

Taylor, C. C. W., 10, 52, 55n17, 110n67, 159n10, 163n34, 164n38, 253, 254, 258n26
teleological
   ethical theories, 6–7, 49
   explanations, 238–9
Trianoski, G., 264

unity
   and justice, 4–8, 150–3
   and society, 150–3
   and virtues, 88–9
Urmson, James, 255, 258n26

value
   conditional, 33–40
   and exchange, 48–9
   and opportunity, 48–51
   and use, 48–9
virtue
   and good, 153–5, 269–74
   and health, 133–8
   and wisdom, 41–2, 274–8
   sovereignty of, 20, 33, 36
virtue ethics, 15, 263–8
virtues
   individual, 113, 125–9

virtues (*cont.*)
  social, 84–103
  unity of, 88–9
Vlastos, Gregory, 20, 22, 53n1, 55n12,
    n22, 56n27, n32, 98–9, 102,
    109n55, 110n67, 114, 164n44, 172,
    174–8, 180, 182, 222n23, 232
von Wright, G. H., 13, 201, 202, 205,
    219n9, 220n13

Watson, Gary, 56n25, 264–7
Wedberg, A., 173, 178, 182, 185, 192n7,
    n10
Wedin, M., 228
White N. P., 54n5, 112, 159n9, 161n19,
    164n41, 173, 193n11, 194

Whiting, J., 256n5
Williams, B., 159n10
wisdom
  and good, 33–42
  and happiness, 45–8, 231–2, 262
  practical, 274–8
  theoretical, 231–2, 262
  and virtue, 41–2, 274–8
Woodruff, Paul, 5, 206
Woods, M., 219n6
Wright L., 69, 257n18

Young, Charles, 247, 258n24, 289n9,
    n13

Zeyl, D., 52n17, 52, 55n17